Data Analytics for Marketing

A practical guide to analyzing marketing data using Python

Guilherme Diaz-Bérrio

Data Analytics for Marketing

Group Product Manager: Kaustubh Manglurkar

Publishing Product Manager: Heramb Bhavsar

Book Project Managers: Farheen Fathima and Shambhavi Mishra

Senior Editor: Rohit Singh

Technical Editor: Rahul Limbachiya

Copy Editor: Safis Editing

Proofreaders: Rohit Singh and Safis Editing

Indexer: Subalakshmi Govindhan

Production Designer: Joshua Misquitta

DevRel Marketing Executive: Nivedita Singh

First published: May 2024

Production reference: 1120424

Published by Packt Publishing Ltd.

Grosvenor House

11 St Paul's Square

Birmingham

B3 1RB, UK.

ISBN 978-1-80324-160-9

www.packtpub.com

To Andreia Lopes, my partner. You are my safe harbor; this book would not have become a reality without your support during the endless hours I thought about giving up. You make me want to be better, and I would not be where I am without you. Love you!

– Guilherme Diaz-Bérrio

Contributors

About the author

Guilherme Diaz-Bérrio is the Head of Marketing Analytics at Kindred Group, one of the 10 largest gambling operators. He helps improve marketing efforts across various platforms. His career started in finance at a hedge fund and moved through the automotive industry at BMW Group and BMW Financial Services, before coming to Kindred Group. He graduated with a degree in economics from ISEG, University of Lisbon, and has additional training in data science and econometrics. He is also the co-founder of Pinemarsh, a data analytics and digital marketing consulting firm.

I want to thank my editor, Rohit Singh, for his help and patience in reviewing my drafts. I also want to thank Birjees Patel and Deepesh Patel, for taking a chance and inviting me to write this book. I would like to thank the reviewers, Devanshu Tayal, Shubham Gupta, and Michael Van Den Reym. Their feedback was incredibly helpful in getting to the final drafts. Finally, I would like to thank Krishna Bhaskaran, for giving me the opportunity to work in marketing analytics and giving me the foundations of what I know today.

About the reviewers

Devanshu Tayal is a highly accomplished data scientist with a master's degree from BITS, Pilani, India. His extensive expertise in data science is evidenced by his contributions to a wide range of industries. Devanshu is deeply committed to mentoring and guiding aspiring data scientists and is an avid researcher of emerging technologies in the field. He is a strong advocate for diversity and inclusion and has shared his insights through various publications. Devanshu is frequently invited to deliver guest lectures at universities throughout India, and his contributions as a technical reviewer have been acknowledged in multiple books. His comprehensive knowledge and experience in the field make him an asset to any team or project.

Shubham Gupta, an accomplished technology leader and a staunch advocate for data-driven decision-making, possesses a vast wealth of expertise spanning analytics, business intelligence, strategic planning, and cutting-edge innovative solutions. His deep comprehension of both technological intricacies and business dynamics equips him to guide business stakeholders from a wide array of industries toward making well-informed, data-backed decisions, thus streamlining operations and fostering substantial growth.

Furthermore, Shubham's significant involvement as a judge for numerous prestigious tech awards highlights his unwavering dedication to promoting excellence and driving innovation within the tech industry.

Michael Van Den Reym is a seasoned professional in the field of digital analytics and search engine optimization, with a rich background in enhancing online visibility for diverse businesses. Currently, he's working at iO, the biggest full-service digital agency in Belgium. Michael has been a speaker on data-driven marketing at industry conferences such as MeasureCamp, MeasureFest, and BrightonSEO. Michael's work primarily revolves around leveraging data-driven insights using Python and data visualization tools to create strategies that significantly improve digital marketing outcomes.

Currently, Michael is working on his first book, *Fundamentals of SEO for Business*, which revolves around search engine optimization for marketing professionals.

Table of Contents

3

Design Principles and Presenting Results with Streamlit   47

4

Econometrics and Causal Inference with Statsmodels and PyMC   75

Part 2: Planning Ahead

5

6

Part 3: Who and What to Target

7

8

9

Customer Survey Analysis 259

10

Conjoint Analysis with pandas and Statsmodels 285

Part 4: Measuring Effectiveness

11

12

13

Preface

When I first started as a marketing data analyst, I felt lost. I already knew how to program in Python, and the basics of statistics and econometrics, but marketing analytics is a surprisingly deceptive field. It feels easy, but due to the nature of the data we work with, it involves more complex models than you initially thought; correlation is often confused with causation, and sometimes, you just feel like you are flying blind. Either that or you feel like a glorified pivot table maker. A lot of my knowledge then came from trial and error: testing techniques, reading up on new methods, and making mistakes… a lot of mistakes.

When I started managing and hiring a team of analysts, I sometimes felt that it would make my life easier if I could just point them to a book that gave them the basics instead of spending hours in one-on-one sessions explaining methods or techniques. This book is my attempt at that: a summary of the fundamentals of marketing analytics, above simple pivot table making.

Marketing analytics is an incredibly complex field, and it is impossible to encapsulate all of it in one book. This book aims to give you, the reader, a grounding understanding of the techniques and tools most used in marketing analytics. The aim is to provide a practical, no-nonsense approach. You will have to have some basic understanding of the theoretical aspects surrounding tools and models so that you know what you are using and why, but we will quickly shift to a practical approach. The ultimate goal of this book is to equip you with the practical knowledge to get operational as a marketing data analyst quickly. This book will present open source libraries that allow you to derive insights quickly and use examples of common questions you will face daily as a marketing analyst.

There are gaps and techniques we will not explore. Marketing analytics is an ever-evolving field, and writing a book to cover everything would take more than 5,000 pages. Each chapter could be, and sometimes is, its own book. This book aims to equip you with fundamental knowledge, give you an overview of what is available, and provide some understanding of how to apply it. It also aims to give you the biggest asset an experienced analyst can have – knowing what to look for and research when facing a new problem. This last point is, for me, the most important. If this book achieves nothing else, let it be that it provides you with the compass to find the tools and techniques you need in your daily life. Even if that means you will disagree with me on a specific technique, that will be a win.

Throughout the book, we will use Python and its rich data analysis and statistics package ecosystem.

Who this book is for

There are some assumptions I have about who you are as a reader. Although an attempt is made to explain the most complex Python code snippets, you need to have a basic understanding of Python and be comfortable with it. By comfortable, I mean you know what a function is, how to define it, how to import a module, and the basic language syntax. Another requirement is you should not be afraid of mathematics. This point is contentious, but some chapters will have some formulation and theory before we get into actual code. Some people might disagree, but while copilots such as GitHub Copilot or ChatGPT can help you produce the code, you still need fundamental theoretical knowledge. In fact, with code copilots becoming better and better, most likely, the distinction between a good and an average analyst will be the theoretical grounding they have. I will attempt to give you the basic toolbelt of math techniques early on, starting from how to calculate a mean, but this book assumes you are comfortable with high-school-level mathematical notation.

This book is primarily aimed at data analysts who want to understand the full suite of techniques available to them in marketing analytics. You can also be a marketing professional aiming to move to the analytical side, but if this is you, I advise you to first brush up on the basics of Python programming, math, and statistics.

What this book covers

Chapter 1, *What is Marketing Analytics?*, delves into what we mean by marketing analytics, breaking down the types of analytics, from descriptive to prescriptive, what value they add to the business, and what questions each of them answers.

Chapter 2, *Extracting and Exploring Data with Singer and pandas*, gives you a brief introduction to ETL and how to extract and handle marketing data, ingestion, and **Exploratory Data Analysis (EDA)**. We will cover the fundamentals of descriptive statistics and go through common data transformations to ensure data normality.

Chapter 3, *Design Principles and Presenting Results with Streamlit*, takes us through how to properly design a dashboard for marketing data, from design principles to actual implementation. This is instrumental in displaying our results in a presentable way to non-technical audiences.

Chapter 4, *Econometrics and Causal Inference with Statsmodels and PyMC*, deals with the fact that, as a marketing analyst, you usually do not have the luxury of big data to feed into machine learning models. The data will be sparse or low-frequency time series or panel data, which will prevent you from brute-forcing your way through. You need a solid understanding of econometrics and the principles of causality to answer common questions your stakeholders will have.

Chapter 5, *Forecasting with Prophet, ARIMA, and Other Models Using StatsForecast*, digs deeper into forecasting. Forecasting is one of the fundamental tasks of a marketing data analyst. It is also one of the most complex fields in statistics. You should understand which models to apply, when to apply them, and what to avoid. We will review the most common models, from ARIMA to ETS, and what are the common pitfalls in forecasting time series.

Chapter 6, *Anomaly Detection with StatsForecast and PyMC*, describes how to perform anomaly detection. In the daily life of an analyst, you will be tasked, more often than not, with finding anomalies before they create business impact. You will also have to understand how to deal with low-frequency data and derive anomalies while avoiding false positives.

Chapter 7, Customer Insights – Segmentation and RFM, helps us discover how to segment customers and create valuable profiles for better marketing. We'll explore customer segmentation and RFM scoring.

Chapter 8, Customer Lifetime Value with PyMC Marketing, builds upon the previous chapter by showing how to assign a value to our customers and segments to optimize our marketing efforts, and to evaluate the ROI of our activities by estimating how much customers are worth.

Chapter 9, Customer Survey Analysis, describes customer satisfaction analysis through surveys. Analyzing customer satisfaction is an integral part of customer satisfaction management, which is an important part of CRM. We'll go through how to analyze survey data to derive insights, how to calculate samples, and the pitfalls of NPS.

Chapter 10, Conjoint Analysis with pandas and Statsmodels, starts with a description of what conjoint analysis is and what it is used for. We'll cover some of the techniques used to derive useful insights, customize your product offering with conjoint analysis, and explain how to build the analysis from the ground up.

Chapter 11, Multi-Touch Digital Attribution, explains in detail what digital attribution is. Marketing attribution is a fundamental problem in marketing analytics. How to attribute outcomes to marketing channels will change the conclusions you derive from channel evaluation. This chapter will describe the most common attribution methods and how to build them.

Chapter 12, Media Mix Modeling with PyMC Marketing, describes the fundamental issue of understanding how to use Media Mix Modeling to optimize your marketing activities. Understanding a marketing channel's performance is important, but of critical importance in modern marketing analytics is understanding how channels interact with each other. The answer to this question allows us, as analysts, to advise marketing teams on optimal budget allocation.

Chapter 13, Running Experiments with PyMC, starts by explaining the fundamentals of what an experiment is. Running experiments in marketing is a fundamental technique for optimization and efficiency. We'll go through the fundamentals of how to run experiments and how to analyze the outcome, while avoiding the most common pitfalls.

To get the most out of this book

The code provided for this book comes in the form of Jupyter Notebooks, with the exception of *Chapter 3*, which is a Python file. All chapters will teach you how to install the required packages for each section.

You should already have a Python distribution installed on your development machine, either via the main Python Website or using Anaconda. An alternative is to use Google Colab.

All source code was developed and tested on MacOS (64-bit) and Google Colab.

Software/hardware covered in the book	Operating system requirements
Python 3.11	Windows, macOS, or Linux
Jupyter lab 4.0	Windows, macOS, or Linux
pandas 2.0.2	Windows, macOS, or Linux
NumPy 1.24.4	Windows, macOS, or Linux
Statsforecast 1.7.3	Windows, macOS, or Linux
Pymc 5.11.0	Windows, macOS, or Linux
Pymc-marketing 0.3.1	Windows, macOS, or Linux
Statsmodels 0.14.0	Windows, macOS, or Linux
Streamlit 1.24.0	Windows, macOS, or Linux

If you are using the digital version of this book, we advise you to type the code yourself or access the code from the book's GitHub repository (a link is available in the next section). Doing so will help you avoid any potential errors related to the copying and pasting of code.

Download the example code files

You can download the example code files for this book from GitHub at `https://github.com/PacktPublishing/Data-Analytics-for-Marketing`. If there's an update to the code, it will be updated in the GitHub repository.

We also have other code bundles from our rich catalog of books and videos available at `https://github.com/PacktPublishing/`. Check them out!

Conventions used

There are a number of text conventions used throughout this book.

`Code in text`: Indicates code words in text, database table names, folder names, filenames, file extensions, pathnames, dummy URLs, user input, and Twitter handles. Here is an example: "To begin, we need to import the required libraries: `streamlit`, `pandas`, `numpy`, `matplotlib`, and `seaborn`."

A block of code is set as follows:

```
import pandas as pd
import numpy as np
import seaborn as sns

pd.set_option('display.float_format', lambda x: '%.2f' % x)
```

```
df = pd.read_csv('data/ trafficsources.csv')
df.describe()
```

When we wish to draw your attention to a particular part of a code block, the relevant lines or items are set in bold:

```
# Define the model
with pm.Model() as model_pymc:
    alpha = 1.0/daily_sales.sales.mean()

    lambda_1 = pm.Exponential("lambda_1", alpha)
    lambda_2 = pm.Exponential("lambda_2", alpha)
```

Any command-line input or output is written as follows:

```
pip install tap-googleads
```

Bold: Indicates a new term, an important word, or words that you see onscreen. For instance, words in menus or dialog boxes appear in **bold**. Here is an example: "Analytics can be split into four areas or pillars: **descriptive**, **predictive**, **diagnostic**, and **prescriptive** analytics."

> **Tips or important notes**
> Appear like this.

Get in touch

Feedback from our readers is always welcome.

General feedback: If you have questions about any aspect of this book, email us at customercare@ packtpub.com and mention the book title in the subject of your message.

Errata: Although we have taken every care to ensure the accuracy of our content, mistakes do happen. If you have found a mistake in this book, we would be grateful if you would report this to us. Please visit www.packtpub.com/support/errata and fill in the form.

Piracy: If you come across any illegal copies of our works in any form on the internet, we would be grateful if you would provide us with the location address or website name. Please contact us at copyright@packt.com with a link to the material.

If you are interested in becoming an author: If there is a topic that you have expertise in and you are interested in either writing or contributing to a book, please visit authors.packtpub.com.

Share your thoughts

Once you've read *Data Analytics for Marketing*, we'd love to hear your thoughts! Scan the QR code below to go straight to the Amazon review page for this book and share your feedback.

https://packt.link/r/1-803-24160-8

Your review is important to us and the tech community and will help us make sure we're delivering excellent quality content.

Download a free PDF copy of this book

Thanks for purchasing this book!

Do you like to read on the go but are unable to carry your print books everywhere?

Is your eBook purchase not compatible with the device of your choice?

Don't worry, now with every Packt book you get a DRM-free PDF version of that book at no cost.

Read anywhere, any place, on any device. Search, copy, and paste code from your favorite technical books directly into your application.

The perks don't stop there, you can get exclusive access to discounts, newsletters, and great free content in your inbox daily

Follow these simple steps to get the benefits:

1. Scan the QR code or visit the link below

https://packt.link/free-ebook/9781803241609

2. Submit your proof of purchase
3. That's it! We'll send your free PDF and other benefits to your email directly

Part 1:
Fundamentals of Analytics

In this part, we will go through the fundamentals of analytics, introducing marketing analytics as a discipline. We will be focusing on data extraction, ingestion, and exploratory data analysis, followed by techniques for effectively presenting results and building dashboards for non-technical audiences. The subsequent discussion shifts toward econometrics and causal inference, providing a foundational understanding of statistics and equipping you with the skills to construct, test, and evaluate statistical models, emphasizing their significance and application in marketing.

This part contains the following chapters:

- *Chapter 1, What is Marketing Analytics?*
- *Chapter 2, Extracting and Exploring Data with Singer and pandas*
- *Chapter 3, Design Principles and Presenting Results with Streamlit*
- *Chapter 4, Econometrics and Causal Inference with Statsmodels and PyMC*

1
What is Marketing Analytics?

Half the money I spend on advertising is wasted; the trouble is I don't know which half.

– John Wanamaker, the forefather of marketing

In this chapter, we will attempt to cover the fundamentals of marketing analytics as a role and discipline. As a marketing analyst, you are faced with common questions during your day-to-day activities. For example, "How did this campaign perform?" or "How can you optimize your budget to achieve a result?".

In this chapter, we will break down the types of analytics (from descriptive to prescriptive), the value they add to a business, and the questions each of them answers.

You will learn about the following topics:

- What is analytics?
- An overview of marketing analytics
- Exploring different types of analytics
- Beyond simple pivot tables
- Why Python?
- Modern challenges in the world of privacy-centric marketing
- The importance of data engineering and tracking

By the end of this chapter, you will understand what marketing analytics is and what it is supposed to measure. You will have a firm grasp of the different types of analytics and why simply using a spreadsheet, while tempting, is sometimes not enough. You will also have an understanding of the importance of data engineering and web tracking.

But before we delve into the tools and techniques that are required of you, to achieve your results, we first need to unpack what we mean by analytics in general and marketing analytics in particular.

What is analytics?

Like any buzzword, analytics can often be overused and hard to define from an exact source. According to the Oxford Dictionary, the textbook definition of analytics is "the systematic computational analysis of data or statistics, in order to describe, predict, and improve business performance". Gartner defines it more broadly as "statistical and mathematical data analysis that clusters, segments, scores, and predicts what scenarios are most likely to happen."

Analytics is commonly known to branch out into four pillars or areas: descriptive analytics, diagnostic analytics, predictive analytics, and prescriptive analytics.

In essence, analytics is the act of extracting meaningful and actionable insights from data by using a set of techniques and tools paired with domain knowledge. Raw data, however large it may be, will not be a silver bullet in your quest for insights in marketing. Neither will advanced techniques and a lack of domain knowledge of how the field you are analyzing operates. It is only in the joining of these three aspects—**domain knowledge**, **data**, and **techniques**—that you will be able to do your job.

An important caveat about analytics is that it is neither reporting nor data science. Your primary job is not to produce a stable, automatically updated dashboard or a machine learning pipeline. In analytics, it helps you to have the right mindset and try to achieve reproducible code for follow-up analysis, or have a stable pipeline. But as an analyst, that is not your primary goal; it is just nice to have in order to achieve your end result. Your primary goal is speed and accuracy; that is, you need to produce meaningful insights that teams easily rely on in a reasonable amount of time with reasonable accuracy.

While it may seem controversial, this distinction bears some thought. Often, analytics will be folded into one of the two extremes. Either it is viewed as simple reporting and/or BI work, meaning you will lose the ability to generate actionable insights due to the rigid nature of datasets and dashboard architecture required. Or, it is viewed as data science, which means you will often use complex models that require a lot of data to learn and are lacking in interpretability. Analytics stands in the middle, although with blurry frontiers:

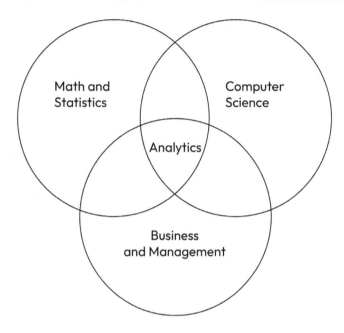

Figure 1.1 – Business analytics as the intersection of several skills

Now let's gain an overview of what is marketing analytics.

An overview of marketing analytics

The quote at the beginning of this chapter illustrates one of the fundamental questions of the marketing manager in their day-to-day activities. The best way to evaluate where to spend and target their efforts to achieve their ultimate target is to obtain new customers or retain current ones.

Marketing analytics is nothing more than the application of analytical methods to said goal, bringing a quantifiable way of guiding investment or consumer targeting decisions. As with any new and growing domain, it is hard to pin an exact definition of it, but we can define it as a "technology-enabled and model-supported approach to harness customer and market data to enhance marketing decision making". Being a domain in the larger field of data analytics, it looks to use mathematics and statistics together with computational tools and techniques to find meaningful patterns and knowledge in data. In this book, we will strive to focus on only the most relevant techniques and models to solve fundamental questions in marketing analytics.

Standard techniques frequently used in marketing include media mix modeling, pricing and promotion analyses, sales force optimization, and customer analytics such as segmentation or lifetime value estimation. The optimization of websites and online campaigns now frequently works hand in hand with the more traditional marketing analysis techniques, coupled with attribution modeling and media mix modeling, to understand channel interactions and optimal budget allocation.

These tools and techniques will allow you to support both strategic marketing decisions—such as how much to spend on marketing and how to allocate budgets across a portfolio of brands and the marketing mix—and more tactical campaign support in terms of targeting the best potential customer with the optimal message in the most cost-effective medium at the ideal time.

The past decades have seen an explosion of data in a digital format, with some estimates pointing to a jump from 6 percent to around 90 percent. That, together with massive improvements in computational tools such as faster databases, inference algorithms, and easier programming languages for statistics means the dramatic improvement and evolution of marketing analytics in recent times. But one might wonder why we should be concerned with marketing analytics, or why it should be regarded as an independent sub-field of greater analytics.

Why should we bother with marketing analytics?

Any business that employs analytics, of any kind, expects that it will improve the performance of said business. Marketing analytics is no different. Evidence supports the claim that marketing analytics improves business performance, be it in the form of increased sales, profits, or market share.

One study states that for a one-unit increase in marketing analytics deployment (measured on a scale of 1–7), there is an increase of 8 percent in **return on assets** (**ROA**) for the business, accounting for $180 million in net income. Businesses in highly competitive industries gain even more; an increase of 21 percent on ROA.

Let's see a simple example of what marketing analytics can do with a mail coupon campaign. Kroger, an American retailer, conducts regular direct mail coupon campaigns. These campaigns to customers delivered a redemption rate of 70 percent within six weeks of mailing compared to an average of 7.93 percent for other companies. How? According to the analytics company working with Kroger, "Demographics can tell you nothing about it. Just because I am the same age as you, live next door, and have 2.2 children does not mean we have the same preferences." What they do is study each customer to see what drives their behaviors individually. Do they have kids, do they skew toward healthy or fun, do they prefer organic or convenience foods, and where are they price sensitive? Is this across all products or only some? "We tell our retailing customers there is no silver bullet. Take data from customers and look at the decisions the business is making and look at their impact on the consumer."

Having discussed the what and why of marketing analytics, we need to take a small detour to explain the different types of analytics in the analytical maturity model to better understand what to apply in each step.

Exploring different types of analytics

As we have seen earlier, analytics is a broad term covering four different pillars in the modern analytics ladder. Each plays a role in how your business can better understand what your data reveals and how you can use those insights to drive business objectives.

The following diagram will help you visualize how the pillars relate to one another:

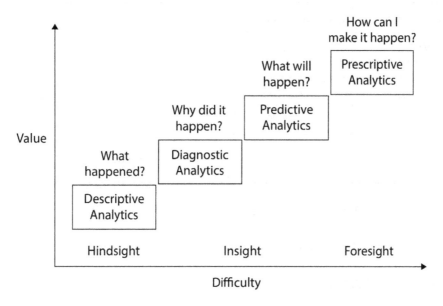

Figure 1.2 – The analytics maturity model

The first step in the process is to always understand the fundamental questions you are trying to answer. All analytical questions can be boiled down into the following categories:

- What happened and when did it happen?
- Why and how did it happen?
- What will happen in the future?
- How can I make something happen?

These categories will define the different areas of analytics involved, which will inform our decision about what tooling and techniques to apply.

Analytics can be split into four areas or pillars: **descriptive**, **predictive**, **diagnostic**, and **prescriptive** analytics.

You can think of the pillars by remembering what questions they try to answer:

Area of analytics	Question answered
Descriptive	What have we done in the past?
Diagnostic	Why have we seen past results?
Predictive	What will happen in the future?
Prescriptive	How should we act in order to achieve a future result?

Table 1.1 – How questions map to areas of analytics

We will look into each of the pillars in detail, starting our journey with descriptive analytics.

Descriptive analytics

The first stage of analytics is descriptive analytics, which is the most common of all analytics activities today. Most management reporting—such as sales, marketing, operations, and finance—uses descriptive analytical tools and techniques. It tries to answer the "What happened?", "How did it happen?", and "When did it occur?" type of questions. It is most commonly associated with reporting or business intelligence work.

If you are in this category, you are attempting to describe groups, categories, and relationships. You are attempting to describe your data and frame it in the context of the domain knowledge. By domain knowledge, we mean a specific understanding of the context to which the data relates. Data does not exist in a vacuum. To understand the financial metrics of a company, you need to understand, to some degree, accounting and how the business operates. Likewise, to understand marketing data, you need to understand its context and operation. How does a digital acquisition campaign work, or how does a user convert through the acquisition funnel?

The descriptive nature of it makes it quite easy to start an analysis. You can essentially start your analysis or insight with an Excel file and the trustworthy PivotTable. For some tasks, that might be enough if the aim is simply an **exploratory data analysis** (**EDA**). As we will see further in this chapter, most likely, the EDA is just the beginning of the analysis, not the final insight you are being asked to give.

Descriptive analytics is, by its nature, the easiest type of analytics to implement and learn for the following reasons:

- First, most likely, you already have the data in such a format that easily allows you, with some work and automation, to correctly group results in the desired dimensions or timeframes, making it an obvious place to start your analytical journey.

- Second, it has the lowest barrier to entry when it comes to skillset. To become competent at this stage of analytics, you need to know the core fundamentals of data extraction and aggregation, visualization and dashboarding best practices, and basic best practices in data engineering, such as the star schema.

- Third, it is intuitive for your stakeholders to get an understanding of what happened and when in a table or visual. Most of your stakeholders already make use of the same techniques to get an understanding of their area.

- Finally, it is very easily automatable and standardizable, which makes the process quick with the correct practice.

Unfortunately, while it is the initial pillar that an analyst starts their journey with, it is also commonly where most stop in the analytics maturity model. The reasons are varied, but it can be argued that it boils down to company culture and the skillset of the teams running the analytical work:

- In smaller companies, this type of analytical work is done by business intelligence teams whose members are experts at aggregating data in SQL and quickly providing dashboards for visualization. To move up the ladder, the skillset shifts more toward people with knowledge of statistics, econometrics, and some form of programming, usually Python or R.

- Even on teams who wish to move up the ladder, there is a maintenance cost to all the existing reports and visualizations that, without careful planning, can end up consuming all the time the team has at its disposal.

A common shortcoming of this type of analysis is that, while it is essential to understand past trends, you will find a general lack of calls to action or actionable insights and inferences. Usually, when someone asks you what happened, what they are really asking is why it happened, which leads us to the next step, diagnostic analytics.

Diagnostic analytics

If in descriptive analytics you are answering what happened based on historical data and trends, in diagnostic analytics, you are attempting to get to the bottom of why. Be it an occurrence, a trend, or an anomaly, you are interested in finding out the key drivers or characteristics of the fact you are analyzing. In the same vein as descriptive analytics, you will make use of historical data.

Diagnostic analytics is where you, as an analyst, usually answer the "What went wrong?" or "Why did this happen?" type of questions. Here, you will frequently be asked, "Why did our cost per acquisition go up in the previous quarter?" or "Why are we seeing an increase in customer churn?". Diagnostic analytics is the home of anomaly detection, outlier analysis, key driver analysis, or causal inference.

Curiously, this stage of analytics is often skipped. Either practitioners stop at descriptive analytics or they jump straight to predictive analytics. A subset will simply fold diagnostic analytics into predictive analytics. This bears some thought; you cannot, and should not, jump to predicting the future without understanding why past patterns or trends happened. If you cannot infer why your cost per acquisition jumped by 25 percent in the previous quarter, it will be a stretch to attempt to forecast what will happen to your cost per acquisition in the next two quarters.

The issue with this type of analytics is that most famous tools and techniques commonly associated with data science focus on forecasting accuracy and not on causal inference. And this is an important distinction; if you are trying to predict, as does Google, whether someone will click an ad, you don't need to understand the causal mechanisms of the action. You just need to find the dimensions that highly correlate with that action, and if you have enough data, you will get good accuracy. We should emphasize here that when we are talking about enough data in this context, we are usually referring to data in the GBs or TBs range. Unless you, as an analyst, are dealing with clickstream data from digital marketing—that is, impression levels showing all interactions with your digital property by your users—you will not be in this range.

Unfortunately, as a marketing analyst, you most often will not have the luxury of big data. You will live in the world of small data, where you will have two years' worth of daily data in the best scenario. It is also the field where you need a good amount of domain knowledge to understand what relationships you should model and what you should avoid.

Another common problem is the often-forgotten aphorism in statistics: correlation does not imply causation.

We will go through this point in greater detail in *Chapter 4, Econometrics and Causal Inference with Statsmodels and PyMC*, but suffice it to say that you will need to understand the causal mechanisms and the data-generating process to provide meaningful and accurate insights.

There are, however, tools and techniques to help you in this area, concentrated around the field of econometrics. Economists have spent the last 70 years developing an entire field devoted to asking the "why" of small data, and marketing analytics derives a lot of its techniques from this field. Economists, like marketing analysts, do not have high-frequency data. Also, like marketing analysts, economists are often tasked with using small data and deriving causal conclusions and policy recommendations with theoretically sound statistical techniques.

Predictive analytics

The next area is predictive analytics, which attempts to determine what is likely to happen. The aim is to provide forecasts or identify the likelihood of future outcomes.

Predictive analytics attempts to answer the question: "What will happen in the future?". This is an entirely different type of question since you are predicting the future. You will combine the historical data and outputs from descriptive and diagnostic analytics, that is, the "what" and the "why," to predict future events.

Common questions you will be asked are "Can we predict customer churn by customer satisfaction?" and "What will my cost per click be in paid searches over the next six months?".

It is in this type of analytics that we need to be mindful of the common, and wrong, assumption that the past will repeat itself. As Mark Twain once famously said, "History doesn't repeat itself, but it often rhymes." You need good modeling practices and a correct workflow, and you should always test your hypothesis. For instance, trying to forecast how much you will spend on marketing and how much return you are going to get is a time-series problem that requires a very specific set of techniques and has a lot of pitfalls.

A common pitfall is focusing solely on the modeling side. While it is important to know which model to use and how to diagnose a bad model, data preparation is essential. A simple outlier in your dataset will throw all your results and efforts into the garbage bin.

Up to now, you have answered "what," "why," and "when" questions. Going one step further, you can ask the following question: what can I do now to achieve a specified result in the future?

This is where prescriptive analytics comes in.

Prescriptive analytics

Considered the final frontier of analytic capabilities, prescriptive analytics extends beyond predictive and diagnostic analytics by specifying both the actions necessary to achieve predicted outcomes and the interrelated effects of each decision. Here, you, as an analyst, are extending beyond predicting outcomes to suggesting actions and showing the implications of such actions.

For instance, in building a media mix model, you started with descriptive analytics by understanding what occurred, then you modeled the relationships between channels to understand how and why channels interact, and you fitted the model to forecast future sales. Now, armed with such a model, you can recommend a budget mix of marketing channels and activities that will result in the desired number of sales.

Prescriptive analytics not only anticipates what will happen and when it will happen but also why it will happen. Further, prescriptive analytics suggests options on how to take advantage of a future opportunity or mitigate a future risk and shows the implication of each decision. Prescriptive analytics can continually take in new data to re-predict and re-prescribe, thus automatically improving prediction accuracy and prescribing better decision options. Prescriptive analytics ingests hybrid data, a combination of structured (numbers, categories) and unstructured data (videos, images, sounds, texts), and business rules to predict what lies ahead and to advise how to take advantage of this predicted future without compromising other priorities.

In essence, it attempts to formalize and quantify educated guesses and domain knowledge in a systematic and repeatable way. There is, however, one large caveat in this field of analytics: you should not skip the ladder. You need the outputs from the previous pillars of descriptive, diagnostic, and predictive analytics.

From the theoretical aspects of analytics and its maturity model to the practical aspects of how to do an analysis, there is a gap. Fitting tools and techniques to questions is a fundamental skill that you, as an analyst, need to master. However, it is easy to get lost in the maze.

Walking through the maze of tools and techniques

It is easy to be overwhelmed at this stage with all the tools, analysis, and techniques for evaluating business objectives and deriving insights. At this stage, we should always keep some first principles in the back of our minds as analysts.

First, you need to understand customer heterogeneity. Second, you need to understand the customer dynamics. Third, you need to understand that, in business, there are always trade-offs to be made with resources.

The principles map to a set of techniques, as seen in the following table:

Applicable techniques	Description
Cluster analysis for segmentation	Identifies groups of similar consumers
Discriminant analysis for targeting and classification	Identifies target customers using data easily available
Preference mapping for competitive positioning	Visual map of consumers' preferences
Recency, frequency, and monetary analysis	Quantitatively separates and ranks groups of customers
Logistic regression models for customer selection	Estimates the effect of one or more predictor variables on a binary outcome
Customer lifetime value analysis	Calculates the value of individual customers or groups of customers
Survey design to derive customer insights	Using factor analysis to identify common factors and dimensions in survey data
Conjoint analysis for product and pricing decisions	Determines the value of different product attributes
Forecasting sales of new products	Predicts new sales and product acceptance
Media mix models to optimize marketing mix	Helps estimate outcome variables based on a mix of product, price, promotion, and medium

Marketing experiments to optimize marketing mix	Determines cause and effect versus correlation and change of output
Topic models to glean customer insights	Provides insight into unstructured text about desires, satisfaction, and emerging product need

Table 1.2 – Some techniques and their uses

Don't think of the preceding table as all of marketing analytics. There are many more techniques and tools that can be applied. Think of it as a starting anchor to help you navigate the maze of what techniques you should use and when. This book aims to build your internal library of techniques such that, when faced with a question, you can think, "This problem is of that category, and one of the techniques I can apply is the following." If this book succeeds at something, let it be to build your intuition and library of what to apply when and what to look for in your quest for insights. Paralysis by analysis is a reality.

Let us now move on to a large topic of debate, namely, why use Python, instead of simply doing all of what is described so far simply in a convenient Excel workbook.

Beyond simple pivot tables

You might wonder why we need a book on *Marketing Analytics Using Python*. Surely you can do the same thing using the trustworthy combination of Excel, some VLOOKUPs, and some PivotTables. This is a widespread misunderstanding, and the problem stems from not realizing what the entire analytical process should look like and why. The following diagram shows the process in a simplified way:

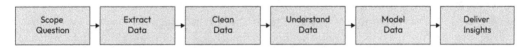

Figure 1.3 – Analytical process

As an analyst, you should have the preceding workflow that will generally go through the following tasks:

1. You should, first and foremost, scope out the question. You need to understand what is being asked of you clearly. Remember that your stakeholders have immense business knowledge and a problem they need to solve, but more often than not, the question might not be clearly defined.

2. You must extract the correct datasets to explore the problem space. This might be as easy as extracting a CSV from Google Ads or as tricky as joining four different spend tables with a customer table in your database. Do not underestimate the time or effort required at this step. You will spend a large part of your time at this stage, but it will save you time in the next steps.

3. After extracting the data, you need to clean the data and sense-check it for obvious problems. Live business data is messy, and you will be faced with non-obvious issues, such as a numerical column that contains a string such as N/A, bad Unicode strings in a survey dataset, or odd DateTime formats. Always remember the aphorism "garbage in, garbage out," no matter how fancy your tech stack is.

4. You have cleaned your data and sense-checked it, and now you must start understanding your data. This is where EDA comes in. At this stage, you will begin to group your data around categories or timeframes of interest. You are exploring the shape of the data, and it is at this step that you should be mindful of outliers. They will wreak havoc on most statistical and analytical models. You need to check quantiles, means and medians, and standard deviations at this stage. It is also at this stage that you start to see whether you have a suitable dataset for the question scoped out in *step 1*.

5. You executed all of the previous steps, and we now get to the interesting part of analytics that gets all the credit—the *model*. If your question is just a matter of describing a dataset, such as the number of conversions on a specific acquisition channel, then EDA is all you need. But, most likely, there are underlying questions beneath, such as "How do the two campaigns compare?", "What is the difference between these two segments of users?", or "What characteristics do my best-converting users have so I can better target them?". It is here that you will choose the proverbial "right tool for the job" and produce the insights you need.

6. Finally, we reach the last stage, the delivery of the insights. You might think this is not a step in the process, but nothing will be actioned if your stakeholders don't understand your results and insights. You should always keep in mind that your stakeholders are business experts first, not analysts. You need to translate the model outputs and the process you took to arrive at them in clear and concise language. Only then will they trust your insights and act on them.

Excel is a very powerful tool that can do almost anything with enough knowledge and experience. Yes, with more or less difficulty, you can execute all of the preceding steps for all types of analytics in Excel. Then again, you can also do a linear regression in SQL directly in the database. The question is, should you?

Remember, your job as an analyst involves the production of meaningful insights that teams can quickly act upon in a reasonable amount of time with good precision. The operative phrase here is "a reasonable amount of time." You need to choose the right tool for the job. Excel is a great tool for EDA and simple aggregations.

If you are dealing with a lot of data, you are going to start having issues with memory consumption. If your goal is more than simple statistical models or EDA, then Excel is not only cumbersome but also error-prone and hard to maintain and debug. We've all had at least one experience of spending an hour going through a gigantic Excel workbook, trying to spot the hidden cell that has the wrong input that is causing a weird calculation.

Finally, Excel has a terrible user experience when attempting to version control. We all know about the miracle of multiplying Excel files. As for running statistical modeling in Excel, it is true that Microsoft did great work in improving the accuracy of the algorithms it used. It is, however, still lacking when compared with languages such as Python or R. But why Python and not another statistical programming language? Let us delve a bit deeper into that.

Why Python?

Python offers a marketing analyst many benefits. First, it is an easy but powerful programming language with a great ecosystem of tools and libraries for data analysis and statistics. Second, as a programming language, it is easily testable, and the code can be made in such a way as to be generalizable and reusable. Do not underestimate this second point. Reusability is a great asset to have. You can reuse them for other datasets or testing purposes, which will massively increase your productivity in the medium to long term. Third, it handles massive amounts of data with modern libraries such as pandas and NumPy. The limit is essentially the physical memory in your machine.

Some of you might wonder, "Why not R?". It is a matter of personal preference. Most marketing analytics was derived from the field of applied econometrics. R is one of the prime tools in econometrics and statistics. As a language, it was built for statisticians who did not want to learn how to program. It has an extensive and deep ecosystem of libraries and support tools. But Python has caught up in the last decade. Libraries such as pandas, statsmodels, scikit-learn, and many others make for an equally pleasant product experience as Python without any of the trade-offs vis-à-vis R. Also, in my personal experience—and your mileage may vary—Python has a nicer user experience than R when dealing with library management and code maintenance.

Although R and Python have most of the market share in the analytics space, there are other languages worth mentioning. First, you have the commercial ones, such as SAS, SPSS, TSP, or MATLAB. Although this is my personal opinion, I tend to shy away from commercial programming languages since they are niche and companies are moving away from some of them, such as SAS. SPSS and TSP are good econometric software tools, which I personally was taught about in college, but there isn't anything you can do with them that you can't do with Python or R. SAS and MATLAB are also curious cases. Although powerful, they tend to be expensive, so companies shy away from them unless they need them. Then comes Mojo, which is a curious case. Although it is a superset of Python, it is commercial in nature. It attempts to remove some of the speed bottlenecks of Python while maintaining the syntax structure. Currently, it is aimed at AI development, where the data requirements are huge and avoiding speed bottlenecks is critical. Finally, there's Julia. Julia is as fast as C or C++ but syntactically as easy as Python. I believe it is a great addition to your toolbelt of languages as an analyst, although the libraries are less mature since Python and R carry a larger open source market share at the moment.

In this book, we will choose some libraries for each specific task or modeling effort. This does not mean they are the only options available. They are, in my opinion, an excellent place to start and are tried and tested. But for each suggestion of a library, there are always alternatives.

Aside from tools, libraries, and languages, as a marketing analyst, you will be concerned with getting good data to analyze. In a world of increased regulations on tracking and privacy concerns, you will have to navigate some challenges on the data collection side.

Modern challenges in the world of privacy-centric marketing

Marketers and marketing analysts have had the chance to swim in a world of data in the last 20 years. In fact, that was one of the main drivers of the spread of marketing analytics in the field, especially in the area of digital marketing, which accounts for almost two thirds of all marketing spending worldwide. However new trends in the attitude toward privacy and tracking online are making it harder for us, as analysts, to quickly derive insights from available data.

As we can see from *Figure 1.4*, for years the trend was clear. The largest proportion of marketing budgets went to online and digital marketing:

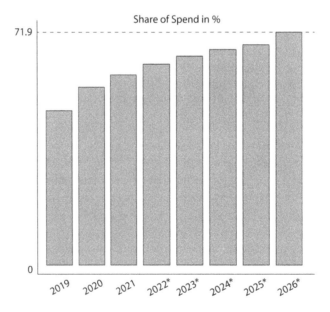

Figure 1.4 – Evolution of digital marketing spend as a percentage of global marketing spend

At our disposal, we had highly granular and vast datasets on our users, encompassing their behaviors, which ads they saw, when they saw them, and how they reacted to them. Clickstream data was a blessing, with its impression-level details. You could tie a user easily to a channel or activity.

The availability of such highly granular datasets made our jobs simpler. Getting insights was more a task of aggregation of individual-level data. Then, we could simply upload all the first- and third-party data we had to the media platform and run look-a-like ads to find similar potential customers. The main challenges were on the tracking front, making sure our users were correctly tagged. For years, we trusted that as long as our UTM parameters were correctly set and the cookies correctly dropped, we would get the visibility we needed.

Consumers are now more privacy-aware. Regulators are rolling out new regulations to protect user data, such as the **General Data Protection Regulation** (**GDPR**) in Europe and cookie consent. Platform vendors, such as smartphone and browser manufacturers (notably Apple), are rolling out new restrictions on third-party cookies and the unavailability of user-level data. The drop of third-party cookies by Apple, followed by first-party cookies, in what is deemed the "Cookiepocalypse," that is set to happen in 2024, as well as the rollout of the restrictions on iOS 14.5, sent shockwaves into the world of digital marketing. This trend will not stop. Yes, some vendors will attempt more advanced tracking and fingerprinting techniques. Still, in the long run, it will be a game of cat and mouse where the consumer will have the final word. Marketing teams are losing the visibility they have become accustomed to. Some feel they are starting to fly blind.

This is where econometrics in general and marketing analytics come back to the fore. The link between econometrics and marketing analytics is an old and acknowledged one. Sir Martin Sorrell, the founder of the British advertising group WPP, described it as the holy grail back in 2005. Some of the techniques you will learn in this book go back 50 to 70 years to the early 20th century.

Having less data, we need to be smarter about how we analyze it. Brute forcing our way with massive datasets using black-box machine learning techniques is no longer possible. Taking the iOS 14.5 update as an example, you won't know for sure what users came from paid media running on Apple devices, but with a media mix modeling approach, you can attempt to estimate the probable range of the effect of your efforts. And with some knowledge of econometrics, you can infer and attribute back, with some probability, which campaigns are proving the best value.

This does not mean we, as analysts, no longer have granular data. We will still have so-called "first-party data," that is, data generated by the direct interactions of your customers with your business. Most of this data will be generated by digital touchpoints, which you can use to enrich your analysis efforts. However, the greater share of data available and the new technologies for a more privacy-friendly environment are proving their own challenges to analysts in areas such as data engineering and web tracking.

The importance of data engineering and tracking

When moving past toy examples, data wrangling and transformation is neither easy nor something to be taken lightly. As described, since most digital marketing spending and interactions are of a digital nature, you are essentially swimming in a sea of data. Your job as an analyst is, as described at the beginning of this chapter, to generate insights in a timely manner. Here, efficient data accessibility is going to become a topic, especially if you work for a larger company with multiple large data sources. While a deeper and thorough walkthrough of data engineering is outside of the scope of this book, as an analyst, you should have a basic understanding of what it is and why it matters.

Don't moonlight as a data engineer

Excel gives us a bit of a bad habit as analysts: we use it simultaneously as a database and a tool to generate insights. The use of it as a database gives us a false sense of understanding of the need for data engineering. We can export data from the platforms and `vlookup` our way to our insights. The problem is that this is not scalable, and it is not sustainable. For one, there will be a limit to the amount of data you can export and store in Excel. Another reason is that, most of the time, you won't have an easy integration or export to get the data from. This is where a data engineer will come in. It is the job of a data engineer to extract, transform, and load the data in a way that is easy to use for the analyst. This is a very important step, and it will save you time if you don't need to be constantly worrying about the consistency of your data. A very simple example to drive the point home is as follows.

You want to export data from Facebook using the API or a lot of CSV exports. A naive approach, where you moonlight as a data engineer, is that you create your own connections, exports, and a database—or worse, you use Excel as a database. At first, everything is fine, but then you find that one day the API endpoints changed and you need to change your code. You need to parse JSON in weird, nested structures, or your improvised database is duplicating rows due to improper use of primary keys. This is before we start discussing the need for data normalization, the need to have a proper data model, and being able to join data from several sources and platforms.

Another important point to highlight is efficiency. Cloud databases have spoiled us a bit. Snowflake, Amazon Redshift, Google BigQuery, and others make it really easy to quickly query data. They also make it very easy to do silly things when querying it, such as doing full table row scans. This is not a problem when you have a few hundred rows, but when you have billions of rows, it can be a problem. A data engineer will make sure that your data is properly indexed and that you are not doing full table scans. This is a very important point, as it can save you a lot of money and it will make your life easier.

Finally, a data engineer will make sure that your data is properly stored. This is a very important point, as it will make sure that you are not storing data that you don't need and that you are not storing data in a way that is not efficient. This is especially important when you do not have a cloud database to work with but instead are dealing with an on-premises database such as Oracle or MySQL. These databases are not as lenient to inefficient data storage as cloud databases are, and getting data is going to become a bottleneck that will slow you down.

The importance of data engineering is not apparent in small datasets or projects. It is only when tables and datasets grow into hundreds of millions of rows that you will start to appreciate the importance of having a data engineer by your side. You also have some new tools available such as Singer for API management or dbt for data transformations, but even those won't save you from the need for a data engineer past a certain point or size.

Adjacent to data engineering, there is the issue of tracking your activities.

Web tracking is hard, and it is becoming harder

Tracking your media activities is of critical importance. You need to understand how many conversions you obtained from a specific media channel, for instance. If you do not have tracking in place, you will essentially be flying blind. However, due to the challenges of more privacy-aware tracking described earlier in this chapter, it is becoming harder to track.

The most basic form of tracking is with URL parameters. You might have seen URLs where, at the end of the page linked, there are parameters after a ?, such as `utm_campaign=` or `channel=`. These allow us to link the follow-up activity to the source that generates it. For instance, you can check which paid search campaign gave rise to the conversion in your website. The most common URL parameters are known as **Urchin Tracking Module** (**UTM**) parameters, introduced by Google Analytics. They are as follows:

- - `utm_source`: The source of the traffic, such as a search engine or a newsletter
- - `utm_medium`: The medium of the traffic, such as email or CPC
- - `utm_campaign`: The name of the campaign
- - `utm_term`: The keyword used to find the site
- - `utm_content`: Used for A/B testing and content-targeted ads

In the present day, these parameters can be blocked by ad blockers, VPNs, or even browsers—Mozilla Firefox famously has an option you can enable to override and strip all UTM parameters from a URL when clicked. This introduces a degree of measurement error in your data. Also, if you are using a third-party tracking tool such as Google Analytics, you need to make sure that you are not blocking the tracking code. This is a very common mistake, and it can lead to a lot of confusion. If you start working in marketing analytics, you will be surprised by the number of times a stakeholder will come to you with the question "Why is the data not showing up in Google Analytics?" or the more common statement of "The data looks funny," and then you realize you have an unexplained drop of 50 to 100 percent in conversions on a specific day. More often than not, a good place to start your analysis is to check tracking.

Another problem is that both GDPR and the move to ban cookies have created an increasingly complex tracking technology landscape. Aside from the most trivial cases, we are past the point of just "placing a tracking code on the website" and generating URLs with UTMs, and we are done. Server-side tracking, tagging management systems, and other technologies are becoming more and more common. This makes the barriers to entry in the field of proper tracking very high, and you require a lot of knowledge and experience to get it right. Like data engineering, don't moonlight as a web tracking specialist.

Like data engineering, web tracking is outside the scope of this book. However, it is important to understand its challenges and importance. When looking at the data for analysis, you need to be mindful that, due to web tracking issues, your data will not be perfectly clean. It will have artifacts, outliers, and other issues that you need to be aware of. Starting your analysis with that knowledge upfront will help you navigate uncertainty and understand the limitations of your data and, by extension, your analysis.

Summary

In this chapter, we delved into what we mean by marketing analytics. We broke down the types of analytics—from descriptive to prescriptive— discussed the value they add to businesses, and learned what questions each of them answers.

We investigated the fundamental questions you are trying to answer—what happened, when did it happen, how did it happen, what will happen in the future, and how can I make something happen. We also covered how they relate to each sub-domain of analytics, and we can now distinguish clearly between descriptive, predictive, diagnostic, and prescriptive analytics.

First, analytics is a complex field that can be summarized as the intersection between statistics, computer science, and analysis. You need to understand that marketing analytics distills those tools and techniques to the efforts of marketing to better optimize spending and obtain a return on investment.

Analytics can be split into question categories that map to areas of analytics:

- Descriptive analytics answers what we have done in the past. It is descriptive in nature and close to reporting and business intelligence.

- Diagnostic analytics answers why we have seen past results, and it is causal in nature. Often skipped, it takes advantage of econometrics to answer "why" questions.

- Predictive analytics answers the question of what will happen in the future. By modeling time series and the causal mechanisms of the data generation process, we can attempt to forecast future events.

- Prescriptive analytics puts it all together and answers how we should act to achieve a particular goal. It combines all the previous steps.

We understood why we could not just use Excel as our only analysis tool. Python allows for the testing and reuse of code and provides us with more statistical methods and tools with ease.

We took stock of the current trends in the digital marketing field, with the restrictions on data availability catering to more privacy-aware consumers. The impact of such restrictions implies a great need for statistical and inferential methods in analyzing marketing data.

Finally, we took a brief look at why we need data engineering and tracking and what the challenges are when we lack either of them.

In the next chapter, we will start our journey by exploring the first step on the analytical ladder. We will delve into the details of data extraction and EDA to prepare us for descriptive analytics.

Further reading

- `https://www.lexico.com/en/definition/analytics`

- `https://www.gartner.com/en/information-technology/glossary/analytics`

- *Performance implications of deploying marketing analytics*, Germann, Frank, Lilien, Gary L., & Rangaswamy, Arvind, 2013. International Journal of Research in Marketing, Elsevier, vol. 30(2), pages 114-128.

- `https://en.wikipedia.org/wiki/Prescriptive_analytics`

- `https://www.forbes.com/sites/forrester/2021/06/25/google-delays-the-cookiepocalypse/`

2

Extracting and Exploring Data with Singer and pandas

It is a capital mistake to theorize before one has data.

– Sherlock Holmes in "A Study in Scarlet," by Arthur Conan Doyle

Usually, in introductory analysis books, the data extraction job is assumed or left as an afterthought. Unfortunately, you will spend a big piece of your time either attempting to extract data or cleaning and preparing it for further analysis.

To bridge that gap, we will spend this chapter going through some data extraction and cleaning basics. We'll provide a brief introduction to data extraction, commonly referred to as the E in **extract, transform, and load** (ETL), and how to extract and handle marketing data ingestion. After that, we will dive into **exploratory data analysis** (EDA). We will explore standard measures of descriptive statistics, such as measures of central tendency and variability, and how to verify common issues such as the normality of data.

In this chapter, we will go through the following topics:

- What is ETL, and why should you care?
- Summarizing data and EDA
- Dealing with common data issues

By the end of this chapter, you will know how to extract data and process it for further steps.

Technical requirements

You can find the code files for this chapter on GitHub at `https://github.com/PacktPublishing/Data-Analytics-for-Marketing/tree/main/Chapter02`.

What is ETL, and why should you care?

ETL is a three-phase engineering process through which you extract data from a source system, transform it, and load it into the target system for further use. A typical example would be to extract data from Google Ads, transform it, and store it in a database system through an API.

Now, before I lose your interest, let's address why you should care. You can surely rely on exporting CSVs from whichever platform you are working on, be it a CRM, a survey platform, or a digital marketing media source, and work from there. And yes, you can do so. But you should not do so in the long run, for two main reasons:

- A proper ETL process will help you trust the data, enforce data types, and reduce errors
- Every time you cut the proverbial corner in the form of a CSV export, you are incurring technical debt for the long run

> **Note**
>
> **Technical debt** is a concept in programming that reflects the extra development work that arises when code that is easy to implement in the short run is used instead of applying the best overall solution. It is the software engineering equivalent of using your credit card to pay a bill. You will have to pay down the interest; the longer you wait, the higher the cost you will incur.

It seems counterintuitive at first. It's quicker to just get the data from the platforms, glue it in Excel, run your analysis on some charts, and ship it. But then, your stakeholder asks for regular weekly updates. Now, you need to take the time to manually update an Excel file that is growing in size. A few weeks later, someone interested in your analysis asks for a further breakdown. What seems to be a simple problem of adding an extra filter is, in fact, a problem of re-doing your entire analysis from the beginning. Manually, I might add. This is not counting potential data errors or duplications that could have been caught in the extraction phase. After a year, you are drowning in "Run the business" data maintenance tasks and wondering why you can't output analysis at the rate you want or need.

A proper ETL process and tool is insurance against part of this problem.

It needs to be said that this is not a book on data engineering and ETL processes, and you can be sure that such fields would fill an entire book. There are also very good ETL and data extraction tools on the market.

Data pipelines

When thinking about extracting data, a core concept to understand is the concept of data pipelines. Like regular water pipelines, the analogy is that it's a process that takes data from one source system to a destination system in a predefined, controlled, and predictable way.

One example is regularly extracting campaign data from a digital media platform into a database, to be consumed later in the form of analysis or reporting.

Data pipelines have vital characteristics:

- **Data frequency**: The speed at which the destination systems require the data – that is, at regular intervals in small batches or in real time. The pipeline should be capable enough to maintain the frequency of data transfer required by the destination system.

- **Resiliency**: How fault-tolerant and resilient is the data pipeline – that is, if the pipeline crashes due to a sudden data load or an overlooked code bug, there should be no data loss.

- **Scalability**: The tools and technology that are utilized in developing the data pipeline must be able to reconfigure it to scale out onto more hardware nodes if the data load increases.

What is Singer?

Before delving into Singer, a word must be said about the ETL tool landscape.

The field is vast, and a multitude of tools are available. Fivetran, Stitch, Keboola, and Airbyte are just some of the tools available on the market to make this task easier. In this section, we will approach Singer since it's open source and accessible to an analyst with Python programming knowledge without extra cost. So, what is Singer?

Singer is an open source standard for ETL created and sponsored by Stitch that lets you write scripts to move data from sources to targets. In essence, it allows us to quickly create a data pipeline.

Figure 2.1 illustrates three basic ETL pipelines in Singer – one for a database, one for a flat file or CSV, and the third for an API:

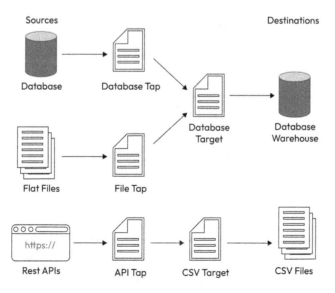

Figure 2.1 – ETL pipeline in Singer

Singer defines some core concepts to handle the common data pipeline abstractions:

- **Taps**: A tap, in Singer terminology, refers to a data extraction script or tool that is responsible for connecting to a data source, such as a database, API, or filesystem. The primary function of a tap is to extract data from its source in a structured format. Taps are designed to be source-specific, meaning each tap is tailored to extract data from a particular type of data source. For instance, there might be a tap for Salesforce, another for MySQL databases, and yet another for Google Sheets.

  Each tap is responsible for authenticating itself with the data source, making the necessary requests to retrieve data, and then outputting that data in a standardized format defined by the Singer specification. This standardized format typically involves a JSON structure that includes schema definitions for the data being extracted, the actual data records themselves, and, optionally, state messages that allow incremental data extraction.

  Singer has taps for most platforms, such as Google Ads, Facebook, or AppsFlyer.

- **Targets**: A target, in Singer parlance, is a data loading script or tool that takes the standardized data output from a tap and loads it into a destination system. Destinations can vary widely and can include databases, data warehouses, analytics platforms, or even other file formats. Like taps, targets are designed to be destination-specific, with each target crafted to load data into a particular type of destination. For example, there might be a target for loading data into PostgreSQL, another for Snowflake, and another for a CSV file.

  The role of the target is to receive the data from the tap, transform it if necessary to fit the destination's requirements, and then manage the process of inserting the data into the destination. This process may involve handling authentication with the destination, managing API requests for web-based destinations, executing SQL commands for databases, or simply writing files in the case of file-based destinations.

  Singer has targets for CSV files, databases such as PostgreSQL, and even ETL platforms such as Keboola.

- **Data exchange format**: A JSON file, with a Singer-specific schema, is used as the data exchange format between taps and targets. While it may seem an unnecessary extra step, it allows us to abstract away the data exchange from the specific tap and target, making it agnostic.

One interesting feature of Singer is that taps and targets can be piped together using the | operator on the command line, making the process quite intuitive once you get the hang of it. Let's see how, in practice, you would use Singer to extract campaign data from Google Ads.

This segment illustrates how to extract campaign data from Google Ads using the Singer ETL library. Here's a step-by-step process:

1. **Install the Google Ads tap**: First, we need to install the Google Ads tap via `pip`, Python's package installer. This can be done by executing the following command in your terminal or command prompt:

   ```
   pip install tap-googleads
   ```

2. **Configure file setup**: Next, we must set up a configuration file in JSON format. This file instructs the Google Ads tap on how to connect to the Google Ads API. The JSON structure is defined by the Singer library, as shown here:

```
{
    "start_date": "2020-10-01T00:00:00Z",
    "login_customer_ids": [{"customerId": "1234567890",
"loginCustomerId": "0987654321"}],
    "oauth_client_id":"client_id",
    "oauth_client_secret":"client_secret",
    "refresh_token":"refresh_token",
    "developer_token":"developer_token"
}
```

3. **Execute the tap**: Once the configuration file is in place, we must run the tap to generate the data catalog file in JSON format. The command to execute this step is as follows:

```
tap-googleads -c my-config.json --catalog catalog.json
```

To provide more context, let's walk through a detailed example of extracting data from a Google Ads account using the Singer tap.

Before we begin, ensure that all the necessary tokens for accessing the Google Ads API have been properly set up in the configuration JSON file, as mentioned earlier. Once that's in place, we are ready to extract data.

To obtain the tokens, you have to grab your developer token from the Google Ads settings area, as seen in *Figure 2.2*:

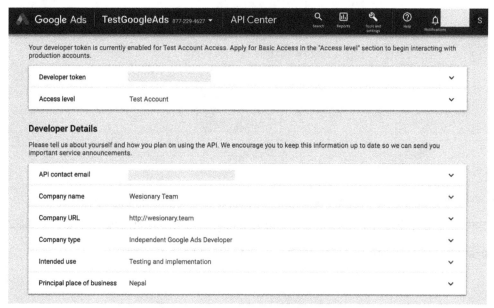

Figure 2.2 – Developer token for Google Ads

You will also need to set up your OAuth client ID and client secrets and generate a refresh token. OAuth tokens have a limited lifespan and need to be refreshed periodically. The refresh token provides a new access token without the need for the user to go through the authentication flow again. This token remains valid until the user revokes access.

You can find further details in the developer documentation at Google.

Let's assume the configuration file (my-config.json) and the catalog file (catalog.json) are stored in the same directory where you're running the tap.

The catalog file is used by the Singer tap to know which data streams and fields to sync from the Google Ads API. A simple catalog file for Google Ads might look like this:

```
{
    "streams": [
        {
            "stream": "campaigns",
            "tap_stream_id": "campaigns",
            "schema": {
                "selected": true,
                "properties": {
                    "id": {
                        "type": [
                            "null",
                            "string"
                        ]
                    },
                    "name": {
                        "type": [
                            "null",
                            "string"
                        ]
                    }
                }
            }
        }
    ]
}
```

This catalog file instructs the Singer tap to fetch id and name for the campaigns stream.

Now, you can run the Singer tap to extract the desired data. In your terminal, run the following command:

```
tap-googleads -c my-config.json --catalog catalog.json
```

This command instructs Singer's Google Ads tap to use the settings specified in `my-config.json` to connect to the Google Ads API and fetch the data defined in the `catalog.json` file.

The output will be a stream of JSON objects, each representing a single row of data from the `campaigns` stream. Let's look at an example:

```
{"type": "RECORD", "stream": "campaigns", "record": {"id":
"123456789", "name": " Summer Sale"}}
{"type": "RECORD", "stream": "campaigns", "record": {"id":
"987654321", "name": " Winter Promotion"}}
```

Here, we have the two example campaigns in the Google Ads account: a campaign named `Summer Sale` with an `id` value of `123456789` and a campaign named `Winter Promotion` with an `id` value of `987654321`. These are the campaign records from the Google Ads account that were specified in the configuration file, and they're ready to be loaded into your destination of choice (for example, a file, database, or data warehouse).

You can "pipe" the output of one tap directly into a target. In command-line jargon, to pipe means to direct the output of a program as the input of the next program by using the | character.

So, let's say you install the CSV target using the following command:

```
pip install target-csv
```

You can then pipe the extraction of Google Ads into a CSV file:

```
tap-google-ads --config config.json | target-csv --config target-config.json
```

Here, `target-config.json` is defined as follows:

```
{
  "destination_path": "./output/",
  "delimiter": ",",
  "quotechar": "\""
}
```

After the run, you will find a CSV file that contains the extracted data. Here's an example:

```
campaign_id,campaign_name,status,budget,clicks,impressions,cost
123456789,Summer Sale,ENABLED,50000,300,9500,45000
987654321,Winter Promotion,PAUSED,100000,0,0,0
```

Remember, always ensure that you have the necessary permissions and rights to access and extract data from the respective platforms. Be mindful of the terms of service and privacy policies of these platforms as well.

This exercise gave us a practical look at how the Singer library facilitates data extraction from media platforms. Applying this process to different platforms will help streamline the extraction process and ensure uniformity in the data you gather.

Upon extracting the data from Google Ads, the next step is storing the output for future analysis. The most effective method to retain the complexity and structure of this data in Python is by utilizing the `pickle` module.

Simply put, pickling allows us to store complex Python data structures, such as lists, dictionaries, and class objects, in a file that can be retrieved later for further use.

Let's consider that we've stored the output of the Singer tap in a variable named `ads_data`. This `ads_data` variable is what we'd like to persist for subsequent use:

```
import pickle
with open('google_ads_data.pkl', 'wb') as file:
    pickle.dump(ads_data, file)
```

In the previous snippet, we're opening a file named `google_ads_data.pkl` in write-binary (wb) mode. If the file does not already exist, Python will create it for us. We then use `pickle.dump()` to transfer the contents of the `data` variable into the file.

Now, to retrieve this data for later use, we can use the `pickle.load()` method:

```
with open('google_ads_data.pkl', 'rb') as file:
    loaded_data = pickle.load(file)
```

Here, we're opening the same file but in read-binary (rb) mode, and then loading the data from the file back into a Python variable. After this step, the `loaded_data` variable should be identical to the original `data` variable, retaining all the structure and details of the extracted Google Ads data.

As you use pickling, it is crucial to be mindful of its potential security risks, particularly when loading data from an untrusted source, as it can execute arbitrary code during the loading process. However, in our current scenario, since we are pickling our own data, it is safe to use.

As highlighted previously, extraction from media platforms is not an easy task, and diving deeper is outside the scope of this book. You will find some references at the end of this chapter, and I advise you to head to the Singer documentation website for more details.

After extracting data, but before running any model or attempting to analyze your data, you need to understand its shape. That is where EDA comes in.

Summarizing data and EDA

Summarizing data and performing EDA is the first task that you, as an analyst, always need to undertake. It will help you to understand the data you are dealing with and know which techniques are appropriate. But EDA is more than just doing some pivot tables. We need to start with a primer on descriptive statistics.

Primer on descriptive statistics

Data can be qualitative (also known as categorical) or quantitative.

Qualitative data can be nominal when, for example, you have two choices, such as "yes" and "no" or "male" and "female," but you do not have an implicit hierarchy in it. It can also be ordinal when a hierarchy has been implied, such as "level of education."

The most common way to describe this type of data is through the use of tabular methods such as frequency distributions or graphical methods with proportions.

When working with statistical models such as linear regression, it is a best practice to convert them into dummy variables – for example, "Yes" = 1, "No" = 0. A simple example of using "Male" and "Female" can be seen in *Table 2.1*:

Qualitative Variable	Dummy Variable
Female	1
Male	0

Table 2.1 – Example of dummy variable correspondence for Male and Female

Quantitative data refers to any data that can be quantified, counted, or measured with a numerical value. Since it's descriptive, it can be discrete in that the number of values can be distinctly counted, such as the number of orders received. Or, it can be continuous, meaning it can be measured but not counted, such as the currency value of sales or temperature readings. The most common way to describe this type of data is by using measures of central tendency and variability.

When starting the EDA process, to analyze our data, we usually start with the `describe()` method of a DataFrame. Let's load an example dataset for conversions per channel:

```
import pandas as pd
import numpy as np
import seaborn as sns

pd.set_option('display.float_format', lambda x: '%.2f' % x)
df = pd.read_csv('data/ trafficsources.csv')
df.describe()
```

Usually, we start with the `.describe()` method of the DataFrame object. It provides us with some summary statistics, as we can see now for our dataset.

```
          Revenue
count      900.00
mean     16441.94
std      13136.76
min          0.00
25%       7720.59
50%      10807.92
75%      17508.41
max      60000.00
```

Percentiles, quantiles, and distributions

25%, 50%, and 75% correspond to the 1st quantile, 2nd quantile (also known as median), and 3rd quantile, respectively. But before we dig deep, we need to make a small pit stop and discuss data distribution. The most basic way to visualize data distribution is using a histogram:

```
sns.histplot(df.Revenue)
```

Let's have a look at the histogram of revenue shown in *Figure 2.3* more closely:

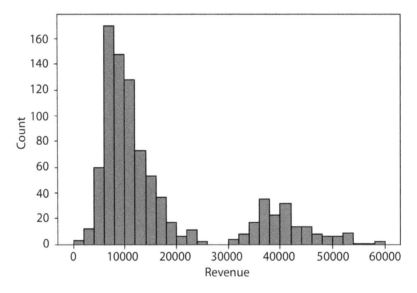

Figure 2.3 – Histogram of revenue

A **histogram** is nothing more than a count of the frequency of the ordered values, in bins of fixed size. This shows us the shape and spread of our data. Now, imagine that we ask the following question: What is the value at above which we have half of the frequency of the data and the other half below it? This value would be the median, as seen previously, and we can easily compute it using numpy:

```
np.median(df.Revenue)
```

You will get the output:

```
10807.925
```

An alternative way is to compute the 50th percentile by using the np.percentile function:

```
np.percentile(df.Revenue, 50)
```

This will produce the following result:

```
10807.925
```

Percentiles, as the name suggests, allow us to split the data from the 1st to the 100th percentile. In numpy, you control the percentile you want by using the q parameter, with a range from 1 to 100. A quantile is simply the percentile that splits the data into quarters and can be calculated with the np.quantile() function, with the difference that the control parameter ranges from 0 to 1:

```
np.quantile(df.Revenue, 0.5)
```

The following result will be observed:

```
10807.925
```

Quantiles are important in assessing outliers and the spread of data. We can do this by looking at the **interquartile range (IQR)**, which is simply computed with $IQR = Q3 - Q1$:

```
Q1 = np.quantile(df.Revenue, 0.25)
Q3 = np.quantile(df.Revenue, 0.75)
IQR = Q3 - Q1
print(f"IQR = {IQR}")
```

This will produce the following result:

```
IQR = 9787.815
```

The IQR is a good method for spotting outliers as we can use a simple heuristic of calculating the upper and lower bounds:

```
lower_bound = Q1 - 1.5 * IQR
upper_bound = Q3 + 1.5 * IQR
```

```
print(f"Lower bound = {lower_bound}")
print(f"Upper bound = {upper_bound}")
```

Any data point outside of the bounds can be classified as an outlier.

A good visualization for this is a **boxplot**, also known as a **box and whiskers plot**. It plots a box that's bounded by the 1st and 3rd quantiles – that is, the 25% and 75% portions of the data. The line in the middle of the box will show you the median. The length of the box is the IQR, and you know that it contains, by definition, 50% of the dataset. The bars at the edges represent the 1.5 * IQR. Everything below, or above, can be considered an outlier:

```
sns.boxplot(x = df.Revenue)
```

A boxplot can be seen in *Figure 2.4*, and it clearly shows some outliers after the edge of the 1.5 * IQR:

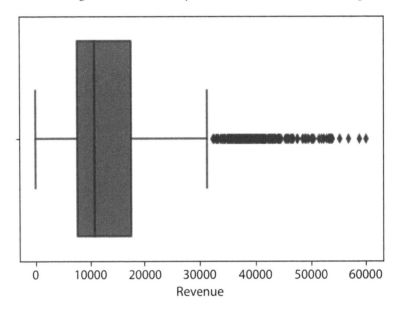

Figure 2.4 – Boxplot chart of revenue

An alternative to using a boxplot, but with the same function, is a violin plot, as seen in *Figure 2.5*. A violin plot blends the characteristics of a box plot with those of a histogram. It will show the distribution of the data, along with the mean, 1st and 3rd quantiles, and the IQR range. The name comes from the shape of how the distribution looks in the chart, shaped like a violin:

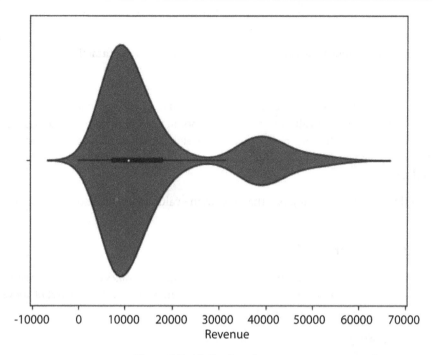

Figure 2.5 – Violin plot of revenue

You might be wondering what the difference is between a boxplot and a violin plot. While a boxplot only shows summary statistics such as the median, interquartile range, and outliers, a violin plot shows the entire distribution of the data. This encompasses additional information, such as the density of the data points around different values, thus providing more nuanced insights into the shape of the data distribution.

You should consider using a violin plot instead of a boxplot when it is important to understand the distribution of the data in greater detail. For instance, if the data is not normally distributed or if there's a need to show the presence of multiple modes in the data, a violin plot can be particularly insightful. It's also helpful when the dataset is large, and the visualization of the distribution's density can inform others about the structure that might not be apparent with box plots. However, you should be cautious when using violin plots for small sample sizes as the kernel density estimation may not accurately represent the underlying data distribution.

Measures of central tendency

A measure of central tendency is a single value that attempts to describe a dataset by identifying the central position within said dataset, be it the most common or the middle point of the dataset. The three main measures of central tendency are the **mean**, the **median**, and the **mode**.

The mean

The most common and popular measure is the mean, specifically the arithmetic mean:

$$\bar{x} = \frac{\sum_{i=1}^{n} x_i}{n}$$

The mean can be used in both discrete and continuous data, although it's most often used in continuous data. It's equal to the sum of all values in a sample or population divided by the total number of values in the dataset. The arithmetic mean can also be weighted, where a value is assigned a weight or proportion, and then you sum the product of all values times the weights and divide by the total number of values.

Means are highly susceptible to outliers – that is, extreme values – as will be demonstrated later in the chapter.

Do not calculate the average of averages

A common mistake in marketing analytics is to do the average of averages or average of proportions. To illustrate this point, consider the following code, which generates a random dataset of conversions of two channels, `paid_search` and `paid_social`:

```
import pandas as pd
import numpy as np

pd.set_option('display.float_format', lambda x: '%.2f' % x)

paid_search = [12, 3, 23, 32, 34, 76, 6, 23, 2, 23, 75, 23, 24, 34,
46, 34, 74, 8, 7, 96, 64]
paid_social = [76, 6, 23, 2]

df = pd.DataFrame(
    {' paid_search ' : pd.Series(paid_search),
     'paid_social' : pd.Series(paid_social)}
    )
```

Calculating the means per channel, using pandas, is straightforward. It's just a matter of invoking the `.mean()` method on the DataFrame object:

```
df.mean()
```

This will give you the following output:

```
paid_search    34.24
paid_social    26.75
dtype: float64
```

Now, if we are asked about the average conversion of all channels, we might be tempted to simply average the averages. It's quick, and sometimes, it can seem intuitive:

```
np.mean(df.mean())
```

So, our average across all channels is 30.49:

```
30.49404761904762
```

But is 30.49 the total average when aggregating both channels? We can quickly check this by unstacking the DataFrame and calculating the mean. Unstack() will simply pivot the columns and collapse them into a single row. Then, we can just chain the .mean() method and find the average:

```
df.unstack().mean()
```

The true average, when not grouping by channel, is 33.04, not 30.49. We are a bit off.

But why is that? The clue is the counts of the items. You don't have the same count of elements in both channels. To calculate the mean of both groups in aggregate, you would need to evaluate the weighted mean. The **weighted mean** is similar to the arithmetic mean, except that the sum of values is weighted by the proportional weight.

Looking at the counts for each channel, we can see the imbalance:

```
df.agg(['mean', 'count'])
        paid_search  paid_social
mean         34.24        26.75
count        21.00         4.00
```

The total mean would only be the same if, and only if, the counts were the same. Since they are not, you cannot do the average of the averages.

Aside from unstacking the original dataset, we could calculate the average by looking at the weight and multiplying it by the average of that channel, as follows:

```
total_counts = df.count().sum()
paid_search_proportion = df.paid_search.count()
paid_search_average = df.paid_search.mean()
paid_social_proportion = df.paid_social.count()
paid_social_average = df.paid_social.mean()

total_average = np.divide(paid_search_proportion * paid_search_average
+ paid_social_proportion * paid_social_average, total_counts)
print(total_average)
33.04
```

As we can see, we recovered the original true mean of the entire dataset.

Both approaches – using unstacking and the weighted mean – yield the same results. Which approach to use comes down to what data you have available. For example, if you are running an analysis where you don't have the original DataFrame to unstack, but only a table with counts and mean per channel, the weighted mean method will help you.

As previously mentioned, means are highly sensitive to outliers – that is, extreme values. This is where the median, the second measure of central tendency, comes in.

The median

The median is the value that splits the dataset in half. It corresponds to the 50th percentile of a dataset. The calculation involves ordering the dataset from low to high and finding the value that splits the dataset in half. If the count of values is even, then the median is the mean of the two values that split the dataset in half.

Let's look at a simple example of the effect of outliers on the mean and median values. We'll take a very simple list of values, `conversions_a`, as an example, to calculate the mean and median:

```
conversions_a = [12, 11, 10, 15, 9, 12]

print(f"mean = {np.mean(conversions_a)}")
print(f"median = {np.median(conversions_a)}")
mean = 11.5
median = 11.5
```

As we can see, the mean and median are the same. This is not always a guarantee, as we will see later in this chapter. Now, let's append a clear outlier to that list and recompute the mean and median:

```
conversions_a.append(100)

print(f"mean = {np.mean(conversions_a)}")
print(f"median = {np.median(conversions_a)}")
mean = 24.142857142857142
median = 12.0
```

As we can see, the mean more than doubled while the median only moved slightly up. This should serve as a cautionary tale. The mean is the usual measure of central tendency, but a single bad data point can lead you astray very quickly and lead you to the wrong conclusion.

Finally, we have the mode.

The mode

The mode is the simplest one and is the most common data point in a dataset. Data can have one or several modes, in which case it is **multi-modal**.

When the mean, the mode, and the median are all the same, we can conclude that the underlying distribution of the data is symmetrical. If the mean is smaller than the median, the data is left skewed, and conversely, if the mean is larger than the median, the data is right skewed:

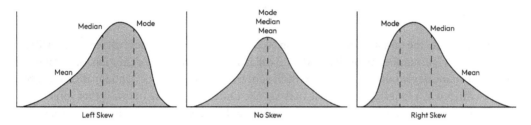

Figure 2.6 – Relationship between the mean, median, and mode and the skewness of data

While this may seem like statistical nitpicking, data skewness is important. Many marketing analytics techniques and methods rely on the assumption of data normality, which we will cover later in this chapter. If the data is not symmetrical and normally distributed, our inferences will be wrong, and we need to transform the data before proceeding with the analysis.

Central tendency measures only tell part of the story about a dataset. Taking a very simple example, you can have two suppliers of a given product. They both have the same average fulfillment time, but, one supplier varies around the mean twice as much as the other, meaning you have more uncertainty about when your order will arrive. This is where measures of variability will help ascertain and capture this uncertainty.

Measures of variability

Measures of variability measure the spread of your data. There are several measures of variability, but the most common ones are range, variance, and standard deviation. Let's begin with the range.

The range

The **range** is quite simply the difference between the largest and smallest values in the dataset. It is similar, in spirit, to the IQR, which we introduced previously, in that it attempts to show you the absolute spread of the data. On its own, it is not the most complete measure of variability, but it is an important input for normalization, specifically min-max normalization, which we will cover later in this chapter.

In Python, it's quite easy to compute the range:

```
def data_range(data):
    return max(data) - min(data)
```

If a measure of central tendency is the most common value, then it is intuitive to follow up by asking what the variability around said central tendency is. Picking the mean as our measure of central tendency, we could ask what the deviation is from the mean, $x_i - \bar{x}$.

The variance

When thinking about the deviation from the mean, as a naïve approach, we could divide the deviation from the mean by the number, n, of elements, and call it a day. However, by definition, on a dataset, the sum of absolute deviations from the mean will sum to zero, so you are essentially dividing 0 by a number, which is 0, rendering the metric useless. The underlying cause of this is that some data points will deviate with a positive sign from the mean, and others with a negative sign, essentially canceling each other out.

The obvious solution is just to square the individual deviations from the mean and sum them. This would turn every negative deviation into a positive number while preserving the magnitude of deviation.

In doing so, we end up with the definition of variance:

$$\sigma^2 = \frac{\Sigma(x_i - \mu)^2}{N}$$

Now, recall that, usually, you are not dealing with full population data, but with a sample, so the sample variance needs to be adjusted for bias:

$$s^2 = \frac{\Sigma(x_i - \bar{x})^2}{n - 1}$$

In both formulas, we have the following:

- x_i represents each value in the sample
- $\bar{x}$ is the sample mean
- n is the sample size
- The numerator, $\Sigma(x_i - \bar{x})^2$, is the sum of the squared deviations of each sample value from the sample mean
- The denominator in the second formula, $n - 1$, is the sample size minus one, to adjust for bias

While a bit more complex, it is still fairly easy to implement in Python when using numpy:

```
import numpy as np

# Population Variance
def pop_variance(data):
```

```
    n = len(data)
    mean = sum(data) / n
    deviations = [(x - mean) ** 2 for x in data]
    variance = sum(deviations) / n
    return variance

# Sample Variance
def sample_variance(data):
    n = len(data)
    mean = sum(data) / n
    deviations = [(x - mean) ** 2 for x in data]
    variance = sum(deviations) / (n - 1)
    return variance
```

We now have a measure of variability around the mean. The problem is that, to get it, we had to square the deviations, meaning we are no longer measuring in the same units as the underlying data. That is where standard deviation comes in.

Standard deviation

To get to the standard deviation, we simply take the square root of variance to reverse the previous squaring operation:

$$\sigma = \sqrt{\sigma^2}$$

The sample standard deviation is the same formula, by convention denoted by s, and involves the square root of the sample variance.

Considering the previously defined functions for variance, we can have the following:

```
# Population Standard Deviation
def pop_std_dev(data):
    return np.sqrt(pop_variance(data))

# Sample Standard Deviation
def sample_std_dev(data):
    return np.sqrt(sample_variance(data))
```

There is also a nice heuristic between range and standard deviation, where we can obtain a rough estimate of the latter from the former:

$$s \approx \frac{range}{4}$$

A word of caution on the last point: the heuristic is based on the assumption that the data is normally distributed, where most values lie close to the mean, and the range is about four standard deviations wide since, in a normal distribution, about 95% of the data falls within two standard deviations of the mean on either side.

Dealing with common data issues

Make no mistake, you will spend a large chunk of your time cleaning data or dealing with messy data, either dealing with mislabeled data, wrong formats, or missing data, among other issues. In this section, we will go through the most common problems that will affect your modeling efforts. Let's start with outliers and missing values.

Bill Gates walks into a bar

The classical example of outlier effects is as follows:

> *"10 men are sitting in a bar. The average income of the 10 men is $50,000.*
> *Suddenly, one man walks out and Bill Gates walks in. Now, the average income of*
> *the 10 men in the bar is $40 million."*

We touched upon this issue when we discussed the difference between the mean and the median. But how do you deal with it? The easiest way is simply to remove the data point. You essentially ignore it and assume it does not exist. If you are dealing with a lot of data points, this might seem reasonable. But as an analyst, you should be wary about throwing away data – especially in our field, where we do not have the luxury of billions of data points. Remember, as a marketing analyst, you live in a world of small data. We will only go through modeling in later chapters, but as food for thought, you need to consider that a rule of thumb for linear regression is 10 data points per variable you are trying to estimate. If time series data is involved, this value might rise to at least 30.

The point is that you usually do not have data points to spare and ignore if you have a lot of outliers. There is, however, another way to approach this problem. If to remove the effect of the outlier, you need to remove it, then you can look at it as a missing data problem. And that brings us to data imputation.

Missing values and data imputation

Sometimes, the data will have gaps or missing values. Imputation is the exercise through which you attempt to estimate a plausible value that the data point could assume. The most basic imputation technique is mean or median imputation, in which you will fill the gap with either the mean or the median of all other datasets. In the case of treating outliers such as missing values, you should avoid mean imputation since that is exactly the metric being affected. Instead, you should use median imputation.

The `sklearn` library provides some useful methods to quickly perform data imputation, in the `impute` module, for both mean and median imputation:

```
from sklearn.impute import SimpleImputer

# Mean Imputer
mean_imputer = SimpleImputer(strategy='mean')
```

```
# Median Imputer
median_imputer = SimpleImputer(strategy='median') ]
```

A common issue we see in statistics and econometrics is that after cleaning the data, we throw it into the model of our choice and wait for the outputs. Why is this an issue? To understand this, we need to dig a bit deeper into variable transformations and why they are needed.

Digging deeper into variable transformations

Statistical models have assumptions, and one of the heaviest is the normality of said data.

If your data does not follow a normal distribution, your estimates will be biased, and your errors will be skewed. In practice, you create a model to forecast sales dependent on spend, and after a month, your estimates are way off from reality, and you are left questioning why. For example, except for tree-based algorithms, the objective function from the Python sklearn library's algorithms assumes data normality of features.

In your EDA work, you should always tend to the shape of your data, skewness, and normality and adjust accordingly. Data transformations can be of three kinds:

- Data standardization or scaling, where you center the data around the mean and the standard deviation

- Power transformations, of which the most common one is the log transformation, where you apply a function that takes an exponent of the original data

- Data normalization, where by using a min-max scaler, you compress all the data points in a range of 0 to 1

Let's start by going through the standardization method.

Data standardization or scaling

This method is usually done when one of the features has a higher variance than the others. It simply involves two steps:

1. Subtracting the mean from all data points, also known as **centering**.
2. Dividing the preceding calculation by the standard deviation, also known as scaling.

This can be accomplished quite easily using sklearn's `StandardScaler`:

```
from sklearn.preprocessing import StandardScaler

scaler = StandardScaler()
data_standardized = scaler.fit_transform(data)
```

> **A word of caution on effectiveness**
>
> Data standardization will work if the features you are standardizing follow a linear distribution. A linear distribution is a pattern where the data is distributed evenly around the mean, resulting in a bell-shaped curve when plotted.
>
> If your features do not follow a linear distribution, it is unwise to attempt to transform the data with the mean and standard deviation. Sales and revenue data are usually examples of data that's ill-suited to this form of normalization due to their highly skewed nature. This is where power transformations come in.

Power transformations

The most common power transformation is to log all values in your dataset. In most cases, this simple operation will force your data to "look normal." There are other transformations that you can do to variables. Listing all of them may seem impossible, but in marketing, you will often see the same type of data in different datasets, be it counts, revenue, or sales. For these, there are some common transformations you can apply, as described in the following table:

Variable	Common Transformation
Unit sales, revenue, income, price	Log(x)
Distance	1/x, 1/x^2
Right tailed distribution (generally)	Sqrt(x) or log(x)
Left tailed distribution (generally)	x^2

Table 2.2 – Common data transformations

Many of the transformations in the preceding table follow some form of taking the power of x, hence the name "power transformations." Remembering high school math, $1/x = x^{-1}$, sqrt(x) $= x^{0.5}$, and so on. Like everything in mathematics, if there is a pattern, a generalization usually exists, and this case is no exception: the Box-Cox transformation. The Box-Cox transformation is defined as follows:

$$y(\lambda) = \begin{cases} \frac{(x^\lambda - 1)}{\lambda} & \text{if } \lambda \neq 0, \\ \ln(x) & \text{if } \lambda = 0, \end{cases}$$

You can think of the Box-Cox transformation as the generalization of the transformations in *Table 2.2*. Essentially, we are trying to find a lambda value that normalizes the data when we use it by taking the power of x to it. We can use the `scipy` implementation for this:

```
from scipy import stats

data_boxcox = stats.boxcox(data)
```

Finally, we have min-max scaling. The effect of this normalization is to compress all data points in a range between 0 and 1. To achieve this, you must complete two steps:

1. Subtract the minimum value from each data point.

2. Divide the preceding calculation by the maximum value – the minimum value. Recall above that max-min is nothing more than the range.

Mathematically, we can write it like this:

$$x_{scaled} = \frac{x - \min(x)}{\max(x) - \min(x)}$$

Looking back at `sklearn`, we can use the following implementation:

```
from sklearn.preprocessing import MinMaxScaler

scaler = MinMaxScaler()
data_minmax_scaled = scaler.fit_transform(data)
```

While this transformation forces the data to follow a normal distribution, the features will not have unit variance and a mean of 0. Also, it's important to note that this transformation doesn't handle outliers well. Outliers are data points that are significantly different from the other data points. Because min-max scaling compresses all the points into the [0,1] range, outliers will become closer to the bulk of the data, and that reduces the ability to detect and handle these extreme values. It is best to handle outliers before applying min-max scaling.

Summary

Throughout this chapter, we embarked on a detailed journey through the realm of ETL processes, specifically how they are applied to extract and handle marketing data. The vital role of data ingestion was discussed, and we emphasized the importance of EDA. Furthermore, we elaborated on the necessity of common data transformations to ensure data normality, thereby safeguarding the validity of any insights or models derived from the data.

After learning how to extract raw data from various sources, we discussed the need to summarize, cleanse, and organize it for subsequent analysis. Techniques for preparing data, including cleaning data and handling missing values and outliers, were explored. We also delved into the significance and methodologies of EDA, enabling you to understand the patterns, anomalies, and structures inherent in the data, laying a solid foundation for any ensuing analysis.

Finally, we engaged in a comprehensive discussion on the array of transformation techniques that are routinely employed in marketing data analysis to maintain normality, a prerequisite for many statistical models. We touched upon a variety of methods, such as data scaling, normalization, and power transformations.

In the next chapter, we will see how we can design dashboards to put the data that we have meticulously prepared and transformed to use.

Further reading

- Singer documentation: `https://github.com/singer-io/getting-started`
- *Building ETL Pipelines with Python*, by Brij Kishore Pandey and Emily Ro Schoof, Packt Publishing
- *R for Marketing Research and Analytics*, by Chris Chapman and Elea McDonnell Feit, Springer
- *Technical Debt*, Techopedia: `https://www.techopedia.com/definition/27913/technical-debt`

3

Design Principles and Presenting Results with Streamlit

Design is not just what it looks like and feels like. Design is how it works.

– Steve Jobs

When discussing how to present your results, few things are more ubiquitous than the trusty dashboard. A dashboard is, at its simplest, a screen that attempts to condense key metrics and KPIs in an easy and intuitive way, to allow for easy digestion of numerical information. We call them dashboards because, just like in a car, the key factor is to display only the fundamental and critical information needed by the user. It can provide a home screen for critical information, be it strategic or operational in nature.

In this chapter, we will go over the types of dashboards and their design principles, how to design good metrics and dimensions, and an example of using Streamlit to build a small dashboard. Specifically, we will cover the following topics:

- Types of dashboards and their design

- Generating effective filters, dimensions, and metrics

- Getting your data into Streamlit and generating a basic dashboard

By the end of this chapter, you will understand what makes a good dashboard and how to set up Streamlit to build dashboards quickly.

Technical requirements

The code files are available on GitHub at `https://github.com/PacktPublishing/Data-Analytics-for-Marketing/tree/main/Chapter03`.

Types of dashboards and their design

There are, commonly, three types of dashboards:

- **Operational dashboards**: These help the user see what's happening right now. The classical example is a call center dashboard, which shows call volumes and service levels. You can think of them as a digital control room. They will have one main driver, that being to give information to the user quickly because they are dealing with time-sensitive tasks that will most likely require immediate action. You want to present data deviations to the user quickly and accurately:

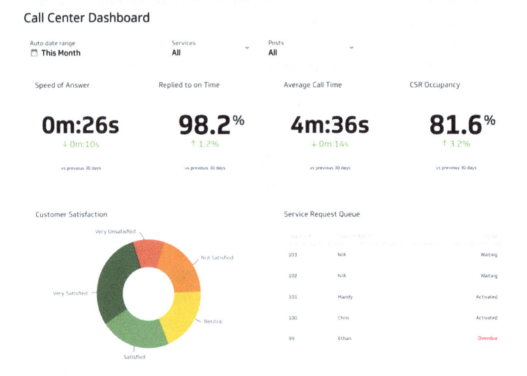

Figure 3.1 – An overview of operational dashboard in a call center application

- **Analytical dashboards**: These help the user understand patterns and trends and have a clear understanding of performance and potential issues for analysis and decision-making. They are not as time-sensitive, nor do they require immediate attention. The goal is to help the user spot trends and make sense of the data. Think of a dashboard showing the daily data for the past quarter on marketing campaign performance from your digital campaigns. As an analyst, these will be your most common type of dashboard to build:

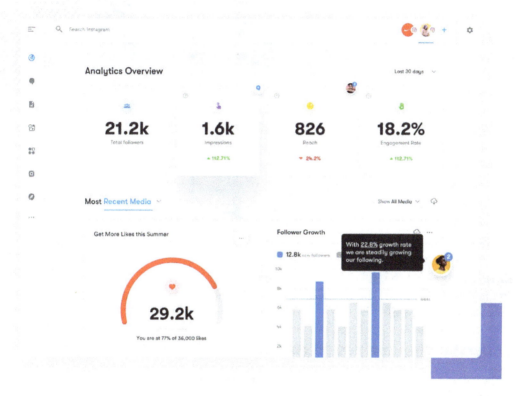

Figure 3.2 – An overview of analytical dashboard from a paid social application, showing social campaign effectiveness

- **Strategic dashboards**: These dashboards will help the user track their strategic decisions by tracking key KPIs of the business:

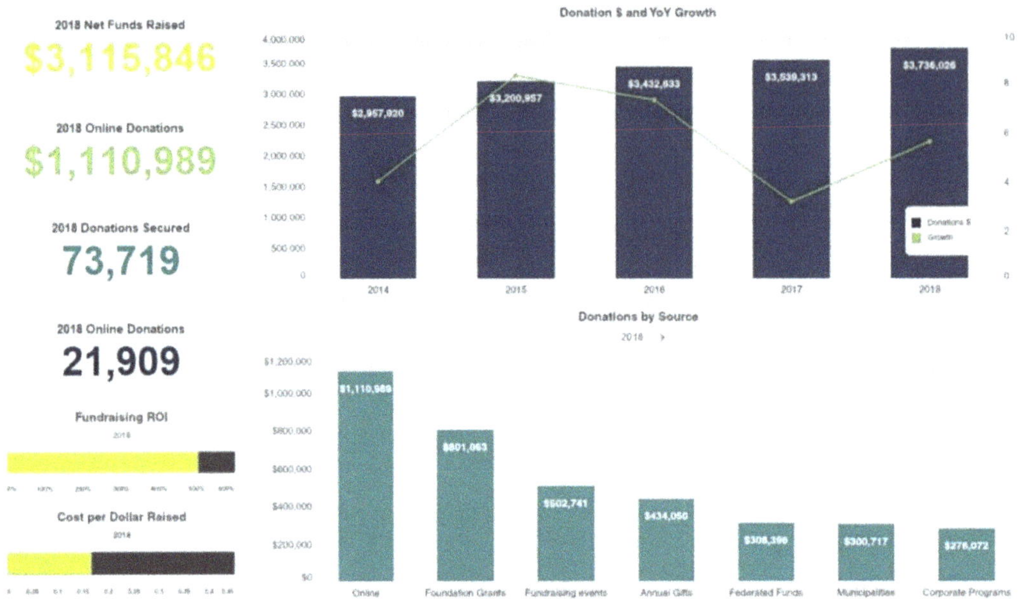

Figure 3.3 – An overview of strategic dashboard showing a non-profit organization's fundraising

There is a key aspect you, as an analyst, need to strive for: a dashboard must always save the user time and, in doing so, help the user become more efficient in the task they are aiming for. But what makes a good dashboard?

Understanding the design concepts of a dashboard

While it does not take a designer or UI/UX expert to design a dashboard, it does help to understand some of the concepts of those fields to design a good dashboard. When thinking about a dashboard design, it is helpful to consider the exercise as if you were designing a product for consumers. In doing so, you should ask yourself what your target audience is and what they care about.

As analysts, we sometimes have a tendency to gloss over or skip this step entirely. It can be argued that due to professional bias, we tend to prefer data modeling to storytelling. But having a key understanding of your key audience is the difference between having a highly used dashboard versus having a dashboard sitting in the BI graveyard or, maybe worse, having your stakeholders constantly asking for changes to it.

When presenting your results, be it in the form of a self-serve data app, a dashboard, or a presentation, you need to understand, first and foremost, that you are telling a story. A story with data, but a story, nonetheless.

Understanding your audience is key:

- Are you talking to the operational side of the business, who need key metrics but a degree of detail to quickly make changes to a marketing campaign on their weekly reviews?

- Or are you talking to management, who do not need, nor have time for, the nitty-gritty details but need a more bird's-eye view to make quarterly resource allocation of budget?

When creating dashboards for marketing analytics, several key heuristics can guide your design process and ensure the effectiveness of your visualizations. Consider the following principles:

- **Define the purpose**: Clearly articulate the objectives and purpose of your dashboard. The intended use and audience should inform the design choices you make. For example, a dashboard designed to track the performance of a new product launch should focus on metrics such as daily signups, conversion rates, and user engagement post-launch. The main objective is to gauge the initial success and growth of the new product.

- **Prioritize important information**: Include only essential elements that support the primary objectives of your dashboard. Avoid cluttering the visualization with unnecessary or distracting elements. If the dashboard's primary goal is to track campaign performance, then metrics such as **click-through rate (CTR)**, **cost per acquisition (CPA)**, and **return on ad spend (ROAS)** should be front and center. Avoid cluttering the space with unrelated metrics such as website uptime or server load.

- **Optimize data-ink ratio**: Minimize the use of decorative elements that do not contribute to the communication of data. Maximize the proportion of ink (or pixels) used to represent meaningful information. A minimalistic line chart showing the trend of website traffic over time with a clear title and axis labels, and without a grid or background images, ensures that the data stands out without unnecessary visual elements.

- **Round numbers for simplicity**: Avoid excessive precision in your numeric values. Instead, round numbers to an appropriate level of granularity that facilitates understanding and highlights significant changes. Displaying revenue as "$25.7K" instead of "$25,739.45" makes the data easier to read and quickly comprehend without losing essential information.

- **Choose the right visualization**: Select visual representations that effectively convey information and can be quickly understood by your audience. Opt for charts and graphs that best represent the underlying data and relationships. Use a bar chart to compare the performance of different marketing channels, a pie chart to show the market share of different product categories, or a funnel diagram to represent the customer journey from awareness to purchase.

- **Group related metrics**: Organize and group related metrics together to enhance discoverability and facilitate comparison. Logical grouping allows viewers to easily identify and analyze related data points. Organize metrics such as social media engagement (likes, shares, and comments) together in one section of the dashboard to allow for easy comparison across different platforms.

- **Maintain consistency**: Consistent use of visualizations, layouts, and color schemes across different sections of the dashboard promotes coherence and simplifies the process of comparing information. Use the same color scheme for similar metrics, such as shades of blue for engagement metrics and shades of green for financial metrics, with consistent font types and sizes across all visual elements.

- **Utilize size and position**: Use variations in size and position to emphasize the hierarchy and importance of different elements within the dashboard. Guide viewers' attention toward critical information by strategically placing it in prominent locations. Place the most critical metrics, such as monthly revenue or lead conversion rates, in the top-left corner of the dashboard, which is often where viewers look first, and make them larger than less critical information.

- **Provide context for numbers**: Accompany numerical values with contextual information to help viewers interpret and evaluate their significance. Provide benchmarks, comparisons, or reference ranges to convey whether a number is good, bad, normal, or unusual. Next to a figure showing a 10% conversion rate, include a small text indicating the industry average is 5%, signaling that the current rate is performing well.

- **Use clear labels**: Keep labels concise, self-explanatory, and tailored to your target audience. Clear labeling enhances comprehension and avoids confusion or misinterpretation. Label a graph showing traffic sources with clear terms such as "Organic Search," "Paid Ads," or "Referrals" instead of acronyms or jargon that might not be immediately understood.

- **User engagement matters**: Remember that dashboards are designed for people. While adhering to best practices, don't be afraid to deviate if it enhances viewer engagement and encourages interaction with the data. Incorporate interactive elements such as filters that allow users to view data for specific time periods or campaigns, and tooltips that provide more information when hovering over data points.

- **Continuous improvement**: Regularly evaluate and evolve your dashboards to ensure they are driving the desired behaviors and delivering actionable insights. Seek feedback, monitor performance, and make iterative improvements over time.

By applying these principles, you can create compelling and impactful dashboards that effectively communicate marketing analytics insights to your audience.

Thinking about how to best present data

All too often, analysts just throw charts at the screen. But not all charts are born equal. Each chart serves a purpose, given the information you intend to convey. We can split charts into four main categories:

- Understanding relationships
- Comparing categories or timeframes

- Seeing the composition of the data

- Seeing the distribution or shape of the data

You can see a short summary of which charts perform better at which function in *Figure 3.4*. Be mindful that the list shows you the most common charts. There are many more options available:

Figure 3.4 – An overview of chart types – each chart has a purpose

Delving a bit deeper into the uses of each chart type, let's start with understanding relationships between variables or dimensions.

Understanding relationships

The best way to understand relationships is by using two-dimensional charts to compare two variables. If the aim is to understand correlation and distribution, a scatter plot is the most efficient at displaying that kind of information. If you need to have another dimension, you can use a bubble chart, where the size of the bubbles will represent a third dimension or variable. Alternatively, you can color code to represent a third variable. You can see an example of a bubble chart in *Figure 3.5*:

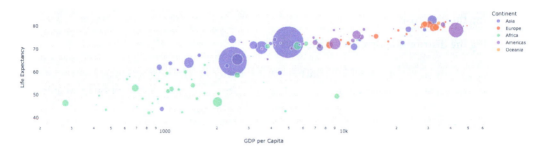

Figure 3.5 – Relationship between life expectancy and GDP per capita

Here, we are observing the relationship between GDP per capita and life expectancy. Notice that the bubbles reflect countries, the colors reflect continents, and the size of the bubble reflects population size, illustrating how this chart type can pack a lot of information in a very clean way.

Comparing categories

When comparing categories, bar and line charts are the most commonly used because of their simplicity in showing the needed information. There are, however, some heuristics to watch out for:

- When one of the dimensions is time, it is best to display it on the *x* axis, making time flow from left to right, from oldest to newest, which matches the human writing pattern

- When using horizontal or vertical bar charts, sort the data by value instead of letting it sit at random

- If a line chart contains more than one category, try to keep the maximum at five lines

- Same for a bar chart, but you can increase the maximum to seven bars

Seeing distribution

Distribution charts will help you understand the shape of data, its normal tendency and range, and outliers. One of the best charts is the histogram chart, which will cut data into ordered bins.

If you wish to convey more information – such as median, quantiles, and range – you can rely on the old boxplot chart. Violin plots are also a good modern update on the boxplot, blending the characteristics of the histogram and boxplot charts.

Seeing composition or parts of the whole

The most common charts for this are the pie chart and donut chart. These charts have a very bad reputation and have the tendency to be the most misused of all the charts. While this book will not make a blanket statement to not use them, they should be used carefully. They should not be used when you have a lot of components – as a rule of thumb, more than three – or very similar values. You need to remember: humans have a hard time differentiating angles and areas.

When having more than three components, treemaps and heatmaps are a great way to quickly show how different parts make up the whole of the data.

Stacked column charts and stacked area charts are good if you need to combine the capability of comparing categories with composition.

Considering things to avoid

There are, however, some red lines when it comes to chart design that will make interpreting the data harder for the end user:

- **3D charts**: Avoid at all costs. Although the idea might look cool, which is debatable, they are very hard to read and interpret given the "perspective" they create to induce the 3D aspect.

- **Over-styled charts**: Avoid using too many colors or too many styles. Keep it simple, and don't distract the user from the core information you are trying to convey. Always consider the data-to-ink ratio.

- **Playing with the y-axis scale on a line chart for a time series**: The oldest trick in the chart book, to show an effect when there is none, is to "zoom in" by using a small scale on the y axis. Think of selecting 95 to 100 as the minimum and maximum value of the y axis when the data goes from 0 to 100. Always keep the scale from 0 to the maximum value.

- A corollary of *point 3* is to keep your y axis consistent across charts, especially if they are on the same view.

On chart design, always consider Edward Tufte's concept of **data-ink ratio**. Edward Tufte was an American statistician who argued for the removal of unnecessary elements on a chart, such as line grid lines, icons, or superfluous colors. When communicating data, you should always aim for simplicity. The reasoning is simple. The more elements in a chart, the more cluttered the space and the more confusing the interpretation. And on the topic of charts, always remember that each chart type serves a purpose. It cannot be stressed enough that the wrong choice of a chart may destroy your efforts in conveying information in a meaningful way.

A good illustration of the data-ink ratio is shown in *Figure 3.6*, where you can compare what a cleaner design for a chart looks like:

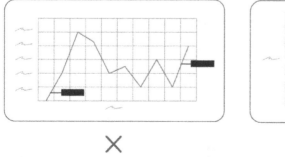 

Figure 3.6 – Data-ink ratio

Aside from which charts to use, we need to consider how your users will read your dashboard, and for that, we need to get our designer-thinking hats on.

Thinking a bit about processing information

Designers think a lot about how human beings process information visually. As analysts, we sometimes forget some interesting lessons from UI design that could help us deliver better storytelling.

One of the key ones is **reading patterns**. We have two fundamental reading patterns: the **F pattern** and the **Z pattern**.

The Z pattern is the easiest to understand and comes as a byproduct of how people read in Western cultures – from left to right. This means your users' eyes will scan a document in a zig-zag pattern:

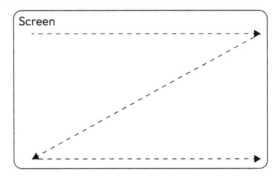

Figure 3.7 – Z pattern of reading

In non-Western languages, such as Arabic, where one writes from right to left, the pattern will become a reversed z.

Through the use of eye-tracking technology, it was found that when reading online or on a digital device, users tend to read based on an F-shaped pattern:

1. They will read the first line with some detail, forming the top part of the F.
2. They will then scan vertically down, on the left, for something interesting to read.
3. Once they find it, they will skim through, drawing the second horizontal line of the F.
4. Lastly, the users will scan vertically the rest of the document.

Such patterns have consequences on how you should structure your dashboard layouts:

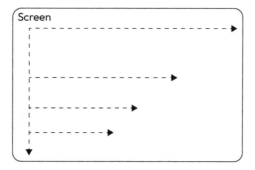

Figure 3.8 – F-shaped reading pattern

A note on the F pattern

While the Z pattern is commonly accepted – even intuitive – the F pattern is more disputed. Recently, Nielsen did a study where it disproved it, in favor of what it called the "layer cake" pattern; that is, users mostly read headings and sub-headings and skim the text. Since we are not writing copy for an ad, our biggest focus is going to be on the Z pattern.

Don't hide information or rely on interactions too much

In relation to the aforementioned content, a common mistake is to design dashboards that are long and require scrolling or rely on filter interactions to get to the data. Try to summarize as much as possible. Do not end up on the other side of the spectrum and overload your user with too much information in a small space. Humans can't process that much information, so overloading will lead to confusion. Use a max of five to seven visuals or widgets per view.

Also, be aware of something designers call the **fold**. The browser has so much space in it that you can present before you need to scroll. The fold is the line before you need to scroll down.

Paying attention to the reading flow and layout

Considering that research shows users tend to follow an F-shaped pattern when reading, analysts should act accordingly. In this regard, analysts should think a bit about design and user experience. The best way to start thinking about the layout is to set up a grid. Grids are common in web design. They help designers create a system that keeps things cohesive and allows us to organize information in a very easy way:

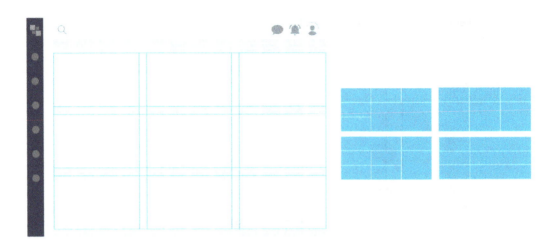

Figure 3.9 – Grid layout creates a cohesive design system

Grid layouts exist for a reason in web design. They keep information neatly packed to the human eye. They create an overall system that keeps things cohesive. Take advantage of it: define your layout and stick with it.

Thinking about the layout will also force you to think about what to show and prioritize accordingly. As an analyst, you may be tempted to show all the information available, but that is a mistake. Remember – when designing a dashboard, you are essentially telling a story – with data, but a story nonetheless. Going back to reading patterns, there is another benefit to a grid layout: it will allow you to easily accommodate a proper flow of information reading. The top left of the screen will get the most attention, so put your most important information there, from left to right.

As pictured in *Figure 3.10*, use grids to create a flow of the most important information to the least important information you want the end user to capture:

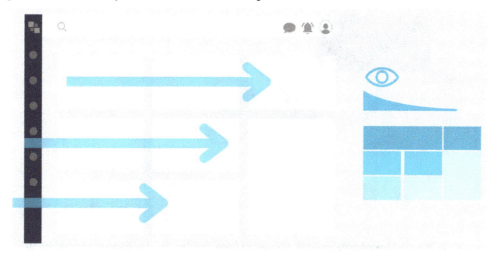

Figure 3.10 – Reading flow and placement of information

And flow is not just defined by paying attention to the human reading pattern. You need to consider progressive information delivery.

What is progressive information delivery?

Tied to the aforementioned point, think about the information you want to supply as a hierarchy, from top-level to more fine-grained details. Again, this book will use the story analogy: when writing a story, you start with the introduction, then development, and finally a conclusion. There is a flow to it that makes you understand the key concepts before the details and not go back and forth to understand them. This last element is key: do not make your users go back and forth through the dashboard to understand what they need to know. That breaks the flow and will break information processing.

You can think of progressive information delivery as going from a broader overview to a more detailed view to an even more detailed view, as seen in *Figure 3.11*:

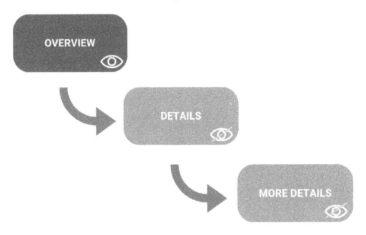

Figure 3.11 – Progressive information delivery: going from a higher-level overview to more details

This means you should design your dashboard either with different views or filter drill-downs to allow the user to progressively get greater and greater detail.

The small details matter

Some small details matter. A lot. Keep your dashboards consistent with regard to the layout. It will help your users learn where to get the information they need. Also, keep consistent formatting of data and naming conventions for variables. Remember the main goal of the dashboard: getting the most information out at a glance.

Generating effective filters, dimensions, and metrics

To create a powerful marketing analytics dashboard, it's essential to carefully choose and define your filters, dimensions, and metrics. These elements play a crucial role in providing insights and enabling data-driven decision-making. Let's explore some best practices for generating effective filters, dimensions, and metrics.

Filters

Filters allow users to slice and dice data based on specific criteria, providing the ability to focus on subsets of information. Here are some tips for creating useful filters:

- **Relevance**: Ensure that your filters are relevant to your dashboard's purpose and the questions you want to answer. Consider the specific needs of your audience and what data subsets they are likely to be interested in. If the main purpose of the dashboard is to monitor the performance of various marketing campaigns, relevant filters could include the following:

- **Campaign name**: Allowing users to select and compare specific campaigns

- **Channel**: Filters for different channels such as social media, email, **pay-per-click** (**PPC**), and so on to see performance by channel

- **Geographic location**: Enabling data selection by country, region, or city to evaluate the campaign performance in different geographical areas

- **Intuitiveness**: Design filters that are intuitive and easy to understand. Use clear and concise labels, and consider using drop-down menus, checkboxes, or sliders to make the selection process smooth and user-friendly. For a dashboard designed to track customer acquisition efforts, intuitive filters could include the following:

  - **Customer segment**: Drop-down menu to select customer segments such as "New Visitors," "Returning Customers," or "Loyal Customers"

  - **Acquisition source**: Checkboxes to select or deselect acquisition sources such as "Organic Search," "Referrals," "Social Media," and so on

  - **Time period**: Sliders to easily select a date range, such as "Last 30 days" or "Q1 2024," to analyze data over specific periods

- **Granularity**: Provide filters at the appropriate level of granularity. For example, if your dashboard displays data at a daily level, include filters to refine the data by date range, but avoid unnecessary filters that may overwhelm users. In a dashboard used for tracking sales and promotions, granularity in filters might include the following:

  - **Product categories**: Allow users to drill down into specific product categories such as "Electronics," "Apparel," or "Home Goods"

  - **Price range**: Providing a filter to view products sold within certain price ranges helps in analyzing the sales performance of different pricing tiers

  - **Promotion type**: A filter to view data for specific types of promotions, such as "Buy One, Get One," "Discount Codes," or "Flash Sales"

- **Interactivity**: Make filters interactive by enabling users to dynamically update the dashboard based on their selections. This flexibility allows users to explore different scenarios and gain deeper insights. For a lead generation dashboard, interactive filters could include the following:

  - **Lead status**: A dynamic filter where users can select to view data on "New Leads," "Contacted," "Qualified," or "Lost," and the dashboard updates in real time

- **Conversion funnel stage**: A filter that allows users to click through different stages of the conversion funnel (Awareness, Interest, Decision, Action) and see the corresponding metrics update instantly

- **Sales representative**: A filter that lets users choose one or more sales representatives to see their performance metrics, with the ability to combine with other filters such as time periods or lead sources for in-depth analysis

Dimensions

Dimensions provide context and categorization to the data, allowing users to analyze and compare different aspects of their marketing efforts. Here's how you can create meaningful dimensions:

- **Relevance**: Select dimensions that align with your dashboard's objectives and the questions you want to answer. Choose dimensions that are critical for understanding your marketing performance and identifying key trends or patterns.

- **Hierarchy**: Organize dimensions hierarchically to provide a structured view of the data. For example, if you have a "Location" dimension, you can break it down into country, region, and city to offer different levels of analysis.

- **Consistency**: Maintain consistency in dimension labels and formats throughout your dashboard. This ensures clarity and facilitates easy comprehension across different sections and visualizations.

- **Contextualization**: Use dimensions to provide additional context to your metrics. For example, if you're analyzing website traffic, dimensions such as "Traffic Source" or "Device Type" can help understand the sources of traffic or the impact of different devices on user behavior.

Metrics

Metrics are the quantitative measures used to assess and evaluate performance. Choosing the right metrics is crucial for tracking progress toward your marketing goals. Consider these guidelines when defining metrics:

- **Relevance to objectives**: Align your metrics with your marketing objectives. Identify KPIs that directly reflect progress toward your goals. For example, if your goal is to increase website conversions, relevant metrics would include conversion rate, **average order value** (**AOV**), and total conversions.

- **Specificity**: Use specific metrics that provide actionable insights. Avoid overly broad metrics that may not provide meaningful guidance for decision-making. Instead, break down complex metrics into more focused sub-metrics to identify specific areas of improvement.

- **Benchmarking**: Establish benchmarks or targets for your metrics to provide context for performance evaluation. These benchmarks can be based on historical data, industry standards, or specific business goals. Tracking progress against benchmarks helps monitor performance and identify areas that require attention.

- **Visualization**: Present metrics in a visually appealing and easily interpretable format. Utilize appropriate charts, graphs, or tables to illustrate trends, comparisons, or performance over time. Visualizations enhance understanding and facilitate data-driven decision-making.

Remember – the effectiveness of your filters, dimensions, and metrics depends on your understanding of your audience's needs and the specific goals of your marketing analytics dashboard. Continuously assess and refine these elements based on feedback and changing business requirements to ensure your dashboard remains relevant and valuable to your users.

By employing these best practices, you can create a marketing analytics dashboard that provides actionable insights and empowers data-driven decision-making within your organization.

Getting your data into Streamlit and generating a basic dashboard

Before going through the practicalities of creating a Streamlit app, we need to look into why we are discussing it in the first place. Usually, dashboards are built in a specialized tool such as Power BI, Looker, Data Studio, or Tableau. Some even use Excel, which has excellent capabilities – and can also be overused. Technically, all these options are excellent.

Firstly, the underlying core of this book is Python. The aim is to provide you, the analyst, with a core set of tools and techniques in one language to be able to do all the facets of your job. And that needs to include dashboarding.

On the other hand, there are increasing limitations to dashboards. They are, by their very nature, static. Streamlit allows you to move into building dynamic data apps in a way that the user can interact with data in a manner not possible with a dashboard. Three reasons stand out when evaluating Streamlit:

- First, Streamlit apps can be set up to reflect changes in real time when the underlying data changes. This means you can create live dashboards that update without user intervention or page refreshes.

- Secondly, Streamlit is built for Python, making it seamless to integrate with Python's extensive ecosystem of data science libraries such as `Pandas`, `NumPy`, and `Matplotlib`, and **machine learning (ML)** frameworks such as TensorFlow and scikit-learn.

- Finally, beyond predefined filters and selections, Streamlit can take text input, file uploads, and other user-generated content to manipulate data or feed models on the fly, providing a more dynamic interaction model.

You can still apply all of the concepts detailed in this chapter to another BI tool. But this section will, hopefully, not keep you tied to BI if you need to design more dynamic data apps. With that introduction out of the way, exactly what is Streamlit?

Starting out with Streamlit

Streamlit is an open source framework that allows data analysts and data scientists to transform Python scripts into web apps quite easily. The R programmer has a very powerful framework in R Shiny. Streamlit attempts to port that concept to Python in a very easy way. You don't need to understand how to deploy a web server, build a Flask app – or what Flask even is. With Streamlit, you can transform data scripts into shareable web apps with minimal effort. The framework deals with that, under the hood, for you. You just need to care about the data modeling part of programming. So, let us start with a simple "hello world" example of how to build a data app with Streamlit.

Installing and running Streamlit

Streamlit is extremely easy to install and run. To install it, just run the following command:

```
$pip install streamlit
```

The source code for a Streamlit app is placed in a `.py` file, and running it is done as follows:

```
$ streamlit run source_file.py
```

A simple Streamlit app would contain the following code:

```
import streamlit as st
import pandas as pd
import numpy as np

st.title('Hello World!')
chart_data = pd.DataFrame(
    np.random.randn(20, 3),
    columns=['a', 'b', 'c'])

st.line_chart(chart_data)
```

You can run this by simply invoking the `streamlit run` command:

```
$ streamlit run streamlit-helloworld.py
```

With the previous code snippet, Streamlit will deploy a Flask web app and display a new web page with the data you instructed it. In this case, it's a line chart with three randomly generated data series:

Hello World!

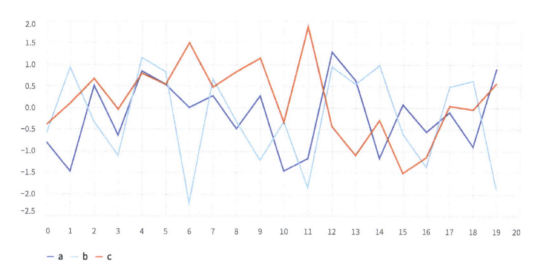

Figure 3.12 – Your first Streamlit app

Now, the **Hello World!** heading is understandably underwhelming, and even breaks some principles, such as the ink-to-data ratio principle described earlier. Let's use the marketing data from *Chapter 2, Extracting and Exploring Data with Singer and Pandas*, and build a simple dashboard with some key metrics.

Creating a marketing data dashboard with Streamlit

In this section, we will explore how to create a store data dashboard using Streamlit, a powerful framework that enables data analysts and data scientists to transform Python scripts into web apps. Streamlit simplifies the process of building web applications by abstracting the complexities of web server deployment and framework setup, allowing you to focus on the data modeling and visualization aspects of your project. Let's start by setting up the necessary libraries and environment.

Setting up the environment

To begin, we need to import the required libraries: streamlit, pandas, numpy, matplotlib, and seaborn. By convention, streamlit is often imported as st, but you can follow your own naming convention:

```
import streamlit as st
import numpy as np
```

```
import pandas as pd
import plotly.express as px
```

When working with a Streamlit application, you can run it initially and keep it running while making changes to the code. Streamlit automatically detects changes and updates the app in real time, providing a seamless development experience. Now, let's create a simple blank version of our dashboard with a title and a wide layout using the st.set_page_config() function:

```
st.set_page_config(
    page_title="Marketing Dashboard",
    layout="wide")
```

Loading the data and creating metrics

Now, let's proceed with loading the data and calculating the metrics. We will use the pd.read_csv() function from the pandas library to read the campaign_data.csv file, create a DataFrame called data_df, and do some manipulation to create a campaign_name column:

```
data_df = pd.read_csv("data/campaign_data.csv", parse_dates=[0])
data_df["year"] = data_df["utc_date"].dt.year
data_df["campaign_name"] = data_df["campaign_url"].str.replace(
    "https://www.example.com/", "", regex=False
)
```

Let's define some of the metrics we want. We want to calculate and return the advertising metrics summarized so that we can build metric cards on the top of the dashboard. We can do this using the following snippet:

```
def get_metrics(data: pd.DataFrame, st_object):
    impressions = data.loc[:, "impressions"].sum()
    clicks = data.loc[:, "page_clicks"].sum()
    ctr = round(
        100.0 * data.loc[:, "page_clicks"].sum() / data.loc[:,
        "impressions"].sum(), 2
    )
    gross_profit = round(data.loc[:, "gross_profit"].sum(), 2)
    avg_cpc = round(data.loc[:, "cpc"].mean(), 2)
    avg_rpc = round(data.loc[:, "rpc"].mean(), 2)

    col1, col2, col3, col4, col5, col6 = st_object.columns(6)

    col1.metric("Total Impressions", impressions)
    col2.metric("Total Clicks", clicks)
    col3.metric("CTR", f"{ctr}%")
```

```
col4.metric("Total Gross Profit", f"{gross_profit/1000:.2f}k $")
col5.metric("Avg Cost Per Click", f"{avg_cpc:.2f} $")
col6.metric("Avg Rev Per Click", f"{avg_rpc:.2f} $")
```

We calculated six metrics:

- `Total Impressions`: Sum of all the impressions from the data. Impressions are the number of times an ad is displayed.

- `Total Clicks`: Sum of all page clicks from the data. This represents how many times users clicked ads.

- CTR: Calculates the CTR as a percentage. It's the ratio of page clicks to impressions, indicating the effectiveness of the advertisements in encouraging viewers to click on them. This value is rounded to two decimal places.

- `Total Gross Profit`: Sum of all gross profit values from the data, rounded to two decimal places. Gross profit typically represents the profit made from the ads after subtracting the cost of selling or producing them.

- `Avg Cost Per Click`: The mean of the **cost per click (CPC)** from the data, rounded to two decimal places. CPC is a billing model where advertisers pay for each click on their ads.

- `Avg Rev Per Click`: The mean of the **revenue per click (RPC)** from the data, rounded to two decimal places. RPC indicates the average revenue generated from each click on the ads.

Additionally, the function uses `st_object.columns(6)` to create a six-column layout in the Streamlit app. This allows for displaying each metric in its own column for a neat presentation.

Each metric is displayed using `colX.metric(label, value)`, where `colX` is one of the six columns created. This method is used to display a key metric with a label (`label`) and its corresponding value (`value`). For the CTR, gross profit, average CPC, and average RPC metrics, specific formatting is applied to the values for better readability (for example, appending `%` to the CTR metric, formatting gross profit in thousands with `k $`, and appending `$` to the average CPC and RPC values).

We can check the result, as shown in *Figure 3.13*:

Total Impressions	Total Clicks	CTR	Total Gross Profit	Avg Cost Per Click	Avg Rev Per Click
482629	285275	59.11%	621.92k $	1.90 $	3.04 $

Figure 3.13 – Output of the get_metrics() function

Designing summaries for platforms and campaigns

Now, we will create some more functions for some summaries for platforms and campaigns.

Let's start with source metrics, as shown in the next snippet:

```python
def top_traffic_source(data: pd.DataFrame) -> pd.DataFrame:
    top_traffic_sources = (
        data.groupby(by=["traffic_source"])
        .agg(
            {
                "impressions": "sum",
                "page_clicks": "sum",
                "revenue": "sum",
                "ad_spend": "sum",
                "gross_profit": "sum",
                "cpc": "mean",
                "rpc": "mean",
                "cpa": "mean",
            }
        )
        .reset_index()
    )

    return top_traffic_sources
```

Here, we are simply aggregating the metrics by `traffic_source` and returning the dataset. You should note that not all metrics are aggregated the same way. While most are sums, CPC, RPC, and CPA should be means. The result can be seen in *Figure 3.14*:

Sources Metrics

	traffic_source	impressions	page_clicks	revenue	ad_spend	gross_profit	cpc	rpc	cpa
0	Facebook Ads	57,078	32,204	115,304.768	40,900.4283	74,404.3397	2.0416	3.0235	3.974
1	Instagram Ads	67,532	38,947	127,074.8119	50,152.0636	76,922.7484	1.8742	2.991	3.6152
2	LinkedIn Ads	80,076	47,457	163,011.0001	61,398.5214	101,612.4787	1.9305	3.0408	3.5286
3	Reddit Ads	71,583	43,750	156,272.9484	54,215.4887	102,057.4597	1.858	3.1872	3.9231
4	TikTok Ads	71,577	42,071	142,015.226	52,494.6794	89,520.5466	1.8147	3.0182	3.7448
5	Twitter Ads	63,295	37,970	133,755.7387	47,774.064	85,981.6747	1.9866	3.0351	3.6161
6	YouTube Ads	71,488	42,876	143,077.8699	51,654.3163	91,423.5536	1.7807	3.0056	3.3393

Figure 3.14 – Platform summary table

On the campaign side, we'll do two things. First, we will make a stacked bar chart of impressions and gross profit per campaign, using a stacked bar chart per month. Second, we will create a summary table with all of the metrics, but this time per campaign. Let's start with the chart in the following snippet:

```
def generated_stacked_campaign_charts(data: pd.DataFrame,
    column: str = "impressions"):
    monthly_data = (
        data.groupby([pd.Grouper(key="utc_date", freq="M"),
            "campaign_name"])
        .agg({column: "sum"})
        .reset_index()
    )

    fig = px.bar(
        monthly_data,
        x="utc_date",
        y=column,
        color="campaign_name",
        title=f"{column} by Campaign",
        labels={column: column, "campaign_name": "Campaign"},
    )

    fig.update_layout(barmode="stack")

    return fig
```

The final result will look like *Figure 3.15*:

Campaign Stats

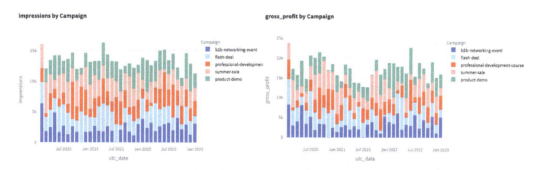

Figure 3.15 – An overview of stacked bar chart of campaign impressions and gross profit

The summary stats for campaigns have the same code as for the platforms, but you are aggregating by `campaign_name` instead of `traffic_source`:

```
def top_campaign(data: pd.DataFrame) -> pd.DataFrame:
    top_campaigns = (
        data.groupby(by=["account_name", "campaign_name"])
        .agg(
            {
                "impressions": "sum",
                "page_clicks": "sum",
                "revenue": "sum",
                "ad_spend": "sum",
                "gross_profit": "sum",
                "cpc": "mean",
                "rpc": "mean",
                "cpa": "mean",
                "roas": "mean",
            }
        )
        .reset_index()
    )

    return top_campaigns
```

Now that we have the aggregate functions for the summary charts done, we will move on to filters.

Creating filters

Now, we need some filters. We will need the following:

- Start date and end date
- Media platform
- Country
- Device
- Account
- Campaign

In Streamlit, the best place to place filters is in the sidebar using `st.sidebar`. We will use `st.date_input()` for the dates and `st.selectbox()` for the other filters. Let's start with the dates, as seen in the following code:

```
with st.sidebar:
    min_date = min(data_df.utc_date)
```

```
max_date = max(data_df.utc_date)
start_date = st.date_input("Pick Start date", min_date)
end_date = st.date_input("Pick End date", max_date)
```

Next, we move on to the other filters. All follow the same basic logic. You first select the unique values of the DataFrame column into a list. Then, you append `"All"` to that list, to have the ability to see all categories. Finally, you create `st.selectbox()`. We will illustrate this with platforms in the next snippet:

```
with st.sidebar:
    platforms = data_df.traffic_source.unique()
    platforms = np.append(platforms, "All")
    default_platform = len(platforms) - 1
    CM_Platform = st.selectbox(
        "Select Media Platform", platforms, index=default_platform
    )
```

All others are analogous. The filter pane will look as shown in *Figure 3.16*:

Figure 3.16 – Filters in sidebar

Now, we need to create the logic to allow these filters to actually filter the DataFrame. Taking the platform filter as an example, the text of the filter is stored in the `CM_Platform` variable, which we can use to filter the data. First, we create a list with filter conditions, as seen in the next snippet:

```
filter_conditions = []
# Update filter_conditions based on user selections
if CM_Platform != "All":
    filter_conditions.append(f"traffic_source == '{CM_Platform}'")

if CM_Country != "All":
    filter_conditions.append(f"country == '{CM_Country}'")

if CM_Device != "All":
    filter_conditions.append(f"device_viewed == '{CM_Device}'")

if CM_Account != "All":
    filter_conditions.append(f"account_name == '{CM_Account}'")

if CM_Campaign != "All":
    filter_conditions.append(f"campaign_name == '{CM_Campaign}'")
```

Then, we combine all filters into a single string and apply the filter to the DataFrame:

```
# Combine all filter conditions into a single string using 'and'
filter_condition = " and ".join(filter_conditions)

# Apply the dynamically constructed filter to the dataframe
if filter_condition:  # Check if there is any condition to apply
    data_filtered = data_df.query(filter_condition)
else:
    data_filtered = data_df  # No filter applied, use the original
DataFrame
```

Finally, let's not forget the date filter:

```
if start_date and end_date:
    data_filtered = data_filtered[
        (data_filtered["utc_date"] >= pd.to_datetime(start_date))
        & (data_filtered["utc_date"] <= pd.to_datetime(end_date))
    ]
```

Now, we have a `data_filtered` DataFrame that we can use on our functions, and assembling the final result is now easy:

```
get_metrics(data_filtered, st)

row1_col1, row1_col2 = st.columns(2)
```

```
row1_col1.plotly_chart(generate_column_charts(data_filtered,
    "impressions"))
row1_col2.plotly_chart(generate_column_charts(data_filtered,
    "gross_profit"))

st.subheader("Sources Metrics")
st.dataframe(top_traffic_source(data_filtered),
    use_container_width=True)

st.subheader("Campaign Stats")
row2_col1, row2_col2 = st.columns(2)
row2_col1.plotly_chart(
    generated_stacked_campaign_charts(
        data_filtered, "impressions")
    )
row2_col2.plotly_chart(
    generated_stacked_campaign_charts(
        data_filtered, "gross_profit")
    )
st.dataframe(top_campaign(data_filtered), use_container_width=True)
```

We can check the final outcome in *Figure 3.17*:

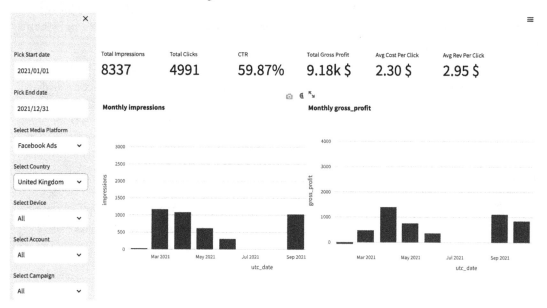

Figure 3.17 – Simple marketing dashboard with filters

By following the design principles we discussed earlier and incorporating appropriate visualizations, we have developed an effective store data dashboard using Streamlit. This dashboard provides key metrics, such as total sales and product sales evolution, and presents them in an easily digestible format. You can further customize and enhance the dashboard based on your specific requirements and preferences.

Remember – designing dashboards is an iterative process. Continuously evaluate and refine your dashboard to ensure it provides the most relevant information and insights to your target audience. Streamlit's real-time updates and intuitive interface allow you to experiment and make changes on the fly, facilitating the creation of dynamic and interactive data applications.

Keep exploring and refining your dashboard to empower data-driven decision-making and gain valuable insights from your store data.

Summary

In this chapter, we embarked on a journey to explore the art of presenting results through interactive dashboards using Streamlit.

We started by learning the principles of designing effective dashboards. By understanding the importance of clarity, purpose, and data-ink ratio, you are now equipped to craft dashboards that deliver key insights without overwhelming non-technical audiences.

Later, you learned how to generate effective dimensions and metrics for your dashboards. Finally, we delved into the world of Streamlit, an open source framework that enables you to transform Python scripts into web applications seamlessly.

Building upon the foundation of presenting results with dashboards, the next chapter will delve into the world of econometrics and causal inference. As a marketing analyst, you often encounter data that presents unique challenges, such as sparsity, time series characteristics, or panel data. You will acquire the skills necessary to navigate these complexities and derive meaningful insights from your marketing data.

Further reading

- Streamlit documentation – `https://docs.streamlit.io/library/api-reference`
- Plotly Express documentation – `https://plotly.com/graphing-libraries/`

4

Econometrics and Causal Inference with Statsmodels and PyMC

All models are wrong, but some are useful.

– George Box

As a marketing analyst, usually you will not have the luxury of big data to feed into machine learning models. The data will be sparce or made up of low-frequency, time series, or panel data, which will prevent you from brute forcing your way through. You need a solid understanding of econometrics and the principles of causality to answer common questions your stakeholders will have.

As you can recall from *Chapter 1, What is Marketing Analytics?*, some questions you will encounter in your daily work will be "Why did something happen?". This is diagnostic analytics. As a marketing data analyst, you will be asked, "What is the impact of X on Y?" or "What is the impact of X on Y, while controlling for Z?" In this chapter, we will cover the basics of how to answer these questions using a linear regression model.

In this chapter, we will cover the following topics:

- What is a linear regression?
- What is a logistic regression?
- What is causal inference?

By the end of this chapter, you will have a solid understanding of econometrics and the principles of causality to answer common questions your stakeholders will have and a basic toolset to conduct causal inference and regression analysis.

Technical requirements

You can find the code files for this chapter on GitHub at `https://github.com/PacktPublishing/Data-Analytics-for-Marketing/tree/main/Chapter04`.

What is a linear regression?

A linear regression is a statistical model that allows us to understand the relationship between two or more variables. The most common use case is for understanding the relationship between a dependent variable and one or more independent variables. The dependent variable is the variable we are trying to explain and the independent variables are the variables we are using to explain the dependent variable. We can use such a model to either predict the dependent variable given the independent variables or compare the predictions for different values of the independent variables to make comparisons.

Before diving into the underpinnings, let's have a look at the intuition for what we are trying to achieve with a linear regression. Let's imagine a simple random dataset:

$$x \sim N(100,50)$$

$$y = 2 * x + error$$

$$error \sim N(10,50)$$

We know the relationship is linear because we have designed the dataset to be so. A linear regression, at its core, is the line that best fits the scattered points. Such a line is our approximation, or prediction, of where the points truly are. Individually, you will either underestimate or overestimate each point, but on an average you will catch the relationship, or formally, this line will minimize the squared sum of errors, as we can see in *Figure 4.1*:

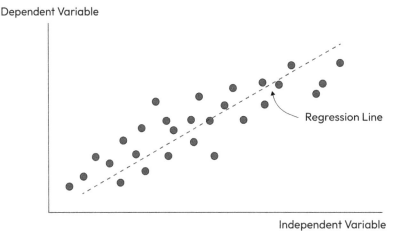

Figure 4.1 – Linear regression example

Essentially, this line is our model. But let's first define what a model is.

What is a model?

Before we dig deeper into the specifics of linear regression, we first need to make a quick stop and address what exactly a model is. A model is a representation of a real world phenomenon. It is a simplification of reality, not reality itself. This distinction is important because it will help us understand the limitations of a model and how to interpret the results we obtain from it. This is the meaning of the quote, *"All models are wrong, some are useful"*. All models are wrong in the sense that they don't represent reality exactly. In the previous simple example, the model fails to predict some individual points. Some models are useful in the sense that they are useful for answering questions about reality, given the assumptions of the model. In our toy model discussed earlier, we captured the essential relationship between *x* and *y*. The dependent variable *y* is two times the independent variable *x*, plus an error. A model needs to be simple enough to be useful but complex enough to be accurate. The more complex the model, the more accurate it will be, but the more difficult it will be to interpret. Always be aware that when building a model, you have assumptions. These assumptions are the simplifications you make to make the model useful. If you violate these assumptions, the model will not be accurate.

> **The difference between a model and an algorithm**
>
> One should be aware of the fact that a model is not an algorithm. A model is an attempt to represent a phenomenon and the relations between variables mathematically. An algorithm, however, is a recipe, a collection of steps, or a set of rules to be followed to achieve a certain certain outcome. So, a linear regression is a model, but a method such as ordinary least squares is an algorithm that fits a linear regression to the data.

What are the assumptions of a linear regression?

When working with statistical models, it is important to be aware of the assumptions of the techniques you are using. Linear regression has a few assumptions that you, as an analyst, need to be aware of:

- First of all, as it's obvious from the name, the model will assume that the relationship between dependent and independent variables is linear in nature. This is a very strong assumption, and one might argue that you will most often deal with non-linear data in real life. However, even with a non-linear relationship, a linear regression might still be useful for estimating an average relationship.

- Closely related with the linearity assumption is the additivity assumption. This means that the effect of each independent variable is independent of the other independent variables. When additivity is violated, it makes sense to transform the data. For example, if $y = a * b * c$, then we can transform the problem with:

$$\log(y) = \log(a) + \log(b) + \log(c).$$

- A third assumption of a linear regression is that the errors from the prediction line are independent from each other. This means that the error of one point does not affect the error of another point. This assumption is violated when you have time series data, or panel data, in a phenomenon called autocorrelation. We will cover time series in *Chapter 5, Forecasting with Prophet, ARIMA, and Other Models Using StatsForecast,* and learn how to deal with this problem.

- The equal variance of errors is our fourth assumption. It is also known as homoscedasticity as opposed to heteroscedasticity, which means we do not have equal variance of errors. This assumption states that the variance of the error is the same for all values of the independent variables. This assumption is violated, for instance, when the relationship between the variables is not linear. While violation of this assumption can be an issue, especially if the regression is to be used for probabilistic prediction, it does not affect the most important aspect of a regression model—how the information is combined and goes into the predictors.

- Our next assumption regarding errors is that they are normally distributed. This assumption is relevant when predicting individual data points. On the other hand, when talking about estimating the regression line, this assumption is not relevant, in most cases. On the topic of the assumption of normality of errors, it is important to emphasize that the normality assumption is for the errors of the regression. The independent variables do not need to be normally distributed. In fact, most of the time, they will not be.

- Finally, the last assumption to be wary of is the absence of multicollinearity. This means that the independent variables are not highly correlated with each other. This assumption is violated when you have a lot of independent variables and some of them are highly correlated. This is a problem because it makes it difficult to estimate the regression coefficients.

A final note on linear regression—as an analyst, you need to be mindful that the model is very sensitive to outliers. You need to handle outliers before running a linear regression or the model will be biased. We covered outlier detection and handling in *Chapter 2, Extracting and Exploring Data with Singer and pandas.*

Exploring different types of regression models

Don't let yourself be fooled by the apparent simplicity of the regression model. Regression models come in a lot of flavors and can be extremely powerful if used correctly. There is a quote attributed to Confucius, *"Don't use a canon to kill a mosquito".* In the same vein, don't use a deep learning neural network to solve a problem that a simple linear regression can handle.

The simplest linear regression is of the following form:

$$y = \beta_0 + \beta_1 x + error$$

Linear regressions can, however, be extended and elaborated in a lot of ways:

- You can add additional predictors or independent variables:

$$y = \beta_0 + \beta_1 x_1 + \beta_2 x_2 + \beta_k x_k + error$$

- If your data is not linear, you can transform it and build a non-linear regression model of the form:

$$\log y = \beta_0 + \beta_1 \log x + error$$

- When additivity does not hold, you can build a non-additive linear regression model. Usually, this happens when you are dealing with discrete outcomes, such as a binary outcome.

- You can build multilevel models, in which the coefficients of the independent variables can vary by situation or group.

- You can also build measurement error models, where both the dependent and independent variables are affected by measurement errors and the model needs to account for this.

In this chapter, we will only cover the simplest form of linear regression, but you should be aware that there are many other types of regression models and that you should choose the right model for the right problem.

The most common method to estimate a linear regression model is the OLS method. **OLS** stands for **ordinary least squares**, which refers to the way the statistical model fits to the data to produce the best-fit line. The best-fit line is the line that minimizes the sum of the squared errors. The errors are the difference between the actual value of the dependent variable and the predicted value of the dependent variable. The squared errors are used to avoid the errors cancelling each other out, when summing them, as described in *Chapter 2, Extracting and Exploring Data with Singer and pandas*, when we had a discussion on variance and standard deviations.

Linear regression is a very powerful tool, but it has some limitations. It assumes that the relationship between the dependent and independent variables is linear and that the errors are normally distributed. It also assumes that the independent variables are not correlated with each other. If any of these assumptions are violated, the results of the regression will be biased.

What we can do when the assumptions break down

Some assumptions of linear regression are more important than others. The other assumptions are less important and the regression will still be useful, even if they are violated. However, if the assumptions are violated, the regression will be less accurate.

When faced with a breakdown in assumptions, there are some things you can do to mitigate the problem. One is extending the model, which relaxes the assumptions you are breaking. However, beware that this increases model complexity. Before you extend the model, you must attempt to do the following:

- **Obtaining cleaner data**: This is the most important step. If you can obtain cleaner data, you can avoid the need to extend the model.

- **Adding predictors**: Sometimes, adding predictors can provide more information, given that the new predictors are not correlated with the predictors already in the model.

- **Adding interactions to model non-linearities**: This is done easily by multiplying predictors together. For example, if you have a predictor x_1 and a predictor x_2, you can add the interaction $x_1 * x_2$ to the model. This will allow the model to capture non-linearities between the predictors.

- **Variable transformation**: You can attempt data transformations of either the predictors, the outcome, or both.

Interpreting the coefficients

The coefficients of a linear regression are often called effects. The terminology can be misleading and lead an analyst astray. As mentioned, quantifying a coefficient as an effect, or worse, a causal effect, requires a lot of assumptions to lead us to causal inference. This is because when speaking of effects, we tend to associate the term with an intervention or treatment. For example, if we are trying to understand the effect of a change to a landing page on conversions, we would like to know how much the conversions are affected by the landing page. This is a causal effect, and it is not possible to quantify this effect without a lot of assumptions. Most analysts remember the aphorism "correlation does not imply causation", but we fall prey to the mistake of interpreting coefficients as effects or causes without thinking about the assumptions that lead us to this conclusion.

The best way to avoid falling into this trap is to be very careful with the language we use. We should not say that a coefficient is an effect or a cause. This is a very important distinction, and it is the first step to avoiding the trap of interpreting coefficients as effects or causes. When you interpret the coefficient as a cause, you are essentially saying, "if I increase the value of a random independent variable by one unit, the effect will be an increase of β units in the dependent variable". In reality, what the model is estimating is the average difference in the dataset of β units. It is a between-data point comparison, not a within-data point comparison.

How to do a linear regression

To start, let's import some requited libraries: `pandas` and `numpy` for data manipulation, `statsmodels` for the regression analysis, and `matplotlib` and `seaborn` for plotting. We then load a test data set. In this case, we will load a satisfaction survey dataset for a fictional park:

```
import pandas as pd
import numpy as np
```

```
import matplotlib.pyplot as plt
import seaborn as sns

import arviz as az
import bambi as bmb

az.style.use('arviz-darkgrid')
sns.set_style("darkgrid")
sat_df = pd.read_csv('data/sat_df.csv')
sat_df.head()
```

Let's see a preview of the data we are working with in *Figure 4.2*:

	weekend	num_child	distance	rides	games	wait	clean	overall
0	no	1	24.605443	73.0	70.0	66.0	79.0	52.0
1	yes	1	31.293988	75.0	74.0	66.0	83.0	54.0
2	no	1	6.077646	65.0	68.0	69.0	78.0	33.0
3	yes	0	25.623529	74.0	72.0	73.0	85.0	30.0
4	yes	2	48.947037	76.0	75.0	74.0	82.0	61.0

Figure 4.2 – First rows of the sat_df data

The data contains the following variables:

- weekend: Indicates if the survey was taken from a user who attended on a weekend or not
- num_child: The number of children in the group
- distance: The distance the customer had to travel to go to the park
- rides: The satisfaction with the rides in the park
- games: The satisfaction with the games in the park
- wait: The satisfaction with the waiting times in the park
- clean: The satisfaction with the cleanliness of the park
- overall: The overall satisfaction of the customer

We will use the overall satisfaction as our dependent variable, and the other variables as our independent variables. Let's first take a look at the data, and it's shape, for some basic EDA:

```
sat_df.describe(include='all')
```

We can see we have 500 rows and no missing data, as shown in *Figure 4.3*:

	weekend	num_child	distance	rides	games	wait	clean	overall
count	500	500.000000	500.000000	500.000000	500.000000	500.000000	500.000000	500.000000
unique	2	NaN	NaN	NaN	NaN	NaN	NaN	NaN
top	no	NaN	NaN	NaN	NaN	NaN	NaN	NaN
freq	262	NaN	NaN	NaN	NaN	NaN	NaN	NaN
mean	NaN	1.688000	31.476842	80.706000	74.596000	73.184000	85.382000	53.488000
std	NaN	1.516329	35.965538	5.624129	8.599109	10.914779	5.229031	16.594596
min	NaN	0.000000	1.048239	62.000000	48.000000	37.000000	67.000000	8.000000
25%	NaN	0.000000	10.727687	77.000000	69.000000	65.000000	82.000000	42.750000
50%	NaN	2.000000	19.856045	81.000000	75.000000	74.000000	85.000000	54.000000
75%	NaN	3.000000	39.524517	85.000000	80.000000	81.000000	89.000000	65.000000
max	NaN	5.000000	300.243254	100.000000	100.000000	100.000000	100.000000	100.000000

Figure 4.3 – Summary statistics of sat_df

Before we go further, we need to check the types of variables in the DataFrame since some of our variables will need to be changed:

```
sat_df.dtypes
```

We can see that the weekend variable is an object:

```
weekend           object
num_child          int64
distance         float64
rides            float64
games            float64
wait             float64
clean            float64
overall          float64
dtype: object
```

We need to change it to a `category` type so that when we do the regression, the library assumes the right type:

```
sat_df.weekend = sat_df.weekend.astype('category')
```

As shown in previous chapters, a good way to quickly glance at the distributions of the data is to use the pair plot, which will give us a quick overview of the data and their relationships with every other variable:

```
sns.pairplot(sat_df, vars = sat_df.columns)
```

We can see the results in *Figure 4.4*:

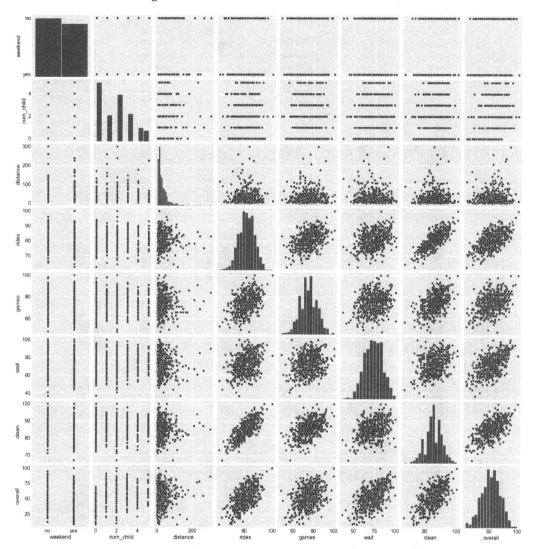

Figure 4.4 – An overview of pair plot of our dataset

We can also use the hue parameter on the pairs plot to see how the data differs when the visit was one per weekend:

```
sns.pairplot(sat_df, hue='weekend')
```

We can see in *Figure 4.5* that the distance is heavily skewed to the right and that the data is not normally distributed:

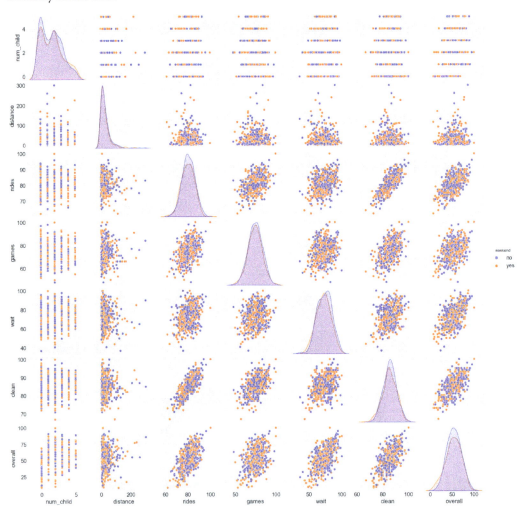

Figure 4.5 – An overview of pair plot with hue on weekend

This will create problems in the future due to the assumptions of the linear regression model. We will have to transform the data to make it more normally distributed and remove the skewness. The easiest way is to attempt to log the data and recheck:

```
sat_df['log_distance'] = np.log(sat_df.distance)
sns.pairplot(sat_df)
```

In *Figure 4.6*, we can see the data is now more normalized:

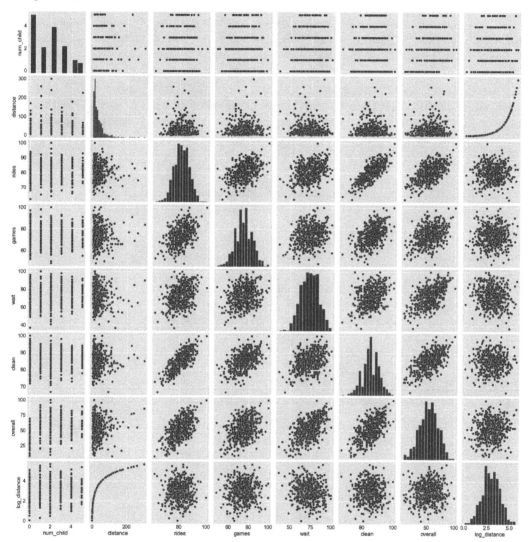

Figure 4.6 – An overview of pair plot to check normalization

Now we can evaluate the correlation matrix to see how the variables are correlated with each other, both as a table and as a heatmap:

```
corr_matrix = sat_df[['num_child', 'distance', 'rides',
    'games','wait','clean','overall',log_distance']].corr()
corr_matrix
```

The output is the correlation matrix, in a Pandas DataFrame, as shown in *Figure 4.7*:

	num_child	distance	rides	games	wait	clean	overall	log_distance
num_child	1.000000	0.046587	0.001207	0.007220	0.078791	0.004446	0.442498	0.051391
distance	0.046587	1.000000	-0.015748	0.013698	-0.113510	-0.004754	0.100449	0.817402
rides	0.001207	-0.015748	1.000000	0.444025	0.334231	0.769007	0.577254	0.004973
games	0.007220	0.013698	0.444025	1.000000	0.230452	0.504474	0.411894	0.036145
wait	0.078791	-0.113510	0.334231	0.230452	1.000000	0.391711	0.576664	-0.130803
clean	0.004446	-0.004754	0.769007	0.504474	0.391711	1.000000	0.591888	0.004057
overall	0.442498	0.100449	0.577254	0.411894	0.576664	0.591888	1.000000	0.081916
log_distance	0.051391	0.817402	0.004973	0.036145	-0.130803	0.004057	0.081916	1.000000

Figure 4.7 – Correlation Matrix of sat_df

Let's turn it into a visual to help us visualize the matrix:

```
mask = np.triu(np.ones_like(corr_matrix, dtype=bool))
mask[np.triu_indices_from(mask)] = True
cmap = sns.diverging_palette(230, 20, as_cmap=True)
sns.heatmap(corr_matrix, mask=mask, cmap=cmap, annot=True,
    vmax = 1, vmin = -1)
```

We can see the correlation matrix in *Figure 4.8*:

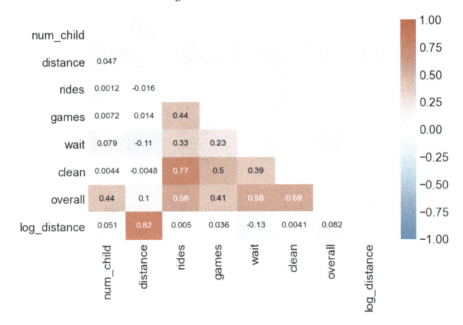

Figure 4.8 – Correlation matrix of our dataset

Let's start by using a simple model, where we see the effect of rides on the overall satisfaction:

```
model_1 = bmb.Model('overall ~ rides', data=sat_df)
results_1 = model_1.fit()
```

Bambi will provide us with a summary of the model fitted, and we can then plot the priors:

```
model_1
Formula: overall ~ rides
Family name: Gaussian
Link: identity
Observations: 500
Priors:
  Common-level effects
      Intercept ~ Normal(mu: 53.488, sigma: 596.7702)
      rides ~ Normal(mu: 0.0, sigma: 7.3765)

  Auxiliary parameters
      sigma ~ HalfStudentT(nu: 4, sigma: 16.578)
------
* To see a plot of the priors call the .plot_priors() method.
* To see a summary or plot of the posterior pass the object returned
by .fit() to az.summary() or az.plot_trace()
results_1
Inference data with groups:
      > posterior
      > log_likelihood
      > sample_stats
      > observed_data
```

Here's a primer on interpreting the output provided by Bambi:

- **Formula**: overall ~ rides indicates that the model is predicting the overall outcome from the predictor rides.

- **Family name**: Gaussian signifies that the model assumes the residuals (differences between observed and predicted values) are normally distributed, which is typical for a linear regression.

- **Link**: identity means the identity function is used to link the mean of the Gaussian distribution to the linear predictor. This is standard for linear regression.

- **Observations**: The dataset contains 500 observations used to fit the model.

Priors represent the beliefs about the possible values of the parameters before observing the data. In Bayesian statistics, priors are updated with data to get the posterior distribution. Here, we have the following:

- **Common-level effects (fixed effects)**:

  - **Intercept ~ Normal(mu: 53.488, sigma: 596.7702)**: This indicates the prior belief about the intercept that it's normally distributed with a mean (mu) of 53.488 and a standard deviation (sigma) of 596.7702. This prior is relatively weak (due to the large standard deviation), meaning it allows for a wide range of possible values for the intercept.

  - **rides ~ Normal(mu: 0.0, sigma: 7.3765)**: The coefficient for `rides` is also assumed to be normally distributed, centered around 0 with a standard deviation of 7.3765. This prior is also relatively weak, suggesting that, before seeing the data, a wide range of values for the effect of `rides` on `overall` is considered possible.

- **Auxiliary parameters**:

  - **sigma ~ HalfStudentT(nu: 4, sigma: 16.578)**: This is the prior to the `sigma` parameter, which represents the standard deviation of the Gaussian distribution of the residuals. The `HalfStudentT` distribution is often used, as it restricts `sigma` to positive values and is more robust to outliers than a normal distribution. The `nu` parameter controls the normality of the distribution; a value of 4 indicates some robustness to outliers. The `sigma` value of 16.578 indicates a belief that most of the residuals will fall within roughly ±33 (2*16.578) of the predicted values.

After fitting the model with data, the posterior distributions of the parameters are available. These distributions give the updated beliefs about the parameters after considering the data. Here we will find the following:

- `posterior`: Contains the samples from the posterior distribution of the model's parameters
- `log_likelihood`: Contains the log-likelihood values for each observation, which can be used for model comparison
- `sample_stats`: Contains summary statistics about the sampling process
- `observed_data`: The actual data that was used in the model fitting

Let's see what parameters were estimated by the regression model and if they converged:

```
az.plot_trace(results_1, kind='rank_vlines');
```

As we can see, all chains converge, and we can see the distributions of the parameter estimates in *Figure 4.9*.

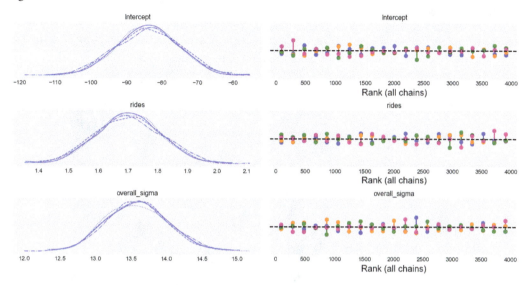

Figure 4.9 – An overview of trace plot of the regression

Arviz provides a simple way to get the summary of the regression estimated parameters:

```
az.summary(results_1)
```

We can see in the following output that the effect of `rides` on overall satisfaction is 1.7, as shown in *Figure 4.10*:

	mean	sd	hdi_3%	hdi_97%	mcse_mean	mcse_sd	ess_bulk	ess_tail	r_hat
Intercept	-83.913	8.806	-99.991	-67.251	0.107	0.076	6794.0	3547.0	1.0
rides	1.702	0.109	1.502	1.905	0.001	0.001	6803.0	3486.0	1.0
overall_sigma	13.592	0.440	12.813	14.416	0.006	0.004	5712.0	3143.0	1.0

Figure 4.10 – Effect of rides on satisfaction

One thing you, as an analyst, should always be careful of is checking the residuals. Remember, the assumption is that the error term is normally distributed and the variance of the errors constant. Let's check the residuals:

```
posterior_predictive = model_1.predict(results_1, kind = 'pps')
y_pred_samples = results_1.posterior_predictive.stack(
    sample = ['chain', 'draw'])['overall'].values.T
```

```
y_pred = y_pred_samples.mean(axis=0)
resid = y - y_pred
print(az.r2_score(y, y_pred_samples))
sns.residplot(x=y_pred, y=resid, lowess=True, color = 'g');
```

We can see from *Figure 4.11* that the line that goes through the residuals is horizontal:

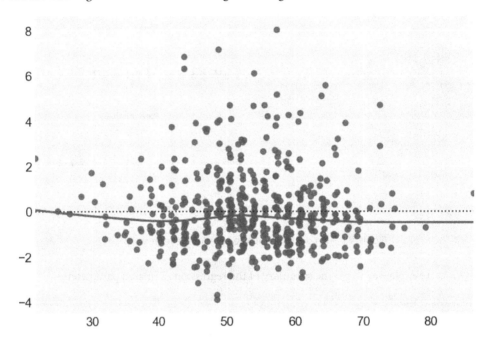

Figure 4.11 – Residual plot

This is an indication that we have homoscedastic errors, which is what we want. Let's try a new model, where we add other variables as predictors:

```
model_2 = bmb.Model('overall ~ rides + games + wait + clean',
    data=sat_df)
results_2 = model_2.fit()
model_2
```

Let's plot the trace to see if it converged:

```
az.plot_trace(results_2, kind='rank_vlines');
```

As seen in *Figure 4.12*, the regressions converged:

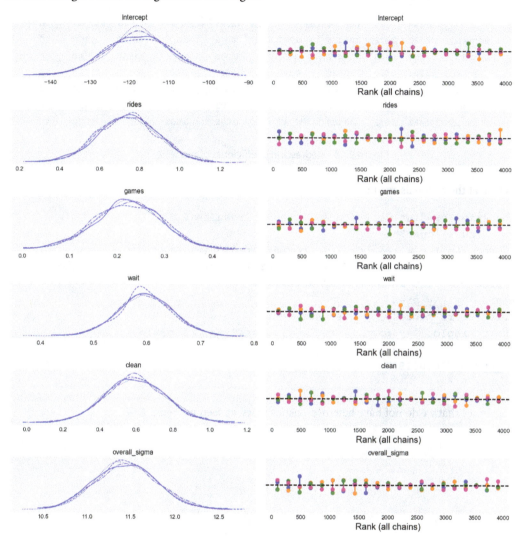

Figure 4.12 – An overview of plot trace of regression coefficients

Like the first model, let's have a look at the coefficients:

```
az.summary(results_2)
```

The output can be seen in *Figure 4.13*:

	mean	sd	hdi_3%	hdi_97%	mcse_mean	mcse_sd	ess_bulk	ess_tail	r_hat
Intercept	-117.330	8.276	-133.275	-101.900	0.119	0.085	4819.0	3215.0	1.0
rides	0.741	0.145	0.472	1.012	0.002	0.002	4285.0	3112.0	1.0
games	0.223	0.070	0.085	0.347	0.001	0.001	5957.0	2985.0	1.0
wait	0.597	0.051	0.501	0.697	0.001	0.001	5175.0	2764.0	1.0
clean	0.594	0.165	0.302	0.925	0.003	0.002	3480.0	2943.0	1.0
overall_sigma	11.453	0.355	10.809	12.143	0.005	0.003	6063.0	3117.0	1.0

Figure 4.13 – Regression coefficients of model 2

Let's look at the residuals again:

```
posterior_predictive = model_2.predict(results_2,
    kind = 'pps')
y_pred_samples = results_2.posterior_predictive.stack(
    sample = ['chain', 'draw'])['overall'].values.T
y_pred = y_pred_samples.mean(axis=0)
resid = y - y_pred
print(az.r2_score(y, y_pred_samples))
sns.residplot(x=y_pred, y=resid, lowess=True, color='g');
r2            0.498329
r2_std        0.001592
dtype: float64
```

We again see that we do not have heteroscedastic errors, as seen in *Figure 4.14*:

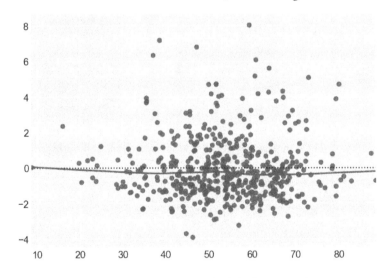

Figure 4.14 – Residual plot to check for heteroscedasty

Let's now compare both models to see how the estimates and their ranges change in *Figure 4.15*:

```
az.plot_forest([results_1, results_2],
    model_names=['Model 1', 'Model 2'],
    var_names=['rides', 'games', 'wait', 'clean'],
    combined=True);
```

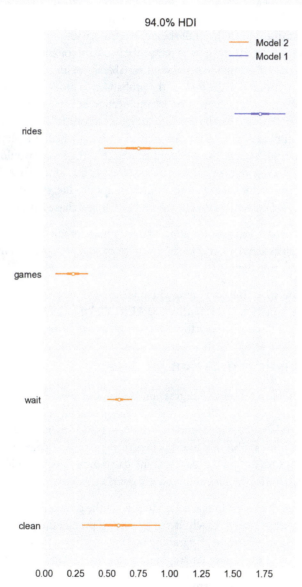

Figure 4.15 – Prediction intervals for both models

Let's now turn our attention to another type of regression model that is very useful in marketing—the logistic regression.

What is logistic regression?

Logistic regression is a type of statistical analysis used to predict the outcome of a binary variable (such as "yes/no" or "0/1" outcomes) based on one or more predictor variables. This method applies the logistic function to estimate the probability of the binary response, with the possibility of being adapted for more complex situations. This technique is particularly useful for cases where the relationship between the independent variables and the dependent variable is not linear, which is often the case in classification problems. In this model, the logit of the probability is modeled as a linear combination of the independent variables. Logistic regression is employed to estimate the likelihood of different outcomes or categories, such as success/failure, victory/defeat, or life/death scenarios. It can also be adapted to classify multiple categories; for instance, identifying whether a photograph features a cat, dog, lion, and so on. In such cases, every identified object in the image would be attributed to a probability ranging from 0 to 1, with the total sum of probabilities equating to one. Logistic regression is also used to predict the probability of a customer purchasing a product or service in the future. This is useful for targeting specific customers that are more likely to purchase a product.

In customer analysis, it is used to estimate the effect of one or more predictor variables on an outcome variable that is binary, such as acquisition expansion and retention strategies, promotion and pricing strategies, and advertising campaigns.

It is very helpful when you want to understand which factors led to specific customer behaviors at each stage (**acquisition, expansion, and retention**, or **AER**). Did they buy or not buy, upgrade or not upgrade, stay or churn? Is it discounted pricing, advertising, or free returns?

Objectives of logistic regression models

Logistic regression is similar to a standard regression model, but the dependent variable is binary. The objective of a logistic regression model is to estimate the probability of a customer belonging to a certain class based on the values of the independent variables. The independent variables can be either continuous or categorical. The variable of interest in logistic regression is a binary one, which is coded as 1 to represent outcomes such as "yes" or "success" and 0 to denote "no" or "failure". The model uses these binary outcomes to predict the probability that Y equals 1, based on the predictor variable X.

Logistic regression is commonly used in marketing to predict the probability of a customer buying a product or service in the future. Alternatively, it can be used to predict the probability of a customer churning or the probability of a customer upgrading or downgrading a product or service. It is also used to predict the probability of a customer responding to a marketing campaign or offer.

The logistic regression model takes the form

$$p = \frac{e^{\beta_0 + \beta_1 x_1 + \beta_2 x_2 + \ldots + \beta_n x_n}}{1 + e^{\beta_0 + \beta_1 x_1 + \beta_2 x_2 + \ldots + \beta_n x_n}}$$

where e is the natural logarithm, and p is the probability of the event. The logistic regression model predicts $P(Y = 1)$ as a function of X, and p will range from 0 to 1. When you have only one independent variable, the logistic regression model is equivalent to the logit function.

Odds of an event

With some simple algebra, we can rewrite the logistic regression model as follows:

$$\frac{p}{1-p} = e^{\beta_0 + \beta_1 x_1 + \beta_2 x_2 + \ldots + \beta_n x_n}$$

This describes the outcome as the odds of the event happening. p is still the probability of an event happening. Probabilities and odds are often used interchangeably, but they are not the same. Odds are the ratio of the probability of an event happening compared to the probability of the event not happening. Probability ranges are always between 0 and 1 and capture the ratio of how often an event of interest occurs. Odds, on the other hand, can range from 0 to infinity and capture the ratio of how often an event of interest occurs over how often it does not occur.

For example, if the probability of a customer buying a product is 0.2, then the odds of the customer buying the product is 0.2/0.8 = 0.25 (or 1:4 odds).

You can easily convert them back and forth:

$$odds = \frac{p}{1-p} \quad p = \frac{odds}{1 + odds}$$

Logistic regressions will also provide the odds ratio for each predictor variable x. The odds ratio captures the increase in the odds of the occurrence of the event as the focal predictor variable x increases by one unit, while holding all other variables constant. This is done by multiplying the odds by the odds ratio.

The odds ratio for a predictor, say x_1, is calculated as:

$$OR_{x_1} = e^{\beta_1}$$

where β_1 is the coefficient for x_1 in the logistic regression equation.

The interpretation is simple:

- $OR_{x_1} = 1$: This indicates that the event's odds are the same regardless of the value of x_1. In other words, x_1 has no effect on the likelihood of the event occurring.

- $OR_{x_1} > 1$: An OR_{x_1} greater than 1 suggests that as x_1 increases, the odds of the event occurring also increase. For example, if $OR_{x_1} = 2$, it means that the odds of the event happening are twice as high for each one-unit increase in x_1. This indicates a positive relationship between x_1 and the likelihood of the event.

- $OR_{x_1} < 1$: Conversely, an OR_{x_1} less than 1 indicates that as x_1 increases, the odds of the event occurring decrease. For example, if $OR_{x_1} = 0.5$, it means that the odds of the event are halved for each one-unit increase in x_1. This signifies a negative relationship between x_1 and the event's likelihood.

First, let's generate a sample dataset representative of churn given variables such as complaints, gender, age, and higher education:

```
import numpy as np
import pandas as pd
np.random.seed(0)  # Setting seed for reproducibility
sample_size = 10000
# Generate other variables
genders = np.random.choice(['Male', 'Female'], sample_size)
ages = np.random.randint(18, 70, sample_size)
higher_education = np.random.choice([0, 1], sample_size,
    p=[0.7, 0.3])  # 1 = Yes, 0 = No
annual_incomes = np.random.randint(20000, 100000, sample_size)
states = np.random.choice(['CA', 'TX', 'NY', 'FL', 'IL'], sample_size)

# Generate number of complaints based on age (older customers complain
less)
complaints = np.random.poisson(5 - ages/20)

# Create a baseline churn probability
base_prob = 0.3

# Define the churn probability
def churn_probability(num_complaints, age, gender):
    odds = base_prob / (1 - base_prob) * (1.5**num_complaints) *
        (0.9**(age/10))
    odds_multiplier = 1.01 if gender == 'Male' else 1
    return odds * odds_multiplier / (1 + odds * odds_multiplier)

# Generate churned based on the above function
probabilities = np.vectorize(churn_probability)(complaints, ages,
    genders)
churned = np.random.binomial(1, probabilities)

# Create the DataFrame
significant_df_2 = pd.DataFrame({
    'Gender': genders,
    'Age': ages,
    'Higher_Education': higher_education,
    'Annual_Income': annual_incomes,
    'State': states,
    'Number_of_Complaints': complaints,
    'Churned': churned
})
```

This code generates a dataset of insurance policy holders over the last five years. This dataset contains the following variables:

- **Gender**: Male or female.

- **Age**: An integer value between 18 and 70.

- **Higher education**: A binary value where 1 indicates that the policy holder has higher education and 0 indicates that they don't.

- **Annual income**: A numeric value indicating the annual income of the policy holder.

- **State**: The state in which the policy holder resides, either CA, TX, NY, FL, or IL.

- **Number of complaints**: Generated based on age; older customers are set to have fewer complaints.

- **Churned**: A binary outcome (1 = churned, 0 = not churned) that indicates whether the customer churned or not. The churn probability is influenced by the number of complaints, age, and gender.

Here's a snapshot of the first few rows of the generated dataset in *Figure 4.16*:

	Gender	Age	Higher_Education	Annual_Income	State	Number_of_Complaints	Churned
0	Male	61	0	85142	TX	2	0
1	Female	27	0	57677	FL	1	1
2	Female	53	0	67848	NY	2	1
3	Male	32	0	50102	FL	3	0
4	Female	50	0	39840	NY	5	1

Figure 4.16 – Complaints snapshot of the first five rows

Let's now fit a logistic regression to estimate churn based on the variables we have:

```
import statsmodels.formula.api as smf

# Fit a logistic regression model
significant_logistic_regression_2 = smf.logit(
    formula="Churned ~ Gender + Age + Number_of_Complaints",
    data=significant_df_2).fit()
```

This code fits a logistic regression model to understand the relationship between the probability of churning (`Churned`) and predictor variables such as `Gender`, `Age`, and `Number_of_Complaints`. We use the `statsmodels` library, which provides a function `logit` to perform logistic regression.

Here is a summary of the logistic regression model in *Figure 4.17*:

```
Logit Regression Results
==============================================================================
Dep. Variable:            Churned   No. Observations:               10000
Model:                      Logit   Df Residuals:                    9996
Method:                       MLE   Df Model:                           3
Date:            Fri, 13 Oct 2023   Pseudo R-squ.:                0.09649
Time:                    08:04:27   Log-Likelihood:               -6228.6
converged:                   True   LL-Null:                      -6893.8
Covariance Type:        nonrobust   LLR p-value:                3.815e-288
=======================================================================================
                          coef    std err          z      P>|z|      [0.025      0.975]
---------------------------------------------------------------------------------------
Intercept              -0.7972      0.093     -8.539      0.000      -0.980      -0.614
Gender[T.Male]          0.0188      0.043      0.438      0.662      -0.065       0.103
Age                    -0.0114      0.002     -7.354      0.000      -0.014      -0.008
Number_of_Complaints    0.3939      0.014     28.118      0.000       0.366       0.421
=======================================================================================
```

Figure 4.17 – Logit regression result

Here are the results from the logistic regression model for this dataset:

- **Intercept**: (-0.7972)

- **Gender (male vs. female)**: (0.0188) (p-value = 0.662)

- **Age**: (-0.0114) (p-value < 0.001)

- **Number_of_complaints**: (0.3939) (p-value < 0.001)

The `coef` column lists the estimated coefficients for the intercept and each predictor variable in the logistic regression model. Each coefficient represents the log odds of the outcome for a one-unit increase in the predictor variable, holding all other variables constant. Let's look at each in turn:

- `Intercept`: The coefficient for the intercept is -0.7972, which is the log odds of the outcome when all predictor variables are at their reference level (often 0 for numerical predictors and the reference category for categorical predictors)

- `Gender[T.Male]`: This coefficient (0.0188) shows the change in the log odds of the outcome when the gender changes from the reference category (presumably female) to male

- `Age`: The coefficient for age is -0.0114, indicating that an increase in age is associated with a decrease in the log odds of the outcome

- `Number_of_Complaints`: The coefficient (0.3939) suggests that an increase in the number of complaints is associated with an increase in the log odds of the outcome

The `stderr` column shows the standard error of each coefficient, which is an estimate of the standard deviation of the coefficient.

The z column shows the z-value, which is the coefficient divided by its standard error. This is used in testing the null hypothesis that the coefficient is equal to zero (no effect).

The p>|z| column gives the p-value for the hypothesis test associated with each coefficient. A small p-value (typically less than 0.05) suggests that the effect of the predictor on the outcome is statistically significant:

- `Intercept`, `age`, and `number_of_complaints`: The p-values for these are 0.000, indicating that their effects are statistically significant

- `Gender[T.Male]`: The p-value is 0.662, which is not less than 0.05, suggesting that gender is not statistically significant in this model

The two columns `[0.025 and 0.975]` provide the 95% confidence interval for the coefficient estimates, meaning we can be 95% confident that the true value of the coefficient is between the lower and upper bounds of the interval.

For instance, for `Number_of_Complaints`, the interval is `[0.366, 0.421]`, indicating a high degree of certainty in the positive effect of the number of complaints on the log odds of the outcome.

We can use this regression to estimate what the probabilities of a user churning are given how many complaints they made:

```
# Generate a range of complaint numbers, from 0 to the maximum number
in the dataset
complaints_range_2 = np.arange(0,
    significant_df_2["Number_of_Complaints"].max() + 1)


# Create a DataFrame for prediction
prediction_df_2 = pd.DataFrame({
    "Number_of_Complaints": complaints_range_2,
    "Age": [significant_df_2["Age"].mean()] * len(complaints_range_2),
    "Gender": ["Male"] * len(complaints_range_2)
})


# Predicting probabilities using the logistic regression model
predicted_probabilities_2 = significant_logistic_regression_2.predict(
    exog=prediction_df_2)
```

This section of the code estimates the probabilities of churning based on the number of complaints. We generate a range of complaint numbers (from 0 to the maximum number of complaints observed in the dataset). For each number of complaints, we estimate the probability of churning using the logistic regression model we fitted earlier. The average age from the dataset is used as a representative age for these estimations.

Here are the estimated probabilities of churning for different numbers of complaints:

Number_of_complaints	Estimated_probability_of_churning
0	0.218
1	0.293
2	0.380
3	0.476
4	0.574
5	0.667
6	0.748
7	0.815
8	0.867
9	0.906
10	0.935
11	0.955
12	0.969

Table 4.1 – Estimated probabilities of churning

Now we need to address an important point: when armed with a regression, as an analyst, you should not throw every variable into it. You need to think causally.

What is causal inference?

The alure of machine learning is strong with complex models that excel in predicting with high precision, as well as in categorizing or grouping your data. However, in diagnostic analytics, you are not forecasting—you're trying to understand why something happened. You are trying to understand the drivers of an outcome. And this is a fundamentally different question. It is not just semantics or academic pedantry. Forecasting something and understanding the effects of something are two different tasks in statistics.

Without a causal understanding of the world, it's often impossible to identify which actions lead to a desired outcome. In business, we are constantly taking actions to achieve a certain outcome (for example, increase sales). So, in order not to waste our time heating our proverbial thermometer, we need a solid understanding of the causal relationships underlying our business processes. This is the premise of decision intelligence.

While machine learning techniques can be highly effective in forecasting future events with remarkable precision, the true usefulness of these predictions is limited if they don't provide insights on the actions necessary to bring about a favorable result.

Correlation, causation, and key drivers

Before we start building models, we need to address some common problems with "why" questions. The first is the very fundamental confusion between correlation and causation. If you ever had a statistics class, the odds are that the professor at one point or another told you the old sentence, "correlation does not imply causation". Or maybe you have seen the anecdote about the correlation between shark attacks and ice cream consumption in Australia. They correlate very well, but does that mean that ice cream consumption causes shark attacks? No, it doesn't. Remember—correlation is a statistical measure of the relationship between two variables. Causation is the relationship between two variables where one variable causes the other. The two are not the same.

Hence that saying, repeated at nauseum in statistics classes. Write it 20 times on a board: "Correlation does not imply causation". This is true, but it is also a bit of a misleading statement, especially if taken to the letter. Correlation does not imply causation, but it can be very strong indicator of causation. The reason for this is that correlation is a measure of the strength of the relationship between two variables. If two variables are correlated, it means that they are related. If they are related, it is very likely that one variable is causing the other. The only way to know for sure is to perform an experiment and control for all other variables. This is the only way to know for sure that one variable is causing the other. But in the real world, we don't have the luxury of performing experiments. We need to use the data we have to infer causation. And the best way to do this is to use a linear regression model.

Going back to the ice cream example, it is absurd to think that ice cream consumption causes shark attacks. But it is not absurd to think that what is causing ice cream consumption to rise is also causing shark attacks to rise. In this case, the correlation between ice cream consumption and shark attacks is a strong indicator of a hidden common cause.

Common sense will tell us that the common cause is the increase in temperature. The increase in temperature is causing both ice cream consumption and shark attacks to rise. This is a very common scenario in the real world. The key is to identify the common cause and use it as a predictor in your model. The same is true for marketing. If you have a variable that is correlated with your dependent variable, it is very likely that this variable is a key driver of your dependent variable. But you need to be careful because correlation does not imply causation. You need to perform an experiment to know for sure. But in the real world, you don't have the luxury of performing experiments. Unlike the ice cream example, in marketing, sometimes common sense cannot saves us from getting to the bottom of things. The common cause is not always obvious. But it helps to think systematically about this with a graph.

In this case, you need to use a linear regression model to identify the key drivers of your dependent variable.

You also need to keep in mind that optimization makes everything endogenous. In the real world, we are often optimizing for a certain outcome. For example, we are optimizing for sales, leads, or clicks. Economic theory teaches us to be warry of correlations that arise from such actions. A correlation, to correctly identify a causal effect, needs to be based on a choice made independent of the potential outcome under consideration. This is called exogeneity. If the choice is made based on the potential outcome, then the correlation is endogenous. This is a problem because it makes it impossible to identify the causal effect. This is the problem of endogeneity, and it is a very common problem in marketing and business. In a business setting, choices are endogenous, and given that, correlations between those choices and outcomes will be spurious and rarely indicate a causal effect. In the heat of the moment, this is often overlooked by marketing teams. It is your job as an analyst to always be aware of this problem and to be able to identify it and correct it. So what tools do we have at our disposal to start dealing with this problem?

Graphs to the rescue

Going back to ice cream's correlation with shark attacks, we can use a graph to identify the common cause. In this case, the common cause is the increase in temperature. The increase in temperature is causing both ice cream consumption and shark attacks to rise. We can put this into a graph called a **directed acyclic graph (DAG)**:

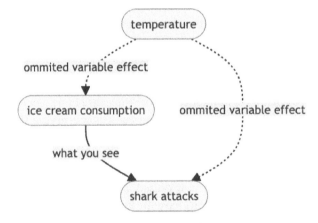

Figure 4.18 – Your first DAG

In this case, we have what's called a confounder—a variable that affects both ice cream consumption and shark attacks. Since we were not accounting for it, we draw the wrong conclusion that ice cream attacks cause shark attacks. But if we account for it, we can see that the common cause is the increase in temperature. This is a very common scenario in the real world. The key is to identify the common cause and use it as a predictor in your model. This is called omitted variable bias. Let's turn our attention to a more practical application, other than ice cream and shark attacks.

A more practical application

We are given the following problem: estimate the impact of Google Ads with TV as a confounder. Simple, right? We just correlate spending with sales. If we want to get fancy, we can use a Bayesian MMM or train a machine learning model.

However, there is an issue: unbeknownst to us, the marketing team is also running TV ads. In order to maximize the effect of TV ads, the marketing team is turning Google Ads on when the TV ads are on and off when they are off to save budget.

This means that TV ads are a confounder, as we can see in *Figure 4.19*:

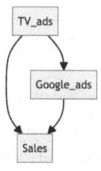

Figure 4.19 – A simple example of Google Ads and TV ads interaction on sales

What does it mean to be a confounder? TV is influencing both sales and Google Ads spend. This means that we can't just correlate Google Ads spend with sales because we would be picking up the effect of TV ads as well. It could even be the case that the effect is totally due to TV ads, making Google Ads are useless because the TV ads are driving search volume.

Before we move further, we need to pause a bit on this example and explain a key concept: the backdoor.

A small detour through the backdoor

Let's take a simple DAG as an example:

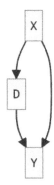

Figure 4.20 – Toy DAG

The variables are of no importance in this example. We want to focus on the structure and paths of the DAG.

The path D to Y is the direct path we want to measure, meaning the causal impact of the variable of interest D onto Y. However, there is another effect path, the path $D <- X -> Y$. This is called a backdoor path.

If you only keep one thing in your mind regarding DAGs, remember the concept of the backdoor path. It is the graphical equivalent of the omitted variable bias. It represents a variable that can also have an effect on the outcome, and not controlling it will introduce bias in your estimates.

Unobserved variables can also introduce backdoor paths, with the added complication of them being unobserved, meaning you cannot control them.

Let's take a look at the Becker human capital model, where we want to represent the effect of a college degree (D) on earnings (Y):

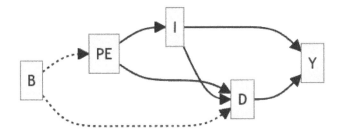

Figure 4.21 – DAG representation of the Becker human capital model

In this model, *B* represents unobserved factors such as genetics, family background, and so on, *PE* is parental education, *I* is family income, *D* is college degree, and *Y* is earnings.

You can see there are four paths from *D* to *Y*:

- *D* -> *Y* (direct path)
- *D* <- *I* -> *Y* (first backdoor path)
- *D* <- *PE* -> *I* -> *Y* (second backdoor path)
- *D* <- *B* -> *PE* -> *I* -> *Y* (third backdoor path)

If we want to estimate the effect of *D* on *Y*, we need to close all backdoor paths. We can do this by controlling *I* and *PE*. This will close the second and third backdoor paths. However, we cannot control *B* because it is unobserved. This means that the first backdoor path will remain open and we will have bias in our estimates.

All these paths are open since none are blocked by a collider. But what is a collider?

Watch out for colliders

A collider is a variable that is caused by its parents instead of causing them. We can see this in *Figure 4.22*:

Figure 4.22 – Example DAG where X is a collider

Notice here the difference is that, instead of *X* affecting *D* and *Y*, the arrows are reversed, that is, both *D* and *Y* have an effect in *X*. This is a collider. A collider automatically blocks that path simply by their presence. This is the graphical explanation of why you should not control all variables in your model. If you control a collider, you will open a backdoor path and introduce bias. So, this leads us to the backdoor criterion.

We need to worry about backdoor paths because, if they are open paths, they will introduce bias into our estimates and create correlations between our variable of interest and the outcome we are worried about. Our goal is then to close all backdoor paths. There are two ways to close a backdoor path:

- The first is conditioning for a confounder variable in the path, which is the equivalent of holding it fixed. This is the same as controlling for a variable in a regression model. You can also condition using other methods such as matching, subclassification, and so on.

- The second is having a collider in the path since colliders always block the path. They should not be controlled for.

Now we are ready to go back to the Google Ads versus TV ads example. As a reminder, the DAG is shown in *Figure 4.23*:

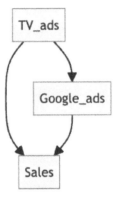

Figure 4.23– DAG for Google Ads versus TV ads

The model represents the interactions as a causal DAG, where we have a binary treatment variable Z (Google Ads, on/off), outcome variable Y (sales), and a confounder C (TV).

Formally, the model will be represented by the following equations:

$$C \sim Normal(0,1)$$

$$Z \sim Bernoulli\left(InvLogit\left(\beta_z 0 + \beta_c zC\right)\right)$$

$$Y \sim Normal\left(\beta_y 0 + \beta_c yC + \beta_z yZ, \sigma_y\right)$$

In this model, we have:

- Random variables C (TV ads spend), Z (Google Ads spend), and Y (sales)

- Observations of C, Z, Y: c, z, y

- A set of latent parameters $\theta = \left\{ \beta_z 0, \beta_y 0, \beta_c z, \beta_c y, \beta_z y, \sigma_y \right\}$

We will now have a set of t regressions: a logistic regression of C on Z and a linear regression of C and Z on Y. Our goal is to estimate the causal effect of Z on Y, which is the $\beta_z y$ coefficient, assuming our DAG is complete.

Now, let's get into the specifics of why Z (Google Ads) is defined as it is:

$$Z \sim Bernoulli\big(InvLogit(\beta_z 0 + \beta_c zC)\big)$$

- **Binary nature of Z**: The first thing to note is that Z (whether Google Ads are on/off) is binary in nature. It can take one of two values: 0 (ads off) or 1 (ads on). Therefore, a Bernoulli distribution is a natural choice for this kind of data.

- **Link function and linear predictor**: The expression inside the Bernoulli function is $InvLogit(\beta_z 0 + \beta_c zC)$. This involves the use of the inverse logit function (often simply called the logistic function). The logistic function maps any real-valued number to a value between 0 and 1, making it suitable to produce the probability parameter for the Bernoulli distribution.

  - $\beta_z 0$ is the intercept, representing the log odds of turning on Google Ads when $C = 0$ (no TV ads spend). If this value is positive, the baseline probability (with no TV ad spend) of turning Google Ads on is greater than 0.5 (since positive log odds correspond to probabilities greater than 0.5).

  - $\beta_c z$ represents the change in log odds of turning on Google Ads for a unit increase in C (TV Ads spend). If $\beta_c z$ is positive, it implies that higher TV ad spend is associated with a higher log odds (and therefore probability) of turning on Google Ads.

- **Why Logit?**: The use of the logistic function here is a common choice in statistics when modeling binary outcomes. In the context of the problem, it allows us to model the probability of turning on Google Ads as a function of TV ad spend in a way that ensures the estimated probability always lies between 0 and 1, irrespective of the value of TV ad spend.

- **Causal inference interpretation**: In causal terms, this model choice acknowledges that the decision to turn on Google Ads might not be random but could depend on the amount of TV ad spend (among other unobserved factors). By using the logistic function, you're allowing for a non-linear relationship between the TV ad spend and the log odds (and hence probability) of turning on Google Ads.

To sum up, the Bernoulli distribution with a logistic link function is a way of modeling the binary decision to turn on Google Ads as potentially being influenced by TV ad spend, and the parameters $\beta_z 0$ and $\beta_c z$ let you quantify that relationship.

We are going to depart from Bambi and use PyMC directly since we need to make use of the do-operator. Let's first import the main libraries we'll need:

```
import arviz as az
import matplotlib.pyplot as plt
import numpy as np
import pandas as pd
import pymc as pm
import pytensor as pt
import pymc_experimental as pmx
import seaborn as sns
from packaging import version
from pymc_experimental.model_transform.conditioning import do, observe
SEED = 42
```

Next, we'll define our PyMC model. We're basically translating what we defined earlier into code:

```
with pm.Model(coords_mutable={"i": [0]}) as model_generative:
    # priors on Y <- C -> Z
    beta_y0 = pm.Normal("beta_y0")
    beta_cy = pm.Normal("beta_cy")
    beta_cz = pm.Normal("beta_cz")
    # priors on Z -> Y causal path
    beta_z0 = pm.Normal("beta_z0")
    beta_zy = pm.Normal("beta_zy")
    # Obs noise on Y
    sigma_y = pm.HalfNormal("sigma_y")
    # core nodes and causal relationships
    c = pm.Normal("c", mu=0, sigma=1, dims="i")
    z = pm.Bernoulli("z", p=pm.invlogit(beta_z0 + beta_cz * c),
        dims="i")
    y_mu = pm.Deterministic("y_mu", beta_y0 + (beta_zy * z) +
        (beta_cy * c), dims="i")
    y = pm.Normal("y", mu=y_mu, sigma=sigma_y, dims="i")
pm.model_to_graphviz(model_generative)
```

Let's take a look at how the model looks from a graphical perspective:

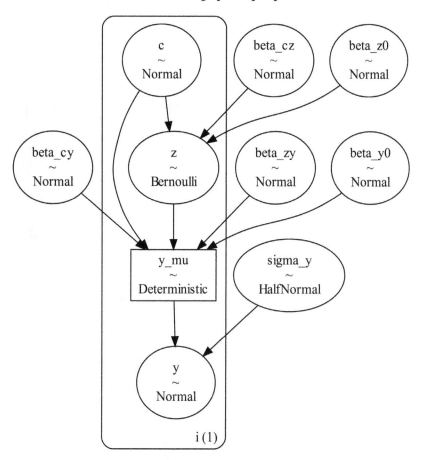

Figure 4.24 – Graphviz representation of the PyMC model

Now, since this is an example, we can define what the true values we are estimating are:

```
true_ATE = 0.0

true_values = {
    "beta_z0": 0.0,
    "beta_y0": 0.0,
    "beta_cz": 1.5,
    "beta_zy": true_ATE,
    "beta_cy": 1.0,
    "sigma_y": 0.2,
}
```

Now that we have defined our true values, let's simulate some sample values from the prior predictive distribution:

```
model_simulate = do(model_generative, true_values)
N = 100

with model_simulate:
    simulate = pm.sample_prior_predictive(samples=N, random_seed=SEED)

    observed = {
        "c": simulate.prior["c"].values.flatten(),
        "y": simulate.prior["y"].values.flatten(),
        "z": simulate.prior["z"].values.flatten(),
    }

    df = pd.DataFrame(observed).sort_values("c", ascending=False)
ax = sns.displot(data=df, x="y", hue="z", kde=True)
ax.set(xlabel="Sales, $y$")
```

As we can see in *Figure 4.25*, if we just take sales when Google Ads are on or off ($z = 0 \mid 1$) then we can clearly see the difference.

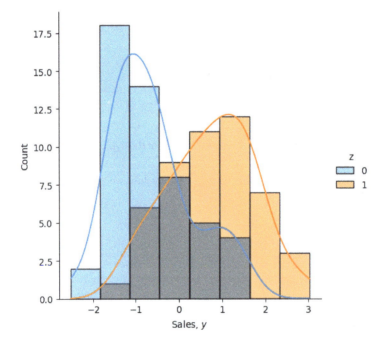

Figure 4.25 – Histogram of sales when Google Ads (z) are on or off

We could even do a t-test or Bayesian significance test to confirm significance.

The key point is that we know for a fact that the true effect size is zero; however, a naive analysis will show an effect.

Let's now try and infer the parameters of our model, also known as inference:

```
model_inference = observe(model_generative, {"c": df["c"],
    "y": df["y"], "z": df["z"]})
model_inference.set_dim("i", N, coord_values=np.arange(N))
with model_inference:
    idata = pm.sample(random_seed=SEED)
az.plot_posterior(
    idata,
    var_names=list(true_values.keys()),
    ref_val=list(true_values.values()),
    figsize=(12, 6),
)

plt.tight_layout();
```

We can see from *Figure 4.26* that our model does a good job of getting back the correct parameters from the sample data that was generated:

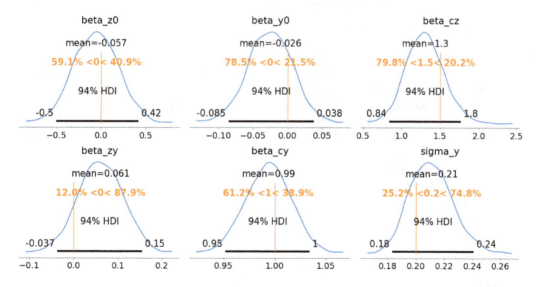

Figure 4.26 – Distribution of parameters in model

Now that we have defined the full join distribution, we are going to use it to simulate data with known causal effect sizes and then test to see if we can recover them.

For that, we need to specify some true parameter values that govern the causal relationships in the data generating process. We will set the true causal influence of Z upon Y to be equal to 0, that is, $\beta_z y$ = 0. This is known as the true **average treatment effect** (**ATE**). This would correspond to the case where Google Ads have no effect on sales.

In the real world, we will not know the true ATE.

One of the main advantages of using the do-operator is the ability to do counterfactual reasoning. This means that we can simulate the effect of interventions, i.e., what would happen if we changed the value of a variable? Essentially, we are asking "what if" questions and answering them with the model.

The question we want to ask is, what if we stopped Google Ads and what if we increased Google Ads spend?

These hypothetical interventions remove any influence of TV on Google Ads because the assumption is that we turn Google Ads on and off irrespective of what TV is doing. This is the logic of the do-operator. Once we have these two hypotheticals, we can estimate how strong the causal influence of Google Ads on sales is, independent of TV.

This is the ATE:

$$ATE = P(Y|c, do(z = 1)) - P(Y|c, do(z = 0)).$$

After running the code, we have the following:

```
model_counterfactual = do(model_inference, {"c": df["c"]})
model_z0 = do(model_counterfactual, {"z": np.zeros(N,
    dtype="int32")}, prune_vars=True)
model_z1 = do(model_counterfactual, {"z": np.ones(N,
    dtype="int32")}, prune_vars=True)
idata_z0 = pm.sample_posterior_predictive(
    idata,
    model=model_z0,
    predictions=True,
    var_names=["y_mu"],
    random_seed=SEED
)


idata_z1 = pm.sample_posterior_predictive(
    idata,
    model=model_z1,
    predictions=True,
    var_names=["y_mu"],
```

```
    random_seed=SEED
)
ATE_est = idata_z1.predictions - idata_z0.predictions
print(f"Estimated ATE = {ATE_est.y_mu.mean().values:.2f}")
```

This produces the following output:

```
Estimated ATE = 0.06
```

Now, you might be tempted to conclude that there is an effect, but as a good Bayesian, you need to be wary of point estimates and always look at the full distribution of outcomes:

```
def plot_causal_estimates(models, ATE_est, model_names):
    fig, ax = plt.subplots(1, 2)

    ret = az.plot_forest(
        [models[0].predictions, models[1].predictions],
        combined=True,
        ax=ax[0],
        model_names=model_names,
    )

    for p in ret[0].patches:
        p.set_color("white") # remove row shading

    az.plot_posterior(
        idata, var_names="beta_zy", ref_val=true_ATE,
            round_to=4, ax=ax[1]
    )

    # formatting
    ax[0].set(
        title="Estimated outcomes under intervention",
        ylabel = "unit, $i$ (ordered)",
        yticklabels=[],
    )

    ax[1].set(title="Average Treatment Effect")
    plt.tight_layout()

    plt.suptitle(
        "unit level estimates with do operator,
        nand estimate of Average Treatment Effect",
        y = 1.05,
```

```
    );
plot_causal_estimates(
    [idata_z0, idata_z1],
    ATE_est,
    model_names=[r"$P(y_i|c_i,do(z_i=0))$",
        r"$P(y_i|c_i,do(z_i=1))$"],
)
```

We can see the estimates of the do-operator in *Figure 4.27*:

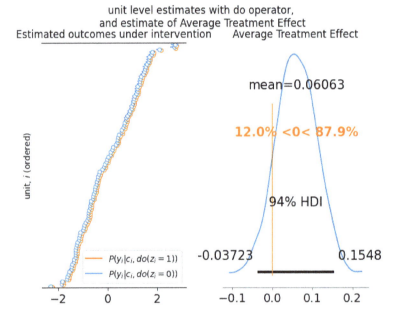

Figure 4.27 – Unit level estimates with do-operator and ATE estimate

So what is the causal effect of Google Ads on sales? We can calculate this with the following:

```
percent = (idata.posterior["beta_zy"] / idata.posterior["beta_cy"]) *
100
print(f"Causal effect of Google Ads on Sales is
    {percent.mean():.1f}% [{az.hdi(percent).x.data[0]:.1f}%,
        {az.hdi(percent).x.data[1]:.1f}%] of the effect of TV")
```

We obtain the following output:

```
Causal effect of Google Ads on Sales is 6.2% [-3.6%, 16.1%] of the
effect of TV
```

We will delve deeper into causal inference later in *Chapter 13, Running Experiments with PyMC*, where we discuss experiments.

Summary

In this chapter, we delved into regression analysis, causal inference, and DAGs. We learned about the basics of linear regressions and logistic regressions. We also walked through DAGs and causal inference and finished on counterfactual analysis.

We have learned the basics of regression models and the differences between a linear regression and a logistic regression. Now you know how to create a DAG for your regression, choose the right regression model, and estimate and interpret the parameters.

We will pick this topic back up in *Chapter 13*, when we discuss experimentation. But for now, we will turn our attention to time series forecasting and the application of regression analysis to time data.

Further reading

Econometrics and causal inference is a very large field, which can't possibly be completely covered in a single chapter. Here are some resources for you to learn more:

- *Causal Inference: The Mixtape* by Scott Cunningham, Yale University Press
- *The Book of Why* by Judea Pearl and Dana Mackenzie, Basic Books
- *Regressions and Other Stories* by Andrew Gelman, Jennifer Hill, and Aki Vehtari, Cambridge University Press
- *Statistical Rethinking* by Richard McElreath, Chapman and Hall
- *Causal Inference and Discovery in Python* by Aleksander Molak, Packt Publishing
- *Causal analysis with PyMC: Answering "What If?" with the new do operator*, `https://www.pymc-labs.com/blog-posts/causal-analysis-with-pymc-answering-what-if-with-the-new-do-operator/`, by Benjamin Vincent and Thomas Wiecki

Part 2: Planning Ahead

This part focuses on preparing for the future and identifying irregularities, starting with an in-depth look at forecasting and time series modeling, a crucial and complex aspect of a marketing data analyst's role. It guides you in choosing the right models, knowing when to use them, and avoiding common mistakes. Following this, the discussion turns to anomaly detection, highlighting its connection to forecasting. It underscores the analyst's frequent task of spotting anomalies before they affect the business and outlines how to manage low-frequency data while reducing false positives.

This part contains the following chapters:

- *Chapter 5, Forecasting with Prophet, ARIMA, and Other Models Using StatsForecast*
- *Chapter 6, Anomaly Detection with StatsForecast and PyMC*

Forecasting with Prophet, ARIMA, and Other Models Using StatsForecast

Gentlemen, you need to put the armor plate where the bullet holes aren't because that's where the holes were on the planes that didn't return.

–Abraham Wald, Hungarian Mathematician

Forecasting is a fundamental tool in any analyst's arsenal. As an analyst, you will be frequently tasked with forecasting **key performance indicators** (**KPIs**) for planning. We will start by understanding the importance of forecasting in marketing analytics and how it helps businesses make informed decisions for future planning. Then, we will learn how to identify the KPIs and other relevant factors that need to be forecasted in marketing analytics. Next, we will go through the fundamental concepts of time series data and basic forecasting methods before closing the chapter by deep diving into more sophisticated forecasting techniques and machine learning based methods, along with when to use these approaches.

We will cover the following topics in this chapter:

- What is forecasting?
- What to forecast
- Basics of time series forecasting
- Advanced forecasting methods

By the end of this chapter, you will have a comprehensive understanding of the various forecasting techniques and their applications in marketing analytics. You will be able to assess the advantages and limitations of each method, choose the appropriate technique for a given task, and effectively apply it to generate accurate forecasts for marketing KPIs and other relevant factors.

Technical requirements

You can find the code files for this chapter on GitHub at `https://github.com/PacktPublishing/Data-Analytics-for-Marketing/tree/main/Chapter05`.

What is forecasting?

Forecasting is the process of making predictions about the future. It is a fundamental task of a marketing data analyst. It is also one of the most complex fields in statistics. You should understand which models to apply, when to apply them, and what to avoid.

Why forecasting is important

Forecasting is important because it allows you to make decisions based on the future. For example, if you are a marketing data analyst, you can use forecasting to predict the number of sales you will have in the next quarter. This will allow you to make decisions about how many products to order, how many people to hire, and how much money to spend on advertising.

Before we begin, we need to understand different types of time series data and how to do some exploratory analysis on them.

Types of times series data

Time series data exhibits a wide variety of patterns, frequencies, and complexities. Understanding the characteristics of different types of time series data is crucial for selecting the appropriate forecasting model and accurately predicting future observations. These types are as follows:

- **Univariate time series**: A univariate time series consists of single observations recorded sequentially over time. For example, the monthly sales of a specific product or the daily closing price of a company's stock can be represented as individual univariate time series. Univariate time series analysis focuses on forecasting future values based solely on the past and present values of a single variable.

- **Multivariate time series**: In contrast to univariate time series, multivariate time series involve multiple variables observed over time. An example could be the daily records of temperature, humidity, and wind speed at a specific location. Multivariate time series analysis considers the relationships between variables and their potential impact on the forecasting process.

- **Panel data**: Panel data (also known as longitudinal or cross-sectional time series data) is a type of time series data where you have multiple time series for the same entity. For example, you might have a time series for the number of sales for each month for each store in a chain of stores. In this case, you have a time series for each store. Panel data analysis aims to understand and model the behavior of the variables across individual entities (such as different stores) and over time, allowing for the identification of both entity-specific and time-specific effects on the forecasts.

- **Hierarchical time series**: Hierarchical time series data consist of time series arranged in a hierarchical structure, where each level of the hierarchy provides additional aggregation or disaggregation of the data. For instance, a retail company might have sales data per product, per category, per store, and per region, creating a multilevel hierarchy. Forecasting hierarchical time series data involves reconciling forecasts at different levels of the hierarchy, which helps to improve the accuracy of predictions and alignment with the overall business strategy.

- **Seasonal time series**: Seasonality is a pattern that repeats at a fixed interval of time, such as daily, weekly, or annually. Seasonal time series data exhibits such recurrent patterns that can be leveraged to improve forecasting accuracy. Examples include monthly sales data influenced by holiday seasons or daily website traffic data affected by weekdays and weekends. Seasonal decomposition and seasonal models, such as SARIMA and Holt–Winters, can be applied to better capture and forecast the underlying seasonal patterns.

- **Non-stationary time series**: Non-stationary time series data exhibits properties that change over time, such as mean, variance, or seasonality patterns. This data often presents more challenges for forecasting, as its statistical properties cannot be assumed constant in the future. Examples include stock prices, economic indicators, and population growth. To improve forecasting accuracy for non-stationary time series, transformations or differencing techniques may be applied to make the data stationary before employing traditional forecasting methods.

As with every piece of new data, we first need to perform some exploratory data analysis to understand our dataset.

Exploratory data analysis

Exploratory data analysis allows us to understand the data and identify any problems with it.

As described in *Chapter 2, Extracting and Exploring Data with Singer and pandas*, we need to begin by checking if the data has nulls, and if there are, then how many. We can do this by using the isna() function and then summing the results:

```
df.isna().sum()
```

When encountering null values in our data, we must determine the appropriate action to handle them. We can either eliminate these nulls or impute them with suitable values. Removing nulls may result in data loss, while filling them in requires choosing a method for imputation. Imputation strategies include using the prior value, subsequent value, or the average of neighboring values. Alternatively, we can replace nulls with a constant value. The fillna() function can be utilized to execute these imputation techniques:

```
df.fillna(method='ffill', inplace=True)
```

Is the data continuous or discrete? Common models such as ETS or ARIMA require the data to be continuous. If the data is discrete, we can use dummy variables or interpolation to convert it to continuous data. Using resampling, you can achieve the interpolation, effectively converting the data to a specified frequency. For example, we can convert the data from daily to weekly. We can do this by using the `resample()` function:

```
df.resample('W').mean()
```

As always, we need to check for outliers. Most methods are sensitive to outliers and that can provide misleading forecasts. Seasonality needs to be taken into consideration. Do not confuse seasonality spikes with outliers. Seasonality spikes are expected and should be taken into account when forecasting. There are several ways to deal with outliers:

- **Winsorization**: This is the process of replacing outliers that exceed a specific percentile. This is useful when the outliers are due to measurement errors. We can do this by using the `clip()` function:

  ```
  df.clip(lower=df.quantile(0.01), upper=df.quantile(0.99),
      inplace=True)
  ```

- **Dummy variables**: This is the process of creating a dummy variable for each outlier. This is useful when the outliers are due to a specific event so you can model them accordingly. We can do this by using the `get_dummies()` function:

  ```
  df = pd.get_dummies(df, columns=['outlier'])
  ```

- **Visualize trend, seasonality, and cyclic behavior**: If cyclic behavior is present, we need to decompose the time series. Be mindful of the distinction between seasonality and cyclic behaviors. Seasonality is periodic behavior that repeats itself every year, month, week, day, and so on. Cyclic behavior is non-periodic behavior that repeats itself every few years. We can do this by using the `seasonal_decompose()` function. We will go over code examples later in the chapter.

What to forecast

Before we begin with forecasting, you need to understand what you are forecasting. For example, if you are tasked with forecasting marketing spend, are we talking about per campaign or groups of campaigns? Is it for every store or group of stores? Are we using daily, weekly, or monthly data? It is also extremely important to consider the forecasting horizon. Are we talking about the next month or five years into the future? This will determine the model we use and the frequency of the data.

There are some common pitfalls to avoid when forecasting. We will discuss some of them here.

Weekly, daily, and sub-daily data

These higher-frequency datasets can be challenging to forecast. Let's start with weekly data. The biggest problem with weekly data is that the seasonal period (that is, the number of weeks in a year) is 52.18. You might notice the decimal part, despite conventional wisdom saying that a year has 52 weeks. A normal year has 365 days, while a leap year has 366 days. So, on average, a year has 365.25 days, so the average number of weeks in a year is 52.18—that is, 365.25 divided by 7. This is both large and not an integer. Why is this a problem? Most methods we will discuss assume the period is a whole number. One might be tempted to round the period to 52, but most methods might struggle with this. The best approach is to first decompose the time series using a method such as **Seasonal–Trend decomposition using LOESS (STL)**, seasonality adjust the dataset by subtracting the seasonal component from the time series, and use a non-seasonal method to forecast.

When looking into daily and sub-daily data frequencies, the challenges arise from different reasons. They often have multiple seasonal patterns, and we need a method that can handle complex seasonality. If the time series is short enough, then the complex seasonality issue won't arise, but if the series is long enough, then the multiple seasonality components will be present. The best approach is to use a method that can handle complex seasonality, such as Facebook's Prophet.

Time series of counts

This chapter primarily deals with time series data that is continuous, or at least can be smoothened to appear so. But in the marketing world, you'll often encounter time series that consist of count data, such as the number of sales, clicks, or ad impressions.

Count-based time series data is just what it sounds like—it tallies occurrences over time. When these counts are high, they start to resemble continuous data, making the distinction less important for our analysis. But when we're working with smaller counts, the gap between continuous and discrete data is more pronounced, and that affects how we should approach our analysis.

For smaller counts, the standard methods we discuss might not be appropriate, and alternative techniques, such as Poisson regression, could be more suitable. These specialized models, however, are not covered in this book. There is a workaround for this issue: **Croston's method**. It's a straightforward technique specifically designed for intermittent demand in time series, which often appears in count data.

Prediction intervals for aggregates

When forecasting aggregates, such as the total number of sales or the total number of clicks, we need to be mindful of the fact that the prediction intervals will be for the individual time forecasts we are aggregating. To illustrate the case, consider a forecast where you have used weekly data and you want to forecast the next eight weeks. The individual point forecasts are the mean, and adding them will yield correct results. However, the prediction intervals will be wider because you will also be adding the errors of the individual forecasts and the correlation between these forecast errors. A simple way to overcome this is by running simulations, where you run the forecast multiple times. Then, you can compute the intervals from the distribution of the forecasts of said simulation.

Long and short time series

When forecasting, you need to be aware that both long and short time series can be challenging for different reasons. With short time series, we are talking about the obvious effect: the more parameters we have to be estimated, the larger the sample size needs to be. And, in an ideal setting, you would split the training dataset from the testing dataset. But in short time series, you will not have enough data to do so. Using a model selection metric such as AICc, which will be discussed in a later section, is helpful in this case since it is a proxy value for the one-step forecast out of sample mean squared error. Choosing the lowest AICc will take into account the number of parameters in the model and the noise of the time series. That is why, when using these criteria, the chosen models tend to be simpler. In practice, anything with more than two parameters will produce very poor forecasts, mostly due to estimation errors.

On the opposite side of the spectrum, one would think that a long time series is a solution for everything. However, the majority of models also do not handle these long series well. The reason is that, when you are forecasting something, you are creating a model to fit patterns. Essentially, you are curve-fitting. You are not, however, modeling the underlying data-generating process. Most of the time, you either do not know it or it is too complex to model. Now, when a time series is not long, that is, up to 200 observations, the models can do a good job at approximating the underlying generating process. When the series becomes too long, the difference between the approximation and the true data generation process becomes apparent. Additionally, you need to be aware that, the more data you have, the more complex the optimization of the parameters will be, which will make the training of the model slower and more time consuming.

A good approach for avoiding such a problem with long time series is to allow the model to change over time. Good models for this are **exponential smoothing** (**ETS**) models. ETS models are built to handle this situation by allowing trend and seasonality components to vary over time.

Transformations

Like any dataset, time series can be transformed. If the data presents, for instance, variations that increase or decrease with time, then a transformation might be useful. Logarithmic transformations are common and useful because they are easily interpretable, as we have seen in previous chapters. A change in the log value is equal to a percentage change in the original value. As discussed in *Chapter 2, Extracting and Exploring Data with Singer and pandas*, a very useful family of transformations is the Box-Cox transformation:

$$y = \begin{cases} \dfrac{sign(y_t)|y^\lambda| - 1}{\lambda} & \lambda \neq 0 \\ log(y_t) & \lambda = 0 \end{cases}$$

An optimal λ value within the Box-Cox transformation is one that achieves similar magnitudes of seasonal fluctuations throughout the series, as it facilitates more accurate forecasting.

What types of patterns are present?

When forecasting, you need to be aware of the type of patterns present in the time series data. This will determine the type of model you will use. Commonly, time series data is described as having trends and seasonality. But what do these terms actually mean?

Trend

A trend is the general direction of the time series. It can be either positive or negative. It can also be constant or it can change over time; for example, a positive trend might change to a negative trend. The trend can be linear, non-linear, multiplicative, or additive. Visual trends are intuitive, as you can see by the dashed line in *Figure 5.1*:

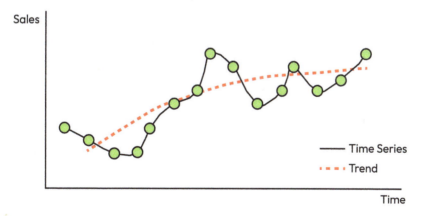

Figure 5.1 – Trend component of a time series

Seasonality

Seasonality is a behavior or pattern that is caused or repeated given some seasonal factor, such as the time of the year or the day of the week. A few good examples from the e-commerce space are Black Friday and Christmas sales. They repeat every year due to a calendar event. One thing to note is that seasonality is always fixed and of a known period. For example, the period of a year is 12 months, and the period of a week is 7 days, which will correspond to the monthly and weekly seasonality periods, respectively. So, in a stylized way, in *Figure 5.2*, we can observe seasonality through the dotted line:

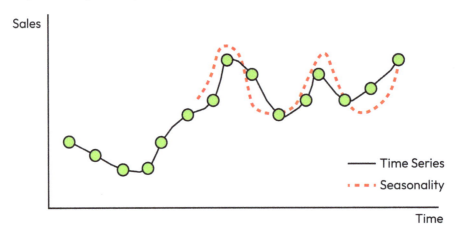

Figure 5.2 – Seasonality component of a time series

A major source of confusion is when people use seasonality to describe cyclic behavior.

Cyclic behavior

A cycle is a behavior or pattern that repeats itself, but the period is not fixed. The reason the period is not fixed is usually due to the influence of an external factor. The most known cycle is the business cycle, caused by economic factors. Another example is cycles induced by competitor activities. In general, cycles are longer than seasonal effects, taking years to complete instead of months or weeks.

It is possible to break time series data into these patterns, known as time series decomposition.

Time series decomposition

Time series decomposition is a method of breaking a time series dataset into its components. Usually, the trend and cyclic components are grouped together, and most statistical packages will output this as a single component called a trend. You will also have the seasonal component. What remains is the residual, which is the noise of the time series. It is essentially the movement from the time series that cannot be explained either by the trend or seasonality. When decomposing time series data, you are not limited to just one seasonal component. A time series can have multiple seasonal components; for example, a time series can have a weekly and a monthly seasonal component.

When breaking down a time series into its basic elements, we can use two approaches: additive or multiplicative decomposition. With an additive model, we simply add the trend, seasonal, and residual components to reconstruct the original time series. This implies that the impact of trend and seasonality does not change over time.

On the other hand, a multiplicative model assumes that the time series is a result of multiplying the trend, seasonal, and residual components. Here, the effect of the trend and the seasonality increases or decreases in direct proportion to the data. So, as the data grows, the influence of the trend and seasonal patterns also grows, and as the data decreases, the influence similarly reduces. This approach is often more appropriate when the seasonal patterns intensify as the time series value rises.

If we are taking an additive decomposition, the time series can be written as:

$$y_t = T_t + S_t + R_t$$

where T_t is the trend, S_t is the seasonal component, and R_t is the remainder part or noise pattern not explained by the other two components.

Multiplicative decomposition is similar, but the components are multiplied together:

$$y_t = T_t \times S_t \times R_t$$

A good mathematical trick to know is that:

$$y_t = T_t \times S_t \times R_t$$

is equivalent to

$$log(y_t) = log(T_t) + log(S_t) + log(R_t)$$

This makes our lives a bit easier in certain cases since it's always easier to work with an additive model than a multiplicative one. We just need to be mindful of the fact that we are working with logs, and we need to take the exponential of the forecast to get the actual forecast.

Seasonally adjusted data

With the components, one can, for instance, seasonally adjust the data. Essentially, we are trying to remove seasonality, and its effects, from the original dataset because we are not interested in analyzing the seasonal effects but the overall trend effects. A good example of when we would want to do so is when looking at unemployment numbers. Employment numbers are seasonal, and the seasonal component is usually due to the fact that, in the summer, people are more likely to be employed in specific industries, while in the winter, people are more likely to be unemployed. So, if we want to compare the unemployment numbers from one year to another, we need to remove the seasonal component so that we can compare apples to apples. The method to do so is to take the original time series and subtract the seasonal component from it if we are dealing with additive decomposition. This will give us the seasonally adjusted data:

$$x = y_t - S_t$$

Similarly to additive decomposition, if we are dealing with multiplicative decomposition, we need to divide the original time series by the seasonal component:

$$x = y_t/S_t$$

You can also do the same with the trend component to give a trend-adjusted dataset, or a detrended dataset.

Detrended data

You are essentially trying to achieve the same as for seasonally adjusted data, but in this case, you want to remove the effect of the trend as opposed to the seasonality. The method of doing so is to take the original time series and subtract the trend component from it if we are dealing with additive decomposition. This will give us the trend-adjusted data:

$$x = y_t - T_t$$

Again, if we are dealing with multiplicative decomposition, we need to divide the original time series by the trend component:

$$x = y_t/T_t$$

The workhorse technique for time series decomposition is STL decomposition. It is a very powerful technique, and it is available in R and Python.

STL decomposition

STL stands for Seasonal-Trend decomposition using LOESS. It is a very powerful technique to decompose a time series into its components. LOESS is a statistical method to estimate non-linear relationships. STL has various advantages:

- It is robust to outliers, so unusual observations will not affect the decomposition with regard to trend or seasonal components. The outliers will be captured in the residual component, however. In the next chapter, we will see how to leverage this feature for anomaly detection.

- You can control the smoothness of the trend component via a window parameter. The smaller the window, the bigger the rate of change allowed in the trend component.

- The seasonal component is allowed to change over time, and like the trend component, it can be controlled via a window parameter. The smaller the window, the bigger the rate of change allowed in the seasonal component.

- Finally, it will be able to handle any type of seasonality at various time scales. For example, it can handle weekly, monthly, quarterly, and yearly seasonality.

An important thing to remember regarding the second and third points is that the window parameter should be an odd number. The trend window will tell STL how many consecutive points to use to estimate the trend. The seasonal window will tell STL how many consecutive points to use to estimate the seasonal component.

Another very important caveat is that STL only handles additive decomposition. If you have a multiplicative decomposition, you need to take the log of the time series and then apply STL. After that, if you want to return to the original scale, you need to take the exponential of the values. If the seasonality is between additive and multiplicative, then the Box-Cox transformation can be used with $0 < \lambda < 1$. $\lambda = 1$ will give you additive decomposition, $\lambda = 0$ will give you multiplicative decomposition.

Aside from patterns, time series have important features that we need to capture.

Time series features

Time series features are essential characteristics extracted from time series data that capture underlying patterns, trends, and relationships within the data. These features provide valuable insights and diagnostics, improve forecasting accuracy, and help identify anomalies and events in the time series. You can think of these features as a form of exploratory data analysis on time series. Let's start with ACF features.

ACF features

The first group of features are autocorrelation features. In the same way as correlation will measure how two variables move together in a linear fashion, autocorrelation will measure how observations move together given lagged values of the time series. For example, if we have a time series of daily sales and we want to know how the sales today are correlated with the sales yesterday, we can calculate the autocorrelation at lag 1. If we want to know how the sales today are correlated with the sales two days ago, we can calculate the autocorrelation at lag 2, and so on.

The autocorrelation coefficient at lag k is denoted by r_k and is defined as follows:

$$r_k = \frac{\sum_{t=k+1}^{T}(y_t - \bar{y})(y_{t-k} - \bar{y})}{\sum_{t=1}^{T}(y_t - \bar{y})^2}$$

The autocorrelation coefficients make up the autocorrelation function or ACF. We can use these autocorrelation coefficients to make new features of interest. As an example, the sum of the first ten squared autocorrelation coefficients is a good feature to capture the overall autocorrelation in the time series, regardless of lag.

There are a few important autocorrelation features to keep in mind:

- The first autocorrelation coefficient derived from the original dataset

- The sum of squared values of the top 10 autocorrelation coefficients from the original data

- The lead coefficient of autocorrelation from data that has been differentiated once, meaning the difference between consecutive data points

- The total squared values of the first 10 autocorrelation coefficients from data differentiated once

- The primary coefficient of autocorrelation from data that has undergone differentiation twice

- The sum of squared values for the top 10 autocorrelation coefficients from data differentiated two times

- For datasets with a seasonal aspect, the autocorrelation coefficient corresponding to the initial seasonal lag is taken into account

In the context of marketing analytics, understanding the dynamics of time series data is pivotal for accurate forecasting and strategic decision-making. A core concept in this arena is the analysis of autocorrelation features, which serve as a compass for navigating the temporal relationships within marketing datasets. In this chapter, we delve into the essence and application of these features, utilizing Python for practical demonstrations.

Autocorrelation coefficients, denoted as r_k, measure the linear relationship between time-lagged observations within a dataset. These coefficients range from -1 to +1, where:

- A value of +1 signifies a perfect positive correlation, indicating that an increase in one observation directly correlates with an increase in another, separated by a specific lag

- A -1 value denotes a perfect negative correlation, suggesting that an increase in one observation corresponds to a decrease in another across the given lag

- A coefficient near 0 implies a lack of a linear relationship between the observations at the specified lag.

Let's go over each important autocorrelation feature and what they mean:

1. **Initial observation correlation** (x_acf1): This represents the immediate linear relationship between successive observations.

2. **Collective influence** (x_acf10): This aggregates the squared autocorrelation coefficients for the first ten lags, offering insight into the overall temporal dependency. Elevated values suggest pronounced autocorrelation, implying that historical data significantly influences future outcomes.

3. **Trend identification through differencing** (diff1_acf1): This applies to once-differentiated data, highlighting trends or non-stationarities. Negative values suggest inverse relationships between consecutive changes, indicative of possible market corrections or overreactions.

4. **Pattern strength in changes** (diff1_acf10): This summarizes the squared autocorrelation of the first differences. Higher totals reveal stronger autocorrelated structures post-differencing, suggesting underlying trends or cycles.

5. **Complex dynamics detection** (diff2_acf1): This focuses on twice-differentiated data, uncovering more intricate patterns that may include seasonal trends or deeper cyclical behaviors.

6. **Underlying structure in second differences** (diff2_acf10): This is similar to diff1_acf10 but for the second differences, indicating even more complex temporal relationships that may necessitate advanced modeling techniques.

7. **Seasonal influence** (**Seasonal ACF**): This examines the autocorrelation at specific seasonal lags, with values close to the extremities indicating significant seasonal effects.

Consider a dataset encompassing various marketing metrics, where each entry is uniquely identified.

There is also a group of STL features to be considered.

STL features

If the data has a strong trend component, the seasonally adjusted data variation will have more variation than the remainder component. Using this fact, we can compute a feature that will capture the strength of the trend component. It is defined as follows:

$$F_t = max\left(0,1 - \frac{var(R_t)}{var(T_t + R_t)}\right)$$

You can reason about seasonality in a similar fashion, but in this case with regards to the detrended data. This ratio is defined as follows:

$$F_s = max\left(0,1 - \frac{var(R_t)}{var(S_t + R_t)}\right)$$

Given the ratio, it will range from 0 to 1. In either case, the higher the value, the stronger the trend or seasonality effect. This will become useful if, given a collection of time series, we want to identify the ones that have the strongest trend or seasonality effect.

A few important STL features to keep in mind are as follows:

- **Seasonal peak year**: This denotes when peaks occur, specifically identifying the month or quarter with the most pronounced seasonal element.

- **Seasonal trough year**: This pinpoints when troughs arise, highlighting the month or quarter with the least prominent seasonal element.

- **Spikiness**: This calculates the frequency of sudden rises in the remainder component R_t. It evaluates the variability of the variances when one observation is omitted from R_t.

- **Linearity**: This assesses how linear the trend-cycle component T_t is, utilizing the coefficient from linear regression on the trend.

- **Curvature**: This evaluates the bend in the trend segment of the STL breakdown, using the coefficient from a quadratic regression that's orthogonal when applied to the trend.

- **stl_e_acf1**: This represents the initial autocorrelation coefficient of the remainder segment R_t.

- **stl_e_acf10**: This totals the squared values of the leading 10 autocorrelation coefficients from the remainder section R_t.

Other features

Other features that can be computed are as follows:

- **Hurst coefficient**: This evaluates a time series' long-term memory. If a series retains memory for an extended period, it displays notable autocorrelations across numerous lags.

- **Spectral entropy (Shannon)**: This gauges the predictability of a time series. A highly predictable series with pronounced trend and seasonality will have entropy nearing 0, while an unpredictable, noisy series will approach an entropy of 1.

- **Box–Pierce and Ljung–Box statistics**: These examine whether a time series is purely random or "white noise."

- **K-th partial autocorrelation**: This scrutinizes the correlation between data points separated by k intervals, but this correlation excludes the influence of data points in between. Notably, when k equals 1, it refers to the first partial autocorrelation.

- **KPSS statistic**: This conducts a test to determine the stability or stationarity of a time series.

- **Phillips-Perron Statistic**: This probes for the presence of non-stationarity in a time series.

- **Differencing count**: This calculates how many times a time series must be differenced to achieve stationarity, using insights from the KPSS statistic.

- **Tiled mean**: This computes the variance of consecutive, non-overlapping blocks of data points' means. Typically, the block length is set to 10 or corresponds to the seasonal period's length. This metric is often dubbed the "stability feature."

- **Tile variance**: This determines the variance of the variances derived from consecutive, non-overlapping blocks of observations. This is occasionally termed "lumpiness."

Remembering the list of features, and how to calculate them, is hard. There is a package called `tsfeatures` that can help us.

Time series features in Python

In this section, we will show how to compute the time series features mentioned earlier using the `tsfeatures` package in Python. Please make sure to first install the necessary package by running the following:

```
!pip install tsfeatures
```

To demonstrate the use of this package, we will use a sample dataset containing a daily time series of sales data. Our goal is to calculate various features that help us understand the underlying dynamics of the time series. Here's an example of how to use the package to achieve this. First, we need to load the libraries and format the data in a specific way. The package expects the data in long format, with columns `ds` for date, `unique_id` for a time series identifier, and `y` for the values:

```python
import pandas as pd
from tsfeatures import (
    tsfeatures, acf_features, stl_features,
    frequency, pacf_features, statistics)

pd.options.display.float_format = "{:,.4f}".format

data_path = '../data'
sales_df = pd.read_csv('../data/superstore.csv',
    encoding = "ISO-8859-1")

sales_df['Order Date'] = pd.to_datetime(sales_df['Order Date'])
monthly_sales = data.groupby([pd.Grouper(key='Order Date', freq='M'),
    'Category'])['Sales'].sum()

features = pd.DataFrame(monthly_sales.copy())
features.reset_index(inplace=True)
features.rename(columns={'Order Date': 'ds', 'Sales': 'y',
    'Category': 'unique_id'}, inplace=True)
```

Once that is done, we can simply run the `tsfeatures` function with our desired feature set. Let's start with basic statistics, for which we can see the output in *Figure 5.3*:

```
tsfeatures(features_df, freq=1, features=[statistics])
```

	unique_id	total_sum	mean	variance	median	p2point5	p5	p25	p75	p95	p97point5	max	min
0	Furniture	1.776357e-15	3.700743e-17	1.0	-0.308431	-1.338507	-1.188439	-0.676709	0.679534	1.778778	2.236840	2.372458	-1.495932
1	Office Supplies	1.731948e-14	3.608225e-16	1.0	-0.232597	-1.482923	-1.196267	-0.713474	0.541197	1.889071	1.972432	2.695727	-1.628910
2	Technology	-2.220446e-15	-4.625929e-17	1.0	-0.212104	-1.363632	-1.299979	-0.744524	0.571026	1.515604	1.709112	3.115816	-1.515907

Figure 5.3 – Basic features

This table represents the output of statistics features extracted for three different product categories: furniture, office supplies, and technology. These statistical features provide a broad overview of the distribution and scale of the time series data for each category. Let's interpret each column:

- `unique_id`: This is the identifier for the time series, in this case, different product categories.

- `total_sum`: This is the sum of all values in the time series. The values are very close to zero, which, depending on the context, could suggest that the data has been normalized or centered around zero.

- `mean`: This is the average value of the time series. These values are also very close to zero, reinforcing the idea that the data might be normalized.

- `variance`: This is the variance of the time series. All categories have a variance of 1, indicating that the data has been standardized to have a unit variance, which is a common preprocessing step in time series analysis.

- `median`: This is the median of the time series. The values are negative for all categories, suggesting that the median value lies below the mean, indicating a skew in the data distribution.

- `p2point5` to `p97point5`: These percentiles provide a detailed look at the distribution of the time series data, from the 2.5th percentile to the 97.5th percentile. The wide range between these percentiles indicates a significant spread in the data points, which can be critical for understanding the variability in the data.

- `max` and `min`: These are the maximum and minimum values in the time series. The range between these values indicates the overall spread of the data and can highlight the presence of outliers or extreme values.

From a marketing analytics perspective, these statistical features can offer several insights:

- **Data normalization**: A mean close to zero and a variance of 1 for all categories suggests that the data has been normalized. This standardization facilitates comparison across categories and the application of certain statistical and machine learning models.

- **Distribution characteristics**: The percentiles and median provide insight into the distribution of the data. For example, the median being less than the mean (given the mean's proximity to zero) suggests a skew in the data distribution. This information can help in understanding sales patterns, such as whether a small number of very high or very low sales days are driving the overall performance.

- **Variability and extremes**: The range between the minimum and maximum values, along with the percentile information, shows the extent of variability within the sales data. High variability might indicate the presence of seasonality, promotional impacts, or other factors that cause sales to fluctuate significantly.

- **Forecasting and planning**: Understanding the statistical distribution of past sales data is crucial for forecasting future sales and planning inventory. For example, knowing the spread and skew of the data can help in setting more accurate inventory levels, minimizing both stockouts and excess inventory.

- **Targeted strategies**: The detailed percentile values can help in identifying targets for improvement. For instance, raising the lower percentiles (for example, p2.5, p5) could be a goal for strategies aimed at reducing the number of low sales days, while strategies aimed at increasing high sales days could focus on the upper percentiles (for example, p95, p97.5).

In summary, the statistical features from the time series data provide a foundation for understanding the underlying patterns and variability in sales across different product categories. This understanding is essential for effective forecasting, inventory management, and the development of targeted marketing strategies.

For the ACF features, the only change is instead of having statistics in the features list, we have `acf_features`, with the output shown in *Figure 5.4*:

```
tsfeatures(features_df, freq=1, features=[acf_features])
```

	unique_id	x_acf1	x_acf10	diff1_acf1	diff1_acf10	diff2_acf1	diff2_acf10	seas_acf1
0	Furniture	0.296613	0.248431	-0.401140	0.482436	-0.587269	0.720740	-0.067398
1	Office Supplies	0.346595	0.273683	-0.419869	0.467545	-0.580794	0.646733	-0.081835
2	Technology	0.209677	0.084553	-0.431491	0.373567	-0.596151	0.660406	-0.031988

Figure 5.4 – ACF features

Analyzing the autocorrelation features across these entries provides insights on autocorrelation features for the same three categories of products: furniture, office supplies, and technology. Let's decode each column:

- `unique_id`: This identifies the product category for which the features are calculated.

- `x_acf1`: This is the autocorrelation at lag 1 of the original time series. It indicates the correlation of the series with its previous value, suggesting momentum or persistence in the series.

- `x_acf10`: This is the sum of squared autocorrelations up to lag 10 of the original series. This gives an idea of the overall memory or dependency structure in the original data over a longer period.

- `diff1_acf1`: This is the autocorrelation at lag 1 after differencing the series once. This transformation is often used to remove trends and make the series stationary.

- `diff1_acf10`: This is the sum of squared autocorrelations up to lag 10 after differencing the series once. It indicates the memory or dependency structure in the differenced data.

- `diff2_acf1`: This is the autocorrelation at lag 1 after differencing the series twice. This further transformation is sometimes necessary for series with more complex trends or seasonal patterns.

- `diff2_acf10`: This is the sum of squared autocorrelations up to lag 10 after differencing the series twice. It shows the dependency structure in the twice-differenced data.

- `seas_acf1`: This is the autocorrelation at the seasonal lag. It provides a measure of the seasonality strength in the series.

Interpreting these features for marketing analytics purposes, we can derive several insights:

- **Persistence in sales**: The positive values in `x_acf1` for all categories indicate a significant persistence in sales; that is, if sales increase (or decrease) in one period, they are likely to do so in the next period as well. This persistence is strongest for office supplies and weakest for technology.

- **Overall dependency**: The `x_acf10` values, which are also positive, suggest that sales in the past have a cumulative effect on future sales, spanning over several periods. This effect is most pronounced for furniture and office supplies, indicating that past sales performance can inform future sales predictions.

- **Impact of differencing**: The negative `diff1_acf1` values across all categories suggest that once the series is differenced to remove a trend, the immediate past no longer offers a straightforward prediction of the future, indicating that the original series had a trend. The positive `diff1_acf10` values indicate that there's still some dependency structure left after differencing.

- **Second differencing**: The `diff2_acf1` and `diff2_acf10` values, which are negative for the first lag and positive for the sum of lags up to 10, suggest that even after removing trends and potential seasonal effects, there's complex dependency in the data that might require sophisticated modeling to capture accurately.

- **Seasonality**: The negative `seas_acf1` values indicate a potential inversion in the seasonality effect from one period to the next at the seasonal lag, albeit the effect is quite mild. This might suggest complex seasonal patterns that are not simply captured by direct correlations over seasonal lags.

The persistence and dependency structure indicated by the autocorrelation features suggests that models such as **autoregressive integrated moving average (ARIMA)**, which can account for these aspects, may be particularly useful. Additionally, the evidence of complex seasonality and trend structures indicates the need for careful preprocessing and potentially the use of models that can accommodate complex seasonal patterns, such as **Seasonal ARIMA (SARIMA)** or machine learning approaches that can model non-linear dependencies.

Finally, let's run the STL features. The output is shown in *Figure 5.5*:

```
tsfeatures(features_df, freq=1, features=[stl_features])
```

	unique_id	nperiods	seasonal_period	trend	spike	linearity	curvature	e_acf1	e_acf10	seasonal_strength	peak	trough
0	Furniture	1	30	1	7.625542e-66	2.635851	-4.718448e-16	0.045461	0.197753	1	6	7
1	Office Supplies	1	30	1	7.541486e-66	3.272922	-5.551115e-16	0.158533	0.278774	1	6	8
2	Technology	1	30	1	1.022913e-65	2.961985	-3.885781e-16	-0.221408	0.359216	1	17	8

Figure 5.5 – STL features

This table shows the output of `stl_features` from the `tsfeatures` library in Python, calculated for three different categories of products: furniture, office supplies, and technology. These features are extracted from time series data to understand various characteristics that could be crucial for forecasting in marketing analytics. Let's break down what each column represents:

- `unique_id`: This is the identifier for the time series, here representing different product categories.

- `nperiods`: This is the number of observed periods in the time series. In this context, all categories have 1, which could imply a single time series per category or potentially a formatting error, as this would typically represent the number of cycles or seasons observed.

- `seasonal_period`: This is the number of observations per cycle/season. Here, it's 30, which could imply monthly data over 2.5 years or another timeframe, depending on the data frequency.

- `trend`: This indicates the presence (1) or absence (0) of a trend within the time series. All categories show a trend.

- `spike`: This measures the sharpness of fluctuations in the time series. The values are extremely low, suggesting minimal sharp spikes, which could be due to the scale of the data or the nature of the time series.

- `linearity`: This quantifies how linear the time series is. The values vary across categories, with office supplies being the most linear. This suggests a more straightforward, predictable trend over time.

- `curvature`: This measures the curvature (second derivative) of the time series. The values are close to zero, indicating a relatively flat or linear trend without much bending.

- `e_acf1`: This is the first lag of the autocorrelation of the residuals. Negative values indicate possible over-differencing, while positive values suggest a trend. Furniture and office supplies show a positive autocorrelation, suggesting a lingering trend in the residuals, whereas technology shows a negative value.

- `e_acf10`: This is the sum of squared autocorrelations of the residuals up to lag 10. Higher values can indicate more complex autocorrelation structures in the residuals, with technology showing the highest complexity.

- `seasonal_strength`: This measures the strength of seasonality in the time series. A value of 1 indicates strong seasonality, consistent across all categories, suggesting that seasonality is a significant component.

- `peak`: This is the time (in periods) to the peak of the seasonal component. Peaks of 6 for furniture and technology suggest their seasonal highs occur at similar times.

- `trough`: This is the time (in periods) to the trough of the seasonal component. This varies slightly between categories, indicating different times for seasonal lows.

Interpreting these features in the context of marketing analytics, we can draw several insights:

- **Trend and seasonality**: All categories exhibit a strong seasonal pattern and a trend component, which is crucial for forecasting and planning marketing strategies around peak sales periods.

- **Linearity and curvature**: The relatively linear trends and minimal curvature suggest that simple linear models may perform well for forecasting, with adjustments for seasonality.

- **Spike and autocorrelation**: The lack of sharp spikes and the positive autocorrelation in furniture and office supplies suggest that past values (and possibly their trends) are good predictors for future values, whereas technology might require a more nuanced approach due to its negative autocorrelation at lag 1.

- **Seasonal peaks and troughs**: Understanding when peaks and troughs occur can help with planning inventory, promotions, and sales strategies, capitalizing on high-demand periods, or stimulating demand during low periods.

Now that we have explored how to extract features from time series, let's move on to get a basic understanding of time series forecasting.

Basics of time series forecasting

When we are trying to forecast a time series, like any other analysis activity, there is a set of steps that we need to follow:

1. **Data cleaning and preparation**: The first step in the process is formatting and cleaning the data. It might involve handling missing data, outliers, or any errors present in the data. It may also involve transforming the data into a format suitable for time series analysis.

2. **Plotting the time series and some exploratory data analysis (EDA)**: In this step, we visualize the data and perform some preliminary analysis to understand the underlying patterns and structures. This might include observing any obvious trends, seasonality, or cyclic behavior.

3. **Defining the model**: Based on insights from the EDA, we select an appropriate model for our time series data. The choice of model depends on the observed components of the time series, such as trend, seasonality, and noise.

4. **Fitting the model**: Once we've chosen a model, we fit it to our data. This involves estimating the parameters of the model.

5. **Evaluating the model**: After fitting, we evaluate the model's performance by comparing the predicted values with the actual values. We might use measures such as **mean absolute error (MAE)**, **mean squared error (MSE)**, or **root mean squared error (RMSE)** for evaluation.

6. **Forecasting**: Once we are satisfied with the model's performance, we use it to forecast future values. We can also provide confidence intervals along with our forecasts to quantify the uncertainty.

This completes the typical workflow for time series forecasting. Each step is vital, and thorough execution can help ensure accurate forecasts.

A good thing to remember when forecasting is a quote from Confucius: *"Do not use a cannon to kill a mosquito"*. Starting with a simple model and then adding complexity is a necessary pattern. As an analyst, you need to remember that when dealing with data, it is a finite resource. Each extra parameter that you add to your model will require more data to estimate. Let's start with a very simple method for forecasting.

Simple methods

Some methods are simple and intuitive. Some will also yield good results when used appropriately. And, as an added feature, they provide a good benchmarking method to compare more complex models against. The simplest possible method you can use or think of is the average method. You are not doing anything fancy; your forecast is simply the average value of the time series. This method will only make sense if the data has no trend or seasonality and has little to no variance. In marketing, we rarely are this lucky, but if a more complex model cannot beat the average method, then it is not worth using.

A step above the average method is to use the aptly named the naive method. This method is not more complex than the average method. It is a simple method that uses the last observation to predict the next one. You might think this is a useless method, but you would be surprised—this will be the best method if the time series you are analyzing follows a random walk. A random walk is a time series where the next observation is a random walk from the previous one. This is a very common pattern in financial time series. In a random walk, there is no information in the past to predict the future. The only thing that matters is the last observation. Now, by definition, random walks have no trend or seasonality, so what would be the baseline for a highly seasonal dataset? We could consider using the last value of the last corresponding season; for example, the same quarter for last year. This is called the seasonal naive method and is calculated as:

$$y_{t+h|t} = y_{t+h-m(k+1)}$$

where m is the seasonal period, h is the forecast horizon, and k is the integer part of $\frac{(h-1)}{m}$.

Another variation of the naive method involves applying a drift to the last observation. This is called the drift method. The drift is a constant that is added to the last observation to get the forecast. The drift is computed as the difference between the last few observations.

While you might consider these methods a bit too simple and naive, probably at one point or another you have used them (or seen them being used). The reason we formalized them and included them is because they are good benchmarking methods. If a more complex model cannot beat these methods, then it is not worth using. Also, given they are easy to implement, your stakeholders will probably use them if left to their own devices.

Now, before we enter more complex methods, we need to discuss how to diagnose and evaluate a time series model.

Fitted values and residuals

When we fit a model to a time series, we are trying to find the best parameters that will minimize the error between the actual values and the predicted values. If you recall from the previous chapter, this error is called the residual. The predicted values are called the fitted values and are the values that the model predicts. The residuals are the difference between the actual values and the fitted values. Plotting these values against each other provides some diagnostics about the model. If you have transformed the variables in any way, sometimes it is useful to look at the residuals on the transformed scale.

Similar to a normal regression model, there are some characteristics that we want to see in the residuals. We want to see that the residuals are normally distributed and that they have a mean of 0. When they don't, it means the model is biased in some way. We also want to see that the residuals are uncorrelated. If the residuals are correlated, then the model is not capturing all the information in the time series. Any model that does not meet these conditions can be improved in some way.

Adjusting for bias

If the residuals have a mean that is not 0, then the model is biased. This means that the model is not capturing all the information in the time series. There is a simple way to adjust for bias: subtract a constant from the fitted forecast values, the constant being the mean m of the residuals. Fixing correlation is a bit more complicated, and we will discuss it later.

The next two characteristics are good to have, but not essential. The first one is a constant variance on the residuals. This is known as homoscedasticity. The second one is a normal distribution of the residuals.

Now, we need to be aware of the impact of not having these two characteristics. A model that does not have a constant variance of residuals and where the residuals are not normally distributed will still be able to make good predictions. However, the model will not be able to properly quantify the uncertainty of the predictions. This means our confidence intervals will be wider. Sometimes these intervals will be wider than what is actually useful. A Box-Cox transformation can be used to fix the variance of the residuals. It is not guaranteed to work, and if it doesn't, there is little you can do.

Correlation and forecasting

At the risk of sounding like a broken record, correlation is not causation. This means that, if you have correlated variables, it is very challenging to infer causality from those correlations because you can't separate the effects on the response variable. While this is true for time series, it does not mean that we can't use correlated variables to make predictions. We don't need to understand the causal relationship between the variables to make predictions. We just need to understand the relationship between the variables. If you recall, in *Chapter 1*, *What is Marketing Analytics?*, that is why I warned you about the dangers of machine learning for causal inference. When you are doing simple forecasts you can get away with correlated variables, but when you conduct causal inference, you need to be very careful. Imagine you are doing scenario analysis and you want to know what would happen if you increased the price of your product. You would need to control all the other variables and provide a causal answer. High correlation between variables will make this very difficult. Another example is when you are trying to understand the impact of a marketing campaign.

A related problem with time series is multicollinearity.

Multicollinearity

Again, imagine you are doing scenario planning. You will have correlated variables with the response variable. In this case, you have correlated variables amongst themselves, or they are a linear combination of others being correlated with another linear combination of variables. There are two consequences for this. The first one is that some statistical software can't handle this, notoriously Excel, and you will get highly inaccurate estimates. The second problem, if you are using more robust packages such as those present in Python or R, is that the estimates of the coefficients are going to have more uncertainty in them. This will lead to more uncertainty in the predictions and forecasts, given that these uncertainties will propagate through the model. As a consequence, your confidence intervals will be wider.

This means we need to have some way of selecting predictors in regression models for time series.

Variable selection in time series regression models

Variable selection in time series regression models is a crucial step in refining your predictions. The essence of this task lies in identifying which predictors (or features) provide valuable information for forecasting the target variable. The overall goal is to include features that improve the model's performance while excluding those that may make it overly complex without providing additional forecasting value.

There are several strategies for variable selection, two of which will be discussed in this chapter: cross-validation and the use of information criteria metrics. Both methods aim to enhance the model's predictive power and generalizability, yet they approach the task from different angles.

Before we dive into these two methods, it's important to note that variable selection in time series models isn't always straightforward. Unlike cross-sectional data, where each observation is assumed to be independent, time series data has an inherent order. This temporal structure means that the value at a given time point is likely dependent on previous values. Therefore, the predictors in our model should reflect this temporal dependency, taking into account not just the values of other potential predictor variables, but also their evolution over time.

Cross-validation

The simplest way to select variables is to use cross-validation. This is a method that is commonly used in machine learning to select the best model. In essence, it is a more developed version of the holdout method. In the holdout method, you split the data into two sets: a training set and a test set. You fit the model on the training set and evaluate it on the test set. The problem with this method is that you are only using a fraction of the data to fit the model. This means that you are not using all the information in the data to fit the model. This is why cross-validation is a better method. In cross-validation, you split the data into k folds. You fit the model on $k - 1$ folds and evaluate it on the remaining folds. You repeat this process k times, using a different fold as the test set every time. The final score is the average of the k scores. This method is more robust because you are using all the data to fit the model and you are not overfitting the model to a specific fold. Now, the splits in time series cannot be random. You need to make sure that the folds are contiguous in time. This is because the data is not independent. The data is dependent on the previous observations. If you split the data randomly, you will be introducing a bias in the model. Most commonly, you will split the model between a test set of one observation and a training set of all the previous observations. For each k fold, you move it one observation forward. This is called a rolling window. You repeat this process until you reach the end of the time series. The result is a set of predictions for each observation. We then average all the test set predictions to get the final score. This method is also known as "evaluating on a rolling forecasting origin" because the origin of the test set is rolling forward one point at a time.

Similar to the previous chapter, we can simplify the calculation process by using leave-one-out cross-validation. In this case, you use all the data except one observation to fit the model, and you use the remaining observation to evaluate the model. You repeat this process for each observation. This is equivalent to using a rolling window with a window size of one:

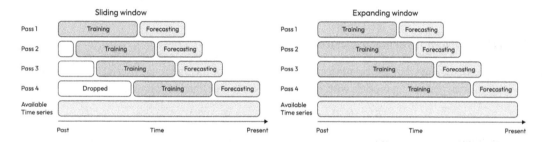

Figure 5.6 – Sliding or rolling window versus expanding window cross-validation

Information criteria metrics

Another way to select predictor variables for your model is to use an information criteria metric. This is a metric that is used to compare models. The most common information criteria metrics are the **Akaike information criterion (AIC)**, the **corrected Akaike's information criteria (AICc)**, and the **Bayesian information criterion (BIC)**. Essentially, they will compare different models for the information they provide and penalize them for the number of parameters they have. The model with the lowest metric is the best model.

Akaike information criterion (AIC)

The AIC is defined as follows:

$$AIC = T\log\left(\frac{SSE}{T}\right) + 2(k+2)$$

In this formula, T is the number of observations we use for estimation and k is the number of variables in the model. As mentioned, this formula will penalize models with more variables. The $2(k + 2)$ term is the penalty term. We want the model with the lowest value. Remember, we will always prefer simpler models to more complex models. An interesting characteristic of the AIC is that it is asymptotically equivalent at large Ts to minimize the cross-validation error. This means that the AIC will select the model that will perform the best on the test set.

Corrected Akaike information criterion (AICc)

When we have a short time series, where T is small, the AIC will still tend to select models with too many variables. In this case, the AICc is a better metric. It is defined as follows:

$$AIC_c = AIC + \frac{2(k + 2)(k + 3)}{T - k - 3}$$

Essentially, the metric attempts to correct for bias. The same interpretation as the AIC applies here: the model with the lowest AICc is the best model.

Schwarz's Bayesian information criterion (BIC)

Finally, we have the Bayesian information criterion. Like both of the previous criteria, it is a measure of the best model, penalizing models with more variables. It is defined as follows:

$$BIC = T\log\left(\frac{SSE}{T}\right) + \left(k + 2\right)\log\left(T\right)$$

The main difference between BIC and AIC is that BIC will either select the same model as AIC or a model with fewer variables. This is because the penalty term is larger, and the criterion will penalize models with more variables more heavily. In the case of the BIC, it is the equivalent of minimizing the leave-one-out cross-validation error for large values of T.

Advanced forecasting methods

We can now move on to more advanced forecasting methods. We will go through four common workhorse models in forecasting: extending regression models to time series, ETS models, ARIMA models, and the Prophet model. Let's discuss each in detail.

Extending regression models to time series

We can start by extending the regression models we learned previously in *Chapter 4, Econometrics and Causal Inference with Statsmodels and PyMC*, for time series. The most basic way to do so is by using the trend as a predictor. One can achieve this by simply regressing the data on time:

$$y_t = \beta_0 + \beta_1 t + \epsilon_t$$

To build upon this, we can incorporate the idea of lagged variables. These are past values of the series we're trying to predict, which are used as predictors in the regression model. This approach forms the basis of the **autoregressive (AR)** model, which is a key part of many more sophisticated time series models.

Before diving into the code, let's prepare a toy dataset:

```python
import pandas as pd
import numpy as np
import statsmodels.api as sm

# Creating a toy dataset
date_range = pd.date_range(start='01-01-2010', end='12-31-2020',
    freq='M')
trend = np.linspace(0, 10, len(date_range))
random_noise = np.random.normal(0, 1, len(date_range))
data = trend + random_noise
df = pd.DataFrame({'date': date_range, 'y': data})

# Adding time as a predictor
df['t'] = range(len(df))

# Adding lagged variable (1 month)
df['y_lag1'] = df['y'].shift(1)

# Remove missing values caused by lag
df.dropna(inplace=True)
```

This code snippet creates a synthetic dataset with a linear trend and random noise. The time (t) and a lagged version of the variable y (one month prior is y_lag1) are added as predictors.

We can now fit a linear regression model to this data:

```python
# Define predictors and target variable
X = df[['t', 'y_lag1']]
y = df['y']

# Add a constant to the predictor variable matrix
X = sm.add_constant(X)

# Instantiate the model
model = sm.OLS(y, X)

# Fit the model
results = model.fit()
```

```
# Print model summary
print(results.summary())
```

In this code block, we first define our predictor variables (`X`) and target variable (`y`). We add a constant to the predictors using `sm.add_constant(X)`, as `statsmodels` does not automatically include an intercept in its models. We then instantiate an **ordinary least squares** (**OLS**) regression model and fit it to our data.

The `summary()` method provides a detailed summary of the model's properties and performance, which includes statistics such as the R-squared value, standard errors of the estimates, and p-values for hypothesis tests for the coefficients. These results can be interpreted to gain insights into the performance of the model and the significance of each predictor.

Linear regression provides a simple and interpretable method for time series forecasting. When combined with feature engineering techniques such as lagged variables, it can offer valuable insights into the temporal dependencies in your data.

ETS models

To introduce ETS models, we need to discuss exponential smoothing. This model is a very simple model that is used to forecast time series. It was introduced in the late 50s by statisticians Bow, Holt, and Winters. In essence, you can think of it as a weighted average of the previous observations. The weights are exponentially decreasing, meaning that the most recent observations have the highest weights and older observations have lower weights. The weights are calculated using the smoothing parameter α. This smoothing parameter is a value ranging from 0 to 1. The higher the value, the more weight given to the most recent observations. The lower the value, the more weight given to the older observations. This method is surprisingly useful for time series data without a trend or seasonality. If you recall, in the naive method, we were taking only the last observation and using it as a forecast, ignoring all previous data points. On the other hand, we also considered a simple average method, where we were taking the average of all the previous observations. We were essentially weighing all previous observations equally. The exponential smoothing method is a combination or compromise of these two methods. By using it, you are assuming that the most recent observations are more important than the older observations, but you are not ignoring all the previous observations.

Formally, you can define the exponential smoothing method as:

$$y_{t+1|t} = \alpha y_t + \left(1 - \alpha\right) y_{t-1} + \left(1 - \alpha\right)^2 y_{t-2} + ... + \left(1 - \alpha\right)^t y_{t-t}$$

where $0 \leq \alpha \leq 1$, y_t is the observed value at time t, and $y_{t+1|t}$ is the forecast for time $t + 1$, based on the data up to time t.

When $\alpha = 1$, the model is the same as the naive method. When $\alpha = 0$, the model is the same as the simple average method. When $\alpha = 0.5$, the model is the same as the simple moving average method. The exponential smoothing method is a weighted average of the previous observations, where the weights are exponentially decreasing.

Now, one step further, if you consider different combinations of trend and seasonal components, you will have several possible methods.

Exponential smoothing methods

Essentially, we are considering different types of seasonal and trend components. Either we don't have either (illustrated by "None") or they can be additive or multiplicative.

Table 5.1 presents a summary of the different possible combinations of trend and seasonal components:

Trend component	Seasonal component
	N (None)
N (None)	(N,N)
A (Additive)	(A,N)
Ad (Additive damped)	(Ad,N)

Table 5.1 – Combinations of trend and seasonal component types

For all of these combinations, we can see, in *Table 5.2*, the corresponding methods and the names they are known by:

Short hand	Method
(N, N)	Simple exponential smoothing
(A, N)	Holt's linear trend method
(Ad, N)	Additive damped trend method
(A, A)	Holt–Winters' additive method
(A, M)	Holt–Winters' multiplicative method
(Ad, M)	Holt–Winters' damped method

Table 5.2 – ETS methods per trend and seasonal component combination

These models are known as state–space models, since they consist of both a description of the observed data and a state equation that will describe the evolution of the state of the system over time. This state equation is then used to model the forecast of the next observation. If you add a third component, the error component, where you can have either additive or multiplicative errors, you will have a third letter on the classification of *Table 5.2*. These are known as ETS models because they are labeled as "ETS(.,.,.)" for the error type, trend type, and seasonality type. ETS is then short for "error, trend, seasonal".

ETS models in Python

In Python, we can use the AutoETS function from the statsforecast library to apply ETS models.

Before we start, ensure you have the statsforecast library installed in your environment. If not, you can do so via pip install statsforecast.

Here's how you can implement an ETS model, grouping all product categories into one:

```
from statsforecast import StatsForecast
from statsforecast.models import (
    AutoARIMA, AutoETS, HoltWinters,
    SeasonalNaive, HistoricAverage)

nixtla_df = monthly_all_df.reset_index()
nixtla_df.rename(columns = {'Order Date': 'ds', 'Sales': 'y'},
    inplace = True)
nixtla_df['unique_id'] = 'all'
test = nixtla_df.iloc[-6:]
train = nixtla_df.iloc[:-6]
models = [AutoETS(season_length=12)]
sf_ETS = StatsForecast(models = models, freq='M')
sf_ETS.fit(train)
```

In this example, we first import the AutoETS function from the statsforecast.models module.

We then initialize our ETS model by providing our data in long format, specifying the frequency of data as M for monthly and season_length as 12 to represent a year. The level keyword in the forecast call specifies that we want a 90% confidence interval around our forecast, and h = 6 means we are specifying the forecasting horizon to be six time units. The output can be seen in *Figure 5.7*:

unique_id	ds	AutoETS	AutoETS-lo-90	AutoETS-hi-90
all	2017-07-31	43986.093750	28107.505859	59864.679688
all	2017-08-31	40872.316406	24659.078125	57085.558594
all	2017-09-30	81991.382812	65450.257812	98532.500000
all	2017-10-31	49274.417969	32411.787109	66137.054688
all	2017-11-30	84976.328125	67798.203125	102154.453125
all	2017-12-31	87223.507812	69735.578125	104711.429688

Figure 5.7 – ETS forecast with 90% confidence interval

We can visually check the forecast in the following snippet, with the output shown in *Figure 5.8*:

```
sf_ETS.plot(nixtla_df, forecast_df, level=[90])
```

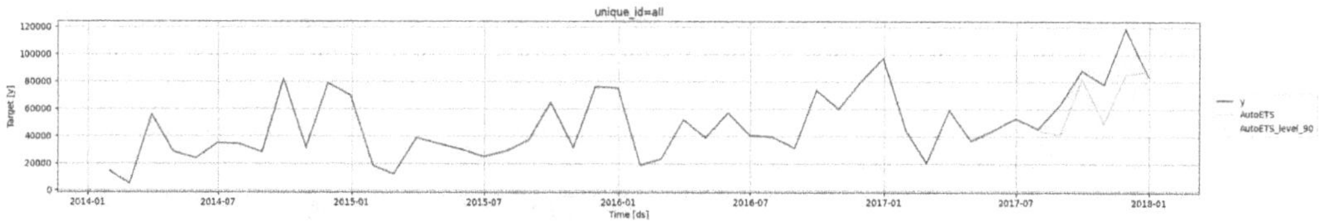

Figure 5.8 – ETS forecast versus actuals

Let's see the results using an ARIMA model.

ARIMA models

Another very common type of model is the ARIMA model. ARIMA stands for **autoregressive integrated moving average**. At its core, it is a combination of autoregressive and moving average models. The main difference between ETS models and ARIMA models lies in what they are modeling. ETS models are modeling the state of the system based on a description of the trend and seasonality, while ARIMA models are modeling the auto-correlations in the time series. To understand ARIMA models, we first need to make a slight detour and discuss stationarity.

What makes a time series stationary?

A time series is stationary if its statistical properties do not change over time. This means that the mean, variance, and autocorrelation structure are constant over time. White noise is a good example of a stationary time series. A non-stationary time series will have trend and seasonality, which will affect the time series at different points in time. Now, recall the warning at the beginning of the chapter: seasonality and cyclic behavior are not the same thing. A time series with cyclic behavior is stationary, provided it has neither trend nor seasonality. The reason behind this is, if you recall, cyclic behavior is not of fixed length. So before we look at the time series, we are not sure where the peaks and valleys will be. In short, a stationary time series will have no distinguishable patterns in it. There are several methods to check for stationarity such as: the augmented Dickey–Fuller test and the Kwiatkowski–Phillips–Schmidt–Shin test. A more visual test is to plot the ACF. If it drops quickly to 0, you are in the presence of a stationary time series.

The question becomes, then, can we turn a non-stationary into a stationary time series?

Differencing a time series for stationarity

The answer is yes. We can turn a non-stationary time series into a stationary time series through a process called differencing. Differencing is a very simple operation. You take the difference between the current observation and the previous observation. This is known as first-order differencing. If you want to difference the differenced time series, you are doing second-order differencing, and so on. The number of times you difference a time series is known as the order of differencing. A variation of this method is when you take the difference between a data point and the previous observation of the same season. This is known as seasonal differencing, or lag-m differences, because we are subtracting the observation of the same season, *m* periods ago.

Autoregressive models

If you remember from *Chapter 4, Econometrics and Causal Inference with Statsmodels and PyMC*, a linear regression model is one where the dependent variable is a linear combination of the independent variables. In the case of an autoregressive model, the dependent variable is a linear combination of the previous observations. This is known as an autoregressive model. The order of the autoregressive model is the number of previous observations that are used to predict the current observation and is usually denoted by p. These types of models are extremely flexible and can be used to model a wide variety of time series.

Moving average models

If instead of using the previous observations to predict the current observation, we use the errors of the previous observations, we get a moving average model. The order of the moving average model is the number of previous errors that are used to predict the current observation and is usually denoted by q. If we combine both of these models, we reach the ARIMA model. The ARIMA model is a combination of autoregressive and moving average models and is denoted by ARIMA(p,d,q). The p is the order of the autoregressive model, the d is the order of differencing, and the q is the order of the moving average model.

SARIMA Models

ARIMA models do not handle seasonality well. This is where SARIMA models come in. SARIMA stands for **seasonal autoregressive integrated moving average**. SARIMA models are a combination of ARIMA models and seasonal differencing. The SARIMA model is denoted by SARIMA(p,d,q) (P,D,Q)m, where the first three parameters are the same as the ARIMA model, and the last three parameters are the seasonal parameters. P is the order of the seasonal autoregressive model, D is the order of seasonal differencing, and Q is the order of the seasonal moving average model. m is the number of periods in a season.

ARIMA models in Python

Let's now move on to ARIMA models in Python. The most efficient approach to identifying the optimal ARIMA model is to leverage the `AutoARIMA` function from the `statsforecast` package.

Now, let's dive into an example. We have already imported the AutoARIMA model in the previous snippet, and using it is analogous to the ETS example:

```
models = [AutoARIMA(season_length=12)]
sf_ARIMA = StatsForecast(models = models, freq='M')
sf_ARIMA.fit(train)
forecast_df = sf_ARIMA.forecast(df=train, level= [90], h = 6)
```

The code interpretation is analogous to the ETS example, with the same `season_length`. We can check the results in *Figure 5.9*:

unique_id	ds	AutoARIMA	AutoARIMA-lo-90	AutoARIMA-hi-90
all	2017-07-31	39261.964844	18463.466797	60060.457031
all	2017-08-31	31115.375000	10316.878906	51913.871094
all	2017-09-30	73410.023438	52611.527344	94208.523438
all	2017-10-31	59687.746094	38889.250000	80486.242188
all	2017-11-30	79411.968750	58613.468750	100210.460938
all	2017-12-31	96999.046875	76200.546875	117797.539062

Figure 5.9 – ARIMA forecast

Again, we can also plot the forecast versus actuals result, with the output shown in *Figure 5.10*:

```
sf_ARIMA.plot(nixtla_df, forecast_df, level=[90])
```

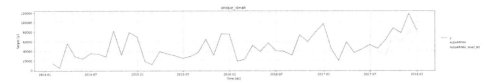

Figure 5.10 – An overview of plot of ARIMA forecast versus actuals

Finally, we reach the Prophet model.

The Prophet model

This model is more recent than the previous two. It was introduced by Facebook and it aims to forecast daily data with weekly and yearly seasonality. Behind the hood, this is an additive model in which a non-linear trend is established, incorporating yearly, weekly, and daily cyclical patterns, as well as impacts from holidays. Its performance is optimal when used with data that exhibits strong seasonal fluctuations and a history featuring multiple seasonal cycles. It is also very easy to use, and it is very fast. It is also very robust to missing data and shifts in the trend, and it handles outliers quite well.

The Prophet model in Python

Now we will dive into implementing the Prophet model in Python. Before we can begin, the Prophet library needs to receive the dataset in long format with the ds column as dates and y column as sales:

```python
from prophet import Prophet
import pandas as pd
import numpy as np

data = pd.read_csv('superstore.csv', encoding = "ISO-8859-1")
data['Order Date'] = pd.to_datetime(data['Order Date'])
monthly_sales = data.groupby([pd.Grouper(key='Order Date',
    freq='M')])['Sales'].sum()
prophet_df = monthly_sales.reset_index()
prophet_df.rename(columns = {'Order Date': 'ds', 'Sales': 'y'},
    inplace = True)
```

Now we generate a Prophet class, which is our model, and fit it with the data:

```python
m = Prophet()
m.fit(prophet_df)
```

Finally, we then specify the number of future periods we want to generate predictions for; in this case, this is the next six months:

```
future = m.make_future_dataframe(periods=6, freq='M')
future.tail()
forecast = m.predict(future)
```

The make_future_dataframe() function helps us create a new DataFrame, which includes these future dates.

The predict() function is then used to generate forecasts for each date in our future DataFrame. This function returns a DataFrame with a column yhat that represents the predicted values.

Finally, we plot the forecast using the plot() function of the Prophet object, which provides a convenient and visually intuitive way to review the forecasted data, as seen in *Figure 5.11*:

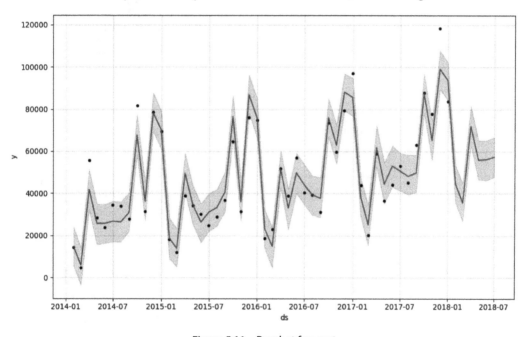

Figure 5.11 – Prophet forecast

Which model to use

So now you might be wondering which model to use. The statsforecast module has some helper libraries for us to do cross-validation. First, let's run a few known models:

```
from statsforecast, in a sf_all model:models = [
    HoltWinters(),
```

```
        SeasonalNaive(season_length=12),
        HistoricAverage(),
        AutoARIMA(season_length=12),
        AutoETS(season_length=12)]
sf_all = StatsForecast(models = models, freq='M',
        fallback_model=SeasonalNaive(season_length=7))
sf_all.fit(train)
forecast_df = sf_all.forecast(df=train, level= [90], h = 6)
```

This will generate a DataFrame with all the forecasts per model and their confidence intervals, which we can plot the usual way. The output is shown in *Figure 5.12*:

```
sf_all.plot(nixtla_df, forecast_df, level=[90])
```

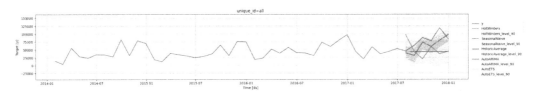

Figure 5.12 – An overview of multiple models compared

Now let's do some cross-validation with all of them. This can be easily done by running:

```
crossvalidation_df = sf_all.cross_validation(
    df=nixtla_df,
    h=6,
    step_size=6,
    n_windows=2
)
```

Now we can use some utilities and a custom `evaluate_cross_validation` function to understand which model has the fewest errors:

```
crossvalidation_df.reset_index().drop(columns=['unique_id', 'ds',
    'cutoff', 'y']).columns.tolist()
from utilsforecast.losses import mse
from utilsforecast.evaluation import evaluate

def evaluate_cross_validation(df, metric):
    df = df.reset_index()
    models = df.drop(columns=['unique_id', 'ds', 'cutoff', 'y']).
columns.tolist()
    evals = []
    # Calculate loss for every unique_id and cutoff.
```

```
    for cutoff in df['cutoff'].unique():
        eval_ = evaluate(df[df['cutoff'] == cutoff],
            metrics=[metric], models=models)
        evals.append(eval_)
    evals = pd.concat(evals)
    evals = evals.groupby('unique_id').mean(numeric_only=True)
# Averages the error metrics for all cutoffs for every combination of
model and unique_id
    evals['best_model'] = evals.idxmin(axis=1)
    return evals


evaluation_df = evaluate_cross_validation(crossvalidation_df, mse)
evaluation_df
```

The output of `evaluation_df` can be seen in *Figure 5.13*:

unique_id	HoltWinters	SeasonalNaive	HistoricAverage	AutoARIMA	AutoETS	best_model
all	1.640303e+09	360456608.0	979267584.0	381157696.0	238694000.0	AutoETS

Figure 5.13 – Evaluation of different models to determine the best one

According to the cross-validation, the model with the lowest errors is the AutoETS model, and that is the one you should use. You should always evaluate models like this, and not just visually, since you can be tricked by patterns that are not there.

Summary

In this chapter, we learned what forecasting is, what types of datasets we regularly deal with, and how to extract features. We then went over forecasting methods, mainly ETS models, ARIMA models, and the Prophet model. This knowledge will ultimately allow you to make strategic decisions based on reliable predictions, leading to improved marketing performance and a better understanding of your target audience and market dynamics.

In the next chapter, we'll take some of the methods discussed here and extend them to trying to identify anomalies in data.

Further reading

- *Forecasting: Principles and Practice* by Rob J Hyndman and George Athanasopoulos, Otexts publishing

- *Exponential smoothing: The state of the art* by E. S. Gardner Wiley online library

- *Forecasting at Scale* by Sean J. Taylor, Benjamin Letham

- Nixtla Documentation: `https://nixtlaverse.nixtla.io/`

6

Anomaly Detection with StatsForecast and PyMC

Data is like garbage. You'd better know what you are going to do with it before you collect it.

– Mark Twain

In the diverse ecosystem of data analysis, one of the most intriguing yet complex areas you will encounter is anomaly detection. It's a challenging task but crucial, as anomalies often signify critical events, such as potential fraud, system errors, or business trends that could impact decision-making.

Throughout this chapter, we'll navigate through the intricacies of identifying these anomalies, honing our focus on how to handle different data types, including low-frequency data. Our exploration will range from understanding the fundamental nature of an anomaly to implementing a variety of techniques to detect anomalies. We will start with the concept of **Seasonal–Trend decomposition using LOESS (STL)** – a powerful technique that can help us discern anomalies from seasonal and trend patterns. We will then proceed to delve into the robust Twitter **Seasonal Hybrid ESD (S-H-ESD)** algorithm, known for its ability to detect both global and local anomalies efficiently.

Further, we will treat anomaly detection as a forecasting problem, employing the StatsForecast library for this purpose. This approach, while having its limitations, especially with low-frequency data, is a flexible tool that can be adapted to a broad range of data scenarios.

Our journey into anomaly detection would be incomplete without addressing change point detection. For this, we'll use the PyMC library for Bayesian modeling, focusing on the rates of arrival of data points. While this approach can seem intricate, it provides a more detailed perspective, proving particularly effective for countable data such as sales records.

We will cover the following topics:

- What is an anomaly?

- Techniques to detect anomalies

- Forecasting as an anomaly detection tool

- Using rates of arrival to identify change points

By the end of this chapter, you'll have a robust understanding of the various techniques for detecting anomalies and their respective strengths and weaknesses. Armed with hands-on Python examples, you'll be well equipped to apply these techniques in your data analytics tasks, enabling you to effectively identify and understand anomalies, thus paving the way for accurate and data-informed decision-making.

Technical requirements

You will find the code files for this chapter on GitHub at `https://github.com/PacktPublishing/Data-Analytics-for-Marketing/tree/main/Chapter06`.

What is an anomaly?

An anomaly is an observation that deviates so much from the expected behavior that it raises suspicions that it was generated by a different data-generating process or mechanism. In other words, an anomaly is an observation that is not expected to happen and that is not expected to happen again.

Anomalies can be due to noise or erroneous data, or they can be due to a change in the data-generating process. A good example of an anomaly due to noise or erroneous data is a sudden drop in conversions from a marketing campaign due to a loss in web tracking. You, as an analyst, want to be able to detect this anomaly and understand that it is due to a loss in tracking, and not due to a change in the data-generating process. Another type of anomaly could be a steep drop in the conversion rate due to a change in the rules that allow your ads to be shown. You still want to detect this anomaly, but here you also want to understand that the data-generating process has changed.

Anomalies can have different types:

- **Anomalies can be point outliers**: A point outlier is a single observation that behaves differently from either the other values in the time series – a global outlier – or in relation to its neighbors – a local outlier

- **You can also have subsequence outliers**: A subsequence outlier is a sequence of observations whose joint behavior is different from either the rest of the time series or from the behavior of the neighboring sequences

You can see the difference between these two different types in *Figure 6.1*:

Figure 6.1 – A point outlier and a subsequence outlier in a time series

Understanding these types of anomalies paves the way for our exploration into various techniques designed to detect them. As we transition into the next section, we'll start exploring these methods, beginning with a familiar tool from our previous chapter.

Techniques to detect anomalies

Before we delve into some of the more statistical and data science-focused techniques for anomaly detection, it's worth reminding ourselves of a method we've already encountered – time-series decomposition. Here's where our earlier discussions come full circle.

Anomaly detection with STL decomposition

As we discussed in the previous chapter, time-series decomposition allows us to extract underlying patterns in our data. STL decomposition, which stands for Seasonal-Trend decomposition using LOESS, is especially useful as it is robust to outliers. The outliers will be left in the residual component, enabling us to use this for anomaly detection.

Residuals in a time series often follow a normal distribution. This assumption is leveraged in anomaly detection techniques, such as the z-score method and Tukey's rule, which we will discuss next.

The z-score

The z-score represents the number of standard deviations a data point is from the mean. It is calculated using the following formula:

$$z = \frac{(x - \mu)}{\sigma}$$

Here, x is the data point, μ is the mean of the data, and σ is the standard deviation of the data.

Given a normal distribution, 68% of the data will be within 1 standard deviation of the mean, 95% will be within 2 standard deviations, and 99.7% will be within 3 standard deviations. We can then use a threshold of 3 standard deviations to detect anomalies, as only 0.3% of the data points will be above or below this value.

Tukey's rule

As we discussed in *Chapter 2, Extracting and Exploring Data with Singer and pandas*, the **interquartile range (IQR)** is the difference between the 75th percentile and the 25th percentile. According to Tukey's rule, observations that fall below the 25th percentile minus 1.5 times the IQR, or above the 75th percentile plus 1.5 times the IQR, are considered outliers. We can use this rule to detect anomalies.

Pros and cons

The primary benefit of these techniques is their simplicity. They can handle a variety of situations and are easy to implement. The main drawback is the lack of flexibility in tweaking parameters, aside from the threshold value.

Now, let's implement these concepts in practice using Python and a marketing analytics dataset.

Python implementation

First, we import the necessary libraries:

```
import pandas as pd
import numpy as np
import matplotlib.pyplot as plt
import seaborn as sns
%matplotlib inline
```

Next, we load the data. For this example, we will use the `anomaly_data` dataset, which represents the sales of a product over time:

```
anomaly_data = pd.read_csv(../data/anomaly_data.csv')
anomaly_data.Date = pd.to_datetime(anomaly_data.Date,
    format='%Y-%m-%d')
anomaly_data.set_index('Date', inplace=True)
```

Our dataset is now ready. Let's take a look at the first few rows to understand its structure:

```
anomaly_data.head()
```

For the purposes of this chapter, we will intentionally introduce some anomalies to our dataset:

```
anomaly_data.loc['1998-12-01', 'Total'] = 10000
anomaly_data.loc["1993-3-1"]['Total'] = 30000
anomaly_data.loc["2003-3-1"]['Total'] = 35000
```

Let's plot our data to visualize the introduced anomalies:

```
anomaly_data.Total.plot(figsize=(12, 6))
```

The plot showcases the total sales over time (*Figure 6.2*), where we can already spot some potential anomalies.

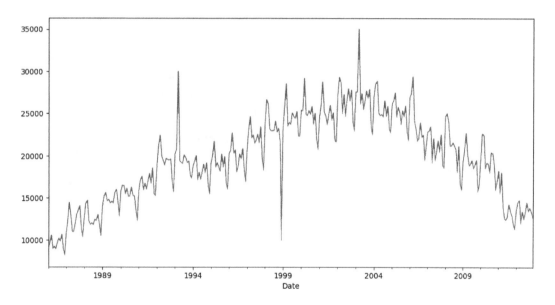

Figure 6.2 – Total sales over time with anomalies

Now, we narrow our analysis to a specific timeframe:

```
lim_anomaly_data = anomaly_data.loc['1996-01-01': '2000-01-01']
lim_anomaly_data.Total.plot(figsize=(12, 6))
```

The plot (*Figure 6.3*) provides a closer look at the sales during this period:

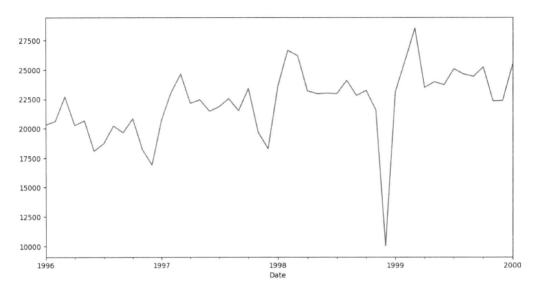

Figure 6.3 – Zooming into the timeframe of sales data

Next, we apply the STL decomposition to our time series data:

```
from statsmodels.tsa.seasonal import seasonal_decompose
result = seasonal_decompose(lim_anomaly_data.Total,
    model='additive')
fig = result.plot()
```

The resulting plot (*Figure 6.4*) showcases the trend, seasonality, and residuals in our data:

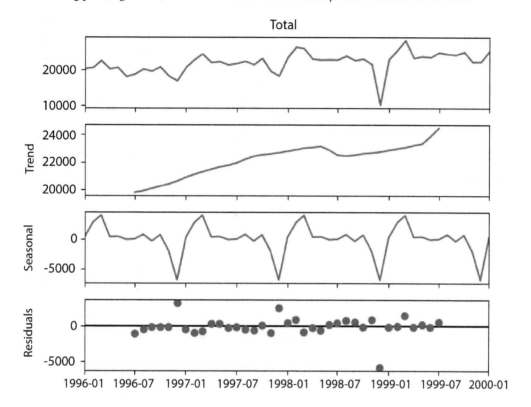

Figure 6.4 – Time-series decomposition of sales data

The residuals can be plotted separately as well:

```
fig, ax = plt.subplots()
x = result.resid.index
y = result.resid.values
ax.plot_date(x, y, '--', color='black')
fig.autofmt_xdate()
```

Figure 6.5 showcases the residuals over time:

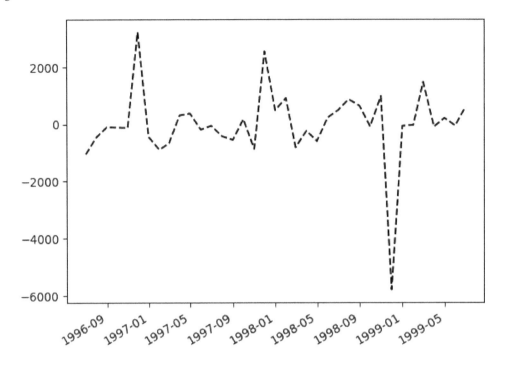

Figure 6.5 – Residuals over time

We can also plot the distribution of the residuals to inspect its shape:

```
sns.displot(result.resid, kde=True)
```

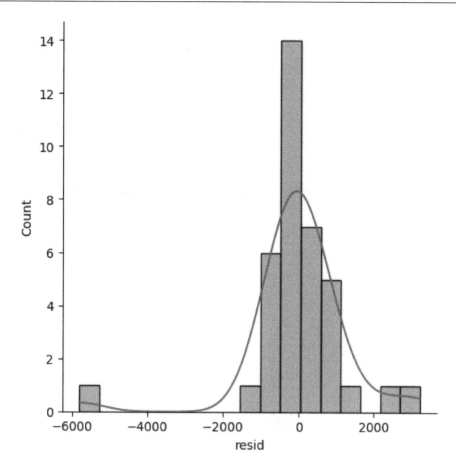

Figure 6.6 – Distribution of residuals

As seen in *Figure 6.6*, our residuals are approximately normally distributed, with some potential outliers.

These outliers can also be visualized using a boxplot:

```
sns.boxplot(result.resid)
```

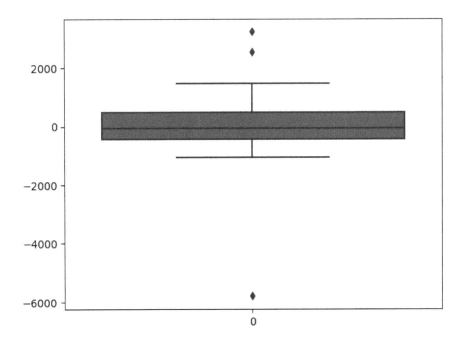

Figure 6.7 – IQR of residuals

The boxplot in *Figure 6.7* shows the IQR of our residuals and potential outliers.

Finally, let's plot the entire dataset with the introduced anomalies:

```
anomaly_data.Total.plot(figsize=(12, 6))
```

In *Figure 6.8*, we can observe the anomalies we introduced earlier in the context of the entire dataset:

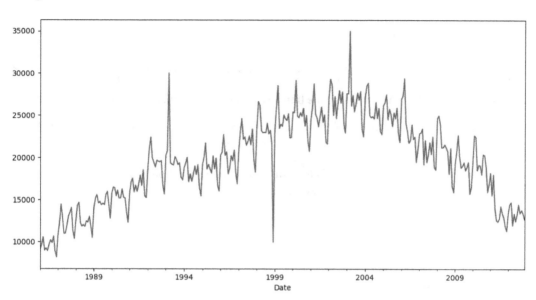

Figure 6.8 – Anomalies introduced earlier

By identifying and inspecting these anomalies, businesses can extract valuable insights and make informed decisions. This process can be applied to various contexts within marketing analytics, from detecting unusual spikes in website traffic to identifying unexpected changes in sales or customer behavior.

Twitter's t-ESD algorithm for anomaly detection

Twitter's **Extended Seasonal Decomposition** (**t-ESD**) is a more advanced method for detecting anomalies. Twitter developed this method specifically for their requirement to detect anomalies in user engagement data, which often exhibited strong periodic patterns.

Twitter's t-ESD

The Twitter t-ESD is a variant of the generalized **Extreme Studentized Deviate** (**ESD**) test for outliers. The ESD test works by iteratively finding the maximum z-score, checking whether it is an outlier, and removing it if it is. The t-ESD extends this by applying it to time-series data with both an underlying trend and seasonality.

Python implementation

In Python, we can create our own implementation of the t-ESD algorithm, based on the R implementation provided by Twitter.

First, we start by importing the necessary libraries and loading our data:

```
import numpy as np
import pandas as pd
from scipy.stats import t
from statsmodels.tsa.seasonal import seasonal_decompose
```

Then, we decompose the time series into the trend, seasonal, and residual components:

```
result = seasonal_decompose(lim_anomaly_data.Total, model='additive')
residuals = result.resid.dropna()  # discard missing values
```

Now, we define the function for the t-ESD test. The inputs to the function will be the residuals and the maximum number of outliers that we want to consider:

```
def t_ESD_test(residuals, max_outliers):
    test_statistics = []
    anomalies = []
    for i in range(max_outliers):
        residuals_mean, residuals_std = np.mean(residuals),
            np.std(residuals)
        z_scores = (residuals - residuals_mean) / residuals_std
        max_z_score = np.max(np.abs(z_scores))
        max_z_index = np.argmax(np.abs(z_scores))
        test_statistic = (len(residuals) - 1) * max_z_score / np.sqrt(
            (len(residuals) - 2 + max_z_score**2) * len(residuals)
        )
        critical_value = t.ppf(1 - 0.05 / (2 * len(residuals)),
            len(residuals) - 2)
        if test_statistic > critical_value:
            anomalies.append(residuals.index[max_z_index])
            residuals = residuals.drop(residuals.index[max_z_index])
            test_statistics.append(test_statistic)
        else:
            break
    return anomalies, test_statistics
```

We can now use this function to detect anomalies in our data:

```
anomalies, test_statistics = t_ESD_test(residuals, max_outliers=10)
```

In this example, we set max_outliers to 10, but this can be adjusted based on your specific needs and understanding of the dataset. The function returns the indices of the detected anomalies and the corresponding test statistics.

Advantages and limitations

The advantage of the t-ESD method is that it is well suited to large datasets with periodic patterns, and it can detect both global and local anomalies.

However, the t-ESD method has its limitations. Since it is based on statistical significance, it assumes that the data is independently and identically distributed after the trend and seasonality have been removed. This may not always be the case. Furthermore, it requires a good estimate of the number of anomalies, which may not always be known in advance.

In conclusion, the Twitter t-ESD algorithm represents an advanced tool in the anomaly detection toolkit. It is especially useful when dealing with large time-series data with both an underlying trend and seasonality, as often happens in marketing analytics.

Please note that this is a simplified version of the t-ESD algorithm and does not include all the features of the full version implemented by Twitter in R, such as the hybrid ESD-Grubbs test and robust time-series decomposition. Nonetheless, it illustrates the main ideas behind the method and provides a starting point for creating a more complete Python implementation.

Isolation forests for anomaly detection

Another effective method for detecting anomalies in our data involves the use of tree-based algorithms, specifically, isolation forests. An isolation forest is an algorithm used to detect anomalies based on the principle that anomalies are observations that are few and different. As such, these points are "isolatable" in fewer steps than "normal" points.

How isolation forests work

The way isolation forests operate is by initially selecting a feature randomly, followed by the selection of a random split value between the maximum and minimum values of that selected feature. The algorithm proceeds to partition the dataset into two sections; one comprising all observations with feature values less than the split value and the other containing all those greater. The partitioning process repeats for a defined number of splits or until each observation sits in a leaf node. The number of splits required to "isolate" an observation serves as an indicator of its anomalousness, with a higher number of required splits signaling a more anomalous observation. We can see an example of three trees, and the isolation points in *Figure 6.9*:

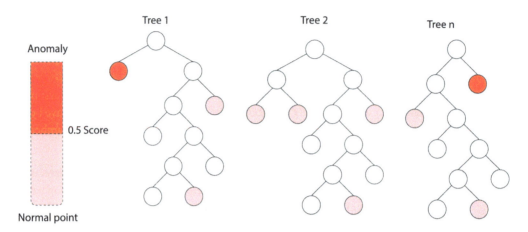

Figure 6.9 – Example isolation forest to isolate anomalous nodes

During training, we can instruct the forest on the expected proportion of outliers, or contamination, in the data. This information assists the algorithm in determining the number of splits needed to isolate an observation; again, the more splits required, the more anomalous the observation.

Pros and cons

Isolation forests exhibit considerable flexibility. The model can handle multiple features or random variables, increasing its potential application to complex datasets. However, the model's computational demand scales with the number of features, and this could be prohibitive for very high-dimensional data. Furthermore, interpretability is limited; understanding why a particular observation is deemed anomalous can be challenging.

Python implementation

Let's see how we can apply isolation forests in Python:

```
from sklearn.preprocessing import StandardScaler
from sklearn.ensemble import IsolationForest
import matplotlib.pyplot as plt

# Define the proportion of outliers expected (contamination)
outliers_fraction = 0.01

# Standardize the data
scaler = StandardScaler()
np_scaled = scaler.fit_transform(anomaly_data)
```

```
data = pd.DataFrame(np_scaled)

# Define and fit the model
model = IsolationForest(contamination=outliers_fraction)
model.fit(data)

# Make predictions (-1 indicates anomalies)
anomaly_data['anomaly'] = model.predict(data)
print(anomaly_data.anomaly.value_counts())

# Plot data and anomalies
fig, ax = plt.subplots()
anomalies = anomaly_data[anomaly_data['anomaly'] == -1]
ax.plot(anomaly_data.index, anomaly_data.Total,
    color='blue', label = 'Normal')
ax.scatter(anomalies.index, anomalies.Total,
    color='red', label = 'Anomaly')
plt.legend()
plt.show()
```

We can see in *Figure 6.10* the anomalies flagged by the algorithm. We can see that it missed one of the anomalies we introduced.

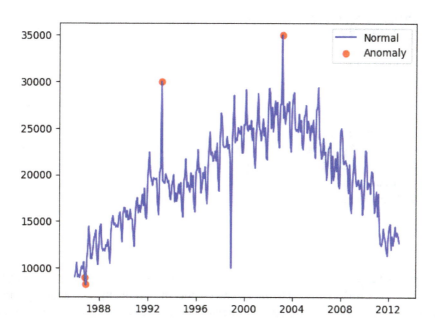

Figure 6.10 – Anomalies flagged with isolation forest

In the example, we first standardize our data using `StandardScaler`, an important step given the algorithm's nature. We then create and fit an `IsolationForest` model to the data, specifying an `outliers_fraction` value of `0.01`, meaning we expect about 1% of the observations to be outliers. The model prediction step labels the observations as either normal (1) or an anomaly (-1). Finally, we plot the results to visually observe the identified anomalies.

In summary, isolation forests provide a powerful tool for anomaly detection, especially when working with high-dimensional datasets or those with complex structures.

Fine-tuning isolation forests

While isolation forests are a potent tool for anomaly detection, it's essential to fine-tune your model for optimal performance. Two main parameters can be tweaked in the isolation forest algorithm:

- `n_estimators`: The number of trees to use in the forest. As with the random forest algorithm, a higher number generally improves performance but at the cost of increased computational load.

- `max_samples`: The number of samples to draw from the dataset to train each decision tree. If there are too few samples, the trees in the forest might not be diverse enough, leading to poor performance. Conversely, using too many samples can make the algorithm computationally expensive and may lead to overfitting.

Here is how in practice you can fine-tune the isolation forest:

```
# Fine-tuning the Isolation Forest
model = IsolationForest(contamination=outliers_fraction,
    n_estimators=200, max_samples='auto')
model.fit(data)
anomaly_data['anomaly'] = model.predict(data)

# Plot data and anomalies
fig, ax = plt.subplots()
anomalies = anomaly_data[anomaly_data['anomaly'] == -1]
ax.plot(anomaly_data.index, anomaly_data.Total,
    color='blue', label = 'Normal')
ax.scatter(anomalies.index, anomalies.Total, color='red',
    label = 'Anomaly')
plt.legend()
plt.show()
```

In this case, we've set `n_estimators` to `200` and `max_samples` to `auto`, which is equivalent to `min(256, n_samples)` according to the `sklearn` documentation. By tuning these parameters, you can achieve a better-performing model that suits your specific dataset and computational resources, as we can see in *Figure 6.11*:

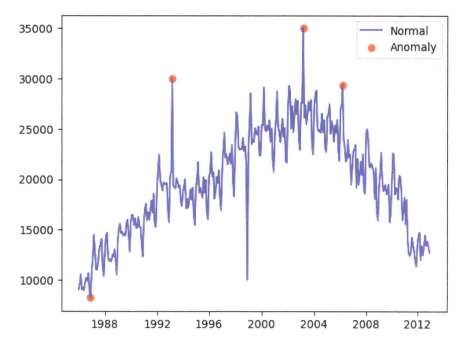

Figure 6.11 – Anomalies after fine-tuning

Notice that after fine-tuning, we now only have one anomaly in 1987, instead of two anomalies as shown in *Figure 6.10*.

Keep in mind that the choice of parameters will depend on the specific characteristics of your dataset and the computational resources available. There's no "one-size-fits-all" solution, and it often involves a bit of trial and error to find the optimal parameters.

In conclusion, isolation forests offer a powerful and flexible method for detecting anomalies in time-series data. While they may require some tuning and can be computationally intensive, their ability to work with high-dimensional data and handle complex data structures makes them a valuable tool in the data analyst's toolbox.

Please note that Python's implementation of isolation forest uses a random sub-sampling of the data instead of the entire dataset. This implementation provides a low memory footprint, an important consideration when dealing with large datasets.

In addition to dedicated methods for anomaly detection, we can also use some of the methods we learned in the previous chapter, and use forecasting to detect anomalies.

Forecasting as an anomaly detection tool

Another approach to anomaly detection involves forecasting. This strategy uses a forecasting model to predict future values and treats any significant deviations from these predictions as anomalies. Facebook's Prophet library, which allows for robust, automatic forecasting, is well suited for this task.

However, one major drawback of this technique is its inefficiency with low-frequency data. If a time series isn't observed frequently enough for a model to accurately forecast, the prediction intervals may be too wide, making anomaly detection challenging. As covered in the previous chapter, forecasting models rely on patterns within the data to make accurate predictions. If these patterns are not well defined due to sparse data, the model's forecasts will have a higher degree of uncertainty.

Prediction intervals are a way of expressing this uncertainty. A prediction interval gives a range within which we expect the actual value to lie, with a certain probability. For instance, a 95% prediction interval means we expect the actual future value to fall within this range 95% of the time. When data is sparse, the model may not be able to tightly constrain the future values it predicts, leading to wide prediction intervals. Wide prediction intervals are less useful for anomaly detection because they make it harder to determine whether a given data point is an anomaly or just part of the normal variability expected due to the uncertainty in the forecast.

In practical terms, if the prediction interval is too wide, many actual values that are not consistent with the historical pattern might still fall within this wide interval. As a result, they wouldn't be flagged as anomalies, even though they might represent significant deviations from the expected behavior. This reduces the sensitivity of the anomaly detection process and can lead to missing out on detecting important anomalies.

Practical implementation with StatsForecast

Here is how we can use StatsForecast, in particular the AutoETS model, to detect anomalies in Python. The first thing we need to do is load Statsmodels and create the DataFrame in the shape the library expects to get the data, that is, a DataFrame with the dates in the DS column, a unique_id column with all in this case for the levels, and the values in a Y column:

```
from statsforecast import StatsForecast
from statsforecast.models import AutoETS

anomaly_data = pd.read_csv('../data/anomaly_data.csv')
anomaly_data.Date = pd.to_datetime(anomaly_data.Date,
    format='%Y-%m-%d')
anomaly_data.set_index('Date', inplace=True)

anomaly_data.loc['1998-12-01', 'Total'] = 10000
anomaly_data.loc["1993-3-1"]['Total'] = 30000
anomaly_data.loc["2003-3-1"]['Total'] = 35000
```

```
nixtla_df = anomaly_data.copy().reset_index()
nixtla_df.rename(columns = {'Date': 'ds', 'Total': 'y'},
    inplace = True)
nixtla_df['unique_id'] = 'all'
```

Now we define a simple model. We define it with additive seasonality, with a 99% interval, and fit it:

```
models = [AutoETS(season_length=12)]
sf = StatsForecast(models = models, freq='M')
sf.fit(nixtla_df)
forecast_df = sf.forecast(df=nixtla_df, level= [99], h = 6,
    fitted=True)
```

Once the model is fitted, we need to recover the in-sample forecasts. Basically, we want to get all the forecasts from the model for all the data points in the original time series. We are now going to take advantage of the confidence intervals of the predictions, by defining that if a forecast is above or below the upper or lower bounds of the forecast, we count it as an anomaly:

```
insample_forecasts = sf.forecast_fitted_values().reset_index()
anomalies = insample_forecasts.loc[
    (insample_forecasts['y'] >= insample_forecasts['AutoETS-hi-99']
    ) | (
    insample_forecasts['y'] <= insample_forecasts['AutoETS-lo-99']
    )
]
anomalies
```

Let's take a look at the forecast first with the 99% confidence interval, as shown in *Figure 6.12*:

	unique_id	ds	y	AutoETS	AutoETS-lo-99	AutoETS-hi-99
86	all	1993-03-01	30000.0	21621.250000	18150.146484	25092.353516
87	all	1993-04-01	19377.0	23516.269531	20045.166016	26987.373047
155	all	1998-12-01	10000.0	20363.175781	16892.072266	23834.279297
156	all	1999-01-01	23107.0	19123.447266	15652.342773	22594.550781
157	all	1999-02-01	25780.0	22082.537109	18611.433594	25553.640625
158	all	1999-03-01	28544.0	25054.363281	21583.259766	28525.466797
206	all	2003-03-01	35000.0	29587.054688	26115.951172	33058.160156
301	all	2011-02-01	15564.0	20473.115234	17002.011719	23944.218750

Figure 6.12 – The table showing the anomaly values from the model

Finally, let's plot the anomalies, as we defined them previously as the data points sitting outside the confidence intervals, as seen in *Figure 6.13*:

```
sf.plot(nixtla_df, forecasts_df=insample_forecasts,
    plot_anomalies = True, level=[99])
```

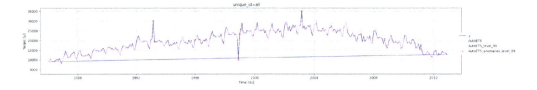

Figure 6.13 – Plot displaying the detected anomalies

This approach provides a flexible and interpretable method for detecting anomalies in time-series data. Although it may not be effective for low-frequency data, it performs well with time-series data with clear trends and seasonality.

Using rates of arrival to identify change points

Another strategy involves analyzing the rate of arrival of data points to spot changes. This subtle method targets less obvious shifts in the data, which may not exactly qualify as anomalies, but represent significant alterations nonetheless. The underlying premise is that changes in the rate of arrival likely indicate a shift in the data-generating process. This technique proves particularly useful in fields such as sales, where a sudden drop in the rate of sales can signal a change in the data-generating process. To model this, we consider the sales data as a Poisson distributed process, and the rate of arrival of sales as an exponential distribution.

A Poisson distribution is a type of probability distribution used to calculate the likelihood of a certain number of events occurring within a specified time or space interval. This calculation assumes that the events take place at a constant average rate and that each event happens independently of the time elapsed since the previous event. An event can be anything that is counted in discrete numbers; for example, the number of customers arriving at a store, the number of emails received per day, or the number of sales transactions in each hour.

The key parameter of the Poisson distribution is the rate (λ), which is the average number of events in the given interval. The distribution is used to model scenarios where events occur independently, and the probability of more than one event happening in an infinitesimally small period is virtually 0.

In this context, change points refer to points in time where the statistical properties of a sequence of observations change. This could mean a shift in the distribution's mean, variance, or other moments that govern the data generation process. In the example provided, change points would indicate a shift in the sales data rate, possibly due to changes in market conditions, consumer preferences, or external events affecting the sales process.

Detecting change points involves testing whether the rate of an event at one point is significantly different from the rate at another. If a change point is detected, it suggests that the process generating the observed data has changed at that time.

The core aim here is two-fold:

1. Estimate the rate of sales at time i, λ_i.
2. Test whether the rate of sales at time i differs from the rate at time j, i.e., $\lambda_i \neq \lambda_j$.

If no change point exists, then $\lambda_i = \lambda_j$ for all i and j. λ_i follows an exponential distribution. An initial choice for α (lambda's rate parameter) is the inverse of the sales data's average. Additionally, we choose a uniform prior for τ, the change point's time period, indicating our uncertainty about the change point's exact timing.

Let's implement this with PyMC:

```
import pymc as pm
import arviz as az
import numpy as np
import pandas as pd


# Load daily sales data
daily_sales = pd.read_csv('../data/anomaly_daily_sales.csv')
daily_sales.rename(columns={0: 'sales'}, inplace=True)


# Plot daily sales
daily_sales.plot(figsize=(12, 4), kind='bar')
```

Figure 6.14 illustrates the sales data plotted as a bar chart. Each bar represents the daily sales count. At this stage, we are visualizing the data to get a sense of the sales pattern and to prepare for the following modeling step.

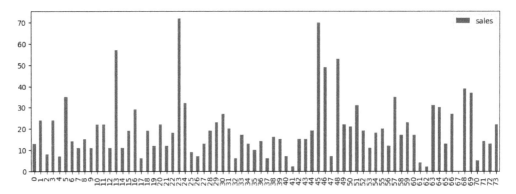

Figure 6.14 – Sales data

Now let's define the PyMC model defined mathematically, where we define the `alpha`, `lambda_1` and `lambda_2`, and `tau` variables:

```
# Define the model
with pm.Model() as model_pymc:
    alpha = 1.0/daily_sales.sales.mean()

    lambda_1 = pm.Exponential("lambda_1", alpha)
    lambda_2 = pm.Exponential("lambda_2", alpha)

    tau = pm.DiscreteUniform("tau", lower=0,
        upper=len(daily_sales.sales)-1)

    idx = np.arange(len(daily_sales.sales))
    lambda_ = pm.math.switch(tau > idx, lambda_1, lambda_2)

    observed = pm.Poisson("observed", lambda_,
        observed=daily_sales.sales)

# Draw samples
with model_pymc:
    trace = pm.sample(10000, tune=5000)
```

Before moving on, let's just briefly explain a key part of the code snippet:

- `tau` represents the change point's time period and is modeled as a discrete uniform random variable. It can take on any integer value from 0 to the length of the sales data minus 1, indicating we do not know a priori when the change point occurred and assume it is equally likely to be at any point in the time series.

- idx is an array of indices corresponding to the time points in the sales data. $lambda\_$ is defined using $pm.math.switch$, a conditional statement that selects $lambda\_1$ if the tau change point has not been reached ($tau > idx$), and $lambda\_2$ otherwise. This creates a piecewise function for the rate parameter that changes its value at the tau change point.

After building the model, we perform Bayesian inference by drawing samples from the posterior distribution of the parameters:

```
# Extract samples
lambda_1_samples = trace.posterior['lambda_1']
lambda_2_samples = trace.posterior['lambda_2']
tau = trace.posterior['tau']

# Plot distributions
az.plot_dist(lambda_1_samples, label='lambda_1', color='red')
az.plot_dist(lambda_2_samples, label='lambda_2', color='blue')
```

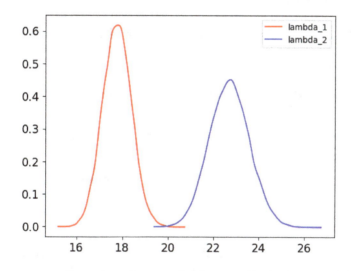

Figure 6.15 – Posterior distributions of lambda

Figure 6.15 displays the posterior distributions of $lambda\_1$ and $lambda\_2$, estimated rates of sales before and after the change point. The different shapes and centers of these distributions provide insights into how the rate of sales changes:

```
# Plot posterior
az.plot_posterior(trace);
```

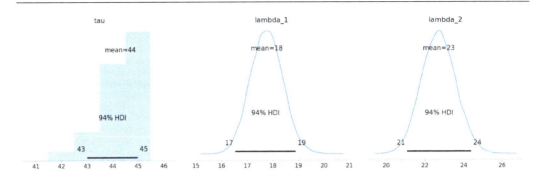

Figure 6.16 – Posterior distributions of lambda_1 and lambda_2, and tau

Figure 6.16 depicts the complete posterior distributions of the model parameters (`lambda_1`, `lambda_2`, and `tau`). It summarizes our inference about the parameters after observing the data. It shows the uncertainty in the values of the parameters, and whether the data provided enough evidence to conclude a significant change in the rate of sales.

Pros and cons of using rates of arrival for change point detection

The pros are as follows:

- **Sensitivity to subtle changes**: This method can detect subtle shifts in the data that traditional anomaly detection might miss
- **Adaptability**: The technique can adapt to various types of count data beyond sales, broadening its applicability
- **Modeling uncertainty**: By utilizing a Bayesian approach, we can quantify uncertainty in the model's parameters

The cons are as follows:

- **Assumption of Poisson and exponential distributions**: These assumptions might not hold true for all datasets, and might lead to incorrect change point detection
- **Computational intensity**: Bayesian methods, such as those used with PyMC, can be computationally expensive, making this approach less suitable for real-time or large-scale applications
- **Necessity of prior knowledge**: To build a useful Bayesian model, some prior knowledge or assumptions are necessary, which might not always be available or correct

By utilizing the rate of arrival, we can effectively detect change points, highlighting subtle variations in the data that could indicate significant underlying shifts.

Summary

This chapter delved into anomaly detection, exploring various strategies to effectively pinpoint unexpected patterns or outliers within data, which often indicate critical events or atypical activities that merit further investigation. It began with the STL method, which breaks down a time series into trend, seasonality, and remainder components, thereby facilitating the identification of anomalies that cannot be accounted for by underlying trends or seasonality. We then shifted to the robust S-H-ESD test, known for its effectiveness in identifying anomalies in time-series data, and the use of forecasting tools such as the StatsForecast library for anomaly detection, which, despite certain limitations with low-frequency data, has proven adaptable and beneficial across diverse data scenarios.

The chapter wrapped up by weighing the pros and cons of each technique discussed, emphasizing the importance of choosing the right method based on the specific nature of the data and business context. Practical Python code examples were provided to demonstrate how these techniques can be implemented, fine-tuned, and interpreted. The chapter also stressed the critical importance of anomaly detection in the field of data analytics and the complexities involved in deciphering the reasons behind these anomalies, paving the way for a deeper understanding of data behaviors.

In the next chapter, we'll build upon our anomaly detection knowledge and use a range of analytics techniques to extract valuable customer insights. These insights can help us uncover the "why" behind the anomalies, enabling us to make better, more informed decisions.

Further reading

- *Outlier Analysis* by Charu C. Aggarwal, Springer publication: This is a comprehensive resource that covers a wide range of topics related to outlier detection techniques

- *Anomaly Detection Principles and Algorithms* by Kishan G. Mehrotra, Chilukuri K. Mohan, and HuaMing Huang, Springer publication: This book provides a deep understanding of various anomaly detection techniques, including statistical, classification-based, cluster-based, and time-series methods

- *Data Mining: Concepts and Techniques* by Jiawei Han, Micheline Kamber, and Jian Pei, Morgan Kaufmann publication: This is a widely recognized textbook in the field of data mining and covers several aspects of anomaly detection

- *Python Machine Learning By Example* by Yuxi (Hayden) Liu, Packt Publishing: This book has a section on anomaly detection and provides Python examples for hands-on learning

- *Practical Time Series Analysis* by Aileen Nielsen, O'Reilly Media: This book, while not exclusively focused on anomaly detection, provides useful insights on handling time-series data, a crucial aspect of many anomaly detection problems

- *Anomaly Detection: A Survey* by Varun Chandola, Arindam Banerjee, and Vipin Kumar: This survey paper provides a structured and comprehensive overview of various research on anomaly detection

- *Twitter's Anomaly Detection Algorithm* by Owen Vallis, Jordan Hochenbaum, and Arun Kejariwal: This paper presents S-H-ESD, a robust method for detecting anomalies in time series data, used at Twitter

Part 3:
Who and What to Target

This part focuses on targeting and understanding customers, beginning with customer segmentation and profile creation for improved marketing strategies, before introducing RFM scoring. It then discusses estimating customer lifetime value through basic and advanced models, including BG-NBD and Gamma-Gamma, followed by an exploration of customer feedback via survey analysis, emphasizing survey design and data interpretation. The part wraps up with conjoint analysis, which seeks to understand customer preferences for products or services, offering techniques for deriving valuable marketing insights.

This part contains the following chapters:

- *Chapter 7, Customer Insights – Segmentation and RFM*

- *Chapter 8, Customer Lifetime Value with PyMC Marketing*

- *Chapter 9, Customer Survey Analysis*

- *Chapter 10, Conjoint Analysis with pandas and Statsmodels*

7
Customer Insights – Segmentation and RFM

In God we trust. All others bring data.

– Barry Beracha, CEO of Sara Lee Bakery Group

As we venture deeper into the complexities of marketing analytics, we now focus on a critical yet frequently evolving concept: customer dynamics. In this chapter, we seek to accomplish several learning objectives to solidify your understanding and practical application of this essential facet of marketing analytics.

We will dig deeper into the role of specific analytic tools in managing customer dynamics: segmentation and **Recency, Frequency, and Monetary Value (RFM)** analysis. These tools provide a mathematical and statistical framework to analyze, predict, and influence customer behavior. Our discussion will cover how these tools work and their implications in the broader context of marketing analytics, using Python to illustrate their application.

We aim to explain the benefits and business potential of RFM and segmentation as instrumental components in a firm's marketing strategy. These tools can transform raw data into actionable insights, enabling businesses to respond effectively to shifting customer dynamics and cultivate a competitive edge.

To achieve these learning objectives, this chapter is structured into the following main sections:

- Understanding the sources of customer dynamics
- Delving deeper into what segmentation is
- Exploring RFM
- ROMI after RFM

By the end of this chapter, you will have a comprehensive understanding of customer dynamics, the analytic tools used to manage them, and how to apply this knowledge using Python. Equipped with these skills, you'll be better prepared to navigate and influence the ever-changing landscape of customer behaviors and preferences, leveraging data-driven insights to drive strategic decisions.

Technical requirements

You can find the code files for this chapter on GitHub: `https://github.com/PacktPublishing/Data-Analytics-for-Marketing/tree/main/Chapter07`.

Understanding the sources of customer dynamics

In marketing analytics, an essential realization for any analyst is that customer behavior is a mutable entity. While assigning customers to a segment provides an organized framework to understand their needs and preferences, this doesn't imply static uniformity. Rather, within each segment, customers continue to undergo changes, individually evolving at varying paces and trajectories. Over time, this evolution led to the manifestation of diverse preferences within what was once a homogeneous customer segment.

To delve deeper into this idea, we can conceptualize five key categories that drive these customer dynamics. Each category is characterized by distinct rates and levels of impact on customer behavior, ranging from individual to environmental influences. These categories, as depicted in *Table 7.1*, provide a broader understanding of the dynamics that underlie shifts in customer behavior and preferences.

Event	Rate of change	Level	Examples
Discrete life events	Rapid	Individual	Parents develop a new purchase pattern, such as gyms that offer daycare
Typical life cycle, maturation	Slow	Individual	Older customers tend to seek reduced risk
Product learning effects	Medium	Individual	By using a product, customers identify additional high-tech features they would like
Product life cycle	Medium	Product market	Initially, users may pay more for new features, before they become price-sensitive
Changes in economy, govt, industry, culture	All	Environment	Recommendations and preferences for healthy food

Table 7.1 – Categories of customer dynamic sources

To further elaborate, discrete life events, such as marriage, childbirth, or retirement, can bring about rapid shifts in an individual's consumption patterns. For instance, new parents might begin to favor gyms that offer daycare facilities.

Life cycle maturation effects encompass gradual alterations in preferences. As customers grow older, their risk tolerance may decrease, prompting them to opt for safer product options. On a similar note, as customers gain more exposure to a product (product learning effects), they may start to recognize and desire additional features, particularly in the case of high-tech goods.

In the broader market, the product life cycle can impact customer dynamics. Early adopters of a product may be willing to pay a premium for innovative features, but as the product matures and becomes commonplace, these customers might become more price-sensitive.

Lastly, macro-environmental changes in the economy, government policies, industry shifts, and culture can all lead to changes in customer behavior. For example, increased public awareness around health and wellbeing, perhaps driven by governmental health campaigns, can lead to a surge in demand for healthier food options.

Understanding these sources of customer dynamics offers invaluable insights for the marketing analyst. It allows us to predict potential shifts in consumer behavior, adapt our marketing strategies accordingly, and ensure we continue to meet the evolving needs of our customers in a targeted, efficient manner.

Analyzing customer dynamics – unveiling segmentation and RFM

Understanding the sources of customer dynamics is just the first step in the complex journey of marketing analytics. The next crucial step involves translating this understanding into actionable insights using a diverse range of analysis techniques.

Two particularly powerful techniques for this purpose are segmentation and RFM analysis. These methodologies offer both descriptive and predictive insights, equipping us to better comprehend and anticipate the ever-changing landscape of customer behaviors and preferences.

Segmentation is the process of dividing a population into groups based on common characteristics. This is a very common practice in marketing, where the goal is to identify groups of customers with similar needs and preferences. This allows marketers to target their campaigns to specific groups of customers rather than to the entire population.

After segmentation, we will discuss RFM analysis. This type of analysis is a behavioral segmentation technique that classifies customers based on three dimensions:

- **Recency**: The time elapsed since a customer's last transaction
- **Frequency**: The number of transactions a customer engages in over a given time period
- **Monetary value**: The total financial contribution a customer makes through their purchases

The guiding principle of RFM analysis is the tendency of customers who have purchased recently, frequently, and with a higher monetary value to continue to exhibit these behaviors in the future. This approach helps us identify and prioritize potentially high-value customers.

Collectively, these techniques allow us to examine and interpret the shifts within our customer segments over time. They help us grasp past and current customer behaviors while equipping us to predict future behaviors. Such insights form the backbone of **crafting** marketing strategies that are pertinent and responsive to our customers' evolving needs.

Let's first dive deep into segmentation in the next section.

Delving deeper into what segmentation is

The difficulty of segmentation is finding actionable business outcomes. It is not difficult to find groups of customers with similar characteristics, but it is difficult to find groups of customers with similar characteristics that are also meaningful.

In computer science, you have the "no free lunch theorem," which states that "for both static and time-dependent optimization problems, the average performance of any pair of algorithms across all possible problems is the same." In other words, there is no algorithm that is better than any other algorithm in all situations. This is true for segmentation. There is no segmentation algorithm that is better than any other segmentation algorithm in all situations. This means you need to evaluate the results of your segmentation to see if they are meaningful, but you cannot do so a priori.

You can break segmentation into two categories: clustering and classification.

The main difference is that clustering is unsupervised, while classification is supervised. Let's review each category in detail.

Clustering

Clustering is the process of grouping data points into clusters. The goal is to find groups of data points that are similar to each other. Clustering is an unsupervised learning technique, which means that the model does not have a target variable. The model is only given the data, and the goal is to find patterns in the data.

We can have different clustering methods: distance-based methods and model-based methods. In distance-based methods, we calculate the distance between each data point and the centroid of the cluster. The data point is assigned to the cluster with the closest centroid. The centroid is the center of the cluster and is calculated as the mean of all the data points in the cluster. The distance between the data point and the centroid is calculated using a distance metric.

The most common distance metric is the Euclidean distance, which is the square root of the sum of the squared differences between the data point and the centroid, as seen in *Figure 7.1*:

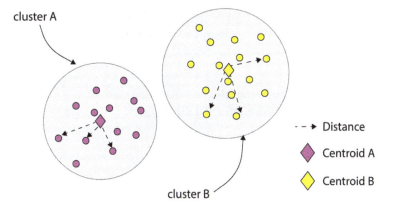

Figure 7.1 – Euclidean distance for clusters

The Euclidean distance is the most common distance metric because it is easy to calculate and is the most intuitive. However, it is not always the best distance metric. For example, if the data is not normally distributed, the Euclidean distance will not be the best distance metric. In this case, you can use the Mahalanobis distance, which is the square root of the sum of the squared differences between the data point and the centroid, divided by the standard deviation of the data. Common clustering algorithms are k-means and hierarchical clustering.

In model-based methods, you view the data as a mixture of groups sampled from different distributions whose original distributions and group membership are lost. These methods attempt to model the data such that a small number of groups with specific distribution characteristics, such as means and standard deviations, can represent the observed variance. The most commonly used model-based methods are Gaussian mixture models.

The steps of clustering are as follows:

1. Transform the data for a particular clustering algorithm. For instance, distance-based methods require the data to be numerical and data to be scaled, while latent class models require the data to be categorical.

2. Apply the clustering method. Some methods require a known number of groups desired, such as k-means.

3. Examine the solution with regard to the underlying data, to check whether it answers a business question.

Gaussian mixture models

Model-based clustering takes a different approach. It assumes that the data is a combination of different groups sampled from different distributions, but whose original distributions and group membership is lost. These methods strive to fit the data in a way that allows the observed variability to be captured by a limited set of clusters, each defined by particular statistical features, such as mean values and standard deviations.

Gaussian mixture models are a popular model-based clustering method. It assumes that the data is a mixture of groups sampled from different normal distributions. It attempts to find the number of groups and the parameters of the normal distributions that best fit the data.

Although you need to specify the number of clusters, that is, distributions, you can use the **Bayesian information criterion** (**BIC**) to compare the models. BIC is a measure of the goodness of fit of a model. The lower the BIC, the better the fit. The difference in BIC values can also be interpreted as the odds of model superiority.

Let's now get a brief overview of hierarchical and k-means clustering.

Hierarchical clustering

Hierarchical clustering is a popular method that groups observations according to their similarity. This method utilizes a dissimilarity matrix, which is an N x N grid quantifying the distance between every pair of data points. Initially, the algorithm treats each individual observation as its own separate cluster. Gradually, it combines adjacent observations or groups incrementally until all data points are interconnected in a single hierarchy. This process is known as an agglomerative method. The distance metric is the Euclidean distance, d, calculated as follows:

$$d = \sqrt{(X - Y)^2}$$

Like k-means, this metric can only be used on numerical data. You cannot compute the distance between male and female, for instance.

The output is what's known as a dendrogram. It is a tree-like diagram that shows the hierarchical relationship between the observations. The height of the tree is the distance between the observations. The leaves of the tree are the observations. The branches are the clusters. The root is the final cluster.

We can check the goodness of fit by looking at the cophenetic correlation coefficient, which evaluates how well the dendrogram matches the true distance metric. The closer the value is to 1, the better the fit.

Groups from hierarchical clustering

A dendrogram can be cut into clusters at any height desired, resulting in different numbers of groups. You draw a horizontal line at the desired height and count how many branches intersect that line. The number of intersections is the number of groups. Because you can cut a dendrogram at any point, you need to specify the number of groups you want. *Figure 7.2* shows an example dendrogram:

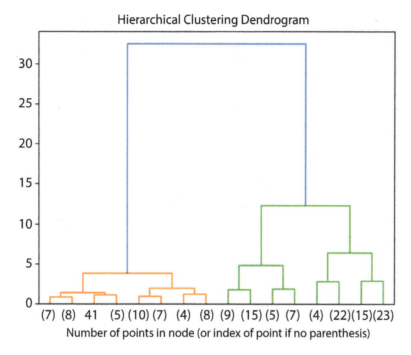

Figure 7.2 – An example dendrogram

K-means clustering

K-means clustering is a mean-based clustering approach. It employs an approach centered around the mean value. The algorithm aims to identify clusters that minimize the sum-of-squares variation between each data point and the center of its corresponding group. Due to its emphasis on calculating this mean discrepancy, the method depends on the Euclidean distance measure. This means that it can only be used with numerical data or data that can be converted to numerical data. So, while categorical data can't, binary outcomes or factors can be coerced to numeric without alteration of meaning. However, it is not optimal to do so with binary factors. It also requires that the data be scaled, because the Euclidean distance is sensitive to the scale of the data.

Let's now look at a practical example of segmentation using the techniques described so far. In this example, we will look at a database from a retailer. We will look to segment the customers into clusters and find the best characteristics with which to target them. Before describing the dataset, we will import the required libraries:

```
import pandas as pd
import numpy as np
import seaborn as sns
import matplotlib.pyplot as plt
```

```
from sklearn.preprocessing import normalize, LabelEncoder
import scipy.cluster.hierarchy as sch
from sklearn.cluster import KMeans, AgglomerativeClustering
from IPython.display import display

import warnings
warnings.filterwarnings("ignore")


seed = np.random.seed(1)
```

Here we are loading the usual libraries for data manipulation (pandas and numpy) and visualization (seaborn and matplotlib). We are also loading some libraries we need for clustering from scipy and scikit-learn. You will learn more about each when we use them. Let's now load the dataset and get some information on it:

```
seg = pd.read_csv("retail_segmentation.csv")
seg.info()
```

The output of the seg.info() function is the following DataFrame:

```
RangeIndex: 2000 entries, 0 to 1999
Data columns (total 16 columns):
 #   Column          Non-Null Count  Dtype
---  ------          --------------  -----
 0   Cust_No          2000 non-null   int64
 1   avg_order_size  2000 non-null   float64
 2   avg_order_freq  2000 non-null   float64
 3   crossbuy         2000 non-null   int64
 4   multichannel    2000 non-null   int64
 5   per_sale         2000 non-null   float64
 6   tenure           2000 non-null   int64
 7   return_rate     2000 non-null   float64
 8   married          2000 non-null   int64
 9   own_home         2000 non-null   int64
 10  household_size  2000 non-null   int64
 11  loyalty_card     2000 non-null   int64
 12  income           2000 non-null   int64
 13  age              2000 non-null   int64
 14  avg_mktg_cnt    2000 non-null   float64
 15  zip_code         2000 non-null   int64
dtypes: float64(5), int64(11)
memory usage: 250.1 KB
```

As we can see, it's essentially a customer database from a retailer with base variables and descriptor variables per user.

Although I am sure that you have seen similar datasets to this before, the distinction between bases and descriptor variables might be a little more obscure. When segmenting users, you don't throw everything at the algorithm. We can call this the "throw the kitchen sink at a problem" method and it does not work. What you want is to cluster for base variables and then find segments on descriptor variables. In short, bases are characteristics that tell us why segments differ (for example, value of order, frequency, or tenure) and descriptors are characteristics that help us find and reach segments (for example, user demographics, are the customers married or do they own a home?).

Usually, base variables can be sourced from your internal systems, such as your data warehouse, while descriptor variables sometimes need to be sourced via external data providers.

Since we are starting with finding out the clusters, we'll define the list of `bases_variables`:

```
bases_variables = ['avg_order_size', 'avg_order_freq',
    'crossbuy', 'multichannel', 'per_sale', 'tenure',
    'avg_mktg_cnt', 'return_rate']
```

Now, before we jump straight into throwing data into a clustering algorithm such as k-means, we first need to decide how many clusters we are going to cluster on.

A good initial place to start is by doing what is called hierarchical clustering on the data and visualizing the dendrogram. As described earlier in the chapter, a dendrogram shows the clusters in a tree form, and the *y*-axis corresponds to the distance between clusters. So, we'll find a horizontal line that crosses the chart at the approximate point of greatest distance. We'll use the hierarchy module from `scipy`, which has the `linkage()` and `dendrogram()` functions that you will need to perform this operation. Let us run the functions and output the dendrogram:

```
plt.figure(figsize=(10, 7))
plt.title("Customers Dendrogram with line")
clusters = sch.linkage(seg[bases_variables], method='ward')
sch.dendrogram(clusters)
plt.axhline(y = 400, color = 'black', linestyle = '--')
```

As we can see in *Figure 7.3*, we can draw a horizontal line at around 400, which splits the dataset into seven clusters:

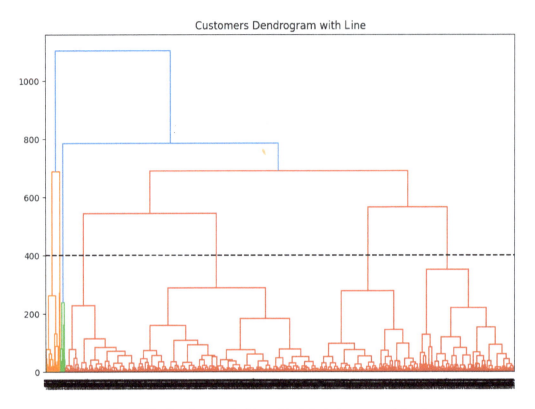

Figure 7.3 – Dendrogram for hierarchical clustering on our dataset

We can also check `KelbowVisualizer` from the `YellowBrick` Python package. `YellowBrick` is a great library with functions and visualizations to test several statistical and machine learning concepts, and `KelbowVisualizer` is a great tool to find out, more or less, programmatically how many clusters we should split the data with. In this case, since `Yellowbrick` is a thin API layer on top of scikit-learn, we'll use the `AgglomerativeClustering` object from that library to instantiate the model. Agglomerative clustering is another name for hierarchical clustering. Let's check what `Yellowbrick` can tell us:

```
from yellowbrick.cluster import KelbowVisualizer
model = AgglomerativeClustering()
visualizer = KelbowVisualizer(model, k = (2, 30), timings = True)
visualizer.fit(seg)
visualizer.show();
```

As we can see in *Figure 7.4*, `KelbowVisualizer` provides us with the same number of clusters. In this method, 7 is the number of clusters that reduces the errors for clustering.

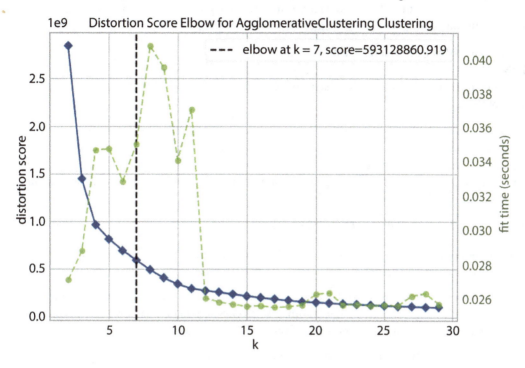

Figure 7.4 – The Yellowbrick KelbowVisualizer

With these two methods agreeing, we'll choose 7 as the number of clusters. Please keep in mind that deciding the number of clusters is as much an art as it is a science, and there is a degree of visual inspection to decide on the cluster number.

Now that we have decided on the number of clusters, we'll run the k-means algorithm, from scikit-learn, to decide how to assign which segment to which user:

```
# cluster size = 7
seg_kmeans = KMeans(n_clusters=7,
    random_state=seed).fit(seg[bases_variables])
segments = seg_kmeans.labels_
segmentation_result = pd.concat([seg, pd.Series(segments,
    name='segment')],
    axis=1)
segmentation_result['segment'] = segmentation_result['segment'] + 1
```

The process is quite simple: just call the `KMeans` object and fit on the `seg` DataFrame filtered by `bases_variables`. To make future tables and visualizations easier, we are going to add 1 to all segments. The reason is that `KMeans` will return an array of integers, one number for each segment, and in Python the numbering starts from 0. Since this is confusing, we'll adjust the segment numbers by 1.

We can now check how well the clusters separate. `Yellowbrick` again has a good function to show the visualization, called `InterclusterDistance`. This function will conduct **Principal Component Analysis** (**PCA**) on the clusters to reduce them to the most informative two dimensions and plot them.

PCA is a technique that applies an orthogonal transformation to transform a collection of potentially correlated variables into a new set of values. These new values are linearly uncorrelated variables known as principal components. This technique is widely used in data analysis and for making predictive models. This approach reduces the complexity found in data with many variables, while maintaining the important trends and patterns.

Here's a step-by-step breakdown of how PCA works:

- **Standardization**: The data is standardized to have a mean of 0 and a standard deviation of 1. This is important because PCA is sensitive to the variances of the initial variables.

- **Covariance matrix computation**: The covariance matrix expresses how the variables vary from the mean with respect to each other. In essence, the matrix captures the variance and correlation between all possible pairs of variables in the dataset.

- **Eigenvalue and eigenvector calculation**: From the covariance matrix, eigenvalues and eigenvectors are computed. Eigenvectors indicate the paths along which there is the greatest spread in the data, while eigenvalues signify the scale of these paths. Eigenvalues are important as they give the amount of variance captured by each principal component.

- **Sorting and selecting principal components**: Eigenvectors are sorted by their eigenvalues in decreasing order. This order determines the importance of the eigenvectors. The first few principal components explain the most variance in the data.

- **Projection**: Finally, the original data can be projected onto the principal components (the eigenvectors with the highest eigenvalues) to reduce its dimensions, often for visualization, further analysis, or as a preprocessing step for other algorithms.

PCA is particularly useful in processing data where multicollinearity exists or when there are too many predictors relative to the number of observations. By reducing the dimensionality of the data, PCA can help improve the performance of models by eliminating redundant features and focusing on the most important features.

Let's see what we get:

```
# Inter cluster distance map
from yellowbrick.cluster import InterclusterDistance
# Instantiate the clustering model and visualizer
visualizer = InterclusterDistance(seg_kmeans)
visualizer.fit(seg)              # Fit the data to the visualizer
visualizer.show();         # Finalize and render the figure
```

We can see in *Figure 7.5* that clusters 4 and 0 are well separated, although cluster 4 is small in size. Also, there is an overlap between all the other clusters, but 5 and 6 seem to have an acceptable separation between them.

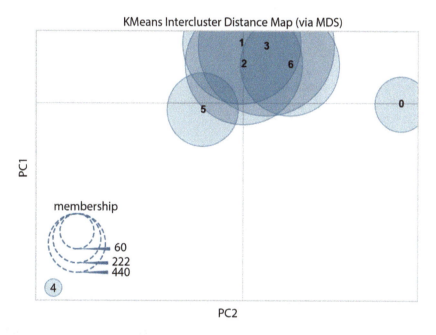

Figure 7.5 – Intercluster distance map

A note on data is important here. As an author, I could have used a more stylized dataset, with a more clear separation between clusters. I chose not to, in order to attempt to show you a simple fact: real data is messy, and you will, more often than not, not find the clear-cut outputs you see in simple and basic tutorials. As an analyst, there is a degree of individual judgment you need to apply when running techniques and insights.

Let's now calculate some financial metrics per segment to visualize how each segment performs from a revenue and profitability point of view.

In this dataset, `Sales` is simply the average order size times the average order frequency. `Profit` is defined as a 52% margin on sales minus a cost of $0.75 per marketing contact.

We will then simply aggregate the segments into a pivot table, where we'll average every base variable, count the users, and add `Sales` and `Profit` per year:

```
segmentation_result['SalesYear'] = \
    segmentation_result['avg_order_size'] * \
    segmentation_result['avg_order_freq'] * \
    (1 - segmentation_result['return_rate'])
segmentation_result['ProfitYear'] = \
    segmentation_result['SalesYear'] * \
    0.52 - segmentation_result['avg_mktg_cnt']*0.75


aggs = dict(zip(bases_variables, ['mean'] * len(bases_variables)))
aggs['Cust_No'] = 'count'
aggs['SalesYear'] = 'sum'
aggs['ProfitYear'] = 'sum'


columns = bases_variables
columns = columns + ['Cust_No', 'SalesYear', 'ProfitYear']


bases_summary = pd.pivot_table(
    segmentation_result,
    values = columns,
    columns = 'segment',
    aggfunc = aggs
)
```

Just for convenience, we'll just change the names of the index to a more readable formation, and reindex it to change the order:

```
bases_summary.index = ['Count of Segment', 'Total Profit per Year',
    'Total Sales per Year', 'avg mktg cnt', 'avg order freq',
    'avg order size', 'avg crossbuy', 'avg multichannel',
    'avg per sale', 'avg return rate','avg tenure']

bases_summary = bases_summary.reindex(index = ['avg mktg cnt',
    'avg order freq', 'avg order size', 'avg crossbuy',
    'avg multichannel', 'avg per sale', 'avg return rate',
    'avg tenure', 'Count of Segment', 'Total Sales per Year',
    'Total Profit per Year'])
```

In *Figure 7.6*, we can see that the segments differ enough for us to derive information from them:

segment	1	2	3	4	5	6	7
avg mktg cnt	135.616667	5.953690	8.716394	8.929943	23.870536	12.266010	38.963591
avg order freq	3.030133	2.085167	0.781351	1.315289	0.317100	0.516159	3.047309
avg order size	38.968040	29.588601	49.755724	23.269489	366.729167	115.390807	34.362015
avg crossbuy	4.050000	3.520879	2.095455	2.142678	1.500000	1.766667	3.545045
avg multichannel	1.900000	1.802198	1.429545	1.461827	1.000000	1.366667	1.680180
avg per sale	0.018593	0.291855	0.042067	0.051372	0.125000	0.053627	0.045873
avg return rate	0.112420	0.203227	0.103691	0.217994	0.000000	0.074208	0.155133
avg tenure	1.900000	32.967033	9.854545	8.846058	11.250000	7.516667	5.878378
Count of Segment	20.000000	455.000000	440.000000	799.000000	4.000000	60.000000	222.000000
Total Sales per Year	1955.886332	22019.802595	14246.806341	20038.597484	479.709957	3027.597665	18565.080482
Total Profit per Year	-1017.189107	9418.600535	4531.929243	5068.802590	177.837570	1022.380321	3166.403870

Figure 7.6 – Aggregation table of segments around base variables

Let's have a quick look at what we can see here: segments 2, 3, 4, and 7 have the most revenue and profit. They also have a decent amount of users, to render the results usable. Segment 3 has almost twice the average order size as segment 2 but half the order frequency, making them equivalent in terms of profitability, but different in types of customers. Segment 7 also looks interesting with a decent profit and sales per year, with a good number of users in the segment.

Let's now see what descriptor characteristics tell these segments apart, such that we can target them. The exercise is similar to the previous one – aggregate and do a pivot table, but this time by the descriptor variables instead of the base variables:

```
descriptors_variables = ['married', 'own_home',
    'household_size', 'loyalty_card', 'income', 'age']
aggs = dict(zip(descriptors_variables,
    (['mean'] * len(descriptors_variables))))
aggs['Cust_No'] = 'count'

columns = descriptors_variables + ['Cust_No']

descriptors_summary = pd.pivot_table(
    segmentation_result,
    values = columns,
    columns = 'segment',
    aggfunc = aggs
)

descriptors_summary.index = ['Count of Segment', 'avg age',
```

```
'avg household size', 'avg income', 'avg Loyalty card',
'avg married', 'avg own home']
```

In *Figure 7.7*, we can see the summary table of descriptor variables:

segment	1	2	3	4	5	6	7
Count of Segment	20.00	455.000000	440.000000	799.000000	4.00	60.000000	222.000000
avg age	37.50	43.936264	39.334091	43.783479	41.75	42.000000	45.707207
avg household size	3.45	2.279121	2.404545	3.458073	1.50	2.216667	3.027027
avg income	71.75	97.010989	71.068182	68.197747	65.00	70.916667	70.833333
avg Loyalty card	0.75	0.589011	0.684091	0.598248	0.50	0.666667	0.599099
avg married	0.50	0.881319	0.293182	0.352941	0.25	0.400000	0.360360
avg own home	0.30	0.375824	0.288636	0.858573	0.25	0.333333	0.563063

Figure 7.7 – Aggregation table of descriptor variables per segment

We can see some interesting factors in this table: the difference between segments 2 and 3 is that segment 2 has an 88% share of married people versus 29% on segment 3. Both have similar average incomes but segment 2 is also younger. Segment 7 has a higher average income compared to segment 3, but an age bracket similar to segment 2. It has the second-highest average household size.

Targeting the right segment with the right marketing efforts

The process of segmentation involves sorting customers from a business into segments. Once completed, it's important to decide which segments are most attractive for us to target with the right marketing message. To do this, we need to evaluate two dimensions: attractiveness and fit.

Segment attractiveness

Several factors come into play when considering the attractiveness of a segment. In this example, we might want to consider the total revenue or profit of each segment.

Let's take a deeper dive into sales per user and profit per user, to zoom in on the segments we might consider attractive:

```
attract_df = pd.pivot_table(
    segmentation_result,
    values = ['Cust_No', 'SalesYear', 'ProfitYear'],
    index = ['segment'],
    aggfunc = {
        'Cust_No': 'count',
        'SalesYear': ['sum', 'mean'],
```

```
        'ProfitYear': ['sum', 'mean'],
    }
)

attract_df.columns = attract_df.columns.to_flat_index()
attract_df.columns = ['Segment Size', 'Avg Profit per Customer',
    'Total Profit', 'Avg Sales per Customer', 'Total Sales']
```

The previous code will produce *Figure 7.8*, with sales and profit per customer:

segment	Segment Size	Avg Profit per Customer	Total Profit	Avg Sales per Customer	Total Sales
1	20	-50.859455	-1017.189107	97.794317	1955.886332
2	455	20.700221	9418.600535	48.395171	22019.802595
3	440	10.299839	4531.929243	32.379105	14246.806341
4	799	6.343933	5068.802590	25.079596	20038.597484
5	4	44.459393	177.837570	119.927489	479.709957
6	60	17.039672	1022.380321	50.459961	3027.597665
7	222	14.263080	3166.403870	83.626489	18565.080482

Figure 7.8 – Sales and profit per customer

When looking at profitability per user, segment 5 is the best, but it only has four users in it, so we need to take that insight with a big grain of salt. Segments 2 and 3 stand out for reasonable profit and sales per customer, while segment 7 has one of the highest average sales per customer but one of the smallest profits per customer.

Segment fit

When judging segment fit, one needs to understand the fit of the customers to the business. Given that the segmentation was done based on that from the CRM database, one would imagine that all of the segments have a degree of fit. More important is being able to determine the message of each segment, and there, we want to understand what types of behavior we want to encourage from each segment we choose.

Classification

Classification uses observations whose status is known to derive predictors and then apply them to new observations to predict their status. Classification is a supervised learning technique, which means that the model has a target variable. The model is given the data and the target variable, and the goal is to find a model that can predict the target variable.

The most common flow of analysis is as follows:

1. Dataset collected with group membership for all observations.

2. Split into test and training sets.

3. Train the model on the training set.

4. Test the model on the test set and evaluate the model.

Naive Bayes

Naive Bayes is a simple but powerful algorithm that leverages training data to ascertain the likelihood of belonging to a particular class, treating each predictor variable as independent — thus the term "naive."

You can evaluate the model's performance by looking at the confusion matrix. The confusion matrix is a table that shows the number of observations in each group that were correctly and incorrectly classified. The confusion matrix is a 2 x 2 matrix, with the rows representing the true group membership and the columns representing the predicted group membership. The diagonal of the matrix shows the number of observations that were correctly classified. The off-diagonal shows the number of observations that were incorrectly classified.

Figure 7.9 shows an example confusion matrix, with a cancer test classifier example:

		Predicted condition	
	Total 8 + 4 = 12	**Cancer** 7	**Non-cancer** 5
Cancer 8		6	2
Non-cancer 4		1	3

Figure 7.9 – An example confusion matrix

The confusion matrix in *Figure 7.9* can be interpreted in the following way:

- **Total**: The number of all predictions made, which is 12 in this case (8 cases of actual cancer + 4 cases of actual non-cancer).

- **Actual condition** (left column):

  - **Cancer**: The true condition of eight patients is that they have cancer

  - **Non-cancer**: The true condition of four patients is that they do not have cancer

- **Predicted condition** (top row):

  - **Cancer**: The model predicted cancer for seven patients

  - **Non-cancer**: The model predicted non-cancer for five patients

- **Correct predictions** (green cells):

  - **True Positive (TP)**: The model correctly predicted cancer for six patients

  - **True Negative (TN)**: The model correctly predicted non-cancer for three patients

- **Incorrect predictions** (red cells):

  - **False Positive (FP)**: The model incorrectly predicted cancer for one patient who actually does not have cancer

  - **False Negative (FN)**: The model incorrectly predicted non-cancer for two patients who actually have cancer

Based on this matrix, several performance metrics can be calculated:

- **Accuracy**: The proportion of true results (both true positives and true negatives) in the total number of cases examined:

$$(TP + TN) \ / \ Total = (6 + 3) \ / \ 12$$

- **Precision**: The proportion of true positive results in the number of cases that were predicted as positive:

$$TP \ / \ (TP + FP) = 6 \ / \ (6 + 1)$$

- **Recall (sensitivity)**: The proportion of true positive results in the number of cases that are actually positive:

$$TP \ / \ (TP + FN) = 6 \ / \ (6 + 2)$$

- **Specificity**: The proportion of true negative results in the number of cases that are actually negative:

$$TN \ / \ (TN + FP) = 3 \ / \ (3 + 1)$$

- **F1 score**: The harmonic mean of precision and recall:

$$2 * (Precision * Recall) / (Precision + Recall)$$

These metrics give us a sense of how well the model is performing, with a particular focus on the balance between correctly identifying cases of cancer and avoiding misclassifying non-cancer as cancer.

The accuracy of the model is the number of correct classifications divided by the total number of observations. The accuracy is a good measure of the model's performance, but it is not always the best measure. For instance, if you have a dataset with 90% of observations in one group and 10% in another, a model that always predicts the first group will have an accuracy of 90%. This is not a good model, because it is not predicting the second group at all. In this case, you would want to look at the precision and recall of the model.

Random forest

Random forest is a classification algorithm that uses a collection of decision trees to make predictions. It is a powerful algorithm that is robust to outliers and non-linear relationships. It is also a good algorithm to use when you have a large number of predictors. It relies on having labeled data to train the trees on.

But what exactly is a decision tree and how does it fit into a forest?

A decision tree is a simple statistical classifier that predicts a target variable by learning simple decision rules that it infers from the structure of the data and its features.

Its simplicity makes it easy to understand and visualize. It is robust to very little data preparation, such as normalization or the removal of blank values. It's also very fast to train, and it's easy to explain the variables. But there are some drawbacks. Decision trees create overly complex trees that fit the data quite well but generalize quite badly. In short, they are very easy to overfit. They can also be unstable.

Now, say instead of fitting a decision tree on all of the data, you were to fit several smaller, simpler decision trees on a subset of the data and a subset of features and then aggregate all of the trees into one classifier. Then, you would have a forest of decision trees. We just need to fit decision trees that are uncorrelated with each other but that add information to the final model. We can see a simple example of three trees in *Figure 7.10*:

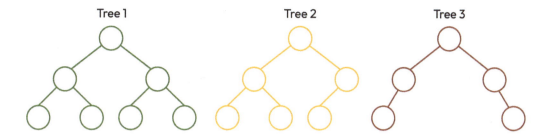

Figure 7.10 – Stylized example of a random forest of three decision trees

The "random" comes from how the model selects the features and data points to fit the individual trees: random forests select them probabilistically. When considering the number of trees to create, you should consider the heuristic of having at least 5 to 10 trees per observation for a small dataset.

A random forest is a simple solution to the drawbacks while maintaining the benefits. The evaluation is the same as the naive Bayes example, that is, the confusion matrix and accuracy.

Random forests are particularly good for estimating the importance of classification variables because each tree can only use a subset of variables.

Discriminant analysis and classification

Now, although we have the segments, we want to be able to understand what characteristics capture segment membership. In essence, we want to be able to discriminate between them. Discriminant analysis involves deriving the linear combination of two or more variables that best distinguishes – or discriminates – between the previously defined segments. Classification entails assigning objects into defined segments, based on the score each object receives from the linear combination of the variables used as part of discriminant analysis.

Discriminant analysis also provides insights into the following:

- How good, or bad, a specific variable or variables are at capturing segment membership
- How the defined segments differ with respect to the variables used to derive the linear combination

Discriminant analysis is commonly used in targeting. Discriminant analysis and classification are used for profiling and classification purposes. A key objective of discriminant analysis is to help identify descriptor variables that are good at predicting cluster membership.

Details on discriminant analysis

Discriminant analysis constructs a combination of the descriptor variables such that the function optimally discriminates among the customer segments. When two segments are compared, one discriminant function is used. When three or more segments are compared, several discriminant functions are at play, assuming enough descriptor variables are available.

Discriminant analysis takes the following form:

$$Y_i(x) = \beta_{11}x_1 + ... + \beta_{1k}x_k$$
$$...$$
$$Y_h(x) = \beta_{h1}x_1 + ... + \beta_{hk}x_k$$

In these equations, there are a total of h segments, and each $Y_h(x)$ is a binary variable that is equal to 1 if a customer belongs to the hth segment, and 0 otherwise, for k descriptor variables x_k used in the analysis.

It's important to note that if there are more descriptor variables, k, than segments, h, then there will be at least $h - 1$ discriminant functions. For example, if there are only two segments, then there will be only one discriminant function. If the number of k descriptor variables is less than segments h, then there will be no more than k discriminant functions. β_{hk} refers to the weights that maximize the ratio of the between-group differences to the in-between-group ratios.

Linear versus quadratic discriminant analysis

Depending on whether the variance-covariance matrix of the segments under analysis is homogeneous, either linear or quadratic discriminant analysis is used.

The term "homogeneous" in the context of a variance-covariance matrix refers to the condition where the variance and covariance are consistent across the different groups or segments being analyzed. This means that each group has similar variability and the relationship between pairs of variables is consistent in all groups. In other words, the data spread and the correlations among variables do not vary from one group to another; they are uniform or homogeneous across the groups. Linear is used when the variance-covariance matrix of the groups is homogeneous, and quadratic is used when the variance-covariance matrix is heterogeneous. Bartlett's test is commonly used to determine this.

With that introduction to LDA, let's take the previously calculated segments and use LDA to decide from a list of prospects which segments we prefer and how to target them.

The `scikit-learn` library again comes to the rescue, with a good module called `Linear DiscriminantAnalysis`, which we'll import. We need to define the descriptor variables as the independent X variables and the y variable as the dependent or target variable. LDA will then fit the regressions as correctly as possible to fit the descriptor variables to the correct segments. The code is simple, as you can see here:

```
## Load Packages and Set Seed
import pandas as pd
from sklearn.discriminant_analysis import LinearDiscriminantAnalysis
as LDA
import statsmodels.api as sm

# Set seed
import numpy as np
np.random.seed(1)

## Read in Segment Data and Classification Data
seg = segmentation_result.copy()
class_data = pd.read_csv('lda/retail_classification.csv')

print("Run Discriminant Analysis")
X = seg[['married', 'own_home', 'household_size', 'income', 'age']]
y = seg['segment']
fit = LDA().fit(X, y)
```

Next, we will compute the group means of the fitted LDA model and display the means and the coefficients for the fit:

```
# Group means
group_means = pd.DataFrame(fit.means_, columns=X.columns,
    index=fit.classes_)
print("Group Means:")
display(group_means) # print the summary statistics of your
discriminant analysis
# Coefficients of Linear Discriminants
coefficients = pd.DataFrame(fit.coef_, columns=X.columns,
    index=fit.classes_)
print("Coefficients of Linear Discriminants:")
display(coefficients)
print(25*"-")
```

We can see the output for the group means in *Figure 7.11* and the coefficients in *Figure 7.12*:

	married	own_home	household_size	income	age
1	0.500000	0.300000	3.450000	71.750000	37.500000
2	0.881319	0.375824	2.279121	97.010989	43.936264
3	0.293182	0.288636	2.404545	71.068182	39.334091
4	0.352941	0.858573	3.458073	68.197747	43.783479
5	0.250000	0.250000	1.500000	65.000000	41.750000
6	0.400000	0.333333	2.216667	70.916667	42.000000
7	0.360360	0.563063	3.027027	70.833333	45.707207

Figure 7.11 – LDA group means

	married	own_home	household_size	income	age
1	0.169557	-1.469454	0.128190	-0.002617	-0.010643
2	2.106469	-0.980776	-0.114889	0.010649	0.003421
3	-0.877408	-1.523522	-0.090005	-0.003138	-0.006643
4	-0.548559	1.552059	0.115065	-0.003239	0.000620
5	-1.086701	-1.740168	-0.280132	-0.006793	-0.000927
6	-0.325908	-1.280135	-0.131846	-0.003316	-0.000947
7	-0.511598	-0.046549	0.028861	-0.002694	0.005153

Figure 7.12 – LDA coefficients

We can calculate the group means and coefficients of the LDA for each segment and each variable. Now, the question becomes, are any of the LDA equations statistically significant?

To answer that, we can quickly use statsmodels MNLogit regression. **MNLogit** stands for **MultiNomial Logistic Regression**, and it's a good fit for this type of data, since the target variable is a classification of seven classes and prints the coefficient p-values:

```
lda_pred = fit.transform(X)
fit_models = []
for i in range(lda_pred.shape[1]):
    print(f"LDA {i}")
```

```
X_const = sm.add_constant(lda_pred[:, i])
mlr_model_sm = sm.MNLogit(seg['segment'], X_const).fit()
fit_models.append(mlr_model_sm)
display(mlr_model_sm.pvalues)
```

As seen in the snippet, the p-values are stored by `statsmodels` in the `mlr_model_sm` model variable. We can check the p-values for the MNLogit in *Figure 7.13*:

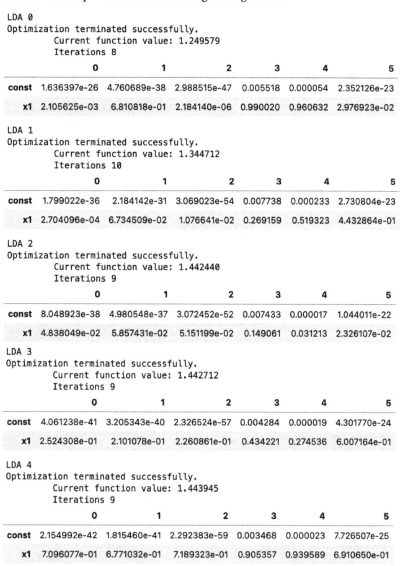

LDA 0
Optimization terminated successfully.
        Current function value: 1.249579
        Iterations 8

	0	1	2	3	4	5
const	1.636397e-26	4.760689e-38	2.988515e-47	0.005518	0.000054	2.352126e-23
x1	2.105625e-03	6.810818e-01	2.184140e-06	0.990020	0.960632	2.976923e-02

LDA 1
Optimization terminated successfully.
        Current function value: 1.344712
        Iterations 10

	0	1	2	3	4	5
const	1.799022e-36	2.184142e-31	3.069023e-54	0.007738	0.000233	2.730804e-23
x1	2.704096e-04	6.734509e-02	1.076641e-02	0.269159	0.519323	4.432864e-01

LDA 2
Optimization terminated successfully.
        Current function value: 1.442440
        Iterations 9

	0	1	2	3	4	5
const	8.048923e-38	4.980548e-37	3.072452e-52	0.007433	0.000017	1.044011e-22
x1	4.838049e-02	5.857431e-02	5.151199e-02	0.149061	0.031213	2.326107e-02

LDA 3
Optimization terminated successfully.
        Current function value: 1.442712
        Iterations 9

	0	1	2	3	4	5
const	4.061238e-41	3.205343e-40	2.326524e-57	0.004284	0.000019	4.301770e-24
x1	2.524308e-01	2.101078e-01	2.260861e-01	0.434221	0.274536	6.007164e-01

LDA 4
Optimization terminated successfully.
        Current function value: 1.443945
        Iterations 9

	0	1	2	3	4	5
const	2.154992e-42	1.815460e-41	2.292383e-59	0.003468	0.000023	7.726507e-25
x1	7.096077e-01	6.771032e-01	7.189323e-01	0.905357	0.939589	6.910650e-01

Figure 7.13 – MNLogit p-values

Since at its core, LDA is a classification model, a good way to inspect how well it performs is by computing a confusion matrix. A confusion matrix will split aggregate the predicted classes versus the actual classes in the data. A perfect classifier will have values only in the diagonal. Let's check our confusion matrix:

```
## Check Discriminant Model Fit
print("Check Discriminant Model Fit")
pred_seg = fit.predict(X)
tseg = pd.crosstab(seg['segment'], pred_seg)
tseg = tseg.reindex(columns=tseg.index.values, fill_value=0)
display(tseg) # print table
accuracy = np.diag(tseg).sum() / len(seg)
print(25*"-")
print(f"Classifier accuracy: {accuracy*100:.2f}% for LDA vs
    {1/seg['segment'].max()*100:.2f}% for Random Allocation")
# print percent correct
print(25*"-")
```

col_0	1	2	3	4	5	6	7
segment							
1	0	7	7	6	0	0	0
2	0	309	31	115	0	0	0
3	0	105	222	113	0	0	0
4	0	81	68	650	0	0	0
5	0	1	2	1	0	0	0
6	0	18	24	18	0	0	0
7	0	43	67	112	0	0	0

```
--------------------------
Classifier accuracy: 59.05% for LDA vs 14.29% for Random Allocation
--------------------------
```

Figure 7.14 – Confusion matrix and classifier accuracy

So, our accuracy is 59%. Not perfect, but we need to compare this with the random allocation. In a random setting, you would have a 1 in 7 chance of getting the class right, or about 14%, so our classifier is better than a pure random setting.

Now that we have a usable model, we'll run it on our list of prospects:

```
## Run Classification Using Discriminant Function
print("Classification Using Discriminant Function")
pred_class = fit.predict(class_data[['married', 'own_home',
    'household_size', 'income', 'age']])
tclass = pd.Series(pred_class).value_counts()
display(tclass) # print table
print(25*"-")


## Add Predicted Segment to Classification Data
class_data['pred_class'] = pred_class
class_data.to_csv('lda/classification_pred.csv', index=False)
```

After running it through our prospects, we can see the output of the number of prospects per class:

```
Classification Using Discriminant Function
4      6497
2      1188
3       315
Name: count, dtype: int64
```

Now we will go through another technique for classifying users called RFM.

Exploring RFM

RFM is a customer segmentation technique that uses recency, frequency, and monetary value to divide customers into groups. RFM is a popular technique because it is easy to calculate and understand. RFM is a good starting point for customer segmentation. It is used to identify clusters of customers based on how much time has passed since their last purchase (recency), how often they purchase (frequency), and how much they spend (monetary). Its uses include the following:

- Segmentation and targeting
- Customer cohort analysis
- Customer lifetime value analysis
- Resource allocation

RFM stands as one of the earliest analytical methodologies in cohort analysis, originating from direct mail marketing strategies in 1995 by Bult and Wansbeek, thus highlighting its longstanding relevance in the field. The technique only needs the most available transactional data, as well as a very simple analysis. The underlying idea is that customers who have purchased more recently made more purchases during a given time period and those who spent more money are more likely to respond to a new offer in the future. One drawback is that the marketing analyst does not have a great understanding of why the customer behaves in a particular way.

RFM analysis, while straightforward in its foundational concepts, can offer complex and nuanced insights when examined more closely. As we delve deeper into this established analytical tool, we uncover its layers and intricacies, helping us maximize its potential in our marketing efforts.

As defined earlier, the underlying idea of RFM is that customers who have purchased more recently made more purchases during a given time period and those who spent more money are more likely to respond to a new offer in the future. Based on this heuristic, RFM analysis is commonly used in marketing campaigns.

Using RFM, some companies rank their customers and use this information when determining how much effort to put into nurturing a customer relationship. For example, a company may decide to spend more time and money on a customer who has a high RFM score than on a customer who has a low RFM score. Some customers make very frequent but low-value transactions, while others might be infrequent but high-monetary-value customers. A simple example is when to send customer communications: if, as a retailer, you know that a group of customers tends to repurchase a product every 30 days on average, you can target that segment of customers and send communications reminding them with promotions in 28 days after their last purchase versus, for instance, every day.

Approaches and techniques – independent versus sequential sorting

The analysis can be conducted via two primary approaches: independent sorting and sequential sorting. These approaches share the common goal of segmenting customers based on RFM values but employ different strategies in processing the RFM components.

Independent sorting

In the independent sorting approach, each RFM component – recency, frequency, and monetary value – is handled separately. Customers are ranked according to recency and divided into equal-sized groups or bins, usually quintiles, that is, five bins ranging from the highest to the lowest. The same procedure is subsequently applied to frequency and monetary value, independent of the previous binning. This results in 125 groups (5 Recency x 5 Frequency x 5 Monetary).

The advantage of this approach lies in its simplicity and direct interpretability. Each RFM component can be evaluated independently. For example, two customers falling within the top quintile for frequency are directly comparable, irrespective of their recency or monetary value scores. However, a drawback of this method is the potential for an imbalanced distribution of combined RFM scores, particularly with smaller datasets. By imbalanced, one means that some segments would contain too few customers to be useful. This is primarily due to the significant correlation that often exists between the three RFM variables.

Sequential sorting

In contrast, sequential RFM, also known as nested sorting, takes a more hierarchical approach. As with independent sorting, customers are initially ranked and grouped according to their recency scores. Then, within each recency group, customers are further segmented based on frequency. Finally, each of these groups is sorted based on the monetary value. This process results in the same 125 distinct customer groups as independent sorting (5 recency x 5 frequency x 5 monetary).

This sequential approach implicitly assumes that recency is more critical than frequency, and frequency more so than monetary value. Of course, this sequence can be altered (for example, FRM or MRF) to suit the unique circumstances and priorities of the business.

Sequential sorting tends to lead to more evenly distributed group sizes, which is particularly beneficial for smaller datasets. However, the interpretability of each RFM component becomes slightly more complex. For example, customers with the same frequency rating are not necessarily comparable, as they may belong to different recency or monetary value groups.

Choosing the right approach

Whether to use independent or sequential sorting often depends on the specific requirements and constraints of your analysis. Sequential sorting often outperforms independent sorting, but this isn't always the case, and it's prudent to test both approaches. Regardless of the method chosen, the goal remains the same: to understand customers better and target them more effectively.

A practical example of RFM analysis

Let's look at a practical example of how to implement RFM and what to use it for on a dataset for a retailer. In this example, we'll look at example data from a potential retailer that sells personal home goods. As an analyst, you were asked to look into a marketing campaign being run, targeting the retailer's customers, with a promotion encouraging the purchase of this season's new offerings. In the past, the company would send catalogs to all of your customer base. The question is, can you, as an analyst, come up with a better approach to target the customers who are more likely to purchase, maximizing the revenue while reducing the cost of the campaign overall?

This exact setting is where RFM shines through as a technique.

The data

The data is a selection of 10,000 customers at random from your customer database, with all the information we will need. Let's go over the columns in the dataset:

- `Customer` is a unique identifier of each of the 10,000 customers in the sample
- `Revenue` is how much the customer spent over the timeframe

- `Number_of_orders` is the number of times the customer has made a purchase during the same timeframe

- `Recency_days` is the number of days since the customer has made the last order relative to the time you are analyzing

- `Purchase` is an indicator (or dummy) variable that is 1 if the customer made a purchase during the campaign and 0 otherwise

- `Zip Code` is the zip code of the customer

Let's now set up the required libraries and load the data file. For now, we'll just be using pandas and numpy:

```
import pandas as pd
import numpy as np
import warnings
warnings.filterwarnings('ignore')

# Set random seed for reproducibility
np.random.seed(1)

data_file = '../data/retail_rfm.csv'

# Read in RFM data
rfm = pd.read_csv(data_file)
```

With the data loaded, we now move to calculate the metrics we'll need to do the analysis, namely recency, frequency, and monetary scores. We'll also create an RFM score, which is nothing more than the following:

$$RFMScore = R * 100 + F * 10 + M$$

This is just concatenating the integers. However, you can add more weight to one of the factors. There is no set rule on the weighting for an RFM score, and as an analyst, you can weigh the factors you consider more important to your business differently.

We'll start with the metrics using independent sort, as described earlier:

```
# Define the number of groups
groups = 5

# Function to calculate ntile
def ntile(x, n):
    return np.ceil(x.rank()/len(x) * n)

# Run RFM Analysis with Independent Sort
```

```
rfm['recency_score_indep'] = ntile(-rfm['recency_days'], groups)
rfm['frequency_score_indep'] = ntile(rfm['number_of_orders'], groups)
rfm['monetary_score_indep'] = ntile(rfm['revenue'], groups)
rfm['rfm_score_indep'] = (rfm['recency_score_indep']*100 + \
    rfm['frequency_score_indep'] * 10 + \
    rfm['monetary_score_indep']).astype(str)
```

Next, we will recalculate the metrics, this time using sequential sort:

```
# Run RFM Analysis with Sequential Sort
rfm['recency_score_seq'] = ntile(-rfm['recency_days'], groups)

# Initialize empty lists
r_groups = []
rf_groups = []
temp = pd.DataFrame()

for r in range(1, groups+1):
    r_group = rfm[rfm['recency_score_seq'] == r]
    r_group['frequency_score_seq'] = ntile
        (r_group['number_of_orders'], groups)
    for m in range(1, groups+1):
        rf_group = r_group[r_group['frequency_score_seq'] == m]
        rf_group['monetary_score_seq'] = ntile
        (rf_group['revenue'], groups)
        temp = pd.concat([temp, rf_group], axis=0)

rfm_result = temp.sort_values('customer_id')
rfm_result['rfm_score_seq'] = \
    (rfm_result['recency_score_seq']*100 + \
    rfm_result['frequency_score_seq'] * 10 + \
    rfm_result['monetary_score_seq']).astype(str)

# Export RFM Results with Independent and Sequential Sort
rfm_result.to_csv('../data/rfm_result.csv', index=False)
```

Before we go further and decide which RFM cells we want to target, we need to understand what our breakeven rate is, which will tell us which RFM cells we can select that will be profitable.

Which customers to target

After doing the RFM clustering, you need to decide which customers to target. You need to calculate the breakeven response rate as in the previous example:

$$Breakeven = \frac{Cost\ to\ do\ campaign}{Profit\ from\ single\ sale}$$

Let's say you have the following costs:

- Cost to carry out the campaign: $5,000

- Profit from a single sale (price – cost): $50

The breakeven response rate is the minimum number of customers who need to respond to your campaign to be profitable. We can do the quick math on this rate:

```
# Define campaign cost and profit per sale
campaign_cost = 5000
profit_per_sale = 50

# Calculate breakeven response rate
breakeven_rate = campaign_cost / profit_per_sale
print(f"The breakeven response rate is: {breakeven_rate}")
```

Another consideration is the **return on marketing investment**, or **ROMI**.

Measuring a simple return on investment

After the campaign, you can calculate the ROMI.

ROMI is the amount of revenue generated for every dollar spent on marketing. Suppose that your campaign results in 150 sales. Then we can quickly calculate the ROMI by simply dividing profit by cost:

```
# Define the number of sales from the campaign
sales = 150

# Calculate the total profit from sales
total_profit = sales * profit_per_sale

# Calculate the Return on Marketing Investment (ROMI)
ROMI = total_profit / campaign_cost
print(f"The Return on Marketing Investment (ROMI) is: {ROMI}")
```

In this example, we'll work with the following data:

- Average purchase amounts from the marketing campaign: 40 USD

- Average cost of the goods: 19.20 USD (equivalent to a 52% gross margin)

- Average cost of shipping the product: 6 USD

- Average cost of the marketing campaign: 2 USD

So this means that the average gross profit is simply 40 – 19.20 = 20.80 USD. Discounting the cost of shipping and the cost of the marketing campaign, we get 20.80 – 6 – 2 = 12.80 USD of profit per customer that made a purchase.

Now, the question becomes, what percentage of customers in each RFM cell needs to purchase if we send the catalog to all customers, which is simply 2/12.80, giving us a breakeven rate of 15.625%?

Visualizing the data

Now we move to visualize the data, plotting the RFM cells versus the average purchase. Since the purchase variable is an indicator variable, its average is the proportion of customers in each RFM cell that made a purchase. The code to achieve this is as follows:

```
import seaborn as sns
import matplotlib.pyplot as plt


# Create a new DataFrame with average purchase value for each RFM
score
rfm_avg_purchase = rfm_result.groupby('rfm_score_indep')['purchase'].
mean().reset_index()


# Create bar plot
plt.figure(figsize=(10, 6))
rfm_plot_indep = sns.barplot(data=rfm_avg_purchase,
    x='rfm_score_indep', y='purchase', palette='viridis')
rfm_plot_indep.axhline(y = 0.15625, color = 'black', linestyle = '--')
plt.title('Average Purchase Value for each RFM Score with Independent
    Sorting')
plt.xlabel('RFM Score')
plt.ylabel('Average Purchase Value')
plt.xticks(rotation=90)   # Rotates X-axis labels if they overlap
plt.show()
```

Let's check the visualization produced by the code in *Figure 7.15*:

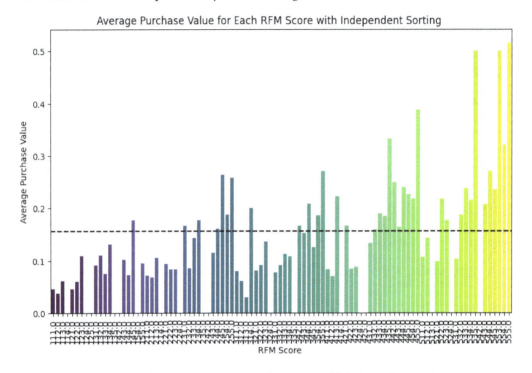

Figure 7.15 – RFM versus average purchase value with independent sorting

We have plotted a horizontal line at 0.15625 to show the breakeven rate. Below that line, those customers will be unprofitable. Let's have a look at the plot using sequential sorting:

```
rfm_avg_purchase = \
    rfm_result.groupby('rfm_score_seq')['purchase'].mean().reset_
index()

# Create bar plot
plt.figure(figsize=(10, 6))
rfm_plot_seq = sns.barplot(data=rfm_avg_purchase,
    x='rfm_score_seq', y='purchase', palette='viridis')
rfm_plot_seq.axhline(y = 0.15625, color = 'black', linestyle = '--')
plt.title('Average Purchase Value for each RFM Score with Sequential
    sorting')
plt.xlabel('RFM Score')
plt.ylabel('Average Purchase Value')
plt.xticks(rotation=90)  # Rotates X-axis labels if they overlap
plt.show()
```

In *Figure 7.16*, we can see the output chart of the RFM score with sequential sorting:

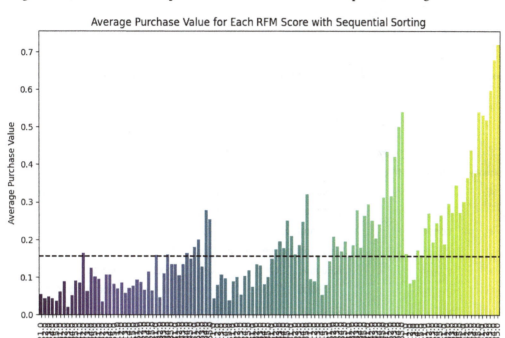

Figure 7.16 – RFM score versus average purchase with sequential sorting

Determining which cells to target

At this stage, we want to calculate the profitability and ROMI, when using either sequential or independent sorting. Later, we will compare the results of targeting users using RFM, with simple random targeting, which in our case will simply be the base case of sending everyone the marketing campaign catalog.

Now, we need to calculate the percentage of purchase rate per RFM cell and the user count per RFM cell. For ease of visualization, we'll apply conditional formatting to the table to see which cells are above the breakeven rate, on the percentage table:

```
# Helper function for conditional formatting
def highlight_cells(val):
    color = '#90EE90' if val > 0.15625 else ''
    return 'background-color: {}'.format(color)

percentage_table = pd.pivot_table(rfm_result,
    values='purchase',
```

```
    index=['recency_score_indep', 'frequency_score_indep'],
    columns='monetary_score_indep',
    aggfunc='mean',
    fill_value=0)

percentage_table_style = percentage_table.style.applymap
    (highlight_cells)
```

We can check the result in *Figure 7.17*:

recency_score_indep	frequency_score_indep	monetary_score_indep 1.000000	2.000000	3.000000	4.000000	5.000000
	1.000000	0.045918	0.037634	0.061224	0.000000	0.000000
	2.000000	0.046154	0.059480	0.108434	0.000000	0.000000
1.000000	3.000000	0.090909	0.109827	0.074766	0.131148	0.000000
	4.000000	0.000000	0.000000	0.101695	0.072289	0.176471
	5.000000	0.000000	0.000000	0.000000	0.000000	0.095238
	1.000000	0.071429	0.068376	0.105263	0.000000	0.000000
	2.000000	0.093525	0.083333	0.083333	0.000000	0.000000
2.000000	3.000000	0.166667	0.085561	0.143357	0.177215	0.000000
	4.000000	0.000000	0.000000	0.114286	0.160000	0.263158
	5.000000	0.000000	0.000000	0.000000	0.187500	0.258333
	1.000000	0.080000	0.060976	0.029412	0.200000	0.000000
	2.000000	0.080645	0.090909	0.136364	0.000000	0.000000
3.000000	3.000000	0.076923	0.090909	0.112727	0.107843	0.000000
	4.000000	0.000000	0.166667	0.152174	0.208861	0.125000
	5.000000	0.000000	0.000000	0.000000	0.186047	0.270531
	1.000000	0.082759	0.069767	0.222222	0.000000	0.000000
	2.000000	0.166667	0.084211	0.088235	0.000000	0.000000
4.000000	3.000000	0.133333	0.159292	0.190217	0.185714	0.333333
	4.000000	0.000000	0.250000	0.163636	0.240106	0.225806
	5.000000	0.000000	0.000000	0.000000	0.217949	0.388298
	1.000000	0.106195	0.142857	0.000000	0.000000	0.000000
	2.000000	0.098765	0.218182	0.176471	0.000000	0.000000
5.000000	3.000000	0.103448	0.187500	0.238372	0.216216	0.500000
	4.000000	0.000000	0.000000	0.206897	0.270677	0.235294
	5.000000	0.000000	0.000000	0.500000	0.321429	0.515748

Figure 7.17 – RFM cells above breakeven percentage for independent sorting

We should also have a look at the customer user count with independent sort:

```
count_table = pd.pivot_table(rfm_result,
    values='purchase',
    index=['recency_score_indep', 'frequency_score_indep'],
    columns='monetary_score_indep',
    aggfunc='count',
    fill_value='')
```

Again, we can check the results in *Figure 7.18*, now with independent sort:

	monetary_score_indep	1.0	2.0	3.0	4.0	5.0
recency_score_indep	frequency_score_indep					
1.0	1.0	588.0	186.0	49.0	11.0	
	2.0	130.0	269.0	83.0	15.0	2.0
	3.0	22.0	173.0	214.0	61.0	7.0
	4.0		4.0	59.0	83.0	17.0
	5.0				5.0	21.0
2.0	1.0	294.0	117.0	19.0	3.0	
	2.0	139.0	180.0	60.0	8.0	
	3.0	18.0	187.0	286.0	79.0	6.0
	4.0		7.0	105.0	275.0	57.0
	5.0				32.0	120.0
3.0	1.0	300.0	82.0	34.0	5.0	
	2.0	62.0	176.0	44.0	10.0	
	3.0	13.0	165.0	275.0	102.0	2.0
	4.0		6.0	92.0	316.0	80.0
	5.0				43.0	207.0
4.0	1.0	145.0	43.0	9.0	2.0	
	2.0	42.0	95.0	34.0	4.0	2.0
	3.0	15.0	113.0	184.0	70.0	3.0
	4.0		4.0	110.0	379.0	93.0
	5.0				78.0	564.0
5.0	1.0	113.0	35.0	1.0		
	2.0	81.0	55.0	17.0	4.0	
	3.0	29.0	112.0	172.0	37.0	6.0
	4.0		4.0	145.0	266.0	51.0
	5.0			4.0	112.0	762.0

Figure 7.18 – Customers per RFM cell with independent sorting

Now we do the same calculations, but for sequential sorting:

```
percentage_table_seq = pd.pivot_table(rfm_result,
    values='purchase',
    index=['recency_score_seq', 'frequency_score_seq'],
    columns='monetary_score_seq',
    aggfunc='mean',
    fill_value=0)

percentage_table_seq = \
    percentage_table_seq.style.applymap(highlight_cells)

count_table_seq = pd.pivot_table(rfm_result,
    values='purchase',
    index=['recency_score_seq', 'frequency_score_seq'],
    columns='monetary_score_seq',
    aggfunc='count',
    fill_value=0)
```

Finally, we can see the percentages in *Figure 7.19*:

recency_score_seq	monetary_score_seq frequency_score_seq	1.000000	2.000000	3.000000	4.000000	5.000000
1.000000	2.000000	0.053571	0.041916	0.047297	0.043011	0.036364
	3.000000	0.061224	0.089109	0.019608	0.051020	0.090000
	4.000000	0.085106	0.163265	0.062500	0.125000	0.102041
	5.000000	0.095238	0.034884	0.105882	0.107143	0.081395
2.000000	1.000000	0.068966	0.085366	0.058140	0.070000	0.076923
	2.000000	0.094118	0.086957	0.064935	0.115385	0.064103
	3.000000	0.159091	0.045455	0.109890	0.160920	0.134831
	4.000000	0.134328	0.104478	0.134328	0.164179	0.149254
	5.000000	0.179487	0.200000	0.128205	0.278481	0.253165
3.000000	1.000000	0.043011	0.079365	0.106383	0.096774	0.038462
	2.000000	0.087719	0.100000	0.051724	0.103448	0.118644
	3.000000	0.073394	0.133929	0.131579	0.081081	0.099099
	4.000000	0.149254	0.173913	0.194030	0.176471	0.250000
	5.000000	0.209877	0.160494	0.185185	0.246914	0.320988
4.000000	1.000000	0.095238	0.088889	0.154930	0.052632	0.078947
	2.000000	0.142857	0.207792	0.181818	0.168831	0.194805
	3.000000	0.157303	0.184783	0.277778	0.177778	0.263736
	4.000000	0.294872	0.250000	0.202532	0.240506	0.312500
	5.000000	0.434211	0.315789	0.421053	0.500000	0.539474
5.000000	1.000000	0.162791	0.083333	0.094118	0.172043	0.159091
	2.000000	0.230769	0.269231	0.192308	0.243590	0.265823
	3.000000	0.187500	0.296296	0.271605	0.345679	0.271605
	4.000000	0.301370	0.364865	0.438356	0.378378	0.540541
	5.000000	0.530864	0.518519	0.597561	0.679012	0.719512

Figure 7.19 – RFM cells above breakeven percentage for sequential sorting

Profitability evaluation

Now the question becomes what is better:

- Target all customers
- Target the RFM cells above the breakeven rate using independent sorting
- Target the RFM cells above the breakeven rate but using sequential sorting instead

First, let's see what RFM cells we want to pick and set them in a DataFrame. The process is simple: we just group by each `rfm_score_seq` and calculate the mean of purchase.

ROMI after RFM

After the campaign, you can calculate the ROMI, or return on marketing investment. First, we are going to extract the users we want from the RFM cell. Given we know our breakeven conversion rate – 15.625% – we will group the data in `rfm_result` using the `purchase` column, and add a new column, named `target`, to indicate whether we have sent a catalog or not to that cell.

We will do this both for the independent and sequential targeting groups and merge them:

```
selection_seq_df = \
    rfm_result.groupby(['rfm_score_seq'])['purchase'].mean().reset_
index()
selection_seq_df['target_seq'] = \
    np.where(selection_seq_df.purchase > 0.15625, 1, 0)

selection_ind_df = \
    rfm_result.groupby(['rfm_score_indep'])['purchase'].mean().reset_
index()
selection_ind_df['target_ind'] = \
    np.where(selection_ind_df.purchase > 0.15625, 1, 0)
targetting_df = rfm_result.merge(
    selection_ind_df[['rfm_score_indep', 'target_ind']],
    on='rfm_score_indep'
    ).merge(
        selection_seq_df[['rfm_score_seq', 'target_seq']],
        on='rfm_score_seq')
```

We now add `target_all`, to simulate the results of sending the campaign to all of the customer base, for comparison:

```
targetting_df['target_all'] = 1
```

Now comes the interesting part. We know from earlier in the chapter what the cost and revenue for the campaign are. We just need to add those columns to the DataFrame and compute the profit, which is simply *Revenue – Cost of Goods Sold – Marketing Costs – Shipping Costs*:

```
targetting_df['marketing_cost'] = 2.00
targetting_df['shipping_cost'] = \
    np.where(targetting_df.purchase == 1, 6.00, 0.00)
targetting_df['revenue_campaign'] = \
    np.where(targetting_df.purchase == 1, 40.00, 0.00)
targetting_df['cost_goods'] = \
    np.where(targetting_df.purchase == 1, 19.20, 0.00)
targetting_df['profit'] = targetting_df.revenue_campaign - \
    targetting_df.cost_goods - \
    targetting_df.marketing_cost - \
    targetting_df.shipping_cost
```

Now we aggregate the data for comparison. The mathematics is easy:

1. We aggregate customers as count, to get the number of total customers targeted by the campaign.

2. The `purchase` column is aggregated as sum, to get the total number of customers who made a purchase. Remember, in this example, purchase is an indicator variable, so it is 1 if the customer makes a purchase and 0 otherwise, which is why we can use it like this.

3. All of the financial metrics are aggregated as sums.

We then aggregate all the targeting models, by the three types under consideration – all customers targeted, independent sorting, and sequential sorting – and processes to calculate the ROMI. Since ROMI is the return on marketing investment, we divide profit by marketing cost. We also need to calculate the conversion or response rate, which is simply purchases divided by the total amount of customers targeted:

```
pd.set_option('display.float_format', '{:.2f}'.format)

agg_dict = {
    'customer_id': 'count',
    'purchase': 'sum',
    'revenue_campaign': 'sum',
    'cost_goods': 'sum',
    'shipping_cost': 'sum',
    'marketing_cost': 'sum',
    'profit': 'sum'
}

# Group by target_ind and target_seq, and aggregate
summary_target_ind = targetting_df[
```

```
    targetting_df['target_ind'] == 1].agg(agg_dict)
summary_target_seq = targetting_df[
    targetting_df['target_seq'] == 1].agg(agg_dict)
summary_all = targetting_df.agg(agg_dict)

# Calculate ROMI
summary_target_ind['ROMI'] = summary_target_ind['profit'] /
    summary_target_ind['marketing_cost']
summary_target_seq['ROMI'] = summary_target_seq['profit'] /
    summary_target_seq['marketing_cost']
summary_all['ROMI'] = summary_all['profit'] /
    summary_all['marketing_cost']

# Calculate Response Rate
summary_target_ind['Response Rate'] = summary_target_ind['purchase'] /
    summary_target_ind['customer_id']
summary_target_seq['Response Rate'] = summary_target_seq['purchase'] /
    summary_target_seq['customer_id']
summary_all['Response Rate'] = summary_all['purchase'] /
    summary_all['customer_id']
```

Finally, we merge all the DataFrames together, and some formatting just to make it easier to read:

```
# Combine into a single DataFrame
summary = pd.DataFrame({
    'All customers': summary_all,
    'Target_ind': summary_target_ind,
    'Target_seq': summary_target_seq
})

# Some formatting

# Create a copy of the DataFrame for formatting
summary_formatted = summary.copy()

# Define the formatting for each cell
for column in summary_formatted.columns:
    for row in summary_formatted.index:
        if row in ['customer_id', 'purchase']:
            summary_formatted.loc[row, column] =
                '{:,.0f}'.format(summary.loc[row, column])
        elif row in ['ROMI', 'Response Rate']:
            summary_formatted.loc[row, column] = \
                '{:.2f}%'.format(summary.loc[row, column] * 100)
        else:
```

```
summary_formatted.loc[row, column] = \
    '${:,.2f}'.format(summary.loc[row, column])
```

Results of using RFM for targeting

The next figure shows how the three strategies behaved:

	All customers	Target_ind	Target_seq
customer_id	10,000	4,563	4,657
purchase	1,779	1,324	1,335
revenue_campaign	$71,160.00	$52,960.00	$53,400.00
cost_goods	$34,156.80	$25,420.80	$25,632.00
shipping_cost	$10,674.00	$7,944.00	$8,010.00
marketing_cost	$20,000.00	$9,126.00	$9,314.00
profit	$6,329.20	$10,469.20	$10,444.00
ROMI	31.65%	114.72%	112.13%
Response Rate	17.79%	29.02%	28.67%

Figure 7.20 – ROMI summary

It will immediately stand out that by using RFM, you ended up targeting around 45% of the original customer base. This leads to an obvious consequence of revenue being lower in those cases. However, we need to be mindful of some other aspects. First, the response rates are much higher (around 18% versus 28-29%). Second, the marketing costs are lower, since you didn't have to spend on marketing for all of the customers. This leads us to the obvious consequence of profits being higher in both targeting strategies and sending to all customers. That can be seen from the return percentage: we went from a 31% ROMI to a ROMI of between 112% and 114%. This was achieved by using RFM to more efficiently choose the right targets for the campaign.

As we have seen, RFM is a very powerful and easy technique for selecting users for targeting that can lead to improvements in the costs and conversion rates of your campaigns.

Summary

Distance-based clustering models focus on grouping similar observations and rely heavily on the definition of the distance metric. These models struggle with categorical values, as it is challenging to calculate distances between categories. On the other hand, model-based clustering methods sort observations by simulating the underlying distributions, often proposing the number of clusters themselves. Comparing these models typically involves using metrics such as the BIC. Whether using distance-based or model-based methods, it's crucial to divide the data into test and training sets in classification models to prevent overfitting. Common challenges in classification models include class imbalance and the need for assessing variable importance, a feature where random forests excel.

RFM analysis serves as a powerful tool in a marketing strategy and is especially useful when the cost of reaching a customer is high. It allows businesses to focus on customers most likely to respond positively to campaigns, optimizing resource allocation and boosting ROMI. The analysis can be executed using either independent or sequential sorting, the latter being preferable for more even bin sizes. Additionally, RFM analysis aids in calculating the ROMI and determining the breakeven response rate, guiding you on which customers to target and how much to allocate for a marketing campaign.

In the following chapter, we will build upon and extend RFM, together with Bayesian statistical modeling, which we learned about in *Chapter 4, Econometrics and Causal Inference with Statsmodels and PyMC*, to evaluate the LTV of our customers.

Further reading

- *Data Analysis Using SQL and Excel – Second Edition*, by Gordon S.S. Linoff, Packt Publishing
- *Marketing Analytics* by Robert W. Palmatier, J. Andrew Petersen, and Frank Germann, Bloomsbury Academic

8

Customer Lifetime Value with PyMC Marketing

Customer Lifetime Value (CLV) is a forward-looking approach that allows analysts to estimate the value and profitability of customers. CLV equals the net present value of the future cash flows from a customer. It is used to estimate the value of a customer over the entire relationship with a company. It is used for customer profitability, segmentation, targeting and retention strategies, customer divestment, promotions, advertising, and pricing campaigns.

In this chapter, we will cover the following topics:

- The fundamentals of CLV and why analysts use them
- What's wrong with the CLV formula
- Beyond the CLV formula
- Implementing the BTYD model with PyMC Marketing

By the end of this chapter, you will be able to use PyMC Marketing's CLV classes to predict the lifetime value and purchase frequency of the users in your business, as well as what the pitfalls of a naïve approach are.

Technical requirements

You can find the code files for this chapter on GitHub at `https://github.com/PacktPublishing/Data-Analytics-for-Marketing/tree/main/Chapter08`.

Diving deeper into CLV

CLV is the net present value of the future cash flows from a customer. It is used to estimate the value of a customer over the entire relationship with a company. One needs to realize that not all customers are equally profitable. The idea behind CLV is fairly intuitive. Once you acquire a customer, you will earn some revenue from services sold to that customer. You will also spend some money on that customer – for example, on marketing, advertising, customer service, and so on. The difference between the revenue and the costs is the profit. The profit is the cash flow from that customer. The CLV is the net present value of all the future cash flows from that customer. Quantifying the CLV can be challenging because you will need to forecast the stream of cash flows generated by the customer over its entire lifetime. This is a difficult task because you will need to make assumptions about the future. You will need to make assumptions about the future revenue, costs, and discount rate.

CLV in practice

Consider the following example – Nick buys a snowboard at the beginning of every season. This year, he paid USD 500. Let's assume it costs USD 150 to make it, so the gross margin is USD 350.

Gross margin (M) = Price - Unit variable cost, that is, M = 500 - 150 = 350.

As Nick buys a snowboard every year, we can estimate the CLV as follows:

$$M_1 + M_2 + M_3 + \ldots = 350 + 350 + 350 + \ldots$$

However, you need to remember that the money you can earn in the future does not have the same value as the value you earn now – that is, you will need to discount the cashflows to account for the time value of money. The discount rate is the interest rate you would earn if you invested the money in a risk-free asset. The discount rate is usually between 5% and 15%. The discount rate is also called the cost of capital. The higher the discount rate, the lower the CLV. The lower the discount rate, the higher the CLV:

$$\frac{M_1}{(1+r)^1} + \frac{M_2}{(1+r)^2} + \frac{M_3}{(1+r)^3} + \ldots$$

where r is the discount rate.

Another aspect to consider is Nick's loyalty over time, which mainly diminishes over time. In other words, Nick's repeat business is not guaranteed, which we can capture by accounting for the probability that Nick will stay as a customer at time t:

$$\frac{M_1 \times p_1}{(1+r)^1} + \frac{M_2 \times p_1}{(1+r)^2} + \frac{M_3 \times p_1}{(1+r)^3} + \ldots$$

where p is the probability that Nick will stay as a customer at time t. This can be estimated from the retention rate, for instance, or a logistic regression.

If the retention rate is constant, then the CLV can be estimated as follows:

$$CLV_{Nick} = \sum_{t=1}^{\infty} \frac{M_t \times p^t}{(1+r)^t}$$

If you remember your mathematics classes, you will recognize the previous formula as a geometric series. The sum of a geometric series always converges to a finite value as long as $r < 1$. So, the preceding formula above can be rewritten as follows:

$$CLV_{Nick} = M\left[\frac{r}{1+r-p}\right]$$

If we assume a constant retention rate of 90% (0.9) for Nick staying as a customer, and 10% (0.1) as the discount rate, we'll have the following:

$$CLV = 350\left[\frac{0.1}{1+0.1-0.9}\right] = 1750$$

A question that frequently arises is, are we not overestimating the CLV? The answer is, no, if we correctly account for the probability of churn and the discount rate.

The preceding is the "standard" CLV formula, which assumes that the customer's margin and retention rate stay constant over time.

An alternative approach also commonly used is to assume that the initial cashflow, M, is certain and received at time $t = 0$. The CLV is then estimated as follows:

$$CLV_{Nick} = \sum_{t=0}^{\infty} \frac{M \times p^t}{(1+r)^t} = M\left[\frac{1+r}{1+r-p}\right]$$

This approach will yield a higher CLV because it assumes that the initial cashflow is certain.

Going back to our example, with the new assumption, we'll have the following:

$$CLV = 350\left[\frac{1+0.1}{1+0.1-0.9}\right] = 1925$$

Using CLV to calculate acquisition costs

A question that follows is, how much are you willing to spend to acquire this customer? Using AA as the acquisition cost, then:

$$CLV_{Nick} - AA \geq 0 \equiv M\left[\frac{1+r}{1+r-p}\right] - AA \geq 0$$

Intuitively, the maximum acquisition cost you are willing to spend is the total value of the CLV of the customer. This is the break-even point. If you spend more than this, you are losing money. If you spend less than this, you are making money. Looking at our example, we have calculated our LTV as 1925, so that is our break-even point. Any acquisition cost above that would lead us to a loss.

CLV and prospects

Not all prospects become customers. If you know your conversion rate α, then you can estimate the CLV of a prospect as follows:

$$CLV_{prospect} = \alpha\left[\sum_{t=0}^{\infty}\frac{M \times p^t}{(1 + r)^t}\right] = \alpha\left(M\left[\frac{1 + r}{1 + r - p}\right]\right)$$

If A is the acquisition cost of a prospect, then, how much you are willing to spend to acquire a prospect is as follows:

$$CLV_{prospect} - A \geq 0 \equiv \alpha\left(M\left[\frac{1 + r}{1 + r - p}\right]\right) - A \geq 0$$

You can also use the preceding logic to calculate what would be your break-even conversion rate. If you know your CLV and your acquisition cost, then you can calculate the break-even conversion rate as follows:

$$\alpha = \frac{A_{prospect}}{CLV_{client}}$$

CLV and incremental value

While it is difficult to calculate the incremental value of a campaign, if you can measure the CLV before and after the campaign, you can estimate the incremental value of the campaign. This is the difference between the CLV before and after the campaign:

$$Incrementalvalue = CLV_{after} - CLV_{before}$$

What's wrong with the CLV formula?

It is common for analysts to learn a formula to calculate CLV that is a generalization of the following:

$$CLV = \sum_{t=0}^{T}m\frac{r^t}{(1 + d)^t}$$

where m is the net cash flow per period, r is the retention rate, d is the discount rate, and T is the number of periods or time horizon.

But what are the pitfalls of this formula? Let's explore them next.

Issue 1

The actual CLV of a client only becomes evident once they cease to be a customer. Thus, any CLV calculation can only serve as an approximation of a customer's true worth.

Issue 2

Setting the summation's upper bound as T might not be ideal unless we intend to conclude our association with the client at that projected future date. Such an approach wouldn't fully capture a customer's projected CLV, as it neglects potential value beyond T. This limited perspective could be termed "truncated CLV."

An optimal upper boundary could be infinity, yielding the formula:

$$E(CLV) = m\sum_{t=0}^{\infty}\frac{r}{(1+d)}^t = \frac{m(1+d)}{1+d-r}$$

Alternatively, setting T to a significantly large value, such as 100 years, would come close to approximating the value obtained using an infinite series.

Issue 3

In the equation, the summation's lower bound is set at 0. A different version could set this bound to 1, resulting in the following:

$$E(CLV) = \sum_{t=1}^{T} m\frac{r^t}{(1+d)^t}$$

Shifting from 0 to 1 implies the omission of the initial transaction that marks the onset of a customer's association. Consequently, while the former equation captures the prospective client's CLV, the latter reflects the CLV of a newly onboarded client.

Issue 4

The equation presupposes a fixed retention rate, denoted by r. On the surface, this seems plausible, given the steady retention rates observed in corporate overviews. Yet, a deep dive into specific customer groups reveals fluctuations. In essence, the longer a customer's tenure, the more likely their continued association. The perceived steady retention rate is a byproduct of averaging across different customer cohorts.

The term r^t represents the likelihood of a customer continuing beyond the t period. Recognizing that retention rates aren't static, it would be apt to replace r^t with $\Pi_{i=0}^{t} r_i$, where r_i symbolizes the retention rate for the i period (and $r_0 = 1$).

Transitioning from assessing potential CLV to residual CLV mandates consideration of a client's "tenure." It implies that a client's residual CLV, after several renewals, will undoubtedly surpass that of a prospective client.

Issue 5

The equation not only presumes a constant retention rate over time but also assumes a definable retention rate. The retention rate is characterized as the proportion of retained clients to those at risk. Computing this metric requires knowing the current customer count and the attrition over a specific period.

For firms with contractual relationships, such as publishers or insurers, the loss of a client is discernible when contracts lapse or require renewal. However, many businesses operate in an environment where the exact point of customer attrition remains unclear. They merely witness purchasing inactivity, leaving them in the dark about whether a customer has ended the relationship or is simply on a purchasing hiatus.

Given this ambiguity, conventional CLV formulas are ill-suited for non-contractual relationships. While you can determine a repeat rate, it's not synonymous with retention. It merely underscores purchasing activity rather than the observed continuity or discontinuity of a customer association.

As highlighted, r^t essentially estimates the probability of a customer continuing beyond the t period. Using a repeat rate in lieu of a retention rate effectively evaluates the likelihood of a customer making subsequent purchases, which might undervalue their ongoing association. So, how can we get around these pitfalls when calculating CLV?

Beyond the CLV formula

What methods can we employ to refine the calculation of CLV? A logical first step is to revisit the definition of CLV, understood as "the present worth of the anticipated cash flows from a customer relationship," which is mathematically represented as follows:

$$E(CLV) = \sum_t expected\ net\ cashflow\ in\ period\ t | alive \times P(alive\ in\ period\ t) \times discount\ factor\ for\ period\ t$$

The formula is basically the expected net cashflow in period t, given that the customer is alive times the probability of the customer being alive at time t times a discount factor for period t.

The formula, as is, is of no practical use. We need to operationalize the terms. The best way to start with that is to look into the **Buy Till You Die (BTYD)** model for a solution.

The BTYD model

Before we delve into the BTYD model, we need to understand customer base classifications. Customer bases can be classified into two axes:

- **Opportunities for transactions**: They be either continuous or discrete
- **Type of relationship with customers**: They can be either contractual or non-contractual

Let's dig a bit deeper into these two axes.

Opportunities for transactions

Opportunities for transactions refer to how and when customers can make purchases, which can be categorized into continuous or discrete:

- **Continuous**: In a continuous setting, customers have the opportunity to make transactions at any point in time. This scenario is common in many retail environments where the store or service is always available, and customers can choose exactly when to make a purchase. The continuous model assumes that purchases can happen at any time, making the prediction of the next purchase time a continuous probability problem.

- **Discrete**: In a discrete setting, transactions occur at specific, often predetermined, intervals. This might apply to businesses that operate on a subscription model, such as monthly subscription boxes, where transactions happen at regular intervals (for example, monthly or quarterly). In this case, the model predicts the likelihood of a transaction within each discrete time period, rather than continuously over time.

Types of relationships with customers

The types of relationships with customers can be as follows:

- **Contractual**: A contractual relationship implies that there is a formal agreement between the business and the customer that specifies the terms of interactions, including the duration. Examples include gym memberships, phone contracts, and other subscription-based services where customers agree to engage over a specified period. In contractual relationships, customer churn (when a customer decides to leave) is clearly defined, as it occurs when a customer chooses not to renew their contract.

- **Non-contractual**: In non-contractual relationships, customers are not bound by a contract and can make purchase decisions freely without any long-term commitment. Retail shopping and dining at restaurants are typical examples. Churn is much harder to identify in non-contractual relationships because there's no explicit point at which a customer decides to "leave" — they simply might stop purchasing for various reasons, and distinguishing between a temporary pause and a permanent cessation of transactions can be challenging.

Understanding these classifications is critical for applying the BTYD model effectively for the following reasons:

- For **continuous, non-contractual** settings, models such as **BG/NBD (Beta-Geometric/ Negative Binomial Distribution)** are often used. They can handle the indefinite transaction opportunities and the lack of a formal customer-business bond.

- In **discrete, non-contractual** scenarios, the Pareto/NBD model might be more applicable, accommodating the regular transaction opportunities without a contractual commitment.

The potential combinations are listed in the following table:

Opportunities for transactions/ relationship	Non-contractual	Contractual
Continuous	Grocery purchases and doctor visits	Credit cards, student meal plans, and mobile phone plans
Discrete	Event attendance and prescription refills	Magazine subscriptions and insurance policies

Table 8.1 – Combinations between opportunities for transactions and relationship

You also need to take into account the purchase history of the customer.

We will explore the family of models, BG/NBD and GG models, to end at the predicted LTV, as shown in *Figure 8.1*:

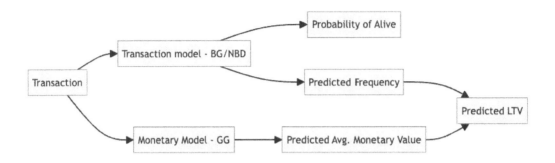

Figure 8.1 – The family of BTYD models to estimate the predicted LTV

Let's start with the Pareto/NBD model.

The Pareto/NBD model

This model was first developed in 1987 in the paper by Schmittlein, Morrison, and Colombo. It has some assumptions, as described next.

The transaction process

While active, the number of transactions made by a customer follows a Poisson process with the mean λ. Heterogeneity in the transaction rates is captured by the Gamma distribution $\Gamma(r, \alpha)$.

The dropout process

Each customer has an unobserved lifetime of length ω, which is distributed according to an exponential distribution with mean μ. Heterogeneity in the dropout rates is captured by the Gamma distribution $\Gamma(s, \beta)$.

The model we are after is actually the BG/NBD model, which is built upon this model.

The BG/NBD model

Introduced by Fader, Hardie, and Lee in 2005, this model is an extension of the Pareto/NBD model. It has some assumptions, as follows:

- **Transaction process**: The transaction process in this model is the same as in the Pareto/NDB model, described in the previous section.

- **Dropout process**: After any transaction, each customer becomes inactive with the probability p. The difference is that, in this model, the heterogeneity in the dropout rates is captured by the Beta distribution β *(a, b)*.

To estimate the model, we will need to use a set of purchase metrics, which will be familiar from the previous chapter, since they are the RFM metrics:

- **Frequency**: This refers to the total number of repeated purchases made by a customer. Specifically, it counts the number of periods in which a purchase was made.

- **T**: This denotes the customer's age in chosen time units. This is the time span between their first purchase and the conclusion of the examined period.

- **Recency**: This represents the age of the customer at the time of their last purchase. Specifically, it's the time elapsed between the initial and the latest purchase.

Assumptions in BG/NBD for frequency

While active, the gap between transactions is exponentially distributed with a transaction rate:

$$f\left(t_j \middle| t_{j-1}, \lambda\right) = \lambda e^{-\lambda(t_j - t_{j-1})},\ t_j \geq t_{j-1} \geq 0$$

Heterogeneity in the transaction rates is denoted by the Gamma distribution with the following pdf:

$$f(\lambda | r, \alpha) = \frac{\alpha^r \lambda^{r-1} e^{-\lambda \alpha}}{\Gamma(r)},\ \lambda > 0$$

Assumptions in BG/NBD for dropout

After any transaction, there's a probability (p) that a customer turns inactive. The differences in these dropout rates are illustrated by the Beta distribution with the pdf:

$$f(p | a, b) = \frac{\Gamma(a + b)}{\Gamma(a)\Gamma(b)} p^{a-1} (1 - p)^{b-1},\ 0 < p < 1$$

The transaction rate (λ) and dropout rate (p) are distinct for each customer and operate independently.

The predicted future purchases are mathematically expressed as follows:

$$E\left[Y(t) \middle| X = x, t_x, T, r, \alpha, a, b\right]$$

Now, we will use PyMC Marketing, which is a very useful port library to PyMC for lifetime.

Implementing the BTYD model using PyMC Marketing

Here's a detailed breakdown of the terms and metrics used in our data models:

- **Frequency**: This refers to the count of repeated purchases made by a customer. It's essential to note that the frequency is always one fewer than the total number of purchases. For instance, if a customer made three purchases in total, the frequency would be two. This is because we're specifically counting how many times they returned to make a purchase after their initial buy.

- **Customer Age (T)**: This metric, denoted as "T," signifies how long a customer has been with us. It's the duration between the customer's very first purchase and the end of the given period under study. For example, if a customer made their first purchase on January 1 and the study period ends on December 31, their customer age would be one year.

- **Recency**: Recency indicates the most recent interaction of a customer with our business, specifically when they last made a purchase. To calculate this, we measure the duration between the customer's first purchase (excluding any subsequent purchases) and their latest purchase. However, there's an exception – if a customer has made only one purchase, their recency is considered to be zero. This is because there hasn't been a subsequent purchase to measure recency against.

- **Monetary value**: This metric provides insight into the average spending of a customer. To calculate it, we sum up all the purchases a customer has made and then divide it by their total number of purchases. For example, if a customer made three purchases of $10, $20, and $30, their monetary value would be $20.

By understanding these terms, we can gain a deeper insight into customer behavior and tailor our strategies to better serve their needs.

Let's first import the necessary libraries we'll need for this exercise:

```
import arviz as az
import matplotlib.pyplot as plt
import numpy as np
import pandas as pd
import pymc as pm
from arviz.labels import MapLabeller
from lifetimes.datasets import
    load_cdnow_summary_data_with_monetary_value
from pymc_marketing import clv
```

PyMC is a Python library for Bayesian statistical modeling and probabilistic machine learning. PyMC Marketing is a python library built by the authors of PyMC to help with CLV modeling. ArviZ is a library for exploratory analysis of Bayesian models, which provides functions to visualize and analyze results.

We will now set up the plotting style and format for the notebook:

```
az.style.use("arviz-darkgrid")
%config InlineBackend.figure_format = "retina"
```

We will use the CDNOW dataset, which contains the purchase history of 2,377 customers who made at least two purchases from CDNOW in the period from June 1997 to February 1998:

```
data = load_cdnow_summary_data_with_monetary_value()
data['customer_id'] = data.index
data
```

As we can see in *Table 8.2*, the data contains the values for customer_id, frequency, recency, T, and monetary_value:

customer_id	frequency	recency	T	monetary_value	customer_id
1	2	30.43	38.86	22.35	1
2	1	1.71	38.86	11.77	2
3	0	0.00	38.86	0.00	3
4	0	0.00	38.86	0.00	4
5	0	0.00	38.86	0.00	5
...	...	...	...	...	...
2353	0	0.00	27.00	0.00	2353
2354	5	24.29	27.00	44.93	2354
2355	0	0.00	27.00	0.00	2355
2356	4	26.57	27.00	33.32	2356
2357	0	0.00	27.00	0.00	2357

Table 8.2 – The CDNOW dataset containing the values for customer_
id, frequency, recency, T, and monetary_value

We will now use the BG/NBD model to infer the frequency of repeat purchases. Let's just review the BG/NBD model. In non-contractual settings, customers make purchases intermittently, and businesses often don't know for certain when (or if) a customer has "churned" or stopped making purchases. The BG/NBD model provides a way to predict the future purchase behavior of customers based on their past purchasing history, allowing businesses to compute the expected number of future transactions and, subsequently, the CLV.

Before we jump into the actual code, let's review the key model components we need to implement:

- **Frequency and recency**:

  - **Frequency (f)**: The number of repeat transactions a customer has made. It's one fewer than the total number of transactions.

  - **Recency (r)**: The age of the customer when they made their most recent purchase. If a customer has only made one purchase, recency is zero.

- **The BG model for dropout**:

  - This component models the probability that a customer has "dropped out" or stopped buying

  - It's based on the observation that if a customer has bought recently, they are less likely to have dropped out than if their last purchase was a long time ago

- **The NBD model for transactions**:

  - This component models the number of transactions a customer is expected to make in a given future period

  - It takes into account the variations in purchasing behavior across customers

Now, you need to understand that this model has some key assumptions you should be aware of:

- While active, the number of transactions made by a customer follows a Poisson process with a transaction rate λ

- This means that customers have a constant transaction rate (λ) over time, which varies across customers

- Heterogeneity in transaction rates across customers follows a gamma distribution

- Customers may become inactive after any transaction, and the dropout process follows a geometric distribution

- The probability of dropping out is constant across transactions but varies across customers

- Heterogeneity in dropout probabilities across customers follows a beta distribution

- Transaction rate and dropout probability are independent across customers

The BG/NBD model is typically fit using historical transaction data, and once the parameters are estimated, it can be used to forecast future purchase behavior and calculate the CLV for individual customers or segments.

In this case, we just need to pass the data to the `BetaGeoModel` class and build the model:

```
bgm = clv.BetaGeoModel(
    data = data
)
bgm.build_model()
bgm
```

As we can see from the output, the model has been built with the following parameters:

```
BG/NBD
a ~ HalfFlat()
b ~ HalfFlat()
alpha ~ HalfFlat()
r ~ HalfFlat()
likelihood ~ Potential(f(r, alpha, b, a))
```

The standard priors for the four parameters use a HalfFlat distribution, which is essentially an unbounded positive uniform distribution. With smaller datasets, this prior might produce unlikely posterior results. To address this, you can employ more informative priors by creating custom PyMC distributions.

In this context, we'll swap out the default HalfFlat with the more stable HalfNormal priors, setting a standard deviation at 10. The shift from HalfFlat to HalfNormal priors when fitting the BG/NBD model in the PyMC marketing library is driven by the need for more informative priors, especially in scenarios involving smaller datasets. Here's why this change is important:

- **More informative priors**: The HalfFlat prior is essentially an unbounded positive uniform distribution. This means it assigns equal probability to all positive values, offering no additional information to guide the estimation of the parameters. This lack of constraint can be particularly problematic with smaller datasets, where the data alone may not be sufficient to accurately estimate the model parameters. The HalfNormal prior, on the other hand, is more informative. By specifying a mean (usually zero for a HalfNormal) and a standard deviation, it introduces additional knowledge into the model, suggesting that parameter values are more likely to be around zero and within a certain range, dictated by the standard deviation.

- **Reduced parameter uncertainty**: With HalfFlat priors, the lack of constraints can lead to high uncertainty in the parameter estimates. This uncertainty might result in a broader range of possible parameter values, making the model's predictions less precise. The HalfNormal distribution, with its specified standard deviation, concentrates more probability mass around lower values, thereby potentially reducing parameter uncertainty and leading to more reliable estimates.

- **Preventing unlikely posterior results**: In the absence of strong data signals (which is common with smaller datasets), models with HalfFlat priors might converge to unlikely or unrealistic posterior distributions. This can affect the reliability and interpretability of the model's outputs. By using HalfNormal priors, you effectively place a soft boundary on the parameter values, making it less likely for the model to produce unlikely posterior results.

- **Improving model convergence**: More informative priors can also aid in model convergence. When the parameter space is very large (as with HalfFlat priors), finding the posterior distribution that best fits the data can be more challenging and computationally intensive. The HalfNormal priors reduce the effective parameter space by focusing the search on more plausible values, which can help to achieve convergence more efficiently.

To customize the priors, you can provide a dictionary where the key represents the name of the prior. The corresponding value is another dictionary with two elements – `dist`, which denotes the PyMC distribution name, and `kwargs`, a potential dictionary detailing any parameters you'd like to incorporate into the distribution:

```
model_config = {
    "a_prior": {"dist": "HalfNormal", "kwargs": {"sigma": 10}},
    "b_prior": {"dist": "HalfNormal", "kwargs": {"sigma": 10}},
```

```
    "alpha_prior": {"dist": "HalfNormal", "kwargs": {"sigma": 10}},
    "r_prior": {
        "dist": "HalfNormal",
    },
}

bgm = clv.BetaGeoModel(data=data, model_config=model_config)
bgm.build_model()
bgm
```

We now have the priors we want to use for the model:

```
BG/NBD
a ~ HalfNormal(0, 10)
b ~ HalfNormal(0, 10)
alpha ~ HalfNormal(0, 10)
r ~ HalfNormal(0, 10)
likelihood ~ Potential(f(r, alpha, b, a))
```

Let's now proceed to fit the model:

```
bgm.fit()
bgm.fit_summary()
```

The table output represents a summary of the posterior distributions for the model parameters after fitting. Each parameter has statistics that help in understanding the model fit in *Table 8.3*:

	mean	sd	hdi_ 3%	hdi_ 97%	mcse_ mean	mcse_ sd	ess_ bulk	ess_ tail	r_hat
a	0.953	0.273	0.524	1.477	0.010	0.007	724.0	726.0	1.0
b	3.116	1.123	1.432	5.195	0.042	0.031	737.0	737.0	1.0
alpha	4.484	0.388	3.720	5.166	0.013	0.009	884.0	966.0	1.0
r	0.244	0.013	0.221	0.267	0.000	0.000	873.0	808.0	1.0

Table 8.3 – A summary of the posterior distributions for the model parameters after fitting.

The table contains the following columns:

- a, b, alpha, r: These are the parameters of the BG/NBD model:

    - a and b: Shape parameters for the Beta distribution of the purchasing behavior

    - alpha and r: Parameters for the Gamma distribution representing the lifetime of the customers

- `mean`: The average value of the sampled values for each parameter from the posterior distribution.

- `sd`: The standard deviation of the sampled values, giving a sense of the spread or uncertainty in the parameter estimates.

- `hdi_3%` and `hdi_97%`: These represent the 3rd and 97th percentiles of the sampled values, effectively giving a 94% **Highest (Posterior) Density Interval (HDI)**. This interval is a region of parameter space where 94% of the sampled values lie, offering a measure of the uncertainty of the parameter estimate.

- `mcse_mean` and `mcse_sd`: The Monte Carlo standard error for the mean and standard deviation. This gives a measure of the uncertainty of the mean and standard deviation estimates due to the finite size of the sample.

- `ess_bulk` and `ess_tail`: The **Effective Sample Size (ESS)** for the bulk and tail of the distribution, respectively. ESS is a measure of the number of independent samples you could expect to get, given the amount of correlation in the sampled values. Higher values indicate more "effective" samples and, typically, better convergence.

- `r_hat`: The potential scale reduction factor. It compares the variance of chains to the variance within chains. For a well-mixed chain, this will be close to 1.0. If it's much above 1.0, it might be a sign that the chains have not mixed well and may not have converged.

In this specific output, all the `r_hat` values are 1.0, indicating good convergence. The HDI gives a range within which we expect the true value of the parameter to lie with 94% probability, and the ESS values seem reasonably high, suggesting the chains are well-mixed.

We can also plot the distributions and parameters of the model, which you can see in *Figure 8.2*:

```
az.plot_posterior(bgm.fit_result);
```

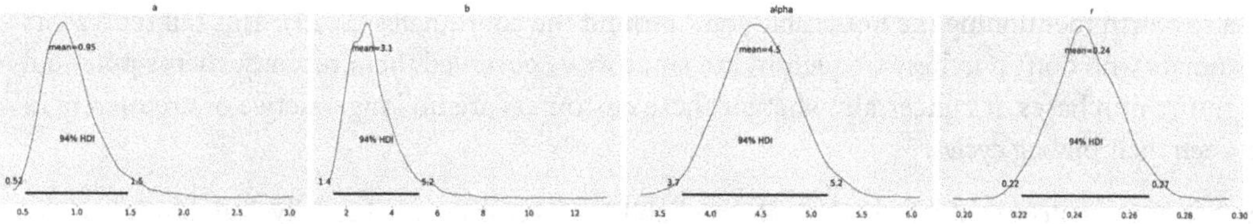

Figure 8.2 – The distributions and parameters of the model

A useful plot is also the expected number of future purchases for 1 unit of time, as shown in *Figure 8.3*:

```
clv.plot_frequency_recency_matrix(bgm);
```

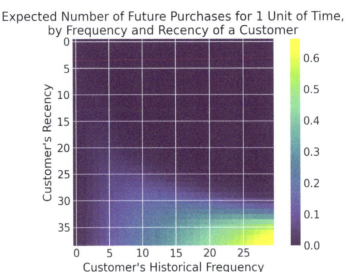

Figure 8.3 – The expected number of future purchases for 1 unit of time

Observing the data, note that a customer who has made 25 purchases and whose most recent purchase occurred at the 35-week mark (assuming the individual's age is 35 weeks) is one of your most valuable customers, situated in the bottom-right quadrant. Conversely, your least engaged customers can be identified in the top-right corner. These customers made numerous purchases in a short span and have been inactive for several weeks.

It's also worth mentioning the noticeable "tail" around the coordinates (5, 25). This tail represents customers who don't purchase frequently, but since we've observed them recently, there's potential for future purchases. It's uncertain whether these customers are no longer active or are merely in between their buying cycles.

An interesting outcome of this model is the probability of a customer being "alive," and by "alive" we mean that the customer is still active or has not churned, which is shown in *Figure 8.4*:

```
clv.plot_probability_alive_matrix(bgm);
```

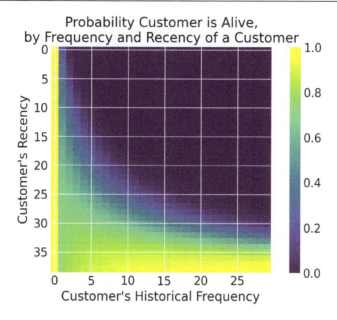

Figure 8.4 – The probability of a customer being alive

From the probability alive matrix, it's evident that users who made numerous purchases in the distant past are probably not coming back. Conversely, customers who have made a few purchases recently are likely to return. This is a useful insight for customer retention strategies.

Finally, this type of model can allow us to forecast the expected number of purchases:

```
num_purchases = bgm.expected_num_purchases(
    customer_id = data.index,
    t = 1,
    frequency=data["frequency"],
    recency=data["recency"],
    T=data["T"]
)
```

Let's extract a copy of the data and add the expected number of purchases to it:

```
sdata = data.copy()
sdata["expected_purchases"] = num_purchases.mean(("chain", "draw")
    ).values
```

Finally, we sort the data by the expected number of purchases and show the top 10 customers, for ease of visualization:

```
sdata.sort_values(by="expected_purchases").tail(10)
```

We can see from *Table 8.4* the expected purchases for the top 10 customers, in the next period:

customer_id	frequency	recency	T	monetary_value	customer_id	expected_purchases
1017	12	32.43	33.43	12.86	1017	0.292810
693	13	34.43	35.00	42.44	693	0.308975
813	13	33.86	34.29	28.62	813	0.315543
1413	14	30.29	31.57	19.01	1413	0.356221
1539	14	29.86	30.86	18.13	1539	0.366560
509	18	35.14	35.86	78.63	509	0.420478
841	19	34.00	34.14	29.49	841	0.470597
1981	17	28.43	28.86	48.23	1981	0.481463
157	29	37.71	38.00	26.26	157	0.657209
1516	26	30.86	31.00	39.97	1516	0.704759

Table 8.4 – The expected purchases for the top 10 customers, in the next period

We can also plot the uncertainty of the expected number of purchases for a subset of customers, as shown in *Figure 8.5*:

```
ids = [841, 1981, 157, 1516]
ax = az.plot_posterior(num_purchases.sel(customer_id=ids),
    grid=(2, 2));

for axi, id in zip(ax.ravel(), ids):
    axi.set_title(f"Customer: {id}", size=20)
plt.suptitle("Expected number of purchases in the next period",
    fontsize=28, y=1.05);
```

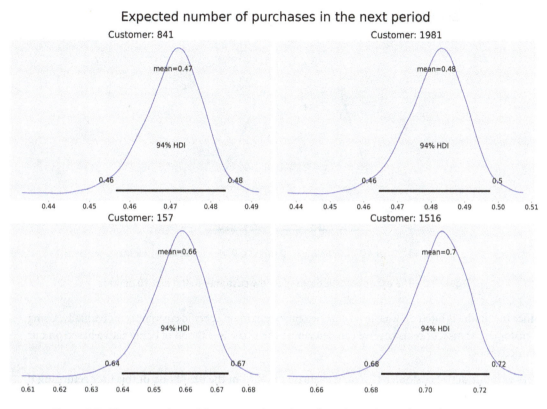

Figure 8.5 – The uncertainty of the expected number of purchases for a subset of customers

Predicting the expected number of purchases for a new customer

We can make use of such a model to forecast what the purchase behavior of a new customer would be. For example, we predict the expected number of purchases of a new customer in the first 10 periods in the following snippet, with the results shown in *Figure 8.6*:

```
az.plot_posterior(
    bgm.expected_num_purchases_new_customer(t=10)
);
plt.title('Expected purchases of a new customer in the first 10
    periods');
```

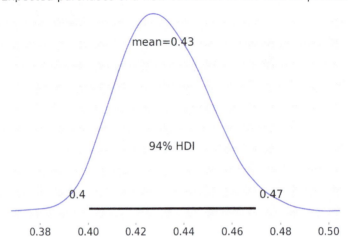

Figure 8.6 – The expected purchases of a new customer in the first 10 periods

Since the model is fitted on user-level data, we can zoom in on specific customers individually. Using a customer's transaction history, we can determine their past likelihood of being active based on our trained model.

Let's examine active customer 1516 and evaluate the shift in the likelihood of this user returning if they make no purchases over the next nine time periods:

```
customer_1516 = data.loc[1516]
customer_1516
```

This will give us the following output:

```
frequency 26.00
recency 30.86
T 31.00
monetary_value 39.97
customer_id 1516.00
Name: 1516, dtype: float64
```

We can see the purchase history of this customer in *Table 8.5* using the following code:

```
customer_1516_history = pd.DataFrame(
    dict(
        ID=np.full(10, 1516, dtype="int"),
        frequency=np.full(10, customer_1516["frequency"], dtype="int"),
        recency=np.full(10, customer_1516["recency"]),
        T=(np.arange(-1, 9) + customer_1516["T"]).astype("int")
```

```
    )
)
customer_1516_history
```

	ID	frequency	recency	T
0	1516	26	30.86	30
1	1516	26	30.86	31
2	1516	26	30.86	32
3	1516	26	30.86	33
4	1516	26	30.86	34
5	1516	26	30.86	35
6	1516	26	30.86	36
7	1516	26	30.86	37
8	1516	26	30.86	38
9	1516	26	30.86	39

Table 8.5 – The purchase history of customer 1516

Now, we are going to compute the probability of this customer being alive in the next nine periods, as shown in *Figure 8.7*:

```
p_alive = bgm.expected_probability_alive(
    customer_id = customer_1516_history["ID"],
    frequency = customer_1516_history["frequency"],
    recency = customer_1516_history["recency"],
    T = customer_1516_history["T"],
)
az.plot_hdi(customer_1516_history["T"], p_alive, color="C0")
plt.plot(customer_1516_history["T"], p_alive.mean(("draw", "chain")),
    marker = "o")
plt.axvline(customer_1516_history["recency"].iloc[0], c="black",
    ls="--", label="Purchase")

plt.title("Probability Customer 1516 will purchase again")
plt.xlabel("T")
plt.ylabel("p")
plt.legend();
```

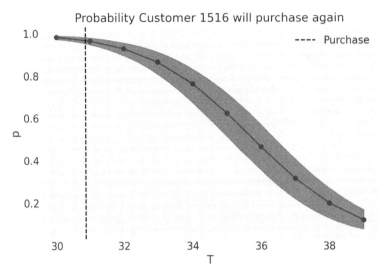

Figure 8.7 – The probability that customer 1516 will purchase again

We can see that, if no purchases are made in the next nine weeks, the model has low confidence that the costumer will ever return. However, if the customer makes a purchase in the next nine weeks, the model will be more confident that the customer will return. Let's try it out, by adding a purchase and changing the history, as shown in *Table 8.6*:

```
customer_1516_history["frequency"].iloc[-3:] += 1
customer_1516_history["recency"].iloc[-3:] = \
    customer_1516_history["T"].iloc[-3] - 0.5
customer_1516_history
```

	ID	frequency	recency	T
0	1516	26	30.86	30
1	1516	26	30.86	31
2	1516	26	30.86	32
3	1516	26	30.86	33
4	1516	26	30.86	34
5	1516	26	30.86	35
6	1516	26	30.86	36
7	1516	28	36.50	37
8	1516	28	36.50	38
9	1516	28	36.50	39

Table 8.6 – The purchase history of customer 1516, with a new purchase in the last three periods

Now, we recompute the probability of this customer being alive in the next nine periods, as shown in *Figure 8.8*:

```
p_alive = bgm.expected_probability_alive(
customer_id = customer_1516_history["ID"],
frequency = customer_1516_history["frequency"],
recency = customer_1516_history["recency"],
T = customer_1516_history["T"],
)
az.plot_hdi(customer_1516_history["T"], p_alive, color="C0")
plt.plot(customer_1516_history["T"], p_alive.mean(("draw", "chain")),
    marker = "o")
plt.axvline(customer_1516_history["recency"].iloc[0], c="black",
    ls="--", label="Purchase")
plt.axvline(customer_1516_history["recency"].iloc[-1], c="black",
    ls="--")

plt.title("Probability Customer 1516 will purchase again")
plt.xlabel("T")
plt.ylabel("p")
plt.legend();
```

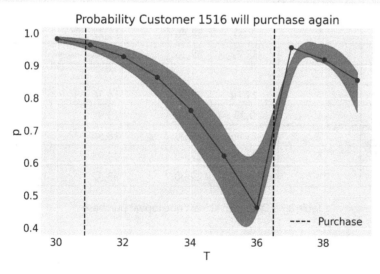

Figure 8.8 – The probability that customer 1516 will purchase again,
with a new purchase in the last three periods

From the preceding graph, note that customer 1516 makes a purchase around week 36.5, approximately 6 weeks after their last logged purchase at 30.86 weeks, as per the data. This results in a swift rise in the likelihood of the customer coming back!

Essentially, with each purchase, the chance of a customer coming back for another purchase intensifies. Conversely, if a period passes without any purchase from the customer, their probability of returning diminishes over time.

Estimating the CLV

In our previous analysis, we concentrated solely on the occurrence of transactions, without considering the monetary worth of each transaction. To evaluate transaction values, the Gamma-Gamma model can be employed. This requires a summary of the monetary values (such as profits or revenues) associated with each transaction.

The model presupposes that we've observed at least one transaction for every customer. Therefore, we exclude those with no repeat purchases, as we can see in *Table 8.7*:

```
nonzero_data = data.query("frequency>0")
nonzero_data
```

customer_ id	frequency	recency	T	monetary_ value	customer_ id
1	2	30.43	38.86	22.35	1
2	1	1.71	38.86	11.77	2
6	7	29.43	38.86	73.74	6
7	1	5.00	38.86	11.77	7
9	2	35.71	38.86	25.55	9
...	...	...	...	...	...
2348	7	24.14	27.00	16.36	2348
2349	1	9.29	27.00	13.97	2349
2350	2	21.86	27.00	18.56	2350
2354	5	24.29	27.00	44.93	2354
2356	4	26.57	27.00	33.32	2356

Table 8.7 – Data with at least one repeat purchase

The Gamma-Gamma model requires a "data" parameter, which is a pandas DataFrame consisting of three columns. These columns capture the group's expected average expenditure and the anticipated individual deviation around this average. Similar to the BG/NBD model, HalfFlat priors are used for these parameters. However, these might be overly broad for smaller datasets. While we'll stick to the default priors in this instance, it's possible to customize them, as demonstrated in the BG/NBD example earlier:

```
dataset = pd.DataFrame({
    "customer_id": nonzero_data.index,
    "mean_transaction_value": nonzero_data["monetary_value"],
    "frequency": nonzero_data["frequency"]
})

gg = clv.GammaGammaModel(
    data = dataset
)
gg.build_model()
gg
```

This produces the following output, showing us the priors:

```
Gamma-Gamma Model (Mean Transactions)
p ~ HalfFlat()
q ~ HalfFlat()
v ~ HalfFlat()
likelihood ~ Potential(f(q, p, v))
```

Let's now fit the model:

```
gg.fit()
```

We can see from *Table 8.8* the estimated parameters of the model:

	mean	sd	hdi_ 3%	hdi_ 97%	mcse_ mean	mcse_ sd	ess_ bulk	ess_ tail	r_hat
p	6.408	1.408	4.110	9.113	0.078	0.057	380.0	363.0	1.0
q	3.787	0.301	3.255	4.365	0.015	0.011	394.0	452.0	1.0
v	16.189	4.518	7.986	24.685	0.236	0.167	347.0	334.0	1.0

Table 8.8 – The estimated parameters of the Gamma-Gamma model

Let's now visualize the parameters of the model, as shown in *Figure 8.9*:

```
az.plot_posterior(gg.fit_result);
```

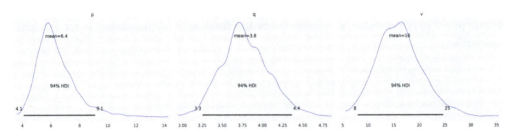

Figure 8.9 – The parameters of the Gamma-Gamma model

Now, in the same way we previously predicted the expected purchase behavior, we can now predict the expected spend of a customer, as shown in *Table 8.9*:

```
expected_spend = gg.expected_customer_spend(
    customer_id = data.index,
    mean_transaction_value=data["monetary_value"],
    frequency=data["frequency"]
)
az.summary(expected_spend.isel(customer_id=range(10)), kind="stats")
```

	mean	sd	hdi_3%	hdi_97%
x[1]	24.720	0.540	23.621	25.670
x[2]	19.024	1.389	16.400	21.692
x[3]	35.205	0.917	33.527	36.980
x[4]	35.205	0.917	33.527	36.980
x[5]	35.205	0.917	33.527	36.980
x[6]	71.370	0.638	70.218	72.626
x[7]	19.024	1.389	16.400	21.692
x[8]	35.205	0.917	33.527	36.980
x[9]	27.328	0.413	26.518	28.072
x[10]	35.205	0.917	33.527	36.980

Table 8.9 – The expected spend of the top 10 customers

Let's plot the expected spend of the top 10 customers, as shown in *Figure 8.10*:

```
labeller = MapLabeller(var_name_map={"x": "customer"})
az.plot_forest(expected_spend.isel(customer_id=(range(10))),
```

```
        combined=True, labeller=labeller)
plt.xlabel("Expected mean spend");
```

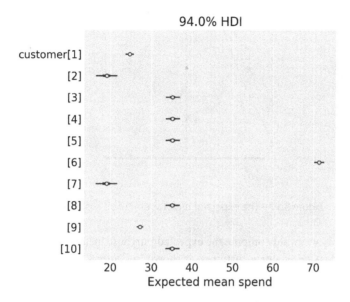

Figure 8.10 – The expected spend of the top 10 customers

We can also look at the average spend across all players, as shown in *Table 8.10*:

```
az.summary(expected_spend.mean("customer_id"), kind="stats")
```

	mean	sd	hdi_3%	hdi_97%
x	35.274	0.623	34.125	36.466

Table 8.10 – The average spend across all players

We can also see it visually, as shown in *Figure 8.11*:

```
az.plot_posterior(expected_spend.mean("customer_id"))
plt.axvline(expected_spend.mean(), color="k", ls="--")
plt.title("Expected mean spend of all customers");
```

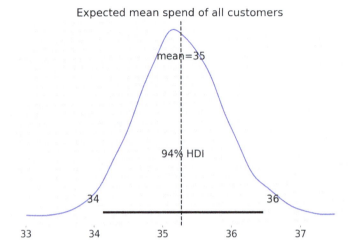

Figure 8.11 – The expected mean spend of all customers

Finally, in the same way we could compute the expected purchase history of a new customer, we can compute the expected spend of a new customer, as shown in *Figure 8.12*:

```
az.plot_posterior(
    gg.expected_new_customer_spend()
)
plt.title("Expected mean spend of a new customer");
```

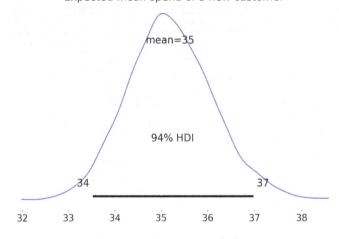

Figure 8.12 – The expected mean spend of a new customer

We can now combine the BG/NBD and Gamma-Gamma models to estimate the CLV of each customer. The CLV is the total value a customer is expected to generate for a business over their lifetime:

```
clv_estimate = gg.expected_customer_lifetime_value(
    transaction_model=bgm,
    customer_id=data.index,
    mean_transaction_value=data["monetary_value"],
    frequency=data["frequency"],
    recency=data["recency"],
    T=data["T"],
    time=12,
    discount_rate=0.01, # monthly discount rate ~ 12.7% annually
    freq="W"
)
```

Note that this relies on the discounted cash flow model, adjusting for the cost of capital. Let's take a look at the estimates, as shown in *Table 8.11*:

```
az.summary(clv_estimate.isel(customer_id=range(10)), kind="stats")
```

	mean	sd	hdi_3%	hdi_97%
x[1]	36.110	1.665	33.009	39.346
x[2]	4.874	0.623	3.858	6.175
x[3]	8.421	0.442	7.591	9.225
x[4]	8.421	0.442	7.591	9.225
x[5]	8.421	0.442	7.591	9.225
x[6]	268.812	29.943	213.217	324.995
x[7]	7.164	0.799	5.670	8.654
x[8]	8.421	0.442	7.591	9.225
x[9]	43.099	1.696	40.219	46.652
x[10]	8.421	0.442	7.591	9.225

Table 8.11 – The estimated CLV of the top 10 customers

We can plot the estimated CLV of the top 10 customers, as shown in *Figure 8.13*:

```
az.plot_forest(clv_estimate.isel(customer_id=range(10)),
    combined=True,
    labeller=labeller)
plt.xlabel("Expected CLV");
```

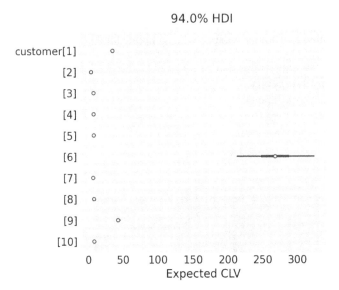

Figure 8.13 – The estimated CLBV of the top 10 customers

We now have the expected lifetime value of our customers, on a per-customer basis.

Summary

In this chapter, we reviewed the basics of CLV, what its uses are, and the basics of how to calculate it, from a merely financial perspective. We then moved on to the pitfalls and issues with such an approach, discussing an alternative family of models, the BTYD models, and how to implement them in Python.

In the next chapter, we will discuss customer satisfaction analysis, where we will dig deeper into how to design and analyze customer surveys.

Further reading

- *"Counting Your Customers" the Easy Way: An Alternative to the Pareto/NBD Model* by Peter S. Fader, Bruce G.S. Hardie, and Ka Lok Lee, 2005

- *Marketing Analytics: Based on first principles* by Robert Palmatier, J. Andrew Petersen, and Frank German, Bloomsbury Academic

- *BG/NBD Model in PyMC* by Juan Orduz

Customer Survey Analysis

Analyzing customer surveys is a vital part of market research, enabling organizations to grasp their customers' needs, preferences, and levels of satisfaction. This process, which involves gathering data via surveys and dissecting the outcomes, aims to enhance the customer experience. By understanding customer sentiments, businesses can pinpoint improvement areas and make strategic decisions to bolster customer satisfaction and loyalty, ultimately improving customer experience, in order to increase customer satisfaction and loyalty. It can also lead to insights into how to improve the product or service and how to better target and acquire new customers.

In this chapter, we will discuss the steps involved in conducting a customer survey and analyzing the results. You will gain a good understanding of the different types of survey methods, how to design a survey, and how to analyze the results. You will also learn about the different types of measurement scales and how to ensure the reliability and validity of the survey data. We will discuss the different types of sampling methods and how to calculate the optimal sample size for a survey. Finally, we'll discuss known issues with NPS as a measure of customer loyalty.

Specifically, we will cover the following topics:

- Steps in customer survey analysis
- Questionnaire construction
- Reliability and validity
- How to do sampling
- Customer loyalty and NPS methodology
- Factor analysis

By the end of this chapter, you will have the knowledge and tools to understand how to conduct a good survey analysis and identify weaknesses in existing surveys.

Technical requirements

The code files for this chapter are available on GitHub at `https://github.com/PacktPublishing/Data-Analytics-for-Marketing/tree/main/Chapter09`.

Steps in customer survey analysis

Customer satisfaction analysis (or customer survey analysis), like any other analysis, is a process that you, as an analyst, need to follow and iterate. There are six steps involved in conducting a customer survey analysis:

1. **Define the objectives of the survey**: The first step in conducting a customer survey analysis is to define the objectives of the survey. This will help you determine the type of data that needs to be collected, the target audience, and the questions that will be asked. The objectives of the survey should be specific, measurable, and aligned with the goals of the organization.

2. **Design the survey questions**: Once the survey method has been selected, the next step is to design the survey questions. The questions should be designed to gather the information needed to meet the objectives of the survey. They should be clear, concise, and easy to understand. Organizations should also consider using a mix of open-ended and closed-ended questions to gather both qualitative and quantitative data.

3. **Choose the right survey method**: There are several survey methods that organizations can use to collect data from customers, including online surveys, phone surveys, and in-person surveys. When choosing the survey method, organizations should consider factors such as the target audience, the amount of time available, and the resources available. Online surveys are often the most convenient and cost-effective option, but organizations may also choose to use a combination of methods to reach a wider range of customers.

4. **Distribute the survey**: The next step is to distribute the survey to the target audience. Organizations can use a variety of channels to distribute the survey, including email, social media, and direct mail. The survey should be distributed to a representative sample of the target audience, and organizations should ensure that the survey is accessible to all participants.

5. **Analyze the results**: After gathering the survey data, the subsequent action is to scrutinize the outcomes. This process entails arranging and summarizing the data, spotting trends and patterns, and deducing the implications of the results. You have various methods and instruments for survey data analysis, such as statistical evaluation, data visualization, and sentiment analysis.

6. **Communicate the results**: Finally, organizations should communicate the results of the survey to stakeholders, including employees, customers, and decision makers. The results should be presented in a clear and concise manner, and organizations should highlight the key findings and recommendations for improvement. The results should also be used to inform decision making and drive action to improve the customer experience.

Step 1 is about defining the objectives of the survey. This is an important step in the process, as it will determine the type of data that needs to be collected, the target audience, and the questions that will be asked. The objectives of the survey should be specific, measurable, and aligned with the goals of the organization. Given this book is about the actual implementation of analysis methods, for this chapter we will focus on *steps 2 to 6*.

Let's look at survey construction and design in more detail.

Questionnaire construction

The right questionnaire is critical to the success of a survey. While it is easy to skip this step, we need to delve deeper into the construction of the questionnaire. If the design is bad, then we will collect bad data, and the analysis will be flawed. The first things we should be aware of are the fundamental principles of design.

Principles of questionnaire design

A questionnaire should have the following characteristics:

- Have a collection of precise inquiries that the participants are both capable and willing to respond to

- Support for efficient data management by streamlining the recording, coding, and analysis of survey responses

- Provide the information and data needed to answer the questions that the researcher seeks to answer

A questionnaire consists of a structured series of questions designed to collect information from participants, thereby providing the essential data needed to achieve the goals of the research inquiry. The various methods of conducting surveys and interviews each have their unique advantages and disadvantages.

- Starting with **personal face-to-face interviews**, they offer several benefits, such as flexibility in obtaining data, the personal nature of a face-to-face encounter, and the ability to immediately clear any doubts. Such interviews help in arousing and maintaining interest, building rapport, and using visual aids. They also allow for clarifying misunderstandings and probing for more complete answers. However, they come with drawbacks such as the potential for interviewer bias, response bias, significant time requirements, and the fact that the cost per completed interview tends to be high.

- **Telephone interviews**, on the other hand, can be conducted quickly and generally have a low non-response rate. They are less expensive than personal interviews and still allow for doubts to be cleared and misunderstandings to be clarified, along with probing for more complete answers. However, they also suffer from interviewer bias, the need to keep calls as short as possible, and difficulty in using visual aids, and they may be viewed as disrespectful by some respondents. Additionally, obtaining an accurate sample can be challenging.

- **Mail surveys** offer the advantage of covering a broad respondent base and are generally lower in cost compared to personal and telephone interviews. They often lead to more thought-out responses, particularly compared to online surveys, and can be more effective in dealing with sensitive topics, especially if anonymity is maintained. The disadvantages include potentially high costs per survey, the possibility of questions being misinterpreted, the inability to control the identity of the respondent, difficulty in compiling an accurate mailing list, and a high non-response rate, as many people do not mail back the questionnaire.

- Finally, **internet surveys** provide a fast turnaround in administering the survey, relatively low costs, immediate return upon completion, and flexible design options, allowing for different questions based on previous answers. There are inexpensive online solutions available as well. However, they too have their downsides, such as a high non-response rate, risk of misinterpretation of questions, respondents not giving answers much thought, and the inability to control for the identity of the respondent.

Types of questions

In survey design, questions are broadly categorized into two types: open-ended and closed-ended, each with unique features and further subdivisions in the case of closed-ended questions.

Open-ended questions

Open-ended questions allow respondents to express themselves in their own words. This trait makes them particularly suitable for exploratory research where detailed and nuanced responses are required. However, the freedom they offer comes with challenges. Analyzing these responses can be difficult and time-consuming due to their varied and unstructured nature. Coding these responses for statistical analysis is also challenging, and comparing answers across different respondents can be problematic due to the diversity in their expressions and points of view.

Closed-ended questions

Closed-ended questions, in contrast, present respondents with a predetermined list of answers to choose from. This structured approach simplifies the analysis process, as the responses are uniform and easier to code and quantify. It also facilitates an easier comparison of responses across different respondents, as each participant is selecting from the same set of options. These qualities make closed-ended questions a practical choice for surveys where quick, straightforward analysis and comparability are important.

Closed-ended questions can be further broken down into specific types:

- Dichotomous questions are the simplest form, offering respondents a choice between two options, often a binary choice such as "Yes" or "No"

- Multiple-choice questions provide a broader range of options, allowing respondents to select from several predetermined answers

- Scaled response questions offer a range of options on a scale, typically used to measure intensity or frequency, such as levels of agreement or satisfaction

Each of these types of closed-ended questions serves different purposes and can be used effectively depending on the survey's objectives.

The scales of closed-ended questions depend on the question being asked. You have four types of scales:

- **Nominal scales**: They are used where the answer choices are named but they do not have an order or direction.

- **Ordinal scales**: They have an order, and said order is important. For example, given a list of brands, the interviewee is asked to rank them in order of preference.

- **Interval scales**: They also have an order, and the difference between each answer choice is known. An example of an interval scale is temperature in degrees Celsius. In marketing research, it is common to use Likert scales, named after social psychologist Rensis Likert. These scales are commonly constructed with five, seven, or nine points and are typically treated as interval scales in analysis.

- **Ratio scales**: They are the same as interval scales but they also have a true zero. For example, "How much do you spend on groceries per month?"

Asking questions

It is critical to make sure that the right kind of questions are asked and that the questions are worded properly. The wording should be clear, the question should not bias the respondent, the question should be easy to understand, and the respondent should be able and willing to answer the question.

The following are examples of badly worded questions and what the best practice should be:

- **Ambiguity in question content**: "Do you own stocks? Yes/No" can be interpreted as livestock ownership rather than financial stock.

  Best practice: Be *specific* to avoid misunderstandings. A better question would explicitly state "financial stocks" to clarify the context.

- **Double-barreled questions**: "Do you think Coca-Cola is a tasty and refreshing soft drink? Yes/No" asks about taste and refreshment simultaneously.

  Best practice: Split complex questions. Consider dividing it into two separate questions about taste and then refreshment.

- **Leading questions**: "Do you think that patriotic Americans should buy imported cars when that would put American workers out of work? Yes/No" nudges towards a particular answer.

> **Best practice**: Maintain *neutrality*. Reword it to "What are your thoughts on Americans buying imported cars?"

- **Lack of contextual clarity**: "How far do you live from campus?" is vague without considering the transport mode.

  Best practice: Include *context*. A clearer question would specify the type of commute.

- **Overgeneralization**: "What is your marital status?" can be too broad.

  Best practice: Offer explicit choices. Provide options such as single, married, divorced, and so on to capture the respondent's status accurately.

- **Recall difficulty**: "How many times in the last six months have you eaten dinner away from home?" demands extensive memory.

  Best practice: Simplify recall requirements. It's more efficient to ask about dining out frequency over the past month with specific frequency options.

- **Assumption of knowledge**: "The National Bureau of Consumer Complaints provides an effective means for consumers to obtain a refund or replacement. Agree/Disagree" presumes respondent awareness.

  Best practice: Avoid assumptions. Include an option for "Don't know" or explain the entity before asking for opinions.

- **Sensitive or personal information**: "How many glasses of alcohol did you consume last Friday?" may inhibit honest answers.

  Best practice: Use third-person framing. Ask how much alcohol the respondent believes people typically consume, which can lead to more candid responses.

- **Simplicity and comprehension**: Consider a question such as "What is your appraisal of the efficacy of the current modalities employed in the facilitation of remote work?". Complex or jargon-filled questions can confuse respondents, so questions should be understandable to all participants.

  Best practice: Use clear, simple language. For example, say "How effective do you find the current methods for working from home?"

By adhering to these guidelines, surveys and questionnaires can be more effectively designed, leading to higher quality and more reliable data.

Questionnaire design—layout

Questionnaires should be designed to appear as short as possible. One common practice is to use a multiple-grid layout where familiar questions and responses are grouped together in a grid format. You should also use a funnel approach, starting from broad questions and moving to narrower questions. This is done to build rapport with the respondent and to make the respondent more comfortable with the survey. Tough and important questions should be placed in the middle of the survey since at that stage the respondent is likely committed to completing the survey. Sensitive and demographic questions should be asked at the end to avoid making the respondent uncomfortable early on in the survey.

You can find a summary of the types of questions to place in which location in *Table 9.1*:

Location	Type	Purpose/function	Example
Starting questions	Broad, general questions	To break the ice	Do you own a DVD player?
Next few questions	Simple and direct	To reassure the respondent that the survey is simple and easy	What brands of DVD players did you consider when you bought it?
Questions up to a third of the survey	Focused questions	Relate more to the research objectives	What attributes did you consider when you bought your DVD player?
Major portion of the survey	Focused questions, may be difficult or complex	To obtain the most information required for the research	Rank the following attributes in order of importance when you bought your DVD player
Last few questions	Personal and sensitive questions	To obtain classification and demographic information	What is the highest level of education you attained?

Table 9.1 – Location versus purpose of questions in a survey

One also needs to be aware of response formats.

Response formats

There are different response formats that can be used in a questionnaire. The most common formats are:

- Thurstone method of equal-appearing intervals
- Guttman's scalogram approach
- Checklist format
- Likert scaling method

The first two are more laborious to implement and are not commonly used, so they will stay out of the scope of this chapter. Let's discuss the remaining two formats:

- **Checklist format**: The checklist format is the simplest format. It is used when the researcher wants to know if the respondent has done something or not. For example, "Have you ever purchased a product from our company? Yes/No".

- **Likert scaling method**: The Likert scaling method is the most common response format. It is used when the researcher wants to know the degree to which the respondent agrees or disagrees with a statement. For example, "I am satisfied with the quality of the product I purchased from your company. Strongly agree / Agree / Neutral / Disagree / Strongly disagree". The scale can be constructed with five, seven, or nine points. The more points, the more granular the scale, but the more difficult it is for the respondent to answer the question.

From a statistical standpoint, Likert scales provide more reliable data than checklist formats. However, they are more difficult to analyze.

An important aspect that you, as an analyst, should not overlook is the reliability and validity of the questionnaire. Let's delve deeper into this in the next section.

Reliability and validity

When we develop questionnaires, it is important to ensure that the data collected is reliable and valid. Reliability refers to the extent to which a measure is free from random error and therefore provides consistent results. Validity indicates how well a question measures what it is specifically designed to assess.

There are different sources of errors and corresponding estimates of reliability as presented in *Table 9.2*:

Source of error	What are we asking?	Estimate of reliability	How to calculate
Time-specific	Is there stability in customer satisfaction over time	Test-retest	Correlation between the same survey on different occasions
Item-specific	Can the items generalize to all possible?	Parallel forms	Correlation between two different forms of the same questionnaire
Internal consistency	Are the items measuring the same construct?	Split-half	Correlation between two halves of the survey

Table 9.2 – Types of error and reliability estimates

Reliability and classical measurement theory

When developing a questionnaire, you want to make sure the data obtained is free from random errors. Reliability is the extent to which a measure is free from random error variance and therefore provides consistent results.

The best you can do when conducting a customer satisfaction survey is ask the person to respond to some questions.

From the answers, you will obtain a score. However, this score will be the observed score, and it will be composed of the true score and the error score. The true score is the score that the respondent would have obtained if the measurement was perfect. The error score E is the difference between the observed score X and the true score T:

$$X = T + E$$

Here's a concrete example in *Table 9.3*:

Customer	X	T	E
1.	5	5	0
2.	3	4	-1
3.	4	3	1
4.	3	2	1
5.	1	1	0
6.	5	5	0
7.	5	4	1
8.	2	3	-1
9.	1	2	-1
10.	1	1	0
	$M X = 3.0 \text{Var}(X) = 2.88$	$M T = 3.0 \text{Var}(T) = 2.22$	$M E = 0.0 \text{Var}(E) = 0.66$

Table 9.3 – Observed score, true score, and error score for 10 customers

You should be aware of the fact you don't know T since T can only be known with perfect measurement, and there is no such thing as perfect measurement.

We can calculate X, T, and E, as follows:

$$X = M_X = \Sigma X_i / n$$
$$T = M_T = \Sigma T_i / n$$
$$E = M_E = \Sigma E_i / n$$

The variances for the same variables are calculated through:

$$X = Var(X) = \Sigma(X_i - M_X)^2/n$$
$$T = Var(T) = \Sigma(T_i - M_T)^2/n$$
$$E = Var(E) = \Sigma(E_i - M_E)^2/n$$

Implementing this in Python, we have the following:

```
import numpy as np

# Data for observed score (X), true score (T), and error score (E)
data = np.array([
    [5, 5, 0],
    [3, 4, -1],
    [4, 3, 1],
    [3, 2, 1],
    [1, 1, 0],
    [5, 5, 0],
    [5, 4, 1],
    [2, 3, -1],
    [1, 2, -1],
    [1, 1, 0]
])

# Calculate means (M_X, M_T, M_E)
means = np.mean(data, axis=0)

# Calculate variances (Var(X), Var(T), Var(E))
variances = np.var(data, axis=0, ddof=0)
```

We can then calculate the correlation between the observed score and the true score, which in this example is 0.88. This suggests that the deltas between true and observed scores are small and that the observed score is a good measure of the true score. This is a form of reliability.

We can also focus on the variance. The variance of the observed score is 2.88, the variance of the true score is 2.22, and the variance of the error score is 0.66. We can then derive

$$\text{Reliability}(r_{xx'}) = \frac{Var(T)}{Var(T) + Var(E)}$$

where $Var(T) + Var(E) = Var(X)$ in Python, this is simply presented as:

```
# Calculate reliability
reliability = variances[1] / (variances[1] + variances[2])
```

In this example, the reliability is 0.77. An interesting point is you can go from this to the correlation between the observed score and the true score, which is 0.88, via the square root of the reliability:

$$r_{XT} = \sqrt{0.77} = 0.88$$

This is trivial to run in Python:

```
# Calculate the correlation between the observed score and the true
score
r_xt = np.sqrt(reliability)
```

There are alternative methods to calculate reliability, such as the split-half reliability estimate and Cronbach's alpha estimate. Let's delve deeper into these methods.

Split-half reliability estimate

This method involves splitting the scale into halves—for instance, odd vs. even items— and then calculating the correlation between the two halves.

A high correlation indicates that the two sets yield consistent information. Hence, they are likely measuring the same construct.

We can then estimate reliability as

$$r_{cc'} = \frac{n\,r_{12}}{1 + (n - 1)\,r_{12}}$$

where $r_{cc'}$ is the corrected reliability estimate of the questionnaire, r_{12} is the correlation between the two halves of the questionnaire, and n is the number of items in each of the halves of the questionnaire.

Cronbach's alpha estimate

Cronbach's alpha is similar to making a split-half reliability estimate of the outcome, but instead of splitting the questionnaire in half, it calculates the correlation between each item and the total score. It is a measure of the internal consistency of the questionnaire.

Cronbach's alpha ranges from 0 to 1 and is calculated as

$$\alpha_{st} = \frac{N.r}{1 + (N - 1)r}$$

where N is the number of items in the questionnaire and r is the average correlation between each item and the total score.

Let's take a look at a toy example in *Table 9.4*:

	good	interesting	exciting	useful
good	1.00000	0.921954	0.873038	0.956183
interesting	0.921954	1.00000	0.946943	0.842665
exciting	0.873038	0.946943	1.00000	0.709566
useful	0.956183	0.842665	0.709566	1.00000

Table 9.4 – Correlation between items of six customers' opinions on product P

Here, $N = 4$ and we have the correlations between items. So, if we take the previous equation, we'll have:

$$r = \frac{0.921954 + 0.873038 + 0.956183 + 0.946943 + 0.842665 + 0.709566}{6} = 0.875058$$

We can calculate the Cronbach's alpha simply with the following:

$$\alpha_{st} = \frac{4 \times 0.875058}{1 + (4 - 1)0.875058} = 0.965$$

To do this in Python, one needs to get the correlation matrix, calculate N and r, and then use the previous equation:

```python
import pandas as pd
import numpy as np

def cronbach_alpha(df):
    df_corr = df.corr()
    N = df.shape[1]
    r = df_corr.values[np.triu_indices(N, k = 1)].sum() / (N * (N - 1)
        / 2)
    cronbach_alpha = (N * r) / (1 + (N - 1) * r)
    return cronbach_alpha
```

A small note on the previous code: when calculating the value of r, the naive approach would be to loop through the correlation matrix, find the values, add them, and divide the sum by the number of values. However, the correlation matrix is symmetrical, and the diagonal is all 1s. We can use the `np.triu_indices` function to get the upper triangle of the matrix, where `k = 1` to offset and remove the diagonal itself. Then, we sum the values and divide by the number of values, which we can get with the following:

$$N*(N - 1)/2$$

Now, we need to understand the concept of standard error of measurement.

Standard error of measurement

The standard error of measurement can be computed for a specific individual by giving the questionnaire n number of times. The person wouldn't give the same answers every time due to measurement error, hence you could form a distribution with a mean and standard deviation. The mean would be our best estimate of the true score.

This standard deviation is called, in this context, the standard error of measurement. In theory, we could calculate it for every individual, but in practice, we don't have the time to do so. However, we can calculate it given the reliability score:

$$SEM = s_x \times \sqrt{1 - r_{xx'}}$$

This begs the question: what are the potential sources of error and reliability estimates?

Sources of error and reliability estimates

An important aspect to remember is that you can never truly calculate the true score, hence having the true reliability is then impossible. However, you can estimate it.

So, first, we need to acknowledge that it is possible to administer the same questionnaire to the same person and get different answers. It can be due to changes in the true score being measured, measurement error, or both. This is the test-retest reliability.

The test-retest reliability is the correlation between the scores of the same person on the same test administered on two different occasions. It is a measure of the consistency of the scores over time. It is a measure of the stability of the scores over time.

The stability will depend, for instance, on the time between surveys. If the time between surveys is short, there might be a carryover effect, that is, the respondent might remember what scores they gave the first time and give the same scores the second time. If the time between surveys is long, the respondent might have changed his mind about the scores they gave the first time and give different scores the second time.

Test-retest reliability is not commonly calculated due to the difficulty of setting the time between surveys.

You can, however, calculate it based on different groups. Imagine that you are administering the same questionnaire to different groups of people in different locations. It would be possible to calculate the correlation between the scores of the different groups.

You will also have another form of reliability: the parallel forms reliability. This form of reliability indicates if two different forms of the same questionnaire produce the same results. It is a measure of the equivalence of the scores obtained from two different forms of the same questionnaire.

We essentially measure two different forms of a questionnaire to answer the same question and use that to measure the error and reliability.

Another important factor to consider is the internal consistency of the questionnaire. By internal consistency, we mean the degree to which the items in a survey are measuring the same construct.

Using scales with high reliability

Using scales with high reliability is important since it allows us to make more accurate inferences about the population:

- It allows us also to make more accurate distinctions between people with closer scores and not have those distinctions be due to measurement error

- It also allows us to more confidently make inferences about relationships between variables that impact satisfaction

On the last point, due to errors in the measurement of variables, the correlation between variables will be impacted, meaning observed correlations are smaller than the true correlations. This is called attenuation. The higher the reliability, the smaller the attenuation.

$$r_{X_0 Y_0} = r_{X_t Y_t} \sqrt{r_{XX'}} \sqrt{r_{YY'}}$$

In this equation, $r_{X_0 Y_0}$ is the observed correlation between variables X and Y, $r_{X_t Y_t}$ is the true correlation between variables X and Y, $r_{XX'}$ is the reliability of variable X, and $r_{YY'}$ is the reliability of variable Y.

Factors impacting reliability

There are a number of factors that impact reliability:

- **Sample size**: The larger the sample size, the higher the reliability.

- **Heterogenous sample**: The more similar the samples between themselves, the lower the reliability.

- **Number of items in the survey**: This is similar to the number of observations in a sample. The more items in the survey, the more reliable the survey.

Let's now move to a fundamental concept in survey analysis: sampling.

How to do sampling

Most often, you will not be able to administer the survey to all of your customers. You will need to sample the population. When conducting a survey, you need to obtain a big enough sample to make valid inferences about the population you are studying. When Nike runs a survey on running shoes, they want the results to be representative of the entire population of people who run. However, it is not possible to survey the entire population. Therefore, you need to sample the population.

Types of sampling

There are three types of sampling:

- **Census**: You survey the entire population. We know the sample is representative because you are surveying the entire population. This is not feasible in most cases.

- **Judgmental**: You select the sample based on your judgment. This is not a random sample, and hence it is not representative of the population in general. For example, you might select the sample based on age or other demographics. You are attempting to make a particular point about a particular group. Since the sample is not representative of the population, you cannot make inferences about the population in general.

- **Statistical**: You select the sample based on a statistical method. This is a random sample, and hence it is representative of the population in general. You can make inferences about the population in general.

Although there are many more sampling methods, the most common statistical sampling methods are:

- **Simple random sampling**: This is the simplest and most common approach. Every member of the population has an equal chance of being surveyed.

- **Stratified sampling**: Before you sample, you break the population into groups, or *strata*, hence the name. After splitting, you will random sample *within* the group. One needs to be careful because membership of the stratum needs to be mutually exclusive, that is, a random person cannot belong to more than one stratum. The advantages are that you can have better precision with the same overall sample size or get the same precision with a smaller sample size. You can get the scores for different strata, allowing you to compare the scores between strata. You also focus on a particular stratum, allowing you to make inferences about that stratum. This is useful if you have a clear imbalance in the population, that is, if you have a large number of customers in one stratum and a small number of customers in another stratum. With a simple random sample, the second stratum would be underrepresented.

- **Cluster sampling**: In cluster sampling, you don't sample based on individual cases. Instead, you sample based on clusters. For example, instead of sampling from 20,000 customers, you decide, given that you have 200 offices, to sample randomly amongst the 200 offices. The population is now your offices, not the users.

You can see a summary of the methods in *Table 9.5*:

Method	Definition	Steps	Important points
Simple random	Each customer has an equal chance of being selected	• Obtain a list of all customers (population) • Randomly select customers from this list	• Simple method • Assume there is some variability in the characteristic being measured
Stratified	Within each stratum, each customer has an equal chance of being selected	• Divide customers into strata (or groups) • Conduct simple random selection within each group	• Each level of the groupings must be mutually exclusive from the others • Each stratum should be treated as if it were a population • Can obtain better precision with the same sample size • Obtain estimates for each stratum • Can target specific strata to ensure they are included in the final overall sample
Cluster	Each cluster (or group) has an equal chance of being selected	• Customers are already "naturally" clustered into groups • Conduct simple random sampling of the clusters	• Clusters must already be formed • Can conduct random sampling within the selected clusters

Table 9.5 – Types of sampling and their definitions

Aside from these methods, there are two types of ways to extract samples from the population: probability sampling and quota sampling.

Probability versus quota sampling

Probability sampling is the most common and well known, and it entails the random selection of respondents. For example, a company has the details of its 10,000 customers and randomly chooses 300 of them, assuming 300 is the desired sample size. Quota sampling is based on quotas. Instead of randomly picking 300 customers, the company contacts every person until they reach said number. This method does not allow researchers to assess estimates resulting from the sampling probabilistically since they are not random samples. Probability sampling should be preferred over quota sampling, and you only revert to the former if it is not possible to do the latter.

Now that we know how to sample, we need to understand how to calculate the sample size to see how many users we need to survey.

Sample size for estimating population mean

Depending on the variable of interest, there are statistical methods to calculate the optimal sample size. If the variable of interest is a close-ended question, these methods can typically be used. Let's say you are interested in understanding US consumers' average attitude toward your brand or product. You can calculate the sample size n using the following formula:

$$n = \frac{1}{\frac{d^2}{z_{\alpha/2}^2 \times \sigma^2} + \frac{1}{N}}$$

N is the population size, σ^2 is the variance of the population's attitude toward the brand, d is the spread around the population estimate (that is, margin of error) you are willing to accept with $100(1-\alpha)\%$ confidence, and $z_{\alpha/2}$ is the z-score for the confidence level you are willing to accept. For example, if you are willing to accept a 95% confidence level, then $z_{\alpha/2} = 1.96$.

Response rate

When you run a survey, it is unlikely that all of the people you contact will respond to the survey. The response rate is the percentage of people who respond to the survey. The response rate is important because it impacts the reliability of the survey. The higher the response rate, the more reliable the survey. Hence, you need to adjust your sample size to account for the response rate. For example, if you want a sample size of 300 and you expect a response rate of 50%, then you need to contact 600 people.

The general formula is simply the following:

$$\text{Distribution size} = \frac{\text{Sample size}}{\text{Response rate}}$$

As an analyst, you should use previous historical data to estimate the response rate. Typically, customer satisfaction surveys and market research surveys have response rates between 10% and 30%. The response rate is typically higher for customer satisfaction surveys since the customers are more likely to respond to a survey from a company they have a relationship with. Employee surveys typically have a response rate between 25% and 60% since the employees are more likely to respond to a survey from their employer.

Let's now move on to how to look at control charts, which are essential for monitoring customer satisfaction.

Control charts

Control charts represent various ways data can be charted. They are useful to identify trends in the data and outliers. Control charts should have, aside from the data itself, a center line, an upper control limit, and a lower control limit. The center line is the average of the data. The **upper control limit** (**UCL**) is the average $\bar{x}_Q$ plus k standard deviations $\sqrt{s_Q^2}$. The **lower control limit** (**LCL**) is the average $\bar{x}_Q$ minus k standard deviations $\sqrt{s_Q^2}$.

$$UCL = \bar{x}_Q + k\sqrt{s_Q^2}$$
$$LCL = \bar{x}_Q - k\sqrt{s_Q^2}$$

In general, it is standard to set k to 3.

Data can be attribute data or variable data:

- **Attribute data**: Attribute data is categorical and binary in nature. Either something is confirming or it is not. For example, a customer is either satisfied or not. We can see the number of conforming occurrences but not the degree to which the data conforms to the standard.

- **Variable data**: Variable data is numerical. We can apply a unit of measurement such as minutes to quantify the data. For example, the time it takes to complete a task. We can see the number of conforming occurrences but also the degree to which the data conforms to the standard.

For control charts for attribute data, we can have two types, the p-chart and the c-chart, as we will discuss next.

p-chart

In the p-chart, for any given sample in the survey, we calculate the percentage of respondents who gave at least 1 negative answer. You can think of calculating the number of "defects" in our sample. The proportion is simply $p_i = D_i/n_i$, where D_i is the number of respondents who gave at least one negative answer in the sample i and n_i is the sample size of sample i.

For every sample, we calculate this proportion or percentage, and we can then calculate the UCL and LCL:

$$UCL = \bar{p} + k\sqrt{\frac{\bar{p}(1-\bar{p})}{n}}$$
$$LCL = \bar{p} - k\sqrt{\frac{\bar{p}(1-\bar{p})}{n}}$$

In Python, using some toy data, we can calculate the UCLs and LCLs as follows:

```
# Define k (number of standard deviations for control limits)
k = 3


# Example data for p-chart (number of negative responses and sample
sizes)
# Number of respondents with negative answers in each sample
D = np.array([5, 2, 1, 3, 4, 2, 6, 1, 3])
n = np.array([100, 80, 90, 110, 100, 120, 80, 95, 105])


# Calculate proportions for each sample (p-chart)
p = D / n


# Calculate the center line (average proportion), UCL, and LCL for
p-chart
p_bar = np.mean(p)
UCL_p = p_bar + k * np.sqrt(p_bar * (1 - p_bar) / n.mean())
LCL_p = p_bar - k * np.sqrt(p_bar * (1 - p_bar) / n.mean())
```

To generate the chart, one would simply do the following:

```
# Creating the p-chart using matplotlib
plt.figure(figsize=(10, 6))
plt.plot(p, marker='o', linestyle='-', color='blue',
    label='Proportion')
plt.axhline(y=p_bar, color='green', linestyle='-',
    label='Center Line (p‾)')
```

```
plt.axhline(y=UCL_p, color='red', linestyle='--', label='UCL')
plt.axhline(y=LCL_p, color='red', linestyle='--', label='LCL')
plt.title('p-Chart')
plt.xlabel('Sample Number')
plt.ylabel('Proportion of Negative Responses')

# Adjust x-axis ticks to match sample numbers
plt.xticks(np.arange(len(p)), np.arange(1, len(p) + 1))
plt.legend(loc='upper left', bbox_to_anchor=(1, 1))
plt.grid(True, which='both', axis='y', linestyle='--', linewidth=0.5)
plt.tight_layout()

plt.show()
```

The code snippet will produce the output seen in *Figure 9.1*:

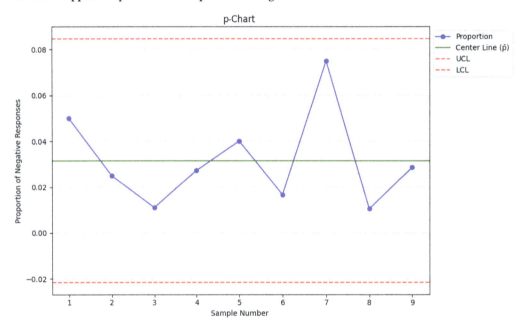

Figure 9.1 – p-chart

c-chart

Now, we may, however, also want to calculate how many negative answers we got in a given sample. A customer may have more than one negative response regarding the service received. This is done with the c-chart

$$UCL = \bar{c} + k\sqrt{\bar{c}}$$

$$LCL = \bar{c} - k\sqrt{\bar{c}}$$

where $\bar{c}$ is the number of negative responses per sample.

In Python, we can calculate it as follows:

```python
# Example data for c-chart (number of negative responses per sample)
c = np.array([10, 12, 14, 13, 9, 11, 15, 8, 10])
# Calculate the center line (average of negative responses), UCL, and
LCL for c-chart
c_bar = np.mean(c)
UCL_c = c_bar + k * np.sqrt(c_bar)
LCL_c = c_bar - k * np.sqrt(c_bar)


# Check for negative LCL and set it to zero if it is negative (since
we cannot have negative counts)
LCL_c = max(LCL_c, 0)
```

Again, generating the chart is simple:

```python
# Creating the c-chart using matplotlib
plt.figure(figsize=(10, 6))
plt.plot(c, marker='o', linestyle='-', color='blue',
    label='Count of Defects')
plt.axhline(y=c_bar, color='green', linestyle='-',
    label='Center Line (ĉ)')
plt.axhline(y=UCL_c, color='red', linestyle='--', label='UCL')
plt.axhline(y=LCL_c, color='red', linestyle='--', label='LCL')
plt.title('c-Chart')
plt.xlabel('Sample Number')
plt.ylabel('Count of Negative Responses')
# Adjust x-axis ticks to match sample numbers
plt.xticks(np.arange(len(c)), np.arange(1, len(c) + 1))
plt.legend(loc='upper left', bbox_to_anchor=(1, 1))
plt.grid(True, which='both', axis='y', linestyle='--', linewidth=0.5)
plt.show()
```

We can see the output in *Figure 9.2*:

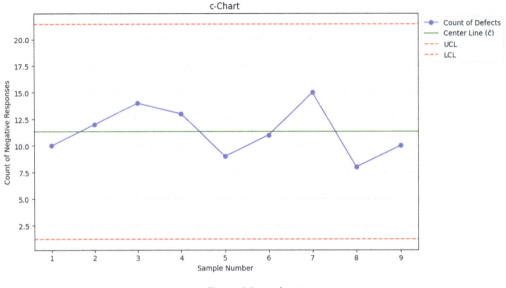

Figure 9.2 – c-chart

In the next section, we will dig deeper into what customer loyalty is and how to measure it, as well as the weaknesses of the net promoter score.

Customer loyalty and NPS methodology

Currently, the most commonly known metric for customer loyalty is the **net promoter score**, or **NPS**. It is a metric that measures customer loyalty. It is based on the idea that customers can be divided into three categories:

- **Promoters** are customers who are loyal to the brand and will recommend it to others
- **Passives** are customers who are satisfied with the brand but are not loyal to it
- **Detractors** are customers who are dissatisfied with the brand and will not recommend it to others

NPS is used by many of the world's leading companies, including Apple, Amazon, and Netflix.

It is calculated by taking the proportion of promoters and subtracting from it the proportion of detractors, where promoters are respondents who answer 9 or 10 to the question "How likely are you to recommend this company to a friend or colleague?" and detractors are respondents who answer 0 to 6 to the same question.

Issues with NPS

There are strong claims made about NPS, such as:

- NPS is the best predictor of growth
- NPS is the single most reliable indicator of a company's ability to grow
- Satisfaction lacks a consistent link to growth

Research has shown that these claims are not entirely true. For example, Keinighham et al. (2007) found that NPS is not the only predictor of growth, and that satisfaction is also a predictor of growth, using the same methods that the creators used to make the case for NPS. Others, namely Morgan and Rego (2006), found that other measures of loyalty, such as satisfaction or likelihood to repurchase, are comparable to NPS in predicting a business's performance on KPIs such as market share or cash flow.

Common questions to measure loyalty

The most common questions to ask when measuring loyalty are as follows:

- Overall, how satisfied are you with the company?
- How likely are you to recommend the company to a friend or colleague?
- How likely are you to repurchase from the company?
- How likely are you to switch to a competitor?

If you average them in a single score, an Advocacy Loyalty Index, you get a score that is comparable to NPS.

Now you may wonder, why are there four questions if with NPS I only get one? The issue is psychological. The distinction between loyalty questions might not be as clear as you believe, and the concept of loyalty itself is not clear. For example, if you ask a customer if they are satisfied with the company, they might answer yes, but if you ask whether they are likely to recommend the company to a friend, they might answer no. By using more questions and aggregating, you are attempting to reduce the noise in the data.

Potential loss of revenue

A potential problem with NPS is overlooking disloyal customers, defined in other ways. For instance, a customer might be a non-detractor but still not loyal. A study conducted with T-Mobile by Bob E. Hayes in *Measuring Customer Satisfaction and Loyalty* found that 31% of customers who scored 7 or above on the NPS scale were likely to switch to a competitor. This is a potential loss of revenue that is not captured by NPS, as seen in *Table 9.6*:

Recommend (NPS)	Percent of T-Mobile customers	Number of T-Mobile customers	Percent highly likely to switch to another provider*	Number of T-Mobile customers highly likely to switch*
0	2%	637,795	52%	375,174
1	3%	850,394	52%	445,444
2	1%	212,598	11%	82,677
3	3%	850,394	8%	94,488
4	1%	212,598	4%	17,008
5	11%	2,976,378	4%	127,196
6	5%	1,275,591	4%	57,116
7	18%	4,889,764	4%	175,891
8	19%	5,102,362	5%	259,442
9	17%	4,464,567	7%	325,233
10	20%	5,527,559	3%	166,321
TOTAL	100%	27,000,000		2,266,321

Table 9.6 – How likely are you to switch to a different provider within the next 12 months?

So what are the alternatives for NPS? Advocacy, purchasing, and retention loyalty, as we will discuss next.

Advocacy, purchasing, and retention loyalty

Loyalty can be broken down using factor analysis into these components:

- **Advocacy**, which has a strong emotional component to it, reflecting the customer's willingness to recommend the company to others
- **Purchasing**, which reflects the customer's willingness to repurchase from the company
- **Retention**, which reflects the customer's willingness to switch to a competitor

We can then construct three indices, one for each component, ALI, PLI, and RLI:

- **ALI** stands for **Advocacy Loyalty Index**
- **PLI** stands for **Purchasing Loyalty Index**
- **RLI** stands for **Retention Loyalty Index**

Studies have shown that these three indices correlate with the following business metrics:

- ALI correlates with new customer growth

- PLI correlates with ARPU growth

- RLI correlates with churn reduction

How do we identify the factors that explain patterns of correlation? Let's have a look at factor analysis.

Factor analysis

Factor analysis is a statistical method used to identify underlying factors that explain the pattern of correlations within a set of observed variables. It is used to reduce a large number of variables into a smaller number of factors, which can then be used to explain the relationships between the variables.

To conduct a factor analysis, the following steps are taken:

1. Collect data on a set of variables.

2. Scale and center the data so that the mean of each variable is 0 and the standard deviation is 1, making all features comparable.

3. Calculate the correlation matrix of the variables.

4. Use **singular value decomposition** (**SVD**) to decompose the correlation matrix into its constituent parts.

5. Interpret the factors.

6. Calculate the factor scores.

If you are familiar with **principal component analysis** (**PCA**), you might be wondering what the difference between PCA and factor analysis is. The main difference is that PCA is primarily used to identify the underlying structure of the data, while factor analysis is primarily used to identify the underlying factors that explain the pattern of correlations within the data.

A good Python library for conducting factor analysis on surveys quickly is the package `FactorAnalyzer`.

Summary

In this chapter, we explored the topic of customer satisfaction analysis and loyalty in the context of marketing analytics. We began by discussing the importance of customer satisfaction and loyalty and how they can be measured. We then moved on to the topic of questionnaire design, covering the different types of questions and response formats, as well as best practices for designing effective questionnaires. Next, we discussed the different methods of administering surveys and interviews, along with their advantages and disadvantages. We then explored the topic of sampling, covering the different types of sampling and their applications. Finally, we discussed the net promoter score (NPS) methodology and its limitations, as well as alternative methods for measuring customer loyalty.

By learning these techniques, you are now able to understand how to conduct survey analysis, how to correctly calculate sample sizes, and how to derive insights from the analysis.

In the next chapter, we will explore what conjoint analysis is and how to conduct it.

Further reading

- *Marketing Analytics* by Robert W. Palmatier, J. Andrew Petersen, Frank Germann, Bloomsbury Academic India

- *Measuring Customer Satisfaction and Loyalty* by Bob E. Hayes, New Age International Private Limited

- *The Value of Different Customer Satisfaction and Loyalty Metrics in Predicting Business Performance* by Neil A Morgan and Lopo L. Rego

- *A Longitudinal Examination of Net Promoter and Firm Revenue Growth* by Timothy L. Keiningham, Bruce Cooil, Tor Wallin Andreassen, and Lerzan Aksoy

10

Conjoint Analysis with pandas and Statsmodels

Conjoint analysis is a multivariate technique used to evaluate customer responses and preferences towards specific combinations of product attributes that simulate potential products.

Just asking customers what they want is not enough. Customers usually want everything, but they are not willing to pay for everything. Conjoint analysis avoids this problem by asking customers to choose between two or more product bundles that differ in the levels of the product attributes. It can also be used to evaluate customers' willingness to pay for different product attributes.

In this chapter, you will cover the following topics:

- An introduction to conjoint analysis
- Setting up a conjoint study
- Conducting conjoint analysis in Python

By the end of this chapter, you will understand the steps needed to conduct a conjoint survey, the fundamentals of the regression model, and how to do the analysis in Python.

Technical requirements

The code files for this chapter are available on GitHub: `https://github.com/PacktPublishing/Data-Analytics-for-Marketing/tree/main/Chapter10`.

An introduction to conjoint analysis

Conjoint analysis provides analysts with insights into customers' product preferences and allows them to identify the most important product attributes and attribute combinations most appealing to customers.

It is based on customer feedback data on a select number of products that are each designed around different levels of the same product attributes (known as product bundles). The product bundles are designed to represent the full range of possible product attribute combinations.

Regression analysis decomposes these product bundles such that the utility (also referred to as value or part-worth) customers assign to the various levels of each of the product attributes can be derived.

Rather than asking directly about their product preferences (*"How much would you like to pay to purchase a mutual fund?"*), conjoint analysis asks customers to choose between two or more product bundles that differ in the levels of the product attributes, such as mutual funds at different price points.

The fundamentals of conjoint analysis

Consider the following problem. You are an analyst at a smartphone manufacturer. Your company has 15 different models on one of their brands. Your task is to understand how to decide at what price points should each model be sold at. Mobile phones have many attributes and differ in different sets of specs of memory, camera, screen size, and so on. So, how do you decide what the right price is for each model and what attributes to bundle into each model?

Examples of companies that have used conjoint analysis include the following:

- **Courtyard by Marriott**: Marriott was among the early users of conjoint analysis. The company wanted to design a new hotel that would be more affordable than its existing hotels. The company used conjoint analysis to identify the attributes that customers valued most in a hotel. The results of the conjoint analysis were used to design the Courtyard by Marriott hotel.

- **Match.com**: Match.com is an online dating service that uses conjoint analysis to help customers find their perfect match. The company uses conjoint analysis to identify the attributes that customers value most in a potential partner. The results of the conjoint analysis are used to match customers with potential partners.

- **Apple versus Samsung**: Conjoint analysis has also been used in patent infringement cases. For example, Apple has used conjoint analysis to determine the value of a stolen touchscreen feature – the ability to recognize a second finger. The results of the conjoint analysis were used to determine the amount of damages that Samsung should pay Apple for infringing on Apple's patents.

Essentially, conjoint analysis provides a way to understand how consumers value different attributes of a product. It is a way to understand how consumers make trade-offs between different attributes of a product.

We need to set some terminology first:

- **Attribute**: A characteristic of a product that can be quantified; for example, the screen size of a mobile phone.

- **Attribute level**: The different values that an attribute can take. For example, the screen size of a mobile phone can be 5.5 inches, 6.0 inches, or 6.5 inches.

- **Product profile or bundle**: A combination of attribute levels; for example, a mobile phone with a 5.5-inch screen, 64GB of memory, and a 12MP camera.

- **Utility of a bundle**: The value that a consumer assigns to a product profile. For example, a consumer might assign a high value to a mobile phone with a 5.5-inch screen, 64GB of memory, and a 12MP camera.

Let's start by discussing how to set up a conjoint study.

Setting up a conjoint study

Conjoint analysis is a five-step process:

1. Select the product attributes to be included.

2. Select the product attribute levels.

3. Create product profiles.

4. Collect data from target customers.

5. Estimate the utility of each product attribute and level using regression analysis.

Let's go over each step in detail.

Step 1 – select the product attributes to be included

The first step in conjoint analysis is to select the product attributes that will be included in the analysis. The product attributes should be those that are most important to customers. The attributes should also be those that are most controllable by the company. For example, if a company is considering launching a new product, the attributes that are most important to customers and that are most controllable by the company should be included in the conjoint analysis.

Analysts should be careful not to include too many product attributes. Typically, it is advisable to keep the number of product attributes at six or less. More than six attributes can make it difficult for customers to make choices between product bundles. Some product attributes are expected by customers. For example, virtually all laptops nowadays have a built-in camera. Such attributes should not be included unless there is a potential opportunity to differentiate the product on that attribute. If the attributes are not included in the survey, it is advisable to inform the participants of the study about the levels these attributes take (for example, assume all laptops have a built-in camera).

Using a simple example of a sandwich, we might consider the following attributes:

- Type of bread
- Type of meat
- Type of cheese
- Type of vegetables
- Price

Step 2 – select the product attribute levels

Using the same sandwich example, we might consider the following levels for each attribute:

- **Type of bread**: White or whole wheat
- **Type of meat**: Ham, turkey, or no meat
- **Type of cheese**: Cheddar or swiss
- **Type of vegetables**: Lettuce, tomato, or lettuce and tomato
- **Price**: $5, $6, or $7

The sandwich is assumed to be identical in all other aspects (for example, brand name and size). It is recommended to include two to five levels per attribute to not overwhelm the participants of the study. Also, it is recommended to keep the number of levels per attribute as consistent as possible across different attributes. Importantly, the meaning of the levels must be unambiguous. Finally, the included attribute levels should be mutually exclusive and the range should be consistent with what customers expect to encounter in real life.

Step 3 – create product profiles

The next step is to create product profiles. A product profile is a combination of the levels of the product attributes. For example, a product profile for the same sandwich example could be: white bread, ham, cheddar, lettuce and tomato, $5. The product profiles are created using a fractional factorial design. The number of product profiles is equal to the product of the number of levels for each attribute. In our toy example, we have 2 x 3 x 2 x 3 x 3 = 108 product profiles. No customer would want to provide feedback on that many profiles. Fortunately, that is not needed.

There are different approaches to conjoint analysis, but two are particularly popular. First is ratings-based or ranking-based conjoint analysis, and second is choice-based conjoint analysis.

In ratings-based conjoint analysis, customers are asked to rate each product profile on a scale from 1 to 7, for example (you can also use a scale of 1 to 100). The ratings are then used to estimate the utility of each product attribute and level. In ranking-based conjoint analysis, customers are asked to rank the product profiles in order of preference. The rankings are then used to estimate the utility of each product attribute and level. Alternatively, customers can be asked to rank the product profiles in order of preference.

Customers do not need to rank all combinations of product profiles. Instead, using experimental design (also known as fractional factorial design), a subset of the product profiles are selected. The number of product profiles that are selected depends on the number of attributes and the number of levels per attribute. The number of product profiles that are selected is typically between 10 and 20.

Importantly, using the subset of rankings in this subset, we can estimate how each customer will evaluate any of the possible product profiles.

In choice-based conjoint analysis, customers are asked to choose between two or more product profiles. The choice data is then used to estimate the utility of each product attribute and level. The customer would be presented with the same choice scenario multiple times with changing attribute levels in each scenario.

Step 4 – collect data from target customers

The next step is to collect data from target customers through a survey. The survey should be designed to collect the data needed to estimate the utility of each product attribute and level. The survey should also be designed to collect demographic data about the customers. The demographic data can be used to control the effects of demographic variables on the utility of the product attributes and levels.

Step 5 – estimate the utility of each product attribute and levels using regression analysis

Once the data is collected, the next step is estimating the customer's utility – also known as part-worths. Conjoint analysis provides two things: the relative importance each customer attaches to each included product attribute and each customer's utility for each level of each product attribute.

Let's now move to an in-depth review of how do to conjoint modeling.

Conducting conjoint analysis in Python

In ratings-based conjoint analysis, standard OLS regression is used. The customers ratings of the various choices form the dependent variable of the OLS regression. Moreover, the respective level of each attribute associated with each rating is captured using dummy variables. These dummy variables form the independent variables of the OLS regressions. For each attribute included, there will be $x - 1$ dummy variables, where x is the total number of attribute levels.

In summary, the OLS regression model is as follows:

$$U(P) = \alpha_0 + \sum_{j=1}^{kj}\sum_{i=1}^{m}\beta_{ij}X_{ij} + \epsilon_{ij}$$

Where:

- *P* is a product to be evaluated

- *U(P)* is the utility of product profile *P*

- β_{ij} is the utility of attribute *i* at level *j*

- *m* is the number of attributes

- k_j is the number of levels for attribute *j*

- X_{ij} is a dummy variable that is equal to 1 if attribute *i* is at level *j* and 0 otherwise

- α_0 is the intercept, or constant of the regression

- ϵ_{ij} is the error term

Once the β_{ij} are estimated, the utility of each attribute and level can be calculated, even for product attribute combinations that were not directly rated as part of the conjoint analysis.

Returning to the sandwich example, the OLS regression model is as follows:

$$U(Product)_{ij} = \alpha_0 + \beta_{j,ij}X_1 + \beta_{Ham,ij}X_2 + \beta_{Cheddar,ij}X_3 + \beta_{Lettuce,ij}X_4 + \beta_{5usd,ij}X_5 + \epsilon_{ij}$$

This equation captures the consumers' *i* rating of sandwich *j*.

We can see the hypothetical coefficients that would come from the results of a linear regression of each attribute in our sandwich example in *Table 10.1*:

Attribute	coefficient
White Bread	0.198
Ham	-0.146
Turkey	-2.153
Provalone	-0.859
American	-0.007
Lettuce	-0.368
Tomato	-0.097
3.99	2.896
4.99	1.243
Intercept	3.443

Table 10.1 – Coefficients of the OLS regression model for the sandwich example

Considering the previous table, the customer values white bread 0.198 units more than whole wheat bread. Note that since you are using dummy variables, the coefficient is interpreted vis-a-vis the baseline. The baseline also always has a part-worth of 0. In this case, the baseline is whole wheat bread.

Using the previous table, an analyst can estimate the rating for each of the 108 possible combinations. For example, the rating for a sandwich with white bread, ham, cheddar, lettuce and tomato, and a price of $5 is 3.443 + 0.198 + (-0.146) + (-0.859) + (-0.368) + 2.896 = 5.4.

A final note regards the intercept that captures the customer's rating of the baseline sandwich. The baseline is the combination of the lowest level of each attribute. In this case, the baseline is a sandwich with whole wheat bread, no meat, Swiss cheese, lettuce and tomato, and a price of $5. The intercept is the rating the customer would give to the baseline sandwich. In this case, the intercept is 3.443.

Now, in isolation, coefficients are meaningless for a concrete analysis. This analysis aims to understand how much the customers value an attribute. If different price levels are included in a conjoint analysis, as in the example, then conjoint analysis can also be used to determine the customer's perceived value of the different attributes.

Determining the value of a product attribute

From the previous example, we see that the customer values a price of 4.99 at 1.243 utility units more than a price of 5.99, which is the baseline. This tells us that for sandwiches that fall into the 4.99 – 5.99 price range, 1.243 utility units are worth $1.00. If we divide 1.00 by the amount of utility units, and multiply by the coefficient of white bread, we get:

$$\frac{1.00}{1.243} \times 0.198 = 0.16$$

Thus the customer is willing to pay about 16 cents more for white bread than whole wheat bread when the customer considers sandwiches that fall into the 4.99 - 5.99 price range. In other words, the sandwich maker can charge this customer about 16 cents more for a sandwich with white bread than for a sandwich with whole wheat bread and they will value it the same.

Now, most often, when dealing with conjoint analysis, the data is not continuous but discrete, and in that case, regression-based analysis is not the best option. For discrete cases, we should look into choice-based models.

Choice-based conjoint analysis

This type of modeling is similar in principle to regular regression-based analysis to predict outcomes, with one exception: the dependent variable is not continuous, but discrete. In other words, the dependent variable is a choice between two or more alternatives.

To accommodate this, we use a logistic regression model, specifically the multinomial logit model. The multinomial logit model is a generalization of the binary logit model. The binary logit model is used when the dependent variable is binary (that is, 0 or 1). The multinomial logit model is used when the dependent variable is categorical, with more than two categories.

Let's have a look at a practical example of a fictitious car company that wants to understand how customers value different attributes of a car. In the data, we have the ratings for different car profiles where we asked customers to make choices between cargo size, engine type, and price. We will use the data to estimate the utility of each product attribute and level using OLS regression.

Let's start by importing the data:

```
import pandas as pd
import numpy as np

data = pd.read_csv('data/conjoint.csv')
data.head()
```

The data is as follows in *Figure 10.1*:

	resp.id	ques	alt	carpool	seat	cargo	eng	price	choice
0	1	1	1	yes	6	2ft	gas	35	0
1	1	1	2	yes	8	3ft	hyb	30	0
2	1	1	3	yes	6	3ft	gas	30	1
3	1	2	1	yes	6	2ft	gas	30	0
4	1	2	2	yes	7	3ft	gas	35	1

Figure 10.1 – Sample of the conjoint data

The DataFrame is structured in a long format, where each row represents a specific choice made by an individual respondent. The target variable is binary, reflecting the respondent's selection or rejection of an option. The explanatory variables correspond to the attributes of the option chosen.

In long format, each option profile is delineated on a separate row, accompanied by a column that specifies the question to which the profile was associated. This format is generally favored in choice modeling as it accommodates variability in the number of profiles per question through the inclusion of additional rows.

Contrastingly, the wide format arranges each question within its own row, offering an alternative organizational structure to long format.

The first step in the analysis is to convert the variables to `Categorical` type. This is done using the following code:

```python
# Convert categorical variables to dummy variables
data["seat"] = pd.Categorical(data["seat"])
data["cargo"] = pd.Categorical(data["cargo"])
data["eng"] = pd.Categorical(data["eng"])
data["price"] = pd.Categorical(data["price"])
```

Now we have two options: we can model price as a numeric variable, or we can model it as a categorical variable. If we model it as a numeric variable, we will get a single coefficient for price. If we model it as a categorical variable, we will get a coefficient for each level of price. In this example, we will model price as a numeric variable.

Fitting a choice model

Fitting a choice model is simply making a regression of the following form:

$$choice \sim 0 + \beta_1 \times attribute_1 + \beta_2 \times attribute_2 + \beta_3 \times attribute_3 + \beta_4 \times attribute_4 + ... + \beta_n \times attribute_n$$

The reason for not having an intercept is that, if we have an intercept, we are essentially getting estimates for the relative preference between positions in the survey, and we don't expect consumers to have a preference for one position over another in the survey. That is, we don't expect consumers to prefer the first option over the second option, or the second option over the third option.

Let's first model price as a categorical variable. We will use the following code:

```python
import statsmodels.api as sm
import statsmodels.formula.api as smf
from statsmodels.stats.anova import anova_lm

# Model 1: Without intercept
m1_formula = 'choice ~ 0 + seat + cargo + eng + price'
m1 = smf.mnlogit(formula=m1_formula, data=data).fit()
print(m1.summary())
```

We can see the results of the model in *Figure 10.2*:

```
Optimization terminated successfully.
        Current function value: 0.558645
        Iterations 6
                          MNLogit Regression Results
```

Dep. Variable:			choice	No. Observations:		9000
Model:			MNLogit	Df Residuals:		8992
Method:			MLE	Df Model:		7
Date:		Tue, 12 Mar 2024		Pseudo R-squ.:		0.1223
Time:			09:03:44	Log-Likelihood:		-5027.8
converged:			True	LL-Null:		-5728.6
Covariance Type:			nonrobust	LLR p-value:		1.702e-298

choice=1	coef	std err	z	P>|z|	[0.025	0.975]
seat[6]	-0.6688	0.067	-9.908	0.000	-0.801	-0.536
seat[7]	-1.1939	0.070	-17.058	0.000	-1.331	-1.057
seat[8]	-0.9617	0.069	-13.938	0.000	-1.097	-0.826
cargo[T.3ft]	0.4386	0.049	9.005	0.000	0.343	0.534
eng[T.gas]	1.4353	0.062	23.218	0.000	1.314	1.556
eng[T.hyb]	0.6748	0.063	10.720	0.000	0.551	0.798
price[T.35]	-0.8223	0.056	-14.562	0.000	-0.933	-0.712
price[T.40]	-1.5866	0.063	-25.359	0.000	-1.709	-1.464

Figure 10.2 – Coefficients of the OLS regression model for the sandwich example

The coefficients are presented in log-odds units, making them not immediately intuitive to understand. To make sense of them, one must convert them into odds ratios by exponentiation.

It's crucial to remember that these estimates are comparative, referencing the baseline levels of each attribute. For instance, the coefficient for seat [7] compares the preference for having seven seats against the default level of six seats.

The direction of the coefficient indicates whether, on average, there is a preference for a higher attribute level over the baseline. The size of the coefficient quantifies the extent of this preference.

Typically, parameter values on the logit scale will vary between -2 and 2, where a value of 0 indicates neutrality.

A key consideration is the choice to omit an intercept from the model. Including an intercept introduces two additional parameters that represent preferences for different positions within a question (such as left, right, or middle). Often, these positional preferences are not of primary interest, as the assumption is that the alternative's position does not significantly influence consumer choice.

Not all predictors need to be categorized as factors. While some predictors are best treated as categorical factors, others, such as price, may be more appropriately modeled as numeric variables. Incorporating price as a numeric variable simplifies the model to a single coefficient for price, rather than separate coefficients for each categorical level.

Let's now run a model where price is a numeric variable. We will use the following code:

```
data['price_numeric'] = pd.to_numeric(data['price'], errors='coerce')

m2_formula = 'choice ~ 0 + seat + cargo + eng + price_numeric'
m2 = smf.mnlogit(formula=m2_formula, data=data).fit()
print(m2.summary())
```

We can see the coefficients produced in *Figure 10.3*:

```
Optimization terminated successfully.
         Current function value: 0.558645
         Iterations 6
                        MNLogit Regression Results
==============================================================================
Dep. Variable:                 choice   No. Observations:                 9000
Model:                        MNLogit   Df Residuals:                     8992
Method:                           MLE   Df Model:                            7
Date:                Sun, 10 Mar 2024   Pseudo R-squ.:                  0.1223
Time:                        18:08:02   Log-Likelihood:                -5027.8
converged:                       True   LL-Null:                       -5728.6
Covariance Type:            nonrobust   LLR p-value:                 1.702e-298
==============================================================================
     choice=1       coef    std err          z      P>|z|      [0.025      0.975]
------------------------------------------------------------------------------
seat[6]           -0.6688      0.067     -9.908      0.000      -0.801      -0.536
seat[7]           -1.1939      0.070    -17.058      0.000      -1.331      -1.057
seat[8]           -0.9617      0.069    -13.938      0.000      -1.097      -0.826
cargo[T.3ft]       0.4386      0.049      9.005      0.000       0.343       0.534
eng[T.gas]         1.4353      0.062     23.218      0.000       1.314       1.556
eng[T.hyb]         0.6748      0.063     10.720      0.000       0.551       0.798
price[T.35]       -0.8223      0.056    -14.562      0.000      -0.933      -0.712
price[T.40]       -1.5866      0.063    -25.359      0.000      -1.709      -1.464
==============================================================================
```

Figure 10.3 – Coefficients of the OLS regression model with price as a numeric variable

The same interpretation applies to the coefficients in this model. The coefficient for `price_numeric` is the utility of a one-unit increase in price.

Reporting findings

Logistical models are not as easy to interpret as linear models. The coefficients are not directly interpretable. So, in choice modeling, instead of presenting the coefficients directly, usually modelers focus on getting the choice share predictions or on computing a willingness to pay.

Once you have the coefficients or the part-worth utilities for every attribute, you can calculate the range. This range is the difference between the maximum and minimum part-worth utilities for each attribute. This range is a measure of the importance of the attribute. The larger the range, the more important the attribute is. Here is a short summary of the main metrics used:

- $R_i = \max(u_{ij}) - \min(u_{ij})$ is used to determine the importance of an attribute. This importance is calculated by finding the difference between the maximum and minimum utility values (u_{ij}) for all levels of a given attribute i. This difference represents the range of utility that the attribute can provide across its different levels. A larger range indicates that the attribute has a more significant impact on the overall utility or preference of a product or service. Essentially, it shows how much the preference changes as you move from the least-preferred level to the most-preferred level of that attribute.

- The relative importance of an attribute ($Rim\,p_i$) is defined as $Rim\,p_i = \frac{R_i}{\sum_{i=1}^{m} R_i}$. This formula calculates the importance of an attribute relative to the importance of all other attributes. It is the ratio of the importance of attribute i to the sum of importances of all attributes. This helps in understanding the attribute's importance in the context of all considered attributes. A higher relative importance indicates that the attribute plays a more critical role in the decision-making process of consumers.

Overall, these formulas are essential in conjoint analysis for quantifying how different attributes and their levels contribute to the overall preference or utility of a product or service, thereby aiding in understanding consumer decision-making processes.

Willingness to pay

The **willingness to pay** (**WTP**) is the amount of money that a consumer is willing to pay for a specific attribute. For example, if a consumer is willing to pay $1.00 for a specific attribute, then the consumer is willing to pay $1.00 more for a product with that attribute than for a product without that attribute.

To calculate willingness to pay, the model has to have a coefficient for price. Then one simply divides the coefficient for that attribute ($\beta_{attribute}$) by that price coefficient (β_{price}):

$$WTP = \frac{\beta_{attribute}}{\beta_{price}}$$

Willingness to pay is a bit of a misnomer. The actual formal interpretation is that it is the marginal utility of the attribute. It is the amount of utility that the consumer gets from the attribute. Or, to put it another way, it is the amount of utility that the consumer is willing to give up to get the attribute, remaining indifferent between having the attribute and not having the attribute.

Let's expand a bit on this last point.

Marginal utility and willingness to pay

Marginal utility refers to the extra satisfaction or advantage a consumer gains from obtaining one more unit of a product or service. In the context of WTP, it specifically refers to the additional utility gained from an attribute of a product.

The indifference point is a key concept in understanding WTP. It represents a situation where a consumer is equally satisfied with two different scenarios and therefore is indifferent between them. In the context of WTP, these scenarios are as follows:

- **Having the product with the desired attribute**: This involves the consumer possessing a product that includes the specific attribute they value

- **Having a monetary equivalent without the product attribute**: This is a scenario where the consumer does not have the product with the desired attribute but has an amount of money equivalent to the utility that the attribute would provide

At the indifference point, the utility derived from the product attribute is exactly balanced by the utility of the monetary amount the consumer is willing to pay for that attribute. This balance is what defines the consumer's WTP for that attribute.

WTP can be understood as a measure of how much utility the consumer is willing to forego (in terms of money) to acquire the additional utility provided by the attribute. This is why it's a bit of a misnomer to just call it "willingness to pay." It's not just about the monetary transaction; it's about the utility trade-off. The consumer is willing to give up a certain amount of utility (money) to gain the utility provided by the attribute, to the point where they have no preference between having the extra utility from the attribute or keeping the money.

Calculating WTP

As the formula indicates, WTP is calculated by dividing the coefficient of the attribute by the coefficient of the price in a conjoint analysis model. This calculation essentially quantifies the trade-off: how much price (or utility in terms of money) a consumer is willing to exchange for the utility gained from the attribute.

By understanding WTP in terms of marginal utility and the indifference point, businesses and researchers can more accurately gauge how much value consumers place on various product attributes, and adjust their offerings or prices accordingly.

In Python, we can calculate the WTP by first extracting the coefficients from the model, and then dividing the coefficient of the attribute by the coefficient of the price. We can use the following code to extract the coefficients from the model:

```
coeff = m2.params.to_dict()
attrarray = {
```

```
    'seat': ['seat[6]', 'seat[7]', 'seat[8]'],
    'cargo': ['cargo[T.3ft]'],
    'eng': ['eng[T.gas]', 'eng[T.hyb]'],
    'price': ['price_numeric']
}

part_worth_utility = {}

for attribute in attrarray:
    for level in attrarray[attribute]:
        part_worth_utility[level] = coeff[0][level]
```

Then we can calculate the WTP using the following code:

```
willingness_to_pay = {}

for attribute in part_worth_utility:
    if attribute != 'price_numeric':
        willingness_to_pay[attribute] = part_worth_utility[attribute]
            / (-part_worth_utility['price_numeric'] / 1000)
```

And now we have the following WTP for each attribute in *Figure 10.4*:

Attribute	WTP
seat[6]	25748.908526652467
seat[7]	22451.33585877174
seat[8]	23907.145057346024
cargo[T.3ft]	2755.802315180679
eng[T.gas]	9015.619377137044
eng[T.hyb]	4236.658666286363

Figure 10.4 – Willingness to pay for each attribute

In *Figure 10.4*, we can see the calculated WTP for each attribute. The WTP for **seat[6]** is higher than for **seat[7]**, which indicates that, according to the model's coefficients, consumers place more value on the attribute associated with **seat[6]** than **seat[7]**.

This higher WTP value for **seat[6]** over **seat[7]** means that **seat[6]** has a higher part-worth utility. This part-worth utility translates into consumers being willing to pay more for the benefits associated with **seat[6]** than those associated with **seat[7]**.

The difference between the two WTP values is a quantitative representation of how much more valuable **seat[6]** is perceived in comparison to **seat[7]**.

Choice share predictions

Choice share predictions are the predicted probability that a consumer will choose a specific product profile over alternatives.

The share of choice for a specific product profile is calculated as follows:

$$share_i = exp(utility_i) / \sum_{i=1}^{n} exp(utility_i)$$

where *utility* is each data point matrix multiplied by the coefficients.

> **A word of caution**
>
> Using survey-based share predictions for forecasting market share is appealing. Although these predictions accurately reflect the potential behavior of respondents when presented with choices (including competitors), this behavior may not directly correspond to actual sales. This discrepancy is due to various other sales-influencing factors, such as brand awareness and brand loyalty.

The algorithm

1. Convert the data to a matrix.
2. Remove the first column because we don't have an intercept.
3. Calculate the utility of each alternative by multiplying the matrix by the coefficients using matrix multiplication.
4. Calculate the choice share predictions using the multinomial logit formula:

$$share_i = \frac{e^{U_i}}{\sum_{j=1}^{J} e^{U_j}}$$

Where U_i is the utility of the alternative, and J is the number of alternatives.

Sensitivity analysis

Sensitivity analysis is a technique used to determine how sensitive the results of a model are to changes in the model's assumptions. In choice modeling, sensitivity analysis is used to determine how sensitive the choice share predictions are to changes in the attributes.

This means a product designer might want to understand how planning a feature or attribute would change the share prediction.

The analysis is simple, you simply loop through all the attribute levels, compute the share predictions, and then save the share prediction of the target design.

First, let's create a small helper function to use the model we created to predict share:

```python
def predict_shares(model, df):
    """
    Predict choice probabilities for each alternative in the dataframe
'df' using the fitted model 'model'.
    """
    # Use the model's predict method directly, which expects the
exogenous variables in the correct format
    probs = model.predict(df)
    # Assuming the choice probabilities are for each row in `df`
     return probs
```

Next, we have our sensitivity function:

```python
def sensitivity_mnl(model, attrib, base_data, competitor_data):
    # Concatenate base and competitor data
    full_data = pd.concat([base_data, competitor_data],
        ignore_index=True)

    # Assuming base_data has the structure expected by the model
(correct dummy variables, etc.)
    # We can modify this base data to explore different attribute
levels
    results = []

    for attr, levels in attrib.items():
        for level in levels:
            # Modify the attribute level in a copy of the base_data
            modified_data = base_data.copy()
            modified_data[attr] = level
            # Predict shares using the modified data
            shares = predict_shares(model, modified_data)[1]

            # Calculate the increase in share compared to the base
            base_share = predict_shares(model, base_data)[1]
            increase = shares - base_share

            results.append({
                'level': level,
                'share': shares.mean(),
                'increase': increase.mean()  # Average increase
            })

    return pd.DataFrame(results)
```

If we take as an example a car with 6 seats, 2ft cargo, a gas engine, and a price of 30,000, and we compare it with 10 other alternatives, we can see how much the share will change given each attribute change as shown in *Figure 10.5*:

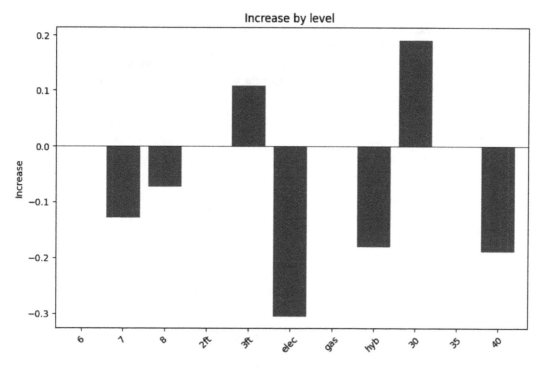

Figure 10.5 – Increase share by attribute level

We can see that changing the cargo from 2ft to 3ft would give us an increased share of this new design.

Now, you need to be careful with this type of analysis, because of the **independence of irrelevant alternatives (IIA)**. Let's break down why this is crucial.

Independence of irrelevant alternatives (IIA)

The IIA assumption, a fundamental aspect of some choice models (notably, the multinomial logit model), posits that the relative preference for any two alternatives is independent of the presence or absence of other alternatives. In simpler terms, adding or removing an option should not affect the relative preferences between the remaining options.

Why must we be careful with IIA in sensitivity analysis?

The following are the reasons for caution with IIA:

- **Unrealistic in certain scenarios**: The IIA assumption can be unrealistic in many real-world situations. For example, if you have two very similar products (such as two models of the same car brand), the introduction of a third, distinct option (say, a bike) shouldn't affect the relative preference between these two car models. However, under IIA, the introduction of the bike can disproportionately influence the choice between the two cars, which is not a realistic depiction of consumer behavior.

- **Impact on predicted choice shares**: When conducting sensitivity analysis to see how changes in attributes affect choice shares, violating the IIA assumption can lead to inaccurate predictions. If your model assumes IIA, it may not correctly account for changes in preferences that occur due to the introduction or modification of similar products.

- **Redistribution of choices**: The IIA problem often manifests as an equal redistribution of choices among alternatives when a new option is added. This can lead to counterintuitive results, such as a new product taking equally from all competitors, regardless of how similar or different they are.

- **Design and attribute overemphasis**: In product design, failure to account for the IIA problem might lead to overemphasizing certain features or attributes, thinking they will have a more significant impact on choice share than they realistically would.

To address IIA concerns in choice modeling, you might consider the following:

- **Using advanced models**: Look into choice modeling approaches that relax the IIA assumption, such as nested logit or mixed logit models. These models can account for similarities between options and offer a more realistic portrayal of choice behavior.

- **Segmenting the market**: Sometimes, segmenting the market and applying separate models to each segment can help mitigate the IIA problem, as similar products may not co-exist in all segments.

- **Careful design of alternatives**: Be mindful of how you design and present alternatives in your analysis. Try to ensure that they are distinct enough to avoid unrealistic substitution patterns.

Understanding and addressing the limitations of the IIA assumption is crucial for obtaining accurate and meaningful insights from sensitivity analysis in choice modeling, especially when predicting how changes in product attributes might influence consumer preferences and market share.

One issue to be careful with is that conjoint analysis is survey based, so sample size matters, as discussed in the previous chapter. Always report on the error of the estimates when doing conjoint analysis.

Summary

In this chapter, we explored the concept of conjoint analysis and its applications in market research and product design. Conjoint analysis is a powerful tool that allows us to understand consumer preferences and make informed decisions about product attributes.

We discussed the process of conducting conjoint analysis, including the creation of choice sets, the estimation of utility values, and the calculation of share predictions. We also highlighted the importance of sample size and the need to report the error of estimates when conducting conjoint analysis.

Furthermore, we addressed the concept of sensitivity analysis and its role in understanding the impact of attribute changes on choice shares. We emphasized caution regarding the IIA assumption and provided strategies to mitigate its limitations, including using advanced models such as nested logit or mixed logit models and segmenting the market.

Overall, conjoint analysis offers valuable insights into consumer preferences and can guide decision-making in product design, pricing, and market segmentation. By understanding the limitations and considerations associated with conjoint analysis, researchers and practitioners can leverage this technique to make informed and effective business decisions.

In the next chapter, we will discuss multi-touch attribution, a technique used to understand the impact of marketing channels on sales.

Further reading

- *Traditional Conjoint Analysis*: `https://github.com/JanisIranee/Traditional-Conjoint-Analysis-with-Python/blob/master/Traditional%20Conjoint%20Analyse.ipynb`

- *Conjoint Analysis: A Powerful Tool for Product Pricing*: `https://medium.com/data-analytics-ai-product-management/conjoint-analysis-a-powerful-tool-for-product-pricing-34278b3ec0f9`

- *Getting Preferred Combination of Attributes With Conjoint Analysis*: `https://www.analyticsvidhya.com/blog/2023/02/getting-preferred-combination-of-attributes-with-conjoint-analysis/`

- *R for Marketing Analytics & Research* by Chris Chapman and Elea McDonnell Feit, Springer

- *Courtyard by Marriott: Designing a Hotel Facility with Consumer-based Marketing Models*, Wind et al. 1989

- *Discrete Choice Methods with Simulation*, Kenneth Tran

Part 4: Measuring Effectiveness

This part examines the challenge of assessing marketing effectiveness, starting with the exploration of multi-touch attribution in digital marketing to understand how different channels contribute to marketing outcomes. It then transitions to discussing media mix modeling, emphasizing the importance of understanding how various marketing channels interact with one another, which is essential for advising on the best ways to allocate marketing budgets. This part also underscores the significance of conducting marketing experiments as a fundamental method for achieving optimization and efficiency, offering insights into experiment design and analysis.

This part contains the following chapters:

- *Chapter 11, Multi-Touch Digital Attribution*

- *Chapter 12, Media Mix Modeling with PyMC Marketing*

- *Chapter 13, Running Experiments with PyMC*

Multi-Touch Digital Attribution

What I cannot create, I do not understand

– Richard Feynman

In marketing, attribution refers to the evaluation of all the marketing touchpoints that a user encounters during their path to conversion from clicking an ad to being acquired as a user. The goal of attribution is to understand the impact of such touchpoints on the conversion from a prospect to an acquired user. This is important because it allows marketers to understand which channels are most effective, assign a value to each channel, and optimize their marketing spend accordingly.

In this chapter, we will cover the following topics:

- An introduction to attribution models
- Heuristic attribution models
- Algorithmic attribution models

By the end of this chapter, you will know what the most commonly used algorithmic attribution models are and how to build them with Python.

Technical requirements

The code files for this chapter are available on GitHub: `https://github.com/PacktPublishing/Data-Analytics-for-Marketing/tree/main/Chapter11`.

An introduction to attribution models

Attribution is fundamental in the world of marketing for several reasons:

- **Optimizing marketing budget**: By understanding which channels are driving conversions, marketers can allocate budget more efficiently to maximize ROI

- **Informing strategy**: Attribution provides insights into which strategies work and which ones need adjustment

- **Enhanced customer understanding**: Attribution offers a clearer picture of the customer journey, helping to refine the marketing approach

Fundamentally, attribution is the act of assigning a value to a channel or touchpoint. A value in this context is simply how much credit for the conversions we give each channel. The question is, how do we, in practice, assign such a value to a marketing channel?

For example, consider the journey depicted in *Figure 11.1*:

Figure 11.1 – An example of a customer journey

Here, we have a user who saw a search ad, then saw a Facebook ad, and, at the end of the journey, went directly to the website and converted. The question becomes, which channel do we assign the value to convert that user?

There are two approaches to solving this problem. On the one hand, we can use heuristics, or rules of thumb, to assign the value. Alternatively, we can use an algorithm to give us that measure of the value.

Let's start with the simplest family of attribution models, heuristic attribution models.

Heuristic attribution models

Heuristic attribution models are based on rules of thumb. They are easy to implement and understand but are not data-driven. The rules are simple, such as, "*Let's give full credit to the last ad the user saw,*" and not being data-driven means that regardless of the user journey, we always apply the same rule or heuristic to give credit to a channel for a conversion. In *Figure 11.2*, you can see a summary of the different heuristic attribution models, where *credit* refers to what channel we give value for the conversion, and to what degree:

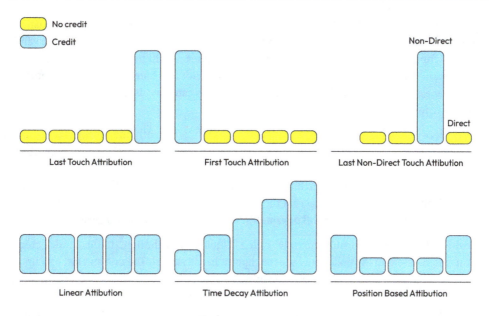

Figure 11.2 – Different heuristic attribution models

Let's have a look at each one of them:

- **Last touch attribution**: In this model, full credit is given to the last touchpoint in the customer journey. This model will maximize efficiency and ROI for **Bottom of Funnel (BoFu)** channels, such as a paid search. If the focus of the marketing team is conversion, most likely this is the model being used. It also requires minimal data and configurations. On the downside, the marketing team will have no visibility on the upper funnel channels, such as display ads, and will not have an indication of assisted conversions – that is, conversions where one channel has aided another in the conversion process. It will also overvalue the last touchpoint, which can often be direct.

- **First touch attribution**: Full credit is given to the first touchpoint in the customer journey. Marketing teams that are focused on demand generation and brand awareness tend to favor this model, since it gives them a way to evaluate the effectiveness of their **Top of Funnel (ToFu)** channels, since this model will have a bias toward ToFu channels, such as display ads. It will reflect the start of the customer journey and help track brand awareness. However, it will neglect the later touch points, such as paid search, which are more likely to be the last touchpoint before conversion.

- **Last touch non-direct attribution**: To account for the point that the last touchpoint can often be the Direct channel, in this model full credit is given to the last touchpoint in the customer journey, excluding direct traffic. It has the same drawbacks and advantages as the last touch attribution model, but it will not overvalue the Direct channel.

- **Linear attribution**: Credit is distributed evenly across all touchpoints in the customer journey. In this model, every touchpoint is considered. It has the drawback of undervaluing key touchpoints while overvaluing less important ones. It will help the marketing team in understanding the full path to conversion, but it will not be of any benefit in evaluating the effectiveness of each touchpoint, since different channels can have different levels of importance in the customer journey.

- **Time decay attribution**: Credit is awarded based on how recently the touchpoint occurred. The more recent the touchpoint, the more credit it is given. The assumption is that the closer a channel is to the conversion, the greater the influence. It makes sense, intuitively, since you can reason that it will be a closer match to the real-life customer journey. This model is useful for heuristically distributing credit across the customer journey, in particular giving some credit to ToFu activities. However, it will devalue such ToFu activities or brand awareness.

- **Position-based attribution**: Sometimes called "U-shaped attribution," in this model, credit is distributed based on the position of the touchpoint in the funnel. The first and last touchpoints may be given 40% credit each, while the middle touchpoints are given 20% credit in total. It promotes budget allocation toward the strategic channels and gives some visibility to both ToFu and BoFu activities. It can undervalue the middle touchpoints, however, especially for long customer journeys. It also has limited flexibility, since the credit distribution is divided evenly among the middle touchpoints.

The implementation of different heuristic attribution models

Let's look at how to use the heuristic attribution method.

We'll start by importing the necessary libraries:

```
import numpy as np
import pandas as pd
import matplotlib.pyplot as plt
import seaborn as sns
from collections import defaultdict
from itertools import combinations

%matplotlib inline
```

We will use the marketing.csv dataset from the book's GitHub repository. Let's import it into a DataFrame:

```
data = pd.read_csv('data/marketing.csv')
```

We can see the first five rows of the data we will work on in *Figure 11.3*:

<	user_id	date_served	marketing_channel	variant	converted	language_displayed	language_preferred	age_group	date_subscribed	date_canceled	subscribing_channel
0	a100000029	1/1/18	House Ads	personalization	True	English	English	0-18 years	1/1/18	NaN	House Ads	True
1	a100000030	1/1/18	House Ads	personalization	True	English	English	19-24 years	1/1/18	NaN	House Ads	True
2	a100000031	1/1/18	House Ads	personalization	True	English	English	24-30 years	1/1/18	NaN	House Ads	True
3	a100000032	1/1/18	House Ads	personalization	True	English	English	30-36 years	1/1/18	NaN	House Ads	True
4	a100000033	1/1/18	House Ads	personalization	True	English	English	36-45 years	1/1/18	NaN	House Ads	True

Figure 11.3 – The first rows of the raw attribution data

Let's do some data cleaning. For this exercise, we only need the `'user_id'`, `'date_served'`, `'data_subscribed'`, `'marketing_channel'`, and `'converted'` columns:

```
data = data[['user_id', 'date_served', 'date_subscribed',
    'marketing_channel', 'converted']]
data.dropna(axis = 0, inplace=True)
data['converted'] = data['converted'].astype('int')
data['date_served'] = pd.to_datetime(data['date_served'],
    format='%m/%d/%y', errors='coerce')
data['date_subscribed'] = pd.to_datetime(data['date_subscribed'],
    format='%m/%d/%y', errors='coerce')
data.head()
```

We now have a shorter DataFrame with only the columns we need in *Table 11.1*:

	user_id	date_served	date_subscribed	marketing_channel	converted
0	a100000029	2018-01-01	2018-01-01	House Ads	1
1	a100000030	2018-01-01	2018-01-01	House Ads	1
2	a100000031	2018-01-01	2018-01-01	House Ads	1
3	a100000032	2018-01-01	2018-01-01	House Ads	1
4	a100000033	2018-01-01	2018-01-01	House Ads	1

Table 11.1 – The first rows of the cleaned attribution data

Now, let's continue to see the implementation of each attribution type.

Last touch attribution

Starting with the most common heuristic attribution model, we can quickly compute the last touch attribution for each channel by simply grouping by channel and summing the conversions:

```
last_touch_attr = data.groupby(['marketing_channel']
    ).agg({'converted': 'sum'})
last_touch_attr
```

marketing_channel	converted
Email	167
Facebook	237
House Ads	298
Instagram	265
Push	83

Table 11.2 – The last touch attribution model

First touch attribution

For the first touch attribution, we need to do some more work:

1. **Sort the data**: Arrange the data in ascending order first by user, and then by the date they were served an ad. This ensures that each user's interactions are processed chronologically.

2. **Group and aggregate**: Group the sorted data by each user. For each user, we need to do the following:

    I.   Identify the earliest (or first) date they were served an ad.

    II.   Capture the marketing channel associated with this earliest date.

3. **Assign conversion**: For each user, attribute a conversion to their first touchpoint. This is based on the assumption of the first touch attribution model, where the first interaction always results in a conversion.

4. **Count conversions by channel**: Calculate the total number of conversions for each marketing channel based on the first touch attribution model.

5. **Prepare the final table**: Generate a table that displays each marketing channel and the number of conversions attributed to it, using the first touch model.

Here is the code to do this:

```
data = data.sort_values(by=['user_id', 'date_served'])
```

```
# Group by user_id and get the earliest date and channel they were
served an ad
first_touch = data.groupby('user_id').agg({
    'date_served': 'first',
    'marketing_channel': 'first'
}).reset_index()

first_touch['converted'] = 1
attribution_table =
    first_touch['marketing_channel'].value_counts().reset_index()
attribution_table.columns = ['marketing_channel', 'converted']
attribution_table
```

	marketing_channel	converted
0	House Ads	497
1	Facebook	180
2	Instagram	141
3	Email	139
4	Push	63

Table 11.3 – The first touch attribution model

Linear attribution

For the linear attribution model, the credit for a conversion is distributed evenly across all the touchpoints that a user interacts with. This means if a user had three touchpoints before converting, each touchpoint would receive 1/3 of the credit for the conversion.

In this code, we do the following:

1. We first calculate the number of touchpoints for each user.

2. We then create a new column called `'credit'` that distributes the conversion credit evenly across all touchpoints for a user.

3. Finally, using the linear attribution model, we aggregate the credits by marketing channel to get the total credit attributed to each channel.

The code to perform these steps is as follows:

```
df = data.copy()

# Find the total number of distinct touchpoints (channels) for each
user
```

```
touchpoint_counts = df.groupby('user_id')['marketing_channel'].
nunique()

# Create a new column 'credit' to allocate the conversion credit for
each touchpoint
df['credit'] = df['user_id'].map(lambda x: 1/touchpoint_counts[x]
    if x in touchpoint_counts else 0)

# Sum the credits for each marketing channel
attribution_table = df.groupby('marketing_channel')['credit'].sum().
reset_index().sort_values(by='credit', ascending=False)

attribution_table
```

	marketing_channel	credit
2	House Ads	526.000000
1	Facebook	246.333333
3	Instagram	233.833333
0	Email	165.500000
4	Push	85.333333

Table 11.4 – The linear attribution model

Time decay attribution

For the time decay attribution model, we'll give more credit to touchpoints that occurred more recently. This will involve assigning weights that increase as we get closer to the conversion point.

One common method to implement time decay attribution is to use an exponential decay formula, where touchpoints further from the conversion receive exponentially less credit than those closer to the conversion.

In this implementation, we do the following:

1. We first calculate the date of conversion for each user.

2. We then calculate the number of days each touchpoint is from the conversion.

3. We apply an exponential decay function to assign credits to touchpoints. The closer the touchpoint is to the conversion, the more credit it receives. Adjusting the base of the exponential function (here, we used 2) allows you to modify the rate of decay.

4. Finally, we aggregate the credits by marketing channel.

Here's how you can implement the time decay attribution model using the given sample data:

```
df = data.copy()

# Compute the maximum date for each user (this represents the
conversion date)
conversion_dates = df.groupby('user_id')['date_served'].max()

# Calculate the days from conversion for each touchpoint
df['days_from_conversion'] = df.apply(
    lambda row: (conversion_dates[row['user_id']] -
    row['date_served']).days, axis=1)

# Apply time decay function. Here, we use an exponential decay.
# You can adjust the base value (2 in this case) to modify the decay
rate.
df['credit'] = df['days_from_conversion'].apply(lambda x: 1 / (2 **
x))

# Sum the credits for each marketing channel
attribution_table = df.groupby('marketing_channel')['credit'].sum().
reset_index().sort_values(by='credit', ascending=False)

attribution_table
```

	marketing_channel	credit
2	House Ads	414.387390
1	Facebook	258.591524
3	Instagram	237.449954
0	Email	185.985185
4	Push	95.544981

Table 11.5 – The time decay attribution model

Position-based attribution

As we discussed, for position-based (or U-shaped) attribution, the first and last touchpoints each receive 40% of the credit, and the remaining 20% is distributed among the middle touchpoints.

In this code, we do the following:

1. We define a function, `assign_weights`, that takes in the touchpoints for a user and assigns credit based on their position:

    *   If there's only one touchpoint, it receives 100% credit

    *   If there are two touchpoints, each receives 50%

    *   For more than two touchpoints, the first and last get 40% each, and the middle touchpoints share the remaining 20% equally

2. We then sort the DataFrame to ensure that touchpoints for each user are processed in order.

3. We apply the position weights to the touchpoints using the `assign_weights` function.

4. Finally, we aggregate the credits by marketing channel to produce the position-based attribution table.

Let's implement the position-based attribution model using the sample data:

```python
df = data.copy()

# Calculate position weights
def assign_weights(touchpoints):
    n = len(touchpoints)
    if n == 1:
        return [1]
    if n == 2:
        return [0.5, 0.5]

    middle_weight = 0.2 / (n - 2)
    weights = [0.4] + [middle_weight] * (n - 2) + [0.4]
    return weights

# Sort the data for sequential processing
df = df.sort_values(['user_id', 'date_served'])

# Apply position weights
df['credit'] = df.groupby('user_id')['date_served'].transform
    (assign_weights).explode().reset_index(drop=True)

# Sum the credits for each marketing channel
attribution_table = df.groupby('marketing_channel')['credit'].sum().
reset_index().sort_values(by='credit', ascending=False)

attribution_table
```

	marketing_channel	credit
2	House Ads	403.165000
1	Facebook	170.250000
3	Instagram	140.318333
0	Email	110.950000
4	Push	60.716667

Table 11.6 – Position-based attribution model

Heuristic attribution models have some limitations and rely on a lot of assumptions. A better approach would be a more data-driven approach, and this is where we can make use of algorithmic attribution models.

Algorithmic attribution models

Algorithmic attribution models are data-driven. They are more complex to implement and understand but are more accurate.

Shapley value attribution

Shapley value attribution is based on game theory, where a game can be a set of circumstances whereby two or more players contribute to an outcome. However, before we delve into how to do Shapley value attribution, we need to understand the concept of Shapley values.

What are Shapley values?

Shapley values are a method used to assign fair importance to each feature in a predictive model, treating each feature as if it were a contributing member in a coalition game, where the final prediction is considered the reward. These values help in quantifying the contribution of each feature to the prediction, ensuring that the total payoff is distributed equitably among all features involved in making the model's decision. You have a machine learning model to predict apartment prices. The model predicts a price of 300,000 USD for a given apartment. The price can be explained by the size of the apartment, the number of rooms, the zip code, and the existence of a balcony. Intuitively, all features play a role in determining the price. But how much does each feature contribute?

For a linear regression, as we have seen in *Chapter 4, Econometrics and Causal Inference with Statsmodels and PyMC*, the answer is simple – *the effect is the weight of the feature times the feature value*. This works because of the linearity of the model.

A possible solution comes from cooperative game theory in the form of the Shapley value, named after its author, Lloyd Shapley, in 1953. Players in a game cooperate in a coalition and receive a certain profit based on their contribution. The Shapley value formally represents the average contribution of a player to all possible coalitions. In our example, the players are the features, and the profit is the difference between the actual and average predictions.

How to calculate Shapley values

Here is how to think about Shapely value – feature values enter a room in random order. All features participate in the game – that is, contribute to the prediction. The Shapley value of a feature is the average change in the prediction that the coalition already in the room receives when the feature joins them.

Let's consider a simplified example of dividing the payout from a cooperative game among different players, based on their contribution. Suppose there is a group of four friends (Alice, Bob, Carol, and David) who decide to work together on a project that yields a payout of $100. The goal is to distribute this $100 among the four of them fairly, based on the value each person contributes to the project. To keep the example manageable, let's say they consider working in pairs, and we know the value that each pair can generate.

Here's how the project payout is generated based on their participation:

- Alone, each person contributes nothing – $0
- Alice and Bob working together can generate $30
- Alice and Carol working together can generate $40
- Alice and David working together can generate $20
- Bob and Carol working together can generate $50
- Bob and David working together can generate $25
- Carol and David working together can generate $45
- All four working together can generate $100

Using the Shapley value, we want to find a fair payout for each individual that considers their individual contribution, as well as their contribution as part of a pair.

To calculate the Shapley value for Alice, we look at all the orders in which the coalition (group of friends) can form and calculate Alice's marginal contribution to each possible coalition.

Here are a couple of examples of how we would calculate the marginal contribution:

- If Alice is the first to join, her marginal contribution is $0 (since she can't generate any payout alone)
- If Alice joins after Bob, her marginal contribution is the additional value that Alice and Bob together can generate compared to Bob alone, which is $30

- If Alice joins after Bob and Carol, her marginal contribution is the value that Alice, Bob, and Carol together can generate minus the value that Bob and Carol can generate without her, which is $100 - $50 = $50

When applying this to marketing, you can think of channels as the friends in the previous example, and instead of dividing the payout, you divide the conversions.

The formula to calculate the shapely value is as follows:

$$\phi_i(v) = \sum_{S \subseteq N \setminus \{i\}} \frac{|S|!\,(n - |S| - 1)!}{n!} (v(S \cup \{i\}) - v(S))$$

Let's review the key notations:

- N = Channels{Display Ads, Facebook, Email, Google} is a set of players. Note that instead of features, we take channels as the "players."

- i = a specific channel or player

- S = coalition, a subset of players that worked together to achieve a conversion

- $|S|$ = cardinality of S, the number of players in the coalition

- n = the number of channels or players in the game

- $v(S)$ = a real-valued function v that is a characteristic function that maps every coalition S to a value $v(S)$, the value of coalition S of channels. In our case, it is the weight of each channel after the calculation

- Weight = $|S|!(n - |S| - 1)!n!$

- Marginal contribution = $v(S \cup i) - v(S)$ – that is, the incremental weighted sum minus the coalition without v(S)

Conversions are credited to the channels by a process of permutating the customer journeys. In each permutation, a channel is given an estimate of how essential it is overall.

Implementing a Shapley value example

Let's start by importing the necessary libraries:

```
import numpy as np
import pandas as pd
import matplotlib.pyplot as plt
import seaborn as sns
from collections import defaultdict
from itertools import combinations

%matplotlib inline
```

We will use the `marketing.csv` dataset from the book's GitHub repository. Let's import it into a DataFrame and have a look at it:

```
data = pd.read_csv('../data/marketing.csv')
data.head()
```

We can see the first rows of the dataset in *Figure 11.4*:

	user_id	date_served	marketing_channel	variant	converted	language_displayed	language_preferred
0	a100000029	1/1/18	House Ads	personalization	True	English	English
1	a100000030	1/1/18	House Ads	personalization	True	English	English
2	a100000031	1/1/18	House Ads	personalization	True	English	English
3	a100000032	1/1/18	House Ads	personalization	True	English	English
4	a100000033	1/1/18	House Ads	personalization	True	English	English

Figure 11.4 – The first few rows of the dataset we'll be working with

As we can see from the table, we have user-level data for which marketing channel they were exposed to and whether they converted or not. We also have the date when they were exposed to the marketing channel. For this exercise, we will only need the `user_id`, `date_served`, `marketing_channel`, and `converted` columns. Let's create a new DataFrame with only those columns:

```
data = data[['user_id', 'date_served', 'marketing_channel',
    'converted']]
data.dropna(axis = 0, inplace=True)
data['converted'] = data['converted'].astype('int')
data['date_served'] = pd.to_datetime(data['date_served'],
    format='%m/%d/%y', errors='coerce')
data.head()
```

We can see the output in *Table 11.7*:

	user_id	date_served	marketing_channel	converted
0	a100000029	2018-01-01	House Ads	1
1	a100000030	2018-01-01	House Ads	1
2	a100000031	2018-01-01	House Ads	1
3	a100000032	2018-01-01	House Ads	1
4	a100000033	2018-01-01	House Ads	1

Table 11.7 – The columns required for the coalitions

Now, we need to create a DataFrame with the coalitions, which in this case are the paths to conversion. We will use the `date_served` column to order this new DataFrame, and then we will group it by `user_id` and `marketing_channel` to create the paths to conversion.

We essentially do the following:

1. **Select and sort**: We select the `user_id`, `marketing_channel`, and `converted` columns from the new `df` DataFrame, and then we sort that DataFrame by `user_id` and `marketing_channel`.

2. **Group and aggregate on a per-user basis**: We group by `user_id` and `marketing_channel` and aggregate the converted column with the `max` function. We then rename the `marketing_channel` column for clarity.

3. **Group and aggregate based on marketing channel combinations**: We simply group by `marketing_channel_subset` and sum the converted column to get the number of conversions for each path to conversion.

Let's see how this is done in Python:

```
ordered_data = data[['user_id', 'marketing_channel',
    'converted']].sort_values(by=['user_id',
        'marketing_channel'])

grouped = ordered_data.groupby(['user_id'], as_index=False).agg({
    'marketing_channel': lambda x: ','.join(sorted(x.unique())),
    'converted': 'max'
})
grouped.rename(columns={
    'marketing_channel': 'marketing_channel_subset'
}, inplace = True)

coalitions = grouped.groupby(['marketing_channel_subset'], as_
index=False).agg({
    'converted': 'sum'
})
```

Let's have a look at the paths to the conversion DataFrame:

	marketing_channel_subset	converted
0	Email	110
1	Email,Facebook	11
2	Email,Facebook,House Ads	8
3	Email,Facebook,House Ads,Instagram	0
4	Email,House Ads	40
5	Email,House Ads,Instagram	3
6	Email,House Ads,Push	1
7	Email,Instagram	10
8	Email,Push	4
9	Facebook	103
10	Facebook,House Ads	72
11	Facebook,House Ads,Instagram	24
12	Facebook,House Ads,Push	4
13	Facebook,Instagram	62
14	Facebook,Push	22
15	House Ads	280
16	House Ads,Instagram	103
17	House Ads,Instagram,Push	12
18	House Ads,Push	46
19	Instagram	57
20	Instagram,Push	21
21	Push	22

Table 11.8 – Coalitions for Shapley value attribution

For the Shapley value calculation, we will need a few auxiliary functions. Let's start by creating a function that returns us the power set of all the sets – in this case, the marketing channels. Essentially, we want all possible combinations of marketing channels:

```
# Create a function that returns all possible combinations of the
channel
def power_set(sets: list) -> list:
    return [list(j) for i in range(len(sets)) for j in
        combinations(sets, i+1)]
```

Then, we need to create a function to calculate all the possible subsets of a set of channels:

```python
def subsets(channels):
    '''
    Returns all possible subsets of a set of channels
    '''
    if len(channels) == 1:
        return channels
    else:
        sub_channels = []
        for i in range(1, len(channels) + 1):
            sub_channels.extend(map(list, combinations(channels, i)))
    return list(map(','.join,map(sorted, sub_channels)))
```

Next comes the characteristic function, $v(s)$, which we will use to measure each coalition. It takes a list of channels – that is, the coalition and a `dict` of the conversions per channel:

```python
# characteristic function v(s)

def v_function(coalition: list, conversions: dict) -> int:
    subsets_coalition = subsets(coalition)
    worth_coalition = 0
    for subset in subsets_coalition:
        if subset in conversions:
            worth_coalition += conversions[subset]

    return worth_coalition
```

Finally, we use a simple function to calculate the factorial of a number:

```python
def factorial(n):
    if n == 0:
        return 1
    else:
        return n * factorial(n - 1)
```

We now have all the necessary functions to calculate the Shapley values. The function to calculate them is as follows:

```python
def calculate_shapley_values(data: pd.DataFrame,
    channel_name: str, conv_name: str) -> defaultdict:
    conversion_values = data.set_index(channel_name).to_dict()
        [conv_name]
    data['channels'] = data[channel_name].apply(
        lambda x: x if len(x.split(',')) == 1 else np.nan)
```

```
channels = list(data['channels'].dropna().unique())

v_values = {}

for A in power_set(channels):
    v_values[','.join(sorted(A))] = v_function(A,
        conversion_values)

n = len(channels)
shapley_values = defaultdict(int)

for channel in channels:
    for A in v_values.keys():
        if channel not in A.split(","):
            cardinal_A = len(A.split(","))
            A_with_channel = A.split(",")
            A_with_channel.append(channel)
            A_with_channel = ",".join(sorted(A_with_channel))
            # Weight = |S|!(n - S - 1)! / n!
            weight = (factorial(cardinal_A) *
                factorial(n - cardinal_A - 1) / factorial(n))
            # Marginal contrib = v(S U {i} - v(S))
            contrib = (v_values[A_with_channel] - v_values[A])
            shapley_values[channel] += weight * contrib
    shapley_values[channel] += v_values[channel] / n

return shapley_values
```

Now, since this function looks a bit complicated, let's break it apart and see what each part does:

- **The input parameters**:

  - data: A Pandas DataFrame containing information about conversions for different marketing channel combinations.

  - channel_name: The column name in data that has the marketing channel names or combinations

  - conv_name: The column name in data that contains the conversion values

- **A conversion values dictionary**: First, we create a dictionary where the keys are the marketing channel combinations and the values are the conversions:

  ```
  conversion_values = data.set_index(channel_name).to_dict()
      [conv_name]
  ```

- **Single channel extraction**: Then, we filter the DataFrame to only consider individual channels (and not combinations). These individual channels are stored in the `channels` list:

```python
data['channels'] = data[channel_name].apply(
    lambda x: x if len(x.split(',')) == 1 else np.nan)
channels = list(data['channels'].dropna().unique())
```

- **V-function value calculation**: For every possible subset of channels (obtained using `power_set`), the function calculates its value using `v_function` and stores it in the `v_values` dictionary:

```python
for A in power_set(channels):
    v_values[','.join(sorted(A))] = v_function(A,
        conversion_values)
```

- **Initialization**:

  - n captures the total number of individual channels

  - `shapley_values` stores the computed Shapley values for each channel:

```python
n = len(channels)
shapley_values = defaultdict(int)
```

- **Shapley value calculation**: The nested `for` loop does the heavy lifting of calculation. The Shapley value for a player (here, a channel) is the average marginal contribution of the player across all possible coalitions. The nested `for` loop ensures each coalition and channel are considered.

- **Return**: Finally, the function returns the computed Shapley values for each channel in the form of a dictionary:

```python
return shapley_values
```

Let's get the results into a variable and create a DataFrame with it so that we can have a look at the results:

```python
shapley_values = calculate_shapley_values(coalitions,
    'marketing_channel_subset', 'converted')
shapley_result = pd.DataFrame(list(shapley_values.items()),
    columns=['channel', 'shapley_value'])
plt.subplots(figsize=(15,8))
s = sns.barplot(x = 'channel', y = 'shapley_value',
    data = shapley_result)
sns.despine(top=True, right=True)
for idx, row in shapley_result.iterrows():
    s.text(row.name, row.shapley_value +5,
        round(row.shapley_value,1), ha='center',
        color='darkslategray', fontweight='semibold')
plt.show();
```

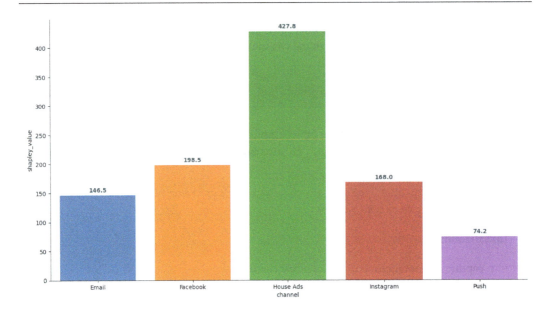

Figure 11.5 – The attribution results from the Shapley values

You can see that the biggest change is that, under Shapley value attribution, a much bigger weight is given to House Ads versus other channels.

There are a few issues with Shapley value attribution:

- The number of permutations grows exponentially with the number of touchpoints, at the rate of 2^n, where n is the number of channels
- It does not take into account the order of the touchpoints in the customer journey
- If order is taken into account, the number of permutations grows at the rate of $n!$, where n is the number of channels
- Touchpoints that are infrequent or are only present in longer journeys have their contributions underestimated

To handle some of the issues of Shapley value attribution, Google developed a closely related and simpler version, called **Fractional Attribution (Fractribution)**, which we'll discuss next.

Fractribution

Fractribution uses a simplified Shapley value method. But first, we need to understand the paths to conversion.

Path transforms

Paths to conversion are often very similar but not exact. It is helpful to apply a path transform before running an attribution algorithm to reduce unnecessary permutations. For example, you may want to group all paths that contain the same channels but in a different order. So, take the journey in *Figure 11.6* as an example:

Figure 11.6 – The original path to conversion

After the path transform, it becomes the shorter path as seen in *Figure 11.7*:

Figure 11.7 – An example path transform

Here, we apply the first path transform, which takes only the first occurrence of any given event. There are five path transforms available:

- **Unique**: Treat all events in a path as unique. It is best if you have a short lookback length, low volume, and specific marketing (and don't do a lot of retargeting).

Figure 11.8 – A unique path transform

- **Exposure**: Collapse repeats events that are immediately in sequence. It's a balance between first and unique and should be the default if you don't know about the type of marketing you are doing.

Figure 11.9 – An exposure path transform

- **First**: Take only the first occurrence of any given event. This is best for cases where attribution is on something new that is being marketed and/or brand awareness-type marketing.

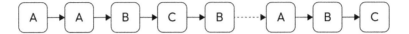

Figure 11.10 – A first path transform

- **Frequency**: Count events from their first occurrence. This is useful when there are retargeting, many follow-ups, and no frequency capping.

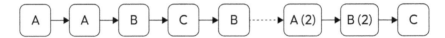

Figure 11.11 – A frequency path transform

- **Recency**: Look at where the event occurred in the timeline before conversion and then do the following:

    I.   Treat the same events differently if they occur in different time buckets

    II.   Collapse events if they are in the same time bucket

    This is useful if there are longer lookback periods (> 30 days) and a tiered marketing strategy.

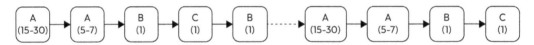

Figure 11.12 – A recency path transform

The fractribution algorithm

The algorithm behind fractribution attribution is as follows:

1. Start with a baseline path:

Figure 11.13 – A baseline path

2. Define its leave-one-out counterfactuals – that is, the alternative potential paths without one of the channels or touchpoints in them.

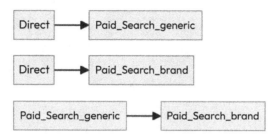

Figure 11.14 – The leave-one-out counterfactuals

3. Calculate the conversion probability for each counterfactual:

path	total_ conversions	total_non_ conversions	conversion_ probability
Direct -> Paid_Search_generic	19	549	0.0335
Direct -> Paid_Search_brand	17	250	0.0637
Paid_Search_ generic -> Paid_Search_brand	7	357	0.0192
Direct -> Paid_ Search_generic -> Paid_Search_brand	1	10	0.0.909

Table 11.9 – Conversion probabilities for fractribution

Where conversion probability $= \frac{\text{total conversions}}{(\text{total conversions + total non conversions})}$

4. The marginal contribution of each event is the conversion probability difference between the baseline (full) path and the counterfactual path without the event in it:

path	total_ conversions	total_non_ conversions	conversion_ probability
Direct -> Paid_Search_generic	19	549	0.0335
Direct -> Paid_Search_brand	17	250	0.0637
Paid_Search_ generic -> Paid_Search_brand	7	357	0.0192
Direct -> Paid_ Search_generic -> Paid_Search_brand	1	10	0.0.909

Table 11.10 – The counterfactual paths to conversion

- Marginal contribution of `Direct` = 0.0909 - 0.0192 = 0.0717

- Marginal contribution of `Paid_Search_brand` = 0.0909 - 0.0335 = 0.0574

- Marginal contribution of `Paid_Search_generic` = 0.0909 - 0.0637 = 0.0272

5. Normalize the fractions so that they add to 1:

Path	Direct	Paid_ Search_ generic	Paid_Search_ brand
Direct > Paid_Search_generic > Paid_Search_brand	0.459	0.174	0.467

Table 11.11 – The normalized marginal contributions

Here, the normalized fraction is calculated as follows:

$$\text{normalized contribution}_i = \frac{\text{marginal contribution}_i}{\sum_{i=1}^{n} \text{marginal contribution}}$$

6. Repeat *steps 1* to *5* for all paths.

The Python implementation

The Python implementation of the fractribution attribution algorithm is as follows:

```
# 1. Define paths and counterfactuals
```

```python
# The baseline path
baseline_path = ['Direct', 'Paid_Search_generic', 'Paid_Search_brand']

# The counterfactual paths
counterfactuals = [
    ['Direct', 'Paid_Search_generic'],
    ['Direct', 'Paid_Search_brand'],
    ['Paid_Search_generic', 'Paid_Search_brand']
]

# The conversion data
conversion_data = {
    tuple(baseline_path): (1, 10, 0.0909),
    tuple(counterfactuals[0]): (19, 549, 0.0335),
    tuple(counterfactuals[1]): (17, 250, 0.0637),
    tuple(counterfactuals[2]): (7, 357, 0.0192)
}

# 2. Calculate the conversion probability
# This function will calculate the conversion probability using the
provided formula
def calculate_conversion_probability(total_conversions,
    total_non_conversions):
    return total_conversions / (total_conversions +
        total_non_conversions)

# 3. Determine the marginal contribution of each event
def calculate_marginal_contributions(baseline_conversion_prob):
    marginal_contributions = {}
    for path, (_, _, conversion_prob) in conversion_data.items():
        for event in baseline_path:
            if event not in path:
                if event not in marginal_contributions:
                    marginal_contributions[event] = 0
                marginal_contributions[event] = \
                    abs(baseline_conversion_prob - conversion_prob)
    return marginal_contributions

marginal_contributions = calculate_marginal_contributions(
    conversion_data[tuple(baseline_path)][2])

# 4. Normalize the fractions
def normalize_contributions(marginal_contributions):
    total = sum(marginal_contributions.values())
```

```
        normalized = {event: value/total for event,
            value in marginal_contributions.items()}
        return normalized

    normalized_contributions = normalize_contributions
        (marginal_contributions)


    print(normalized_contributions)
```

Let's go over the code in further detail.

Defining paths and counterfactuals

Let's go through the code snippet for the fractribution algorithm in greater detail, highlighting the key steps and transformations:

- **Baseline path**: The code sets a baseline path, named `baseline_path`, which is an ordered list of events leading to the conversion. This path is `Direct > Paid_Search_generic > Paid_Search_brand`.

- **Counterfactual paths**: `counterfactuals` is a list containing alternative paths that leaves one event out from the baseline path at a time.

- **Conversion data**: The `conversion_data` dictionary contains conversion data for each path. It uses the path as the key (converted to a tuple) and a tuple as the value. The tuple consists of total conversions, total non-conversions, and the calculated conversion probability for that path.

Calculating the conversion probability

A function named `calculate_conversion_probability` is defined to compute the conversion probability, based on given total conversions and total non-conversions:

```
def calculate_conversion_probability(total_conversions,
    total_non_conversions):
    return total_conversions / (total_conversions +
        total_non_conversions)
```

Determining the marginal contribution of each event:

The `calculate_marginal_contributions` function computes the marginal contributions of each event in the baseline path. It uses the difference between the baseline conversion probability and the conversion probability of each counterfactual path, without the event in question:

```
def calculate_marginal_contributions(baseline_conversion_prob):
    marginal_contributions = {}
    for path, (_, _, conversion_prob) in conversion_data.items():
```

```
        for event in baseline_path:
            ...
```

Normalizing the fractions

The `normalize_contributions` function is responsible for taking the marginal contributions of each event and normalizing them so that they sum up to 1.

```
def normalize_contributions(marginal_contributions):
    total = sum(marginal_contributions.values())
    normalized = {event: value/total for event,
        value in marginal_contributions.items()}
    return normalized
```

Finally, the code calls these functions in sequence and prints out the normalized contributions of each event.

There are other more complex algorithms, such as Markov chain attribution, but they are outside of the scope of this book. There are references at the end of the chapter for the more curious among you.

Summary

In this chapter, we explored marketing attribution. We discussed the two main families of models – heuristic and algorithmic. We then explored the most common heuristic models, what their limitations are, and why you should use algorithmic models. Finally, we delved deeper into the Shapley value and fractribution and how they can be used to calculate attribution.

You can now distinguish between the heuristic and algorithmic attribution models, explain the different types of heuristic models available, and implement the three most common algorithmic attribution models.

In the next chapter, we will look at how we can optimize media spending when we don't have the level of granularity and detail for algorithmic attribution, with the use of media mix models.

Further reading

- Fractribution – Google: `https://github.com/google/fractribution`
- RBA – Google: `https://github.com/google/rba`
- *Finite Markov Chains* – Quant Econ: `https://python.quantecon.org/finite_markov.html`

- *Building an attribution model with markov chains*: `https://www.avayant.com/post/building-an-attribution-model-with-markov-chains`

- *Introduction to Markov Chains*: `https://towardsdatascience.com/introduction-to-markov-chains-50da3645a50d`

- *Introduction to Algorithmic Marketing* by Ilya Katsov

12

Media Mix Modeling with PyMC Marketing

In the previous chapter, we discussed how to assign credit to marketing channels, understand their value, and optimize our budget. However, a big caveat of the topics discussed in the previous chapter is the availability of granular-level data that shows which ads the user saw and clicked, and where they ended up converting.

This data is only available in digital channels, leaving out activities such as sponsorship or offline marketing, which, by definition, cannot be easily tracked. Adding to this issue, cookies are being slowly deprecated across major vendors, implying that even on digital channels, the availability of granular data is reducing. For example, many advertisers struggled when Apple released iOS 14.5 with enhanced privacy protections as this prevented companies from having access to the type of data needed for multi-touch attribution.

The solution to these measurement issues is a type of modeling called **media mix modeling (MMM)**. It is an econometric model that aims to measure the impact of marketing and non-marketing activities on a pre-defined KPI, commonly sales.

In this chapter, you will learn about the following topics:

- Understanding MMM
- Steps toward implementing MMM
- Selecting a model
- A synthetic data example of MMM

By the end of this chapter, you will have a solid understanding of MMM and how to start implementing it in Python.

Technical requirements

The code files for this chapter are available on GitHub: `https://github.com/PacktPublishing/ Data-Analytics-for-Marketing/tree/main/Chapter12`.

The code in this chapter was tested on PyMC-Marketing version 0.3.1. Version 0.4.0 introduced some breaking changes that were still being addressed by the library maintainers at the time of publishing.

Understanding MMM

A media mix model is a statistical analysis technique that's used by marketers to quantify the effectiveness of different marketing strategies on sales and to predict the outcomes of applying future strategies. This approach is frequently employed to fine-tune advertising expenditures to enhance the **return on investment** (**ROI**) or to meet other key marketing objectives.

It is a privacy-friendly approach where you neither have nor need access to user-level data. It is a top-down approach where the model is fitted to aggregated data, and the results are then used to inform future marketing decisions.

Let's see why we should use MMM:

- **Privacy-friendly and signal-resilient**: It is privacy-friendly and resilient to cookie deprecation. Compared to multi-touch attribution, it is less reliant on online signals.

- **Holistic**: It takes into account all marketing (both online and offline) and non-marketing activities (seasonality, events, promotions), and how they interact with each other.

- **Flexible**: It can be used to measure the impact of marketing activities on a variety of KPIs, such as sales, leads, app installs, and so on.

Media mix models have a lot of moving parts and requirements that an analyst needs to be aware of:

- **Data collection**: MMM requires historical data on sales and marketing efforts across different channels, such as television, radio, print, digital, social media, and out-of-home advertising

- **Variable isolation**: It takes into account not only the direct effects of marketing activities but also indirect factors such as economic conditions, seasonality, competition, and market changes

- **Statistical analysis**: Using regression analysis or more sophisticated econometric models, MMM evaluates how various elements of the marketing mix contribute to sales outcomes

- **Attribution**: By attributing sales to different marketing inputs, MMM helps in understanding the effectiveness of each media channel

- **Optimization**: Marketers can use the insights from the MMM to allocate future spending in a way that maximizes sales or achieves other campaign objectives

The main uses of MMM are as follows:

- **Budget allocation**: Determining how to allocate the marketing budget across different media channels to achieve the best results

- **ROI analysis**: Understanding which campaigns or media channels give the best return on investment

- **Forecasting**: Predicting future sales based on different levels of spending across media channels

- **Scenario planning**: Testing various "what if" scenarios to anticipate the outcomes of changes in the marketing strategy

- **Long-term planning**: Informing strategic decisions about long-term marketing investments and brand positioning

- **Price elasticity**: Understanding how sensitive consumers are to price changes and how pricing interacts with marketing efforts

- **Market response modeling**: Analyzing how different markets respond to various marketing strategies

- **Cross-channel synergies and cannibalization**: Identifying the synergistic effects of multiple media channels working together and instances where different marketing strategies may cannibalize each other's effectiveness

Here are some common questions that MMM can answer:

- **Quantifying media channel impact**: To what extent did each media channel contribute to both online and offline sales?

- **Evaluating marketing channel ROI**: What ROI did each marketing channel yield?

- **Budget allocation strategy**: How should the marketing budget be distributed across channels to optimize key performance indicators?

- **Optimal use of marketing funds**: Where is the most effective place to invest the next marketing dollar?

- **Determining ideal spending levels**: What is the ideal expenditure for each primary marketing channel?

- **Assessing sales impact of marketing changes**: How would alterations in the marketing strategy affect sales outcomes?

- **Strategic budget reductions**: In the event of a marketing budget cut by a certain percentage, in which areas should the reductions be made?

- **Performance analysis of specific channels**: How does the execution method (such as buying objectives, frequency, creative quality, or targeting strategy) influence the performance of channels such as Facebook?

- **Price adjustment considerations**: Is there a need to increase prices, and if so, by what margin?

- **Competitor advertising impact**: What effect does competitors' advertising have on the performance of our brands?

- **Revenue influence of trade and promotions**: How much additional revenue is generated by trade and promotional activities?

Before we dive further into the details of MMM, I would like to clarify a common misunderstanding that occurs when discussing MMM and MTA or A/B testing, and how they relate to one another.

MMM versus MTA versus lift analysis and A/B testing

There is a common misconception when doing an MMM. An MMM *does not require* attribution. As you may recall from the previous chapter, attribution – be it heuristic or algorithmic – is the process of assigning credit to conversions or revenue. If you take a step back, and consider that an MMM is a regression model, you can reason that this model is doing the same thing. The regression coefficients are going to be the channel share of the outcome variable, given every other channel or variable fixed. Essentially, an MMM is doing attribution and assigning credit, but at a macro level, and not at a micro level. In lift analysis, which we will cover in the next chapter, you use A/B testing to understand the incremental effect of a channel by closing it down and checking the effect. Again, you are answering the same question – that is, how much is this channel worth and how much should I credit it with? However, here, you are doing it via a randomized control trial.

You can think about this as answering the same question from three different points of view. The question is, how much is this channel worth?

- **MMM**: The answer is given by the coefficient of a regression that attempts to calculate the share of the outcome variable that is explained by the channel in question

- **Multi-touch attribution**: The answer is given by the algorithm that attempts to calculate the credit that should be awarded to the channel in question, given the granular path to conversion

- **Lift analysis and A/B testing**: The answer is given by using the gold standard of causal inference, literally stopping the channel in question and measuring the difference in the outcome variable

You are measuring the same thing; you are just using three different techniques. Due to the nature of statistics, they will not give you the same values, but they should be in the same vicinity, which means you can use them to validate each other. If you are getting very different results, then you need to investigate why that is the case. It could be that the data is not good enough, or that the model is not good enough. For example, a very common way to test and calibrate an MMM model is to stop a channel, conduct an A/B test, and verify if the results are in line with the MMM – that is, that the drop is the outcome is the percentage predicted by the coefficient. Now, let's turn our attention to what we need to do to perform MMM.

Steps toward implementing MMM

There are several steps involved in implementing MMM:

1. **Define business questions and scope**: Like any other analysis, defining the scope and what questions you are trying to answer is critical as a first step. This will help you define what data you need to collect and what data you need to have access to, to get the best value out of an MMM.

2. **Data collection**: MMM requires historical data on sales and marketing efforts across different channels, such as television, radio, print, digital, social media, and out-of-home advertising. It takes into account not only the direct effects of marketing activities but also indirect factors such as economic conditions, seasonality, competition, and market changes. Inaccurate or incomplete data will lead to misleading results.

3. **Data analysis and review**: Before modeling begins, you need to check the data for any issues, such as missing values, outliers, or data quality issues. This is a critical step as it will impact the quality of the results.

4. **Modeling**: Now, you can run the models. This will be an iterative process where you will need to check the results and make adjustments to the model until the results are satisfactory.

5. **Recommendations**: The final step is to analyze the data and produce recommendations. This is where the analyst needs to use their business knowledge to interpret the results and provide recommendations to the business.

The first step of understanding the business problem is common to any data analysis and sits outside the scope of this chapter. We will start with the topic of data collection.

Data collection

The first thing to keep in mind when collecting data is to remember that you will need data that reflects what happened, not what the business wanted to happen. This means, for instance, that you need actual spend data, not planned spend data. If, however, actual data is not available, it may be acceptable to use planned data if we consider the variable in question has an effect on the outcome or KPI we are optimizing towards.

The dependent variable – that is, the outcome we are optimizing our budget toward – will be a primary KPI. Usually, it's sales, but as an analyst, you need to think about the following question: what KPI or metric is critical for your business's financial performance?

The independent variables are going to be all the variables we expect to have an impact on the dependent variable. These can be marketing variables, such as spend, impressions, clicks, and so on, but also non-marketing variables, such as seasonality, events, promotions, and so on.

First, we'll focus on the media activities; then, we'll discuss non-marketing activities.

Media activities

For media activities, in the ideal world, you want to capture data that reflects how many people have seen or have been exposed to your ads. This can be impressions, for digital activities, **gross rating points** (**GRPs**) or **target audience rating points** (**TARPs**) for TV and radio, and readership from print. One note on digital activities – it is not advised that you use clicks as a metric since clicks can be highly correlated with impressions – leading to co-linearity problems – and will not reflect view through conversions – that is, conversions where someone saw the ad but did not click on it.

There is also the question of paid versus organic. Modeling data for paid activities only usually leads to more actionable results since organic is very hard to control and influence. However, with more options, there could be a good reason to include organic data, given currently you have more and more options available to directly contact consumers through organic channels. The variables to be collected can be reach or impressions on blog posts, impressions on organic social media, SEO improvements, and so on.

Non-media activities

Seasonality and holidays also need to be modeled since they can have big effects on the dependent variable, and as such should be included in the model.

Macroeconomic variables can also be included in the model, such as GDP, unemployment rate, and so on. These variables can be used to capture the effect of the economy on the dependent variable, and you need to choose those that you believe are relevant to your business. However, be careful of choosing correlated variables as this can lead to colinearity problems.

How much data to collect

The more data you have, the better. However, some rules of thumb can be used to determine how much data is enough. The first rule of thumb is to have at least 10 to 20 observations per feature in the model. Less than that and the standard errors of the coefficients will become too wide. The second rule of thumb is to have at least 2 years' worth of weekly data. If you only have monthly data, then the timeframe should be expanded to 4 or 5 years' worth of data.

Data granularity

While these models were designed to be robust without a great degree of granular data, there are advantages to getting granular data if you can. Studies have shown that MMM models can be greatly improved by the use and modeling of granular data, such as campaign attributes. Aside from model performance and accuracy, you can also benefit from more actionable results. As an example, digital platforms work with different algorithms and behave differently. If you have granular data, you can model the performance of each platform separately, and then use the results to optimize your spend across platforms, instead of just having a model that averages out digital spend.

Note that granular data is not always available, and it can be costly to collect. So, if you are just starting out, it is recommended that you start with aggregated data, and then move to granular data once you have a good understanding of the model and how it works. You also have to deal with concerns regarding data variation and volume. MMM is a regression model, and any regression model relies on looking at the correlation between the dependent and independent variables. If there is little variation in the data, fitting the model will be hard, and in some cases downright impossible.

For example, if there is a weekly variation in your revenue, but the TV spend stays fixed, then it will be difficult for the model to infer how TV has impacted sales. The same goes for volume. Even if there is a lot of variation in the variables, if the volume is low, can you say that the variable had an impact on the outcome? As a rule of thumb, if you don't have enough volume and variation, it is best to exclude the data in question from the model. The presence of such data will only create noise for the model, and will not lead to robust and accurate results. If you are unsure, you can always run the model with and without the data in question, and see if the model fit statistics consider it beneficial to include said variables.

Usually, digital channels will be where you have the most granular data. You should be able to break digital down at least to the channel or publisher level. In certain cases, you can go deeper – for instance, how does static versus video on Facebook, or brand versus non-brand in search, impact sales? The same thought process can be applied to brands, products, or business units if your business has any of those characteristics. We can see a summary of these potential variables in *Table 12.1*:

Variable Type	Bucket	Variable
Dependent variable	Sales	Sales
Independent variables	Promotions	Price discounts
		Bundle offers
	Media – online	Facebook
		Google search
		YouTube
		Display
	Media – offline	TV
		Radio
		Print
		OOH
	Competitor activity	Competitor media activity
	Macroeconomic factors	Seasonality/holidays
		Economic growth
		Government policy changes
		COVID-19 impact

Table 12.1 – Summary of potential variables for MMM

Modeling

Once we start the modeling process, the first step is to do some feature engineering. The first obvious step is to decompose the times series seasonality. This usually involves decomposing the time series into trend, seasonality, holiday, and weekday effects, usually through the use of dummy variables in the model.

The **model** window is also an important consideration to make. The model window is the period that is used to fit the model. The model window should be long enough to capture the effect of the variables, but not so long that it captures too much noise. A good rule of thumb is to use 2 years' worth of data, but this can be adjusted depending on the data and the business. The window can also be fixed or rolling.

Impressions versus spend

The recommended approach for modeling is to use impressions as the independent variable, and not spend. The reason for this is that impressions are a better proxy for reach, and reach is what drives sales. However, you will require spend data to calculate the ROI and simulate budget allocations.

Some frameworks, such as Meta's Robyn, will fit a non-linear model with Michaelis Menten's function between exposure and spend to get to the relationship. The function is defined as follows:

$$exposure = V_{max} * \frac{spend}{spend + K_m}$$

In this scenario, the function is used to model the relationship between the amount spent on advertising (spend) and the exposure or attention it generates. Let's break down the components, V_{max} and K_m, in more detail within this context:

- V_{max} represents the maximum potential exposure (or impact) that can be achieved with infinite advertising spend on a particular media channel. It's a theoretical ceiling where, beyond a certain point, additional spending does not significantly increase exposure. This concept acknowledges that there's a limit to how effective ad spend can be; after saturating a market or audience, the effectiveness of additional spend decreases.

   In marketing terms, V_{max} could be thought of as the maximum level of awareness, reach, or engagement that your advertising can achieve in your target audience through a specific channel, regardless of how much more you spend.

- K_m represents the spend level at which half of V_{max} is achieved. It's a measure of the efficiency or efficacy of your advertising spend on that channel. A lower K_m value indicates that less spend is needed to achieve significant exposure, making the channel highly effective up to a certain point. Conversely, a higher K_m suggests that more spend is required to get to half of the maximum exposure, indicating a less efficient channel for converting spend into exposure.

   In practical terms, K_m helps marketers understand how much they need to invest in a particular media channel to achieve a substantial portion of their potential reach or impact. It provides a benchmark for comparing the efficiency of different channels: channels with a lower K_m are more efficient at converting advertising dollars into exposure, up to the point of diminishing returns marked by V_{max}.

Here, V_{max} and K_m need to be estimated.

To do so, you need to loop through media channels; for each media channel, it calculates V_{max} (the maximum exposure) and K_m (half of V_{max}):

```
#define the response function based on the Michaelis-Menten equation
calculate_exposure = lambda spend_amt, max_response,
    half_saturation_const: max_response * spend_amt / (half_
saturation_const + spend_amt)

# Lists of mediaexposures and spends
media_exposure_metrics = ["facebook_impressions", "search_clicks"]
media_spend_metrics = ["facebook_spend", "search_spend"]

# Initialize DataFrame to store results
media_performance_df = pd.DataFrame()
```

```
# Loop through each media channel to calculate exposure
for (exposure_metric, spend_metric) in zip(media_exposure_metrics,
    media_spend_metrics):
    # Find the maximum exposure value
    max_exposure = final_data[exposure_metric].values[
        START_ANALYSIS_INDEX:END_ANALYSIS_INDEX].max()
    # Calculate the half-saturation constant as half the maximum
exposure
    half_saturation = max_exposure / 2

    # Get the spend data
    spend_data = final_data[spend_metric].values[
        START_ANALYSIS_INDEX:END_ANALYSIS_INDEX]

    # Get the actual exposure data
    actual_exposure = final_data[exposure_metric].values[
        START_ANALYSIS_INDEX:END_ANALYSIS_INDEX]
    # Fit the Michaelis-Menten model to the data
    optimized_params, _ = optimize.curve_fit(
        f=calculate_exposure, xdata=spend_data,
        ydata=actual_exposure, p0=[max_exposure,
        half_saturation])
    # Append the results to the DataFrame
    media_performance_df = pd.concat([media_performance_df,
        pd.DataFrame({
            'spend_metric': [spend_metric],
            'exposure_metric': [exposure_metric],
            'max_response': [optimized_params[0]],
            'half_saturation_const': [optimized_params[1]]
        })
    ]).reset_index(drop=True)

# Display the DataFrame
media_performance_df
```

Now, we need to make a small detour and consider some of the critical aspects of the internals of an MMM – the concepts of adstock, saturation, and diminishing returns.

How to measure the adstock effect

You may have several challenges when measuring the effect of marketing activities. While we can measure the current effect of an activity, customer responses can have a delay, depending on the channel in question. Another consideration is that you can have multiple activities at the same time, so we can only measure the cumulative effects.

For example, a TV ad can affect sales, but that effect can take a few days to be seen. This is called the **carryover effect**, and it is a common problem in MMM. Another problem is that the effect of a marketing activity can be short-lived and can decay over time. This is called the **decay effect**, and it is also a common problem in MMM. Finally, there is the problem of saturation. The effect of a marketing activity can reach a point where it stops having an effect, and any additional spend will not lead to any additional sales. This is called the **saturation effect**, and it is also a common problem in MMM.

One popular way of dealing with the saturation effect is the adstock model.

The adstock model

The key assumption of the adstock model is that each period will retain a share of the previous period's stock of advertising. For now, let's assume we are only working with one channel, for simplicity. If we have y_t as the sales volume, x_t as the advertising spend, a_t as the current effect induced by advertising on sales, and λ as a decay factor, we can write the following equation:

$$a_t = x_t + \lambda a_{t-1}$$

It boils down to saying that current period adstock, a_t, is equal to the current media spend and a share, λ, of the previous period's adstock, a_{t-1}.

You can also call λ a decay parameter. It is a number between 0 and 1, and it represents the percentage of the previous period's adstock that will be retained in the current period. If λ is 0, then there is no carryover effect, and the current period's adstock is only equal to the current period's media spend. If λ is 0, then there is no decay effect.

Expanding the recursive equation, we can write the following:

$$a_t = x_t + \lambda x_{t-1} + \lambda^2 x_{t-2} + \lambda^3 x_{t-3} + \dots$$

Essentially, we are applying a smoothing filter to the input sequence. Another assumption we can make, reasonably, is that the treatment effect is finite and limited by n periods. For this, we can write the following equation:

$$a_t = x_t + \sum_{i=0}^{n} \lambda^i x_{t-i}$$

We are interested in estimating sales as a function of adstock:

$$\^y_t = \beta_0 + \beta_1 a_t$$

Here, we have β_1 as the weight and β_0 as the baseline when there is no adstock. If we want to move away from a single channel, and assuming adstock is additive, we get the following equation:

$$\hat{y}_t = \beta_0 + \sum_{i=1}^{n}\beta_{i1}\,a_{it}$$

Here, each channel will have its own λ decay parameter. The fitted model will allow us to estimate the contribution of each channel to the outcome variable and estimate the impact of increasing or decreasing the spend on each channel, as follows:

$$z_{it} = \frac{\beta_{i1}\,a_{it}}{\sum_i \beta_{i1}\,a_{it}}$$

This formula is a measure of impact because it quantifies the relative contribution of each advertising channel to the overall effect on sales. This formula is crucial for understanding the effectiveness of different advertising channels in a multi-channel marketing strategy. Here's a breakdown of why this formula serves as a good measure of impact:

- **Channel-specific contribution**: The numerator, $\beta_{i1}\,a_{it}$, represents the contribution of a specific advertising channel (indexed by i) at time t. Here, a_{it} is the adstock for channel i at time t, and β_{i1} is the weight or effectiveness of that adstock in influencing sales. This product gives the estimated increase in sales attributable to the adstock from a specific channel.

- **Total advertising effect**: The denominator, $\sum_i \beta_{i1}\,a_{it}$, is the sum of contributions from all advertising channels at time t. It provides a measure of the total impact of advertising across all channels on sales.

- **Relative importance**: By dividing the channel-specific contribution by the total advertising effect, z_{it} gives the proportion of the total sales impact that is attributable to each channel. This allows for a comparison of the effectiveness of different channels relative to each other.

- **Strategic decision-making**: Understanding the relative impact of each channel is crucial for optimizing marketing strategies. If a channel has a higher z_{it} value, this means it has a more significant impact on sales compared to other channels. This information can guide decisions on where to allocate resources for maximum return on investment.

- **Dynamic analysis**: Since z_{it} is calculated for each period, t, it allows for dynamic analysis of how the impact of different channels changes over time. This is particularly important in adjusting strategies in response to market changes or varying consumer behaviors.

Other types of adstock

The adstock described previously is called geometric adstock. It is the simplest form of adstock, with the added benefit of being the best. However, it can be considered too simplistic and not suitable for digital media.

The alternative is the Weibull adstock model, which uses the Weibull survival function. This function gives more flexibility in terms of shape and distribution. It is also more computationally expensive.

Saturation and diminishing returns

While the adstock model will account for simultaneous activities and delayed effects, it will not account for saturation. Though, intuitively, an increase in marketing intensity will lead to greater outreach, that relationship is usually not linear. You will often face diminishing returns, and at some point, you will reach a point where any additional spend will not lead to any additional sales.

All marketers need to keep in mind there is a trade-off between spend and efficiency. The rationale is fairly straightforward: the low-hanging fruit of cheap conversions, which have the highest intent, will be captured in the first run of ads. Then, as you increase spend, you will start to capture less intentful conversions, which will be more expensive. Finally, at one point, you will reach ad fatigue or saturation, and people will stop paying attention to your ads, and you will not capture any additional conversions. We can see this graphically in *Figure 12.1*:

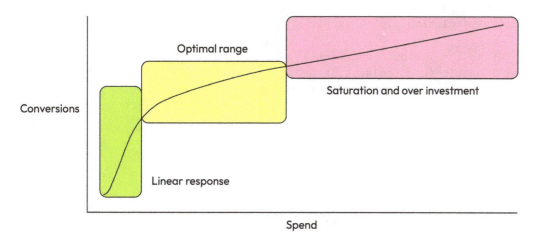

Figure 12.1 – Saturation in media spend

To account for this, we can use a logistic function to model the relationship between marketing intensity and sales. The logistic function is a sigmoid function and is generally defined as follows:

$$f(x) = \frac{L}{1 + e^{-k(x-x_0)}}$$

Here, x_0 is the function's midpoint, L is the maximum of the function, and k is the logistic growth rate – that is, the steepness of the curve. This function is called sigmoid because of its shape – it's an S-shaped curve.

Applying this to our example, we can rewrite adstock a_t as follows:

$$a_t = \frac{1}{1 + e^{-k(x_t)}} + \lambda\, a_{t-1}$$

An alternative to the logistic function is the Hill function. This function takes the following form:

$$hill(x; \alpha, \gamma) = \frac{x^\alpha}{\gamma^\alpha + x^\alpha}$$

The advantage of the Hill function is that due to its parameters, γ and α can have both the S-shape and the C-shape:

- The α parameter controls the shape. It can go between exponential and S-shape. The larger α is, the more S-shaped the curve.

- The γ parameter controls the inflection point. The larger the γ value, the more to the right the inflection point.

We can visualize a simple logistic function in Python using the following code snippet:

```
import numpy as np
import matplotlib.pyplot as plt

# Define the logistic function
def logistic_function(x, L, k, x0):
    return L / (1 + np.exp(-k * (x - x0)))

# Parameters
L = 1     # Maximum value
k = 1     # Growth rate
x0 = 0    # Midpoint

# Generate x values
x = np.linspace(-10, 10, 300)

# Compute y values
y = logistic_function(x, L, k, x0)

# Plotting
plt.figure(figsize=(8, 4))
plt.plot(x, y, label='Logistic Function')
plt.xlabel('x')
plt.ylabel('f(x)')
plt.title('Logistic Function Plot')
plt.legend()
plt.show()
```

We can see the results in *Figure 12.2*:

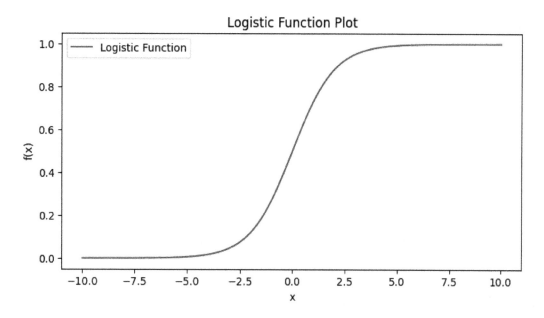

Figure 12.2 – Example logistic function

We can also easily visualize a simple Hill function with different alphas in Python:

```
# Define the Hill function
def hill_function(x, alpha, gamma):
    return x**alpha / (gamma**alpha + x**alpha)


# Parameters
gamma = 0.5  # EC50
alphas = [0.1, 0.5, 1, 2]  # Different values of alpha (Hill
coefficients)

# Generate x values
x = np.linspace(0, 1, 100)

# Plotting
plt.figure(figsize=(8, 6))
for alpha in alphas:
    y = hill_function(x, alpha, gamma)
    plt.plot(x, y, label=f'Alpha = {alpha}')

plt.xlabel('x')
```

```
plt.ylabel('Hill Function Value')
plt.title('Hill Function Plot with Different Alphas')
plt.legend()
plt.show()
```

Here are the results:

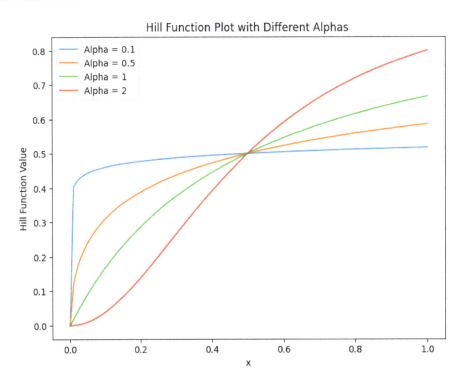

Figure 12.3 – Hill function with different alphas

Alternatively, we can generate a different Hill function with different gammas in Python:

```
# Parameters
gammas = [0.1,0.3,0.5, 0.7, 0.9]  # EC50
alpha = 2  # Different values of alpha (Hill coefficients)

# Generate x values
x = np.linspace(0, 1, 100)

# Plotting
plt.figure(figsize=(8, 6))
for gamma in gammas:
```

```
    y = hill_function(x, alpha, gamma)
    plt.plot(x, y, label=f'Gamma = {gamma}')

plt.xlabel('x')
plt.ylabel('Hill Function Value')
plt.title('Hill Function Plot with Different Gammas')
plt.legend()
plt.show()
```

Here are the results:

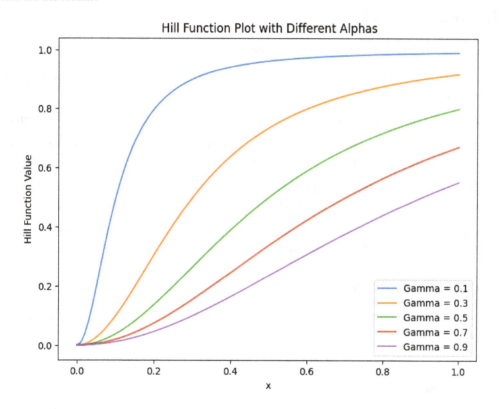

Figure 12.4 – Hill function with different alphas

Which comes first?

Adstock and saturation are not commutative. This means that the order in which you apply them matters. There is, however, a useful rule of thumb to follow:

- **Adstock first** if the spend in each period is small compared with the cumulative spend
- **Saturation first** if the spend is concentrated in a few periods and has an on-and-off pattern

MMM is complex. But how do you select a good candidate model? Let's review that next.

Selecting a model

There are some considerations to take when selecting a final model:

- **Experimental calibration**: Integrating experimental results into the MMM is the gold standard approach
- **Business insights**: Evaluate the model by investigating if the outcomes match your business context
- **ROAS convergence**: Looking at the distribution of ROAS over multiple iterations and how it evolves can be a good indicator of higher confidence in results if the distributions are peaky
- **Statistical parameters**: Looking at the model fit statistics, such as R2, RMSE, AIC, BIC, and so on, can be a good indicator of higher confidence in results if the values are good

After creating the model, you need to see how accurate it is. In MMM, the gold standard for this is via experimenting and calibrating the model.

Experimenting and calibrating

Using experiments to calibrate the model is the best way to achieve accurate results. Several methodologies can be used:

- **People-based**: For example, Meta conversion lift
- **Geo-based**: For example, Meta geo lift

We will explore these methodologies in the next chapter when we cover A/B testing, but essentially, you want to establish the true incrementality of your advertising.

If you think of a Bayesian approach, you are using the results of these experiments to update your priors to calibrate the coefficients of the models.

To ensure that you are accurately calibrating and deriving the right changes, there are some things to watch out for:

- Make sure that your incrementality studies are measuring the same things as your MMM – that is, the same metrics and periods

- Avoid results that have low power and confidence

- Longer is better to be able to capture tail conversions and reduce bias.

Now, let's put everything together and implement a small media mix model based on synthetic data.

A synthetic data example of MMM

First, we'll begin with the necessary imports and setup:

```
import warnings
import arviz as az
import matplotlib.pyplot as plt
import numpy as np
import pandas as pd
import pymc as pm
import seaborn as sns

from pymc_marketing.mmm.transformers import geometric_adstock,
    logistic_saturation
from pymc_marketing.mmm.delayed_saturated_mmm import
    DelayedSaturatedMMM
warnings.filterwarnings("ignore")

az.style.use("arviz-darkgrid")
plt.rcParams["figure.figsize"] = [12, 7]
plt.rcParams["figure.dpi"] = 100

%load_ext autoreload
%autoreload 2
%config InlineBackend.figure_format = "retina"
```

Synthetic data generation

Let's generate some synthetic data to test the model. We will generate data for two media channels, with adstock and saturation effects, and a trend and seasonality component. We'll start by generating a DataFrame containing weekly dates within a specified range, along with the corresponding year, month, and day of the year for each date:

```
# Date Ranges

seed: int = sum(map(ord, 'mmm'))
rng: np.random.Generator = np.random.default_rng(seed=seed)

min_date = pd.to_datetime("2018-04-01")
max_date = pd.to_datetime('2021-09-01')

df = pd.DataFrame(
    data = {"date_week": pd.date_range(start=min_date, end=max_date,
        freq="W-MON")}
).assign(
    year = lambda x: x["date_week"].dt.year,
    month = lambda x: x["date_week"].dt.month,
    dayofyear = lambda x: x["date_week"].dt.dayofyear
)

n = df.shape[0]
print(f"Observations: {n}")
```

The output should be as follows:

```
Observations: 179
```

Next, we will generate the media costs data. We will generate two media channels, both drawn from the uniform random distribution, with a few modifications. We will set a threshold for the first channel so that 10% of the values are drawn from the uniform distribution and the remaining 90% are divided by 2. This will give us a distribution with a long tail. For the second channel, we will set a threshold of 20% so that 20% of the values are drawn from the uniform distribution and the remaining 80% are set to 0. This will give us a distribution with a lot of 0 values:

```
# Media Costs
x1 = rng.uniform(low=0.0, high=1.0, size=n)
df["x1"] = np.where(x1 > 0.9, x1, x1 / 2)
x2 = rng.uniform(low=0.0, high=1.0, size=n)
df["x2"] = np.where(x2 > 0.8, x2, 0)
```

We can visualize the result with the following snippet:

```
fig, ax = plt.subplots(
    nrows=2, ncols=1, figsize=(10, 7), sharex=True, sharey=True,
    layout="constrained"
)
sns.lineplot(x="date_week", y="x1", data=df, color="C0", ax=ax[0])
sns.lineplot(x="date_week", y="x2", data=df, color="C1", ax=ax[1])
ax[1].set(xlabel="date")
fig.suptitle("Media Costs Data", fontsize=16);
```

Here's the output:

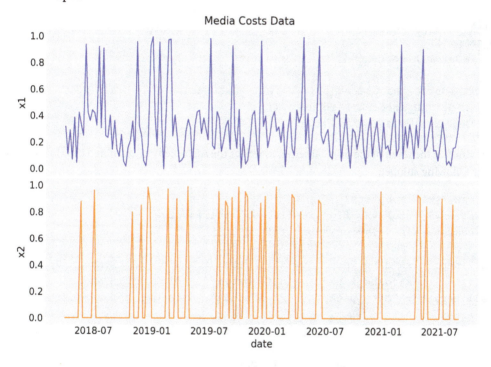

Figure 12.5 – Media cost data x1 and x2

Now, we will apply the adstock transformation to both series. In this case, we will keep it simple and apply a geometric adstock:

```
# apply geometric adstock transformation
alpha1: float = 0.4
alpha2: float = 0.2
```

```
df["x1_adstock"] = (geometric_adstock(x=df["x1"].to_numpy(),
    alpha=alpha1,
    l_m"x=8, normalize=True).eval().flatten())

df["x2_adstock"] = (geometric_adstock(x=df["x2"].to_numpy(),
    alpha=alpha2, l_max=8, normalize=True).eval().flatten())
```

After applying saturation, we will saturate the adstocked series using a logistic function:

```
# apply saturation transformation
lam1: float = 4.0
lam2: float = 3.0

df["x1_adstock_saturated"] = logistic_saturation(x=df["x1_adstock"].
to_numpy(),
    lam=lam1).eval()

df["x2_adstock_saturated"] = logistic_saturation
    (x=df["x2_adstock"].to_numpy(),
    lam=lam2).eval()
```

We can visualize the result of the original series, as well as the adstocked and saturated transformations, with the following snippet:

```
fig, ax = plt.subplots(
    nrows=3, ncols=2, figsize=(16, 9), sharex=True,
    sharey=False, layout="constrained"
)
sns.lineplot(x="date_week", y="x1", data=df, color="C0", ax=ax[0, 0])
sns.lineplot(x="date_week", y="x2", data=df, color="C1", ax=ax[0, 1])
sns.lineplot(x="date_week", y="x1_adstock", data=df, color="C0",
    ax=ax[1, 0])
sns.lineplot(x="date_week", y="x2_adstock", data=df, color="C1",
    ax=ax[1, 1])
sns.lineplot(x="date_week", y="x1_adstock_saturated", data=df,
    color="C0", ax=ax[2, 0])
sns.lineplot(x="date_week", y="x2_adstock_saturated", data=df,
    color="C1", ax=ax[2, 1])
fig.suptitle("Media Costs Data - Transformed", fontsize=16);
```

Here's the output:

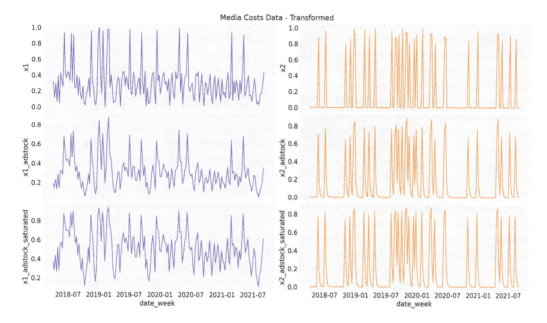

Figure 12.6 – x1, adstocked x1, and saturated adstock x1

Finally, on the media variable side of things, let's apply a trend and seasonal component to the data. We will use a simple polynomial function for the trend and a cosine function for the seasonality:

```
#Trend and Seasonal components
df["trend"] = (np.linspace(start=0.0, stop=50, num=n) + 10) ** (1/4) -
1


df["cs"] = -np.sin(2 * 2 * np.pi * df["dayofyear"] / 365.5)
df["cc"] = np.cos(2 * 2 * np.pi * df["dayofyear"] / 365.5)
df["seasonality"] = 0.5 * (df["cs"] + df["cc"])
```

To visualize the trend and seasonality components, we can use the following snippet:

```
fig, ax = plt.subplots()
sns.lineplot(x="date_week", y="trend", color="C2", label="trend",
    data=df, ax=ax)
sns.lineplot(
    x="date_week", y="seasonality", color="C3",
    label="seasonality", data=df, ax=ax
)
ax.legend(loc="upper left")
```

```
ax.set(title="Trend & Seasonality Components", xlabel="date",
    ylabel=None);
```

Here's the output:

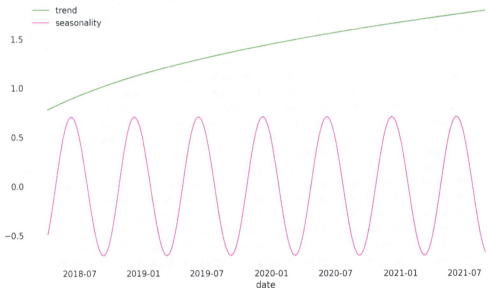

Figure 12.7 – Trend and seasonality

Now, let's add some special events to the data. We will add two events: one in 2019 and one in 2020. We will use a simple indicator variable to represent the events:

```
# Control variables

df["event_1"] = (df["date_week"] == "2019-05-13").astype(float)
df["event_2"] = (df["date_week"] == "2020-09-14").astype(float)
```

Now, let's generate the target variable:

```
# Target Variable

df["intercept"] = 2.0
df["epsilon"] = rng.normal(loc=0.0, scale=0.25, size=n) # White noise
amplitude = 1
beta_1 = 3.0
beta_2 = 2.0
betas = [beta_1, beta_2]
```

```
df["y"] = amplitude * ( df["intercept"] + df["trend"] +
    df["seasonality"] + 1.5 * df["event_1"] +
    2.5 * df["event_2"] + beta_1 * df["x1_adstock_saturated"] +
    beta_2 * df["x2_adstock_saturated"] + df["epsilon"] )
```

We can now take a look at our target data by using the following snippet:

```
fig, ax = plt.subplots()
sns.lineplot(x="date_week", y="y", color="black", data=df, ax=ax)
ax.set(title="Sales (Target Variable)", xlabel="date",
    ylabel="y (thousands)");
```

Here's the output:

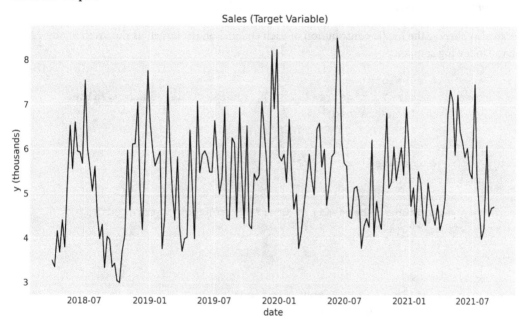

Figure 12.8 – Target variable sales

From the synthetic data we've generated, we can see the actual media contribution of each channel on the target that MMM needs to recover:

```
# [x] Explain this formula from contribution share

contribution_share_x1: float = (beta_1 *
    df["x1_adstock_saturated"]).sum() / (beta_1 *
    df["x1_adstock_saturated"] + beta_2 *
```

```
        df["x2_adstock_saturated"]).sum()

contribution_share_x2: float = (beta_2 *
    df["x2_adstock_saturated"]).sum() / (beta_1 *
    df["x1_adstock_saturated"] + beta_2 *
    df["x2_adstock_saturated"]).sum()

print(f"Contribution Share of x1: {contribution_share_x1:.2f}")
print(f"Contribution Share of x2: {contribution_share_x2:.2f}")
```

This will give us the following contribution shares:

- **Contribution share of x1**: 0.81

- **Contribution share of x2**: 0.19

We can also observe the media contribution of each channel on the target, as shown in *Figure 12.9*, with the following snippet:

```
fig, ax = plt.subplots(
    nrows=2, ncols=1, figsize=(12, 8), sharex=True, sharey=False,
        layout="constrained"
)

for i, x in enumerate(["x1", "x2"]):
    sns.scatterplot(
        x=df[x],
        y=amplitude * betas[i] * df[f"{x}_adstock_saturated"],
        color=f"C{i}",
        ax=ax[i],
    )
    ax[i].set(
        title=f"$x_{i + 1}$ contribution",
        ylabel=f"$\\beta_{i + 1} \cdot x_{i + 1}$
            adstocked & saturated",
        xlabel="x",
    )
```

Figure 12.9 provides us with some details regarding how media contributes to sales:

- The adstock effect can be seen in the charts by the fact that even at zero spend, media still affects sales

- The saturation effect can be seen in the charts by the fact that the effect of media on sales is not linear, and at some point, additional spend will not lead to additional sales:

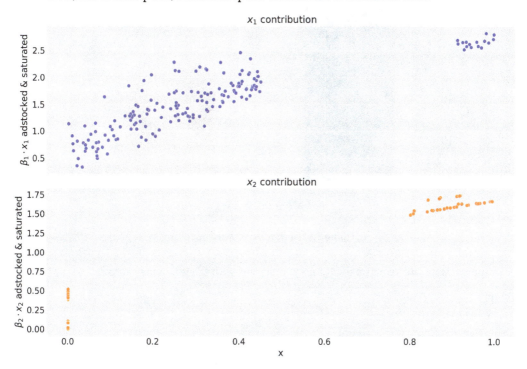

Figure 12.9 – Media contribution to the target variable

We can visualize the total media spend per channel on our synthetic data by using the following snippet:

```
fig, ax = plt.subplots(figsize=(7, 5))
df[["x1", "x2"]].sum().plot(kind="bar", color=["C0", "C1"], ax=ax)
ax.set(title="Total Media Spend", xlabel="Media Channel",
    ylabel="Costs (thousands)");
```

Here's the output:

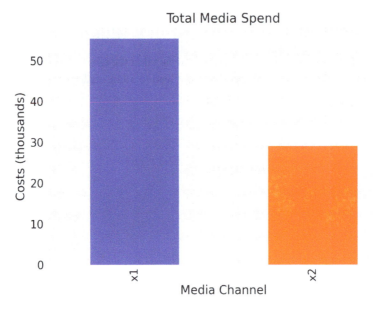

Figure 12.10 – Total media spend

We can approximate and visualize the ROAS per channel with the following snippet:

```
# ROAS approximation
[ ] Explain this formula for ROAS
roas_1 = (amplitude * beta_1 * df["x1_adstock_saturated"]).sum() /
    df["x1"].sum()
roas_2 = (amplitude * beta_2 * df["x2_adstock_saturated"]
    ).sum() / df["x2"].sum()
fig, ax = plt.subplots(figsize=(7, 5))
(
    pd.Series(data=[roas_1, roas_2], index=["x1", "x2"]).plot(
        kind="bar", color=["C0", "C1"]
    )
)

ax.set(title="ROAS (Approximation)", xlabel="Media Channel",
    ylabel="ROAS");
```

Here's the output:

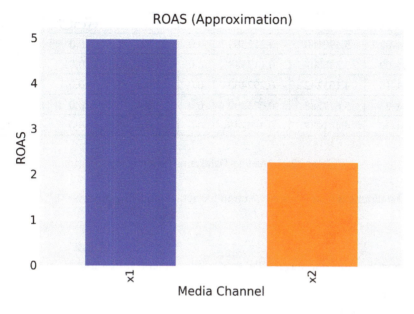

Figure 12.11 – ROAS approximation

Lastly, we can clean up the DataFrame, leaving only the variables we need for the model. These are the variables we expect to have access to in the real world:

```
columns_to_keep = [
    "date_week",
    "y",
    "x1",
    "x2",
    "event_1",
    "event_2",
    "dayofyear",
]
data = df[columns_to_keep].copy()
data.head()
```

Here's the output:

	date_week	y	x1	x2	event_1	event_2	dayofyear
0	2018-04-02	3.490150	0.318580	0.0	0.0	0.0	92
1	2018-04-09	3.345307	0.112388	0.0	0.0	0.0	99
2	2018-04-16	4.153242	0.292400	0.0	0.0	0.0	106
3	2018-04-23	3.677788	0.071399	0.0	0.0	0.0	113
4	2018-04-30	4.401077	0.386745	0.0	0.0	0.0	120

Table 12.2 – The final DataFrame for modeling

Now that the DataFrame is ready, let's move on to the actual modeling process.

Modeling

Now that we are at the modeling stage, will need to add another feature variable, for the trend:

```
# trend feature
data["t"] = range(n)
data.head()
```

Here's the output:

	date_week	y	x1	x2	event_1	event_2	dayofyear	t
0	2018-04-02	3.490150	0.318580	0.0	0.0	0.0	92	0
1	2018-04-09	3.345307	0.112388	0.0	0.0	0.0	99	1
2	2018-04-16	4.153242	0.292400	0.0	0.0	0.0	106	2
3	2018-04-23	3.677788	0.071399	0.0	0.0	0.0	113	3
4	2018-04-30	4.401077	0.386745	0.0	0.0	0.0	120	4

Table 12.3 – Modeling data with the trend feature variable

Modeling assumptions

Since we don't know much about the channels, we'll start with a simple heuristic:

- The channel contributions should be positive so that we can, for example, use a HalfNormal distribution, as we did previously. We need to set the sigma parameter per channel. The higher the sigma, the more "freedom" it has to fit the data. To specify the sigma, we can use the following point.

- We expect channels where we spend the most to have more attributed sales, before seeing the data. This is a very reasonable assumption (note that we are not imposing anything at the level of efficiency!).

It is important to note that the `DelayedSaturatedMMM` class scales the target and input variables through a `MaxAbsScaler` transformer from `scikit-learn`. It's important to specify the priors in the scaled space (that is, between 0 and 1). One way to do it is to use the spend share as the sigma parameter for the HalfNormal distribution. We can add a scaling factor to take into account the support of the distribution.

So, first, we must calculate the actual spend share per channel:

```
total_spend_per_channel = data[["x1", "x2"]].sum(axis=0)
spend_share = total_spend_per_channel / total_spend_per_channel.sum()
spend_share
```

We get the following output:

```
x1     0.65632
x2     0.34368
dtype: float64
```

Now, we must specify the sigmas per channel by calculating a scaling factor for the half-normal distribution, which is a special case of the normal distribution where all the values are non-negative (hence "half"):

```
# specify sigma per channel
# [ ] explain this formula?
HALFNORMAL_SCALE = 1 / np.sqrt(1 - 2 / np.pi)
n_channels = 2
prior_sigma = HALFNORMAL_SCALE * n_channels * spend_share.to_numpy()
prior_sigma.tolist()
```

The result will be:

```
[2.1775326025486734, 1.1402608773919387]
```

The scale of a half-normal distribution is related to the standard deviation of the underlying normal distribution. Here, `1 / np.sqrt(1 - 2 / np.pi)` is used to compute this scaling factor. This formula adjusts the scale so that the half-normal distribution reflects the properties of the underlying normal distribution correctly.

Now, let's drop the target variable and start assembling our model:

```
X = data.drop("y", axis=1)
y = data["y"]
dummy_model = DelayedSaturatedMMM(date_column= "", channel_columns="",
    adstock_max_lag = 4)
dummy_model.default_model_config
```

We will see the default model configuration, which is a dictionary with the following structure:

```
{'intercept': {'mu': 0, 'sigma': 2},
 'beta_channel': {'sigma': 2, 'dims': ('channel',)},
 'alpha': {'alpha': 1, 'beta': 3, 'dims': ('channel',)},
 'lam': {'alpha': 3, 'beta': 1, 'dims': ('channel',)},
 'sigma': {'sigma': 2},
 'gamma_control': {'mu': 0, 'sigma': 2, 'dims': ('control',)},
 'mu': {'dims': ('date',)},
 'likelihood': {'dims': ('date',)},
 'gamma_fourier': {'mu': 0, 'b': 1, 'dims': 'fourier_mode'}}
```

Let's adjust the model configuration with the priors we defined earlier:

```
custom_beta_channel_prior = {"beta_channel": {"sigma": prior_sigma,
    "dims": ("channel",)}}
my_model_config = {**dummy_model.default_model_config,
    **custom_beta_channel_prior}
my_model_config
```

This results in the following model configuration:

```
{'intercept': {'mu': 0, 'sigma': 2},
 'beta_channel': {'sigma': array([2.1775326 , 1.14026088]),
   'dims': ('channel',)},
 'alpha': {'alpha': 1, 'beta': 3, 'dims': ('channel',)},
 'lam': {'alpha': 3, 'beta': 1, 'dims': ('channel',)},
 'sigma': {'sigma': 2},
 'gamma_control': {'mu': 0, 'sigma': 2, 'dims': ('control',)},
 'mu': {'dims': ('date',)},
 'likelihood': {'dims': ('date',)},
 'gamma_fourier': {'mu': 0, 'b': 1, 'dims': 'fourier_mode'}}
sampler_config = {"progressbar": True}
```

Now, let's define our variable, mmm, which will contain the model:

```
mmm = DelayedSaturatedMMM(
    model_config = my_model_config,
    sampler_config = sampler_config,
    date_column="date_week",
    channel_columns=["x1", "x2"],
    control_columns=[
        "event_1",
        "event_2",
        "t",
    ],
    adstock_max_lag=8,
    yearly_seasonality=2,
)
```

We can now fit the model by using the following snippet:

```
mmm.fit(X=X, y=y, target_accept = 0.95, chains = 4, random_seed=rng)
```

Model results

We're finally ready to fit the results and check the summary statistics:

```
az.summary(
    data=mmm.fit_result,
    var_names=[
        "intercept",
        "beta_channel",
        "alpha",
        "lam",
        "gamma_control",
        "gamma_fourier",
        "sigma",
    ],
)
```

Here's the output:

Parameter	mean	sd	hdi_3%	hdi_97%	mcse_mean	mcse_sd	ess_bulk	ess_tail	r_hat
intercept	0.343	0.013	0.318	0.366	0.000	0.000	3003.0	2922.0	1.0
beta_channel [x1]	0.354	0.018	0.323	0.390	0.000	0.000	2790.0	2991.0	1.0
beta_channel [x2]	0.266	0.089	0.189	0.381	0.003	0.002	1333.0	994.0	1.0
alpha[x1]	0.397	0.030	0.343	0.453	0.001	0.000	3230.0	2890.0	1.0
alpha[x2]	0.192	0.040	0.112	0.265	0.001	0.001	1975.0	2244.0	1.0
lam[x1]	4.061	0.364	3.400	4.759	0.006	0.004	3465.0	2534.0	1.0
lam[x2]	3.169	1.189	0.986	5.401	0.030	0.021	1355.0	1000.0	1.0
gamma_control [event_1]	0.241	0.030	0.186	0.299	0.000	0.000	5869.0	2687.0	1.0
gamma_control [event_2]	0.320	0.030	0.264	0.376	0.000	0.000	4868.0	2464.0	1.0
gamma_control [t]	0.001	0.000	0.001	0.001	0.000	0.000	3707.0	2993.0	1.0
gamma_fourier [sin_order_1]	0.003	0.003	-0.003	0.009	0.000	0.000	4817.0	2784.0	1.0
gamma_fourier [cos_order_1]	0.003	0.003	-0.003	0.009	0.000	0.000	6479.0	2437.0	1.0
gamma_fourier [sin_order_2]	-0.056	0.003	-0.062	-0.050	0.000	0.000	5351.0	3039.0	1.0
gamma_fourier [cos_order_2]	0.061	0.003	0.055	0.067	0.000	0.000	5057.0	3357.0	1.0
sigma	0.029	0.002	0.026	0.032	0.000	0.000	4760.0	2727.0	1.0

Table 12.4 – Summary statistics for the model fit

We can also visualize the trace of the model with the following snippet:

```
_ = az.plot_trace(
    data=mmm.fit_result,
    var_names=[
        "intercept",
        "beta_channel",
        "alpha",
        "lam",
```

```
        "gamma_control",
        "gamma_fourier",
        "sigma",
    ],
    compact=True,
    backend_kwargs={"figsize": (12, 10), "layout": "constrained"},
)
plt.gcf().suptitle("Model Trace", fontsize=16);
```

Here's the output:

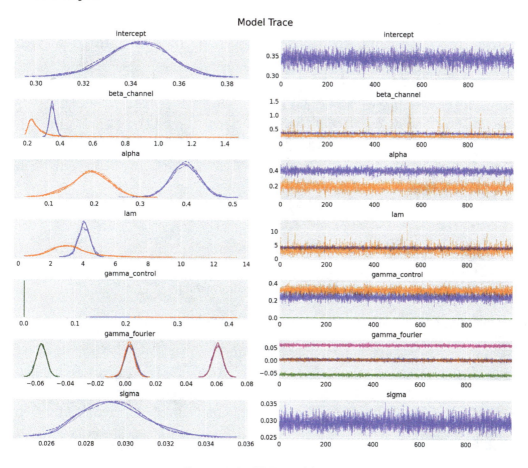

Figure 12.12 – MMM model trace

Now, we can sample from the posterior predictive distribution and plot the results with the following snippet:

```
mmm.sample_posterior_predictive(X, extend_idata=True, combined=True)
mmm.plot_posterior_predictive(original_scale=True);
```

Here's the output:

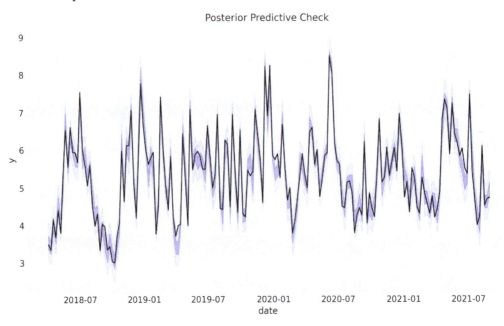

Figure 12.13 – Posterior predictive check

We can also check the component contributions with the following snippet:

```
mmm.plot_components_contributions();
```

This is what we'll get:

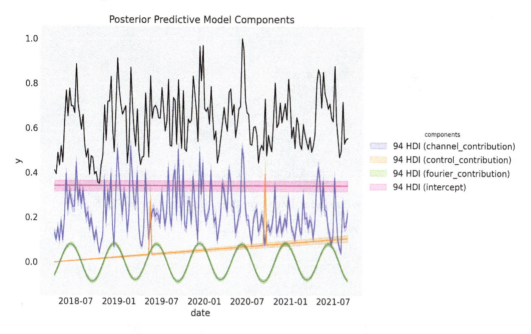

Figure 12.14 – Component contributions

Another way to plot the decomposition of the target variable is to use an area chart:

```
groups = {
    "Base": [
        "intercept",
        "event_1",
        "event_2",
        "t",
        "sin_order_1",
        "sin_order_2",
        "cos_order_1",
        "cos_order_2",
    ],
    "Channel 1": ["x1"],
    "Channel 2": ["x2"],
}

fig = mmm.plot_grouped_contribution_breakdown_over_time(
    stack_groups=groups,
    original_scale=True,
```

```
    area_kwargs={
        "color": {
            "Channel 1": "C0",
            "Channel 2": "C1",
            "Base": "gray",
            "Seasonality": "black",
        },
        "alpha": 0.7,
    },
)


fig.suptitle("Contribution Breakdown over Time", fontsize=16);
```

This will provide us with a contribution breakdown over time, as seen in *Figure 12.15*:

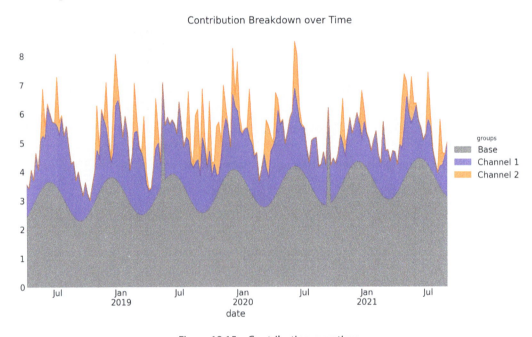

Figure 12.15 – Contribution over time

If you want to extract the mean contributions over time, you can use the following snippet:

```
get_mean_contributions_over_time_df = mmm.compute_mean_contributions_
over_time(
    original_scale=True
)


get_mean_contributions_over_time_df.head()
```

This will result in the following output:

date	x1	x2	event_1	event_2	t	sin_order_1	cos_order_1	sin_order_2	cos_order_2	intercept
2018-04-02	1.115799	0.0	0.0	0.0	0.000000	0.027161	-0.000271	0.011226	-0.515176	2.911508
2018-04-09	0.854125	0.0	0.0	0.0	0.005094	0.026925	-0.003024	0.124081	-0.497401	2.911508
2018-04-16	1.325983	0.0	0.0	0.0	0.010189	0.026300	-0.005733	0.229773	-0.450915	2.911508
2018-04-23	0.808261	0.0	0.0	0.0	0.015283	0.025294	-0.008359	0.322203	-0.378402	2.911508
2018-04-30	1.575895	0.0	0.0	0.0	0.020378	0.023922	-0.010864	0.396035	-0.284047	2.911508

Table 12.5 – Mean contributions over time

Now, let's take a deeper dive into the channel parameters and plot the posterior distributions of the channel parameters. We'll start with the α parameter by using the following snippet:

```
fig = mmm.plot_channel_parameter(param_name="alpha", figsize=(9, 5))
ax = fig.axes[0]
ax.axvline(x=alpha1, color="C0", linestyle="--", label=r"$\alpha_1$")
ax.axvline(x=alpha2, color="C1", linestyle="--", label=r"$\alpha_2$")
ax.legend(loc="upper right");
```

Here's the output:

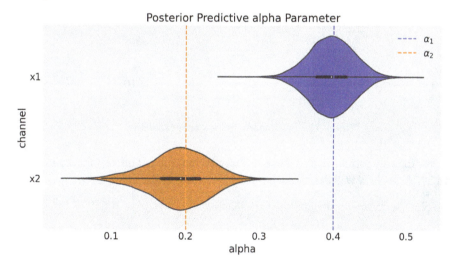

Figure 12.16 – α parameter posterior predictive

Now, we'll visualize the λ parameter:

```
fig = mmm.plot_channel_parameter(param_name="lam", figsize=(9, 5))
ax = fig.axes[0]
ax.axvline(x=lam1, color="C0", linestyle="--", label=r"$\lambda_1$")
ax.axvline(x=lam2, color="C1", linestyle="--", label=r"$\lambda_2$")
ax.legend(loc="upper right");
```

Here's the output:

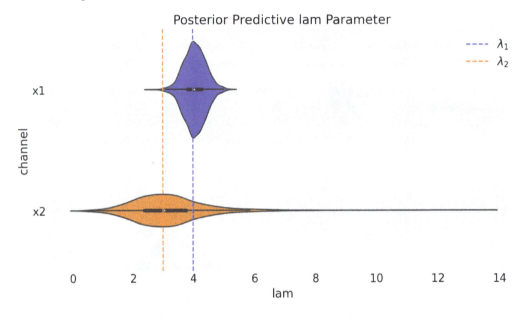

Figure 12.17 – λ parameter posterior predictive

Since we know the true parameters, we have also plotted the true parameters for α and λ in *Figures 12.16* and *12.17* to see how well the model has recovered the true parameters.

We can also plot the channel contribution share, like so:

```
fig = mmm.plot_channel_contribution_share_hdi(figsize=(7, 5))
ax = fig.axes[0]
ax.axvline(
    x=contribution_share_x1,
    color="C1",
    linestyle="--",
    label="true contribution share ($x_1$)",
)
```

```
ax.axvline(
    x=contribution_share_x2,
    color="C2",
    linestyle="--",
    label="true contribution share ($x_2$)",
)
ax.legend(loc="upper center", bbox_to_anchor=(0.5, -0.05), ncol=1);
```

Here's the output:

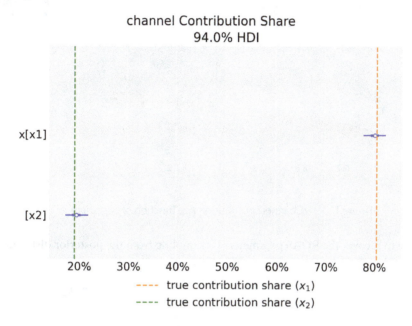

Figure 12.18 – Channel contribution share

A common output of the model is the contribution share of each channel across different spend levels. We can plot this with the following snippet:

```
mmm.plot_channel_contributions_grid(start=0, stop=1.5, num=12);
```

This is what we'll get:

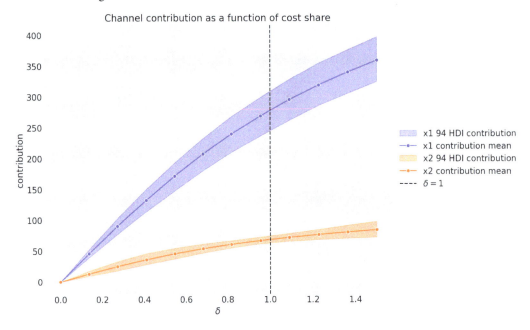

Figure 12.19 – Channel contribution as a function of cost share

Finally, let's try to recover the ROAS parameters by sampling from the posterior distribution and plotting the results:

```
channel_contribution_original_scale = mmm.compute_channel_
contribution_original_scale()

roas_samples = (
    channel_contribution_original_scale.stack(sample=("chain",
    "draw")).sum("date")
    / data[["x1", "x2"]].sum().to_numpy()[..., None]
)

fig, ax = plt.subplots(figsize=(10, 6))
sns.histplot(
    roas_samples.sel(channel="x1").to_numpy(), binwidth=0.05,
        alpha=0.3, kde=True, ax=ax
)
sns.histplot(
    roas_samples.sel(channel="x2").to_numpy(), binwidth=0.05,
        alpha=0.3, kde=True, ax=ax
)
```

```
ax.axvline(x=roas_1, color="C0", linestyle="--",
    label=r"true ROAS $x_{1}$")
ax.axvline(x=roas_2, color="C1", linestyle="--",
    label=r"true ROAS $x_{2}$")
ax.legend(loc="center left", bbox_to_anchor=(1, 0.5))
ax.set(title="Posterior ROAS distribution", xlabel="ROAS");
```

This results in the following output:

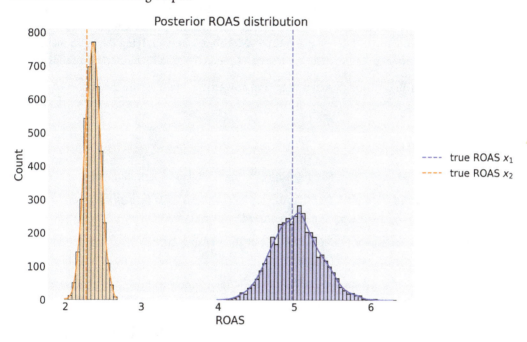

Figure 12.20 – Posterior ROAS distribution

With that, we have achieved our main aim of MMM, which was to understand ROAS and get an accurate picture of our true returns per channel.

Summary

In this chapter, we dove deeper into what a media mix model is and what it is used for. We discussed what data we should gather and how to transform it. We also discussed different adstock models and how to account for media saturation. Finally, we went through an example of how to fit a media mix model using PyMC Marketing with synthetic data, to understand how we could recover the original parameters.

You now know how to discuss and evaluate a media mix model, understanding its strengths and limitations. You can extract the correct data needed to operationalize one, ensuring reliable inputs. You can also implement a simple media mix model by using the PyMC library and applying Bayesian methods, as well as calibrate the model to improve its accuracy and predictive quality in marketing analysis.

In the next chapter, we will go through A/B testing, and how to use it to measure the impact of media on sales.

Further reading

- *Bayesian methods for media mix modeling with carryover and shape effects*, Jin, Yuxue, et al. (2017)

- *Media Effect Estimation with PyMC: Adstock, Saturation & Diminishing Returns*, Juan Orduz, `https://juanitorduz.github.io/pymc_mmm/`

- *Media Effect Estimation with Orbit's KTR Model*, Juan Orduz, `https://juanitorduz.github.io/orbit_mmm`

- *Media Mix Models: A Bayesian Approach with PyMC*, Juan Orduz, `https://juanitorduz.github.io/html/mmm.html#/title-slide`

13

Running Experiments with PyMC

It is hard in marketing to prove the effectiveness of an action. However, we can arrange experiments and analyze the data in such a way that we can properly isolate the causes of the outcome. Running experiments in marketing is a fundamental technique for optimization and efficiency. In this chapter, we'll go through the fundamentals of how to run experiments and how to analyze the outcome.

In this chapter, we'll review experimentation and walk through the following topics:

- What makes a good experiment?
- Delving deeper into some pitfalls
- Experimentation
- Observational studies
- Quasi-experiments

By the end of this chapter, you will have the technical background required to assess and plan good experiments. You will also be able to plan, conduct, and debug reliable testing and experimentation.

Technical requirements

You can find the code files for this chapter on GitHub: https://github.com/ PacktPublishing/Data-Analytics-for-Marketing/tree/main/Chapter13.

What makes a good experiment?

The gold standard of causal inference is the **Randomized Control Trial** (**RCT**). In marketing, we refer to it as A/B testing.

An A/B test, also known as a split test, is a method to compare two versions of a web page or app against each other and determine which one performs better. Unlike an A/A test, where both groups are exposed to the same conditions, in an A/B test, the test and control groups are exposed to different variations. The key purposes and benefits of an A/B test are as follows:

- **Evaluating the effectiveness of changes**: By comparing two versions (A and B), where typically one is the original and the other contains one or more changes, you can understand the impact of these changes on user behavior

- **Data-driven decision making**: A/B testing provides empirical data on how a small change impacts user interaction, helping in making informed decisions

- **Optimizing user experience and conversion rates**: By testing how different versions perform in real-world scenarios, you can optimize elements of a web page or app to improve user experience and increase conversion rates

- **Reducing risk**: Before implementing a major change, A/B testing allows you to test its impact on a smaller scale, reducing the risk of making a decision that could negatively affect user engagement or revenue

- **Understanding user preferences and behavior**: A/B testing gives insights into user preferences and behavior, helping in tailoring the content, design, and functionality to meet user needs better

In A/B testing, randomization ensures that each group is representative of the overall population, and statistical analysis is used to determine whether the differences in outcomes between the two groups are statistically significant, implying that the changes had a real effect rather than being due to random chance. Let's now review the fundamental aspects of proper A/B testing, what A/A testing is, Type I and Type II errors, and the infamous p-value.

A/A testing

An A/A test is a test where the test and control groups are the same. The purpose of this test is to ensure that the randomization is working as expected and that the groups are comparable. If the randomization is working, then the conversion rate of both groups should be the same.

The reason why you want to test your experimentation platform this way is to ensure the following:

- **Type I errors are controlled as expected**: Sometimes standard variance calculations are not accurate and you want to ensure that the variance is as expected, or the normality assumption is not met and you want to ensure that the distribution is as expected.

- **Checking variability**: You want to make sure that the variability of the conversion rate is as expected. If the variability is too high, then you might need to increase the sample size.

- **Checking for bias between test and control groups**: This is especially important if you are reusing populations from previous tests.

- **Estimating variance metrics for power calculations**: Using A/A tests, you can estimate the variance of the conversion rate and use it to estimate the sample size and how long is needed for a future test.

Before we go deeper into the details, we need to explain what Type I and Type II errors are.

Type I and Type II errors

In statistics, Type I and Type II errors are concepts related to hypothesis testing, where a hypothesis is tested against available data to determine whether there's enough evidence to reject it:

- **Type I error**: This occurs when the hypothesis test incorrectly rejects a true null hypothesis. In other words, it is the error of finding evidence for a difference or effect when in fact there is none. A Type I error is often denoted by the Greek letter alpha (α) and is equivalent to the significance level of the test. For example, in a medical trial, a Type I error would occur if a drug is concluded to be effective when it is not.

- **Type II error**: This happens when the hypothesis test fails to reject a false null hypothesis. Essentially, it's the error of not detecting a difference or effect when one actually exists. A Type II error is represented by the Greek letter beta (β). The power of a test ($1 - \beta$) is the probability of correctly rejecting a false null hypothesis. In the same medical trial example, a Type II error would occur if the drug is effective, but the test fails to show this effectiveness.

A Type I error is a **false positive**, wrongly indicating that a significant effect or difference exists, and a Type II error is a **false negative**, failing to detect an effect or difference that is truly present. Balancing these errors is a key aspect of designing statistical tests, as minimizing one type of error typically increases the risk of the other type.

Looking at an example

First, let's define our null hypothesis (H0) and alternative hypothesis (H1):

- **H0**: The coin is fair (probability of heads = 0.5)

- **H1**: The coin is not fair (probability of heads ≠ 0.5)

We'll simulate flipping a coin a number of times and use a significance level (alpha) for our test. The significance level is the threshold for Type I error – the probability of rejecting the null hypothesis when it's actually true:

- **Type I error example**: We'll simulate a fair coin but set our alpha low. If our test incorrectly rejects the null hypothesis, that's a Type I error.

- **Type II error example**: We'll simulate an unfair coin but use a test that's not very powerful. If our test fails to reject the null hypothesis, that's a Type II error.

Here is the Python code that exemplifies Type I and Type II errors in the context of testing whether a coin is fair using a binomial test:

```python
import numpy as np
from scipy.stats import binom_test

# Parameters
n_flips = 100   # Number of coin flips
p_fair = 0.5    # Probability of heads for a fair coin
alpha = 0.05    # Significance level for Type I error

# Simulate a fair coin (Type I Error demonstration)
fair_coin_heads = sum(np.random.binomial(1, p_fair, n_flips))

# Perform binomial test
p_value_fair = binom_test(fair_coin_heads, n_flips, p_fair)

# Check for Type I Error
type_1_error = p_value_fair < alpha

# Simulate an unfair coin (Type II Error demonstration)
p_unfair = 0.55  # Slightly unfair coin
unfair_coin_heads = sum(np.random.binomial(1, p_unfair, n_flips))

# Perform binomial test
p_value_unfair = binom_test(unfair_coin_heads, n_flips, p_fair)

# Check for Type II Error
type_2_error = p_value_unfair >= alpha

# Results
print("Fair Coin - Type I Error:")
print(f"Number of heads: {fair_coin_heads}, p-value: {p_value_fair},
    Type I Error: {type_1_error}")

print("\nUnfair Coin - Type II Error:")
print(f"Number of heads: {unfair_coin_heads},
    p-value: {p_value_unfair},
    Type II Error: {type_2_error}")
```

This code simulates two scenarios:

- A fair coin is simulated, and a binomial test is performed to see whether the result leads to a Type I error (rejecting a true null hypothesis)

- An unfair coin is simulated, and the binomial test is used to check for a Type II error (failing to reject a false null hypothesis)

Here are the results of our simulation:

- For the fair coin (Type I error scenario):

  - Number of heads in 100 flips: 43.

  - p-value from binomial test: 0.193.

  - Since the p-value (0.193) is greater than our significance level (0.05), we do not reject the null hypothesis. In this case, we did not commit a Type I error (false).

- For the unfair coin (Type II error scenario):

  - Number of heads in 100 flips: 55.

  - p-value from binomial test: 0.368.

  - Here, the p-value (0.368) is also greater than our significance level (0.05), so we again do not reject the null hypothesis. However, since the coin was actually unfair (probability of heads = 0.55), not rejecting the null hypothesis is incorrect. This is a Type II error (true).

The results include the number of heads observed, the p-value from the binomial test, and whether a Type I or Type II error occurred.

Our test did not commit a Type I error in the first scenario but did commit a Type II error in the second scenario. This exemplifies how statistical tests can sometimes fail to detect real effects (Type II error) or incorrectly suggest effects that aren't there (Type I error).

Now that we know what Type I and II errors are, let's discuss and dig deeper into the infamous p-value.

p-values

The p-value is the probability of observing the data, or something more extreme, under the assumption that all the modeling assumptions are true, including that the null hypothesis is true.

The key part is that you are conditioning on the null hypothesis being true. The p-value is expressed as follows:

$$p_{value} = Pr(\Delta \text{ observed or more extreme} | H_0 \text{ is true})$$

A common misunderstanding about p-values is that a statistically significant result of 0.05 has a 5% chance of being a false positive. This is not true. The p-value is the probability of observing the data, or something more extreme, if the treatment and control were actually the same.

Vendors provide an alternative concept called **confidence**, that is, $(1 - \text{p-value})*100\%$, which again is misinterpreted as the probability that the result of the test is a true positive.

These interpretations are not the definition of the p-value. Formally, they represent the following:

$$Pr(H_0 \text{ is true}|\Delta \text{ observed})$$

You can use Bayes' rule to alternate between the two, but you need to specify a prior for the null hypothesis:

- Although it is a common misconception, the p-value is not the probability that the results are due to random chance. The p-value can be better understood as the measure of the probability of observing data at least as extreme as the data actually observed, assuming that the null hypothesis is true.

- It does not directly tell us the probability of the null hypothesis being true or false. Instead, it indicates how unusual the data is, assuming the null hypothesis is correct.

False positive risk

One can calculate the probability that a statistically significant result is a false positive, that is, the probability that the result is statistically significant, but the treatment and control are actually the same.

We have the following:

- SS: Statistically significant result

- α: Significance level, the threshold used to determine whether the result is statistically significant (usually 0.05)

- β: Type II error, the probability of a false negative, that is, the probability of not detecting a true effect (usually 0.2 for 80% power)

- π: The prior probability that the treatment and control are the same, that is, the probability that the null hypothesis is true $Pr(H_0)$

To calculate π, we can do the following:

1. Replicate borderline results (for example, near your p-value). For instance, we set alpha to 0.01 and replicate anything between 0.01 and 0.10.

2. You know the value of P(SS). If you're running your experiments consistently with some level of power (beta), then you can use $P(SS) = \alpha^* \pi + (1 - \beta)^* (1 - \pi)$ to derive pi.

3. The value of π can be calculated as follows:

$$\pi = \frac{(\text{power} - P(SS))}{(\text{power} - \alpha)}$$

Then, the probability that the result is a false positive is as follows:

$$Pr(H_0|SS) = P(SS|H_0)\frac{P(H_0)}{P(SS)}$$

$$= \frac{P(SS|H_0)P(H_0)}{P(SS|H_0)P(H_0) + P(SS|\neg H_0)P(\neg H_0)}$$

$$= \frac{\alpha * \pi}{\alpha * \pi + (1 - \beta) * (1 - \pi)}$$

Statistical power is the probability of detecting a true effect, given that the effect is there. It is the probability of correctly rejecting the null hypothesis when it is false and you have a true difference of δ.

When running experiments, it is recommended that you have a sample size that gives you enough statistical power to detect the minimum δ you are interested in. For example, if you take the industry standard of 80% power and a p-value threshold of 0.05, then you can calculate the minimum sample size n in each variant you can detect with the following formula:

$$n = \frac{16\sigma^2}{\delta^2}$$

Here, σ is the standard deviation of the metric of interest, and δ is the minimum difference you want to detect.

How to calculate σ^2

The formula $\sigma^2 = p(1 - p)$ is used to calculate the variance (and hence the standard deviation, σ, as the square root of variance) of a binary outcome, which is common in scenarios such as conversion rates in A/B testing. For example, for a 5% conversion rate, that is, p = 0.05, you would have $\sigma^2 = 0.5$ $(1 - 0.5) = 0.5 * 0.95 = 0.0475$.

Here's why:

- **Binary outcome**: In your example, the outcome of interest (conversion) is binary; it can only take two values: converted (1) or not converted (0). This kind of data is modeled using a Bernoulli distribution.

- **Bernoulli distribution**: The variance of a Bernoulli-distributed random variable, where p is the probability of one of the two outcomes (for example, conversion), is given by $p(1 - p)$. This is because the Bernoulli distribution has an expected value (mean) of p and its variance is calculated as the expected value of the squared deviation from the mean:

  - For a Bernoulli random variable, X, with outcomes 0 and 1, the mean is p

  - The squared deviations from the mean are $(1 - p)^2$ for $X = 1$ and $(0 - p)^2$ for $X = 0$

  - Since the probability of $X = 1$ is p and the probability of $X = 0$ is $1 - p$, the variance is $p(1 - p)^2 + (1 - p)p^2$, which simplifies to $p(1 - p)$

- **Standard deviation**: The standard deviation, σ, is the square root of the variance. However, in many statistical formulas, such as the one provided for sample size calculation, the variance itself (σ^2) is used directly.

In summary, the formula $\sigma^2 = p(1 - p)$ is derived from the properties of the Bernoulli distribution, which is appropriate for binary outcomes such as conversion rates in A/B testing. It represents the inherent variability in the outcome due to the probabilistic nature of each individual observation either being a success (conversion) or a failure (no conversion).

When the power goes below 0.1, the probability of getting the sign wrong approaches 50%. That means you have a coin-flip chance of identifying a positive effect when it is actually negative. This is why it is important to have a high power.

Beware of p-hacking

p-hacking, also known as data dredging or fishing, refers to the practice of manipulating data analysis to achieve statistically significant results, specifically to obtain a p-value below a predefined threshold (commonly 0.05). It undermines the integrity of statistical analysis and can lead to misleading, unreliable, or false conclusions. The key elements of p-hacking include the following:

- **Multiple comparisons**: Conducting numerous tests on the same dataset and only reporting those results that yield significant p-values. The more tests performed, the higher the likelihood of finding at least one statistically significant result by chance.

- **Selective reporting**: Choosing to report only those outcomes or variables that demonstrate significant results, while ignoring or not disclosing others that do not.

- **Data mining**: Continuously testing various combinations of data or models until a significant result is found. This includes adding or removing variables, adjusting the model, or changing the subset of data analyzed.

- **Stopping rules**: Deciding when to stop collecting data based on the results obtained at that point, often stopping when a significant result is achieved.

- **Cherry-picking data**: Selecting specific data points or time periods that support a desired outcome, while excluding others that do not.

The consequences of p-hacking are significant:

- It inflates the Type I error rate (false positives) – believing there is an effect when there isn't

- Leads to spurious and non-reproducible research findings

- Erodes trust in scientific research, as results are more likely to be artifacts of the analysis process rather than true findings

Combatting p-hacking involves transparent reporting of all hypotheses, analyses, and data manipulations; pre-registering study designs and analysis plans; adjusting for multiple comparisons; and promoting replication studies. The scientific community is increasingly aware of the issues surrounding p-hacking and is working toward more robust and reproducible research practices.

Consider the following A/B test running for 35 days where traffic was split 50/50:

Variant	Visitors	Conversions	Conversion rate	Lift
Control	82	3	3.7%	-
Treatment	75	12	16.0%	337%

Table 13.1 – Example of an A/B test on conversions

Consider that the p-value for this treatment is 0.009.

The first thing to note is that the p-value is not the probability that the treatment is better than the control. It is the probability of observing the data, or something more extreme, if the treatment and control were actually the same.

Second, note that, for small values, the test should be **Fisher's exact test**.

Fisher's exact test is a statistical significance test used to determine whether there are non-random associations between two categorical variables in a contingency table. It's particularly useful when sample sizes are small, as it provides an exact p-value, unlike other tests that provide an approximation. The test was developed by R.A. Fisher in the early 20th century.

Here's how it works and why it's used:

- **Context of use**: Fisher's exact test is primarily used for 2x2 contingency tables. These tables represent two categorical variables, each with two levels or categories. In the context of A/B testing, these categories are often **converted** and **not converted** for two different groups (such as control and treatment groups).

- **Calculation method**: The test calculates the probability of observing the data in the table (or something more extreme) under the null hypothesis that the variables are independent (that is, there is no association between the variables). It does this by calculating the hypergeometric distribution of the observed data.

- **Applicability in small samples**: Unlike the Chi-squared test, which approximates p-values and can be inaccurate for small sample sizes, Fisher's exact test calculates the exact probability of the observed outcome. This makes it particularly reliable when dealing with small numbers of observations, where the assumptions underpinning larger-sample tests (such as normality) may not hold. While there's no hard cutoff, a total sample size where the smallest expected cell frequency is greater than 5 is often mentioned as a practical point where the Chi-squared test becomes preferable. This typically occurs with total sample sizes well into the hundreds, depending on how evenly distributed the observations are across the categories.

- **Interpretation of results**: A significant result (typically $p < 0.05$) indicates that there is evidence to reject the null hypothesis of independence between the variables. In the context of A/B testing, it would suggest a non-random association between the treatment and the conversion rate.

In the example provided, where the A/B test involves small sample sizes, Fisher's exact test would be appropriate to accurately assess whether the observed difference in conversion rates between the control and treatment groups is statistically significant, without relying on the approximations that larger-sample tests employ.

Given the data presented, you should assume that the study is underpowered, that is, the sample size is too small to detect the effect. The reason is that the conversion rate of the control group is too low, and the conversion rate of the treatment group is too high. This means that the variance of the conversion rate is too high, and the sample size is too small to detect the effect. You should do a replication run.

Let's take an example. We assume that the historical data shows a 3.7% conversion rate for the control group, and we want to detect a 10% lift in the conversion rate. We can calculate the standard deviation of the conversion rate as follows:

$$\sigma^2 = p(1 - p) = 0.037^*(1 - 0.037) = 0.03563$$

We calculate δ as follows:

$$\delta = 0.037^*0.1 = 0.0037$$

We can calculate the minimum sample size needed for each variant as follows:

$$n = \frac{16\sigma^2}{\delta^2} = \frac{16^*0.03563}{0.0037^2} = 41642$$

We clearly do not have a large enough sample size to detect the effect. In the example given, we have 82 visitors in the control group and 75 visitors in the treatment group.

Surprising results require strong evidence – lower p-values

With a power of 3%, even assuming a success rate of 33%, we'll have a **false positive rate** (**FPR**) of 63%. To override the low power, we need a lower p-value. If we want $Pr(H_0|SS) < 0.05$, then we need a p-value of the following:

$$\alpha/2 = \frac{0.05^*(1 - \beta)^*(1 - \pi)}{0.95^*\pi} = 0.0008$$
$$\alpha = 0.0016$$

This is much lower than the p-value of 0.009 reported in the experiment. We can see the standard success rates and FPR at different levels of power, from known sources that conduct regular testing, in *Table 13.2*:

Company/source	Success rate	FPR @ 80% power	FPR @ 50% power	FPR @ 20% power
Microsoft	33%	5.9%	9.1%	20%
Avinash Kaushik	20%	11.1%	16.7%	33.3%
Bing	15%	15%	22.1%	41.5%
Booking.com, Google Ads, Netflix	10%	22%	31%	52.9%
Airbnb search	8%	26.4%	36.5%	59%

Table 13.2 – Running rates at 20% with success rates similar to Google or Netflix will lead to more than half false positives

As a side note, Ioannidis (2005) argues that most published research findings are false, given exactly this reason; that is, given the low power of most studies, the probability of a false positive is high.

Common pitfalls

Be careful about multiple comparisons and inflating the Type I error rate.

Take, for example, comparing the results of an experiment before and after removing outliers from the data. Outlier removal within a variant, rather than across the whole data, can result in FPRs up to 43%.

Researcher degrees of freedom

Another common issue in flexibility is data collection and analysis, which also increases the FPR. When faced with non-significant results, the researcher or analyst might be confronted by some questions:

- Should more data be collected or should we stop?

- Should some observations be excluded?

- Should there be segmentation by variables significant ones be reported?

Don't peek and stop

Some platforms show you real-time results, so you are tempted to stop the experiment early as soon as you have a statistically significant check mark. This is a bad idea, as it will inflate the Type I error rate.

Why is this a problem? The issue is what statisticians call repeated significance testing errors.

In statistical significance testing, it's assumed that the number of observations, or sample size, is determined before the experiment begins. This means you decide on a specific number of observations to collect, such as 5,000, before starting the experiment. However, if you conduct the experiment with the mindset of *"I'll continue until I achieve statistical significance"* rather than sticking to a pre-determined sample size, the significance levels you obtain can become unreliable. This is because the calculations for statistical significance are based on the initial plan of having a fixed sample size. This is, admittedly, counterintuitive. So, let's work through an example.

Let's say you have an experiment. Four things can happen, as seen in *Table 13.3*:

	Scenario 1	**Scenario 2**	**Scenario 3**	**Scenario 4**
After 200 observations	Not significant	Not significant	Significant	Significant
After 500 observations	Not significant	Significant	Not significant	Significant
End of experiment	Not significant	Significant	Not significant	Significant

Table 13.3 – Possible scenarios for different occurrences when running an A/B test

Now imagine you stop at the sight of the significance, meaning you'll stop after 200 observations. You will get the following scenarios, as seen in *Table 13.4*:

	Scenario 1	**Scenario 2**	**Scenario 3**	**Scenario 4**
After 200 observations	Not significant	Not significant	Significant	Significant
After 500 observations	Not significant	Significant	Experiment stopped	Experiment stopped
End of experiment	Not significant	Significant	Significant	Significant

Table 13.4 – Possible scenarios for different occurrences when running an A/B test with early stop

Notice the third row, you've increased the ratio of significant results. By peeking and stopping, you have increased the likelihood of the experiment returning a false significant result.

Repeated significance

Repeated significance increases the FPR. The more you peek and stop, the more your significance levels will be off. For example, if you peek 10 times, then what you see as a 1% significance is really just 5%. We can see a summary of this effect in *Table 13.5*:

You peeked…	To get 5% actual significance, you need…
1 time	2.9%
2 times	2.2%
3 times	1.8%
5 times	1.4%
10 times	1.0%

Table 13.5 – How peeking throws the significance levels off

The solution is simple: don't do it. Always set the sample size in advance, and don't peek.

Instead of calculating the significance in the middle of the experiments, you are better off calculating how large of an effect can be detected with the current sample size. This is called the **minimum detectable effect**.

$$\delta = \left(t_{\alpha/2} + t_{\beta}\right)\sigma\sqrt{2/n}$$

Here, $t_{\alpha/2}$ is the critical value of the t-distribution for the significance level $\alpha/2$, t_{β} is the critical value of the t-distribution for the power β, σ is the standard deviation of the metric of interest, and n is the sample size.

Delving deeper into some pitfalls

Theoretically, a single control can be shared across multiple treatments. The theory also says that a larger control can have benefits in terms of reducing the variance.

Assuming equal variances, the sample size of a two-sample t-test is given by $\frac{1}{\frac{1}{x_t}+\frac{1}{x_c}}$, which translates into the harmonic mean of the sample sizes. When one has one control with x users, k equally sized treatments with size $\frac{1-x}{k}$, the optimal control size is given by minimizing the sum $\frac{k}{1-x} + \frac{1}{x}$.

The solution is $x = \frac{1}{\sqrt{k}+1}$. For example, if you have three treatments, the optimal control size is not 25% but 36.6%, and the optimal treatment size is 21.1% each. With $k = 9$, the control should get 25%, and each variant only 8.3%.

However, one needs to be careful, in practice, of the following:

- **Triggering**: If you run more targeted experiments, where you'll have stronger signals for lower population sizes, it is too hard to share a control across multiple treatments

- **Cookie churn**: If you have unequal variants, this will cause a larger percentage of users in the small variants to become contaminated and be exposed to multiple variants

If you run unequal variants, and when the distributions are skewed, the t-test cannot maintain the nominal Type I error rate. The solution is to use Welch's t-test, which does not assume equal variances.

When a metric is positively skewed, and the control is larger than the treatment, the t-test will have a higher Type I error rate on one tail and smaller on the other tail.

Common sources of skewness are as follows:

- **Heavy tail measurements**: Revenue and counts

- **Binary metrics**: Conversion metrics with a small positive rate

The skewness of a metric decreases with the rate $\sqrt{n}$, where n is the sample size. The sample size in each variant should be large enough to reduce the skewness to be no greater than $1\sqrt{355}$.

Lazy assignment

Running experiments with proper power is hard. The sample size requirements can get quite big, and the time to run the experiment can be long. This is why some platforms use lazy assignment, where the users are assigned to the treatment or control groups only when they are exposed to the treatment.

Sales funnel example

Imagine you have a multistep sales funnel. In this funnel, 10% of your users will reach the final checkout page, and 5% of those will convert. You want to test a new checkout page, to see whether it improves the conversion rate.

Armed with the knowledge from this chapter, you are tasked with calculating what is the required sample size for the experiment. You set the power level at the standard 80%, the statistical significance at 5%, and a predefined minimum detectable effect of 10%.

You run the math and find that you will need more than 30,000 users per variant to run the test. This is a lot of users, and it will take a long time to run the experiment. The question is, can you reduce the number of users needed?

Lazy assignment

Let's think it through. It's true that only 10% of your users reach the checkout, and of the total, half convert. However, you can reason that what you actually need to test is of the users who reach the checkout, what is the conversion rate of the new checkout page versus the old checkout page? Of these users, 50% will convert, and what you are actually testing is whether they increase to 55%. This will greatly reduce the sample size needed. We can see how the sample size required per variant changes once we change the assignment from start of funnel to checkout in *Table 13.6*:

Experiment	Old rate	New rate	Sample size per variant
Assign at start of funnel	5%	5.5%	30,244
Assign at checkout	50%	55%	1,567

Table 13.6 – Sample size needed for the experiment

So, knowing that only 10% of users reach the checkout page, you need $1,567/0.1 = 15,670$ users per variant to run the experiment. This is a 50% reduction in the sample size needed.

Why is this reasonable? Because of dead weight; if you assign at the start of the funnel, 90% of those users will never be exposed to the treatment. These users then become indiscriminate noise, since they will be lumped with the users who were exposed to the treatment but did not convert.

It's the equivalent of assigning the entire population of Earth to your test and counting them as failed conversions. It's not a fair comparison.

This is called lazy assignment.

How much efficiency can you get?

You can calculate the efficiency gains of lazy assignment as follows:

$$E = \frac{1 - p_1}{1 - p_2}$$

Here, p_1 is the probability of converting when you start the funnel, and p_2 is the probability of converting after you reach the checkout page.

The efficiency gains will depend on how well you can isolate the users in an experiment prior to the KPI you are measuring.

Taking the previous example, the efficiency gains are as follows:

$$E = \frac{1 - 0.05}{1 - 0.5} = 1.9$$

This is equivalent to approximately a 50% reduction in the sample size needed.

Table 13.7 shows the efficiency gains for different conversion rate percentages at the start of the funnel:

p1 / p2	80%	50%	20%	10%	5%
50%	2.5				
20%	4.0	1.6			
10%	4.5	1.8	1.13		
5%	4.75	1.9	1.19	1.06	
1%	4.95	1.98	1.23	1.1	1.04

Table 13.7 – Efficiency gains for different conversion rates

Statistical power

Understanding the concept of power in A/B testing is crucial for interpreting test results effectively. Let's use intuitive examples to grasp this concept better.

In the context of A/B testing, power is the probability of correctly rejecting the null hypothesis when it is false. In simpler terms, it's the test's ability to detect a true effect when there actually is one.

Consider, for example, we're evaluating whether a new website layout, referred to as version B, boosts sales in contrast to the existing layout, version A. The null hypothesis (H0) posits that version B does not lead to an increase in sales compared to version A.

The alternative hypothesis (H1), on the other hand, suggests that version B does enhance sales. If in reality version B does lead to better sales, but our test's power is merely 50%, it indicates that there's just a 50-50 chance of recognizing this true improvement and dismissing the null hypothesis. Consequently, there exists a significant risk – precisely 50% – that we might wrongly assume version B doesn't offer any improvement, hence missing out on potential gains.

In example 2, we see that the power of a test can be augmented. By extending the duration of the test and expanding the sample size, such as increasing the number of visitors, we can improve the test's sensitivity to actual increases in sales. If we enhance the test's power to 80%, it means that should version B genuinely elevate sales, we now have an 80% probability of detecting this true effect and rightfully rejecting the null hypothesis. You've significantly reduced the risk of missing a true effect.

Let's apply these concepts to the real world:

- **Marketing campaigns**: Consider testing two different marketing campaigns.
- **Low-power test**: If your test has low power, say due to a small sample size, you might not detect the effectiveness of the better campaign. This could lead you to stick with a less effective campaign incorrectly.
- **High-power test**: With a higher sample size or a longer test duration, the test's power increases, improving your chances of accurately identifying the more effective campaign.

So by now, you should understand that low power means that the probability of detecting the true effect is small. However, there is another side effect, usually unrecognized, which is that a statistically significant effect size will be exaggerated in the size of said effect.

There is an aphorism for this, the winner's curse, meaning that in a low-powered test, a "lucky experimenter" who finds an effect is cursed with an exaggerated effect size.

Gelman and Carlin (2014) showed that when power is below 50%, the exaggeration ratio, that is, the ratio between the absolute value of the effect and the true effect size, becomes so high that it becomes meaningless. The effect can be seen in *Figure 13.1*:

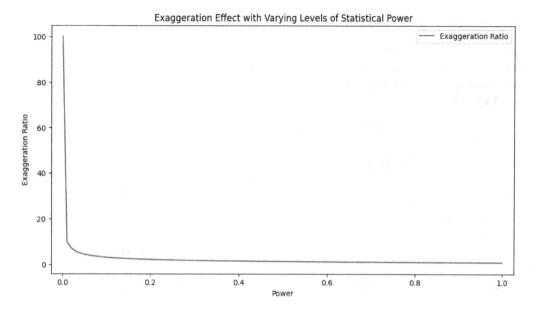

Figure 13.1 – Exaggeration effect

So, when conducting an experiment, do not start a low-powered test. If you do, with high probability, nothing of statistical significance will come out of it, and if it does, it will be exaggerated.

How to calculate power

If you have a treatment effect, δ, and assume it is the true effect, you can compute the observed power or post hoc power:

$$Z_{1-\beta} SE = \delta - Z_{1-\alpha/2} SE$$
$$Z_{1-\beta} = \delta/SE + Z_{1-\alpha/2}$$
$$1 - \beta = \Phi\left(\delta/SE + Z_{1-\alpha/2}\right)$$

Here, δ/SE is the observed Z-value used for the test statistic, meaning it's $Z_{1-pval/2}$. We can derive ad hoc power as follows:

$$1 - \beta = \Phi\left(Z_{1-pval} + Z_{1-\alpha/2}\right)$$

Be careful with post hoc power

The post hoc power is misleading. Power is a function of α and p-value. With a p-value of 0.009, as we saw in the example, the post hoc power is 74%. But we know that the power of the test was 3%.

The reason for the discrepancy is that, in low-powered studies, the variability of the p-value is high, making it a very noisy estimate, skewing the post hoc power calculations.

This means your power calculations should be done before the experiment, not after.

One simple way to think about it is through thinking conceptually of the probability of correctly estimating the true effect. Since the effect can exist or not, and can be estimated to exist or not, we will have four occurrences with probability. Power and significance can then be seen as described in *Table 13.8*:

True effect	Estimated effect	Probability of occurring	Comment
Effect exists	Effect exists	A	A/(A + B) is power
Effect exists	No effect	B	A/(A + B) is power
No effect	Effect exists	C	C/(C + D) is significance
No effect	No effect	D	C/(C + D) is significance

Table 13.8 – Thinking of significance and power in terms of the probability of estimating and effect

Ignoring power ignores half of the table, where the effect exists.

Conversion rate

Assuming that the number of people who receive a treatment, n, is known, and that the number of users who convert, k, is also known, we can calculate the conversion rate as follows:

$$R = \frac{k}{n}$$

Depending on the number of people who are exposed to the treatment and convert, this rate can be statistically reliable, or not. If the samples are small, we can expect a lot of variance in the conversion rate. If the samples are large, we can expect a more stable conversion rate.

Given that the total number of promotions, n, is a non-random value we choose before the experiment, our aim is to understand the distribution of the conversion rate, R, given the number of conversions, k, $p(R|k)$. If we can understand this distribution, we can calculate the probability that the results of hypothetical repeated experiments would deviate from the observed results and conclude whether the estimated rate is reliable or not.

Let's take Bayes' rule:

$$p(R|k) = \frac{p(k|R)p(R)}{p(k)}$$

Here, note the following:

- $p(k|R)$ is the likelihood, that is, the probability, of observing k conversions given a conversion rate, R

- $p(R)$ is the prior likelihood

- $p(k)$ is the marginal likelihood and can be viewed as a normalization constant

The marginal likelihood ensures that the posterior distribution is a proper probability distribution, that is, it integrates to 1, so it can be expressed as follows:

$$p(k) = \int p(k|R)p(R)dR$$

In layman's terms, all this means is that we begin with some prior belief, and then we update that belief based on the data we observe.

Under the assumption that the conversion rate is fixed, then the probability k conversions given n trials is a binomial distribution:

$$p(k|R) = \binom{n}{k} R^k (1 - R)^{n-k}$$

$$= \frac{n!}{k!(n - k)!} R^k (1 - R)^{n-k}$$

The prior $p(R)$ will be assumed uniform for the time being, or it can be estimated from observed historical data.

Uniform prior

If we assume $p(R)$ is uniform in the range from 0 to 1, then $p(R|k)$ is a function of R instead of k, so the normalizing constant is different. If we denote the constant as $c(n, k)$, then we have the following:

$$p(R|k) = c(n, k) R^k (1 - R)^{n-k}$$

This is also known as the beta distribution, and we can alternatively write it as follows:

$$P(R|k) = Beta(k + 1, n - k + 1)$$

Here, beta is the beta function, defined as follows:

$$beta(\alpha, \beta) = \frac{1}{B(\alpha, \beta)} \cdot x^{\alpha-1} (1 - x)^{\beta-1}$$

We have the following:

$$B(\alpha, \beta) = \int_0^1 x^{\alpha-1} (1 - x)^{\beta-1} dx$$

Non-uniform prior

If the conversion rate is not uniform, we can model it as a beta distribution, where we can use historical data to estimate the α and β parameters. There are some intuitive cases where the conversion rate should not be assumed as uniform. Conversion rates can vary over time due to seasonality, marketing campaigns, changes in user interface, or other time-sensitive factors. This temporal variability will make the assumption of a uniform conversion rate unrealistic.

In this case, the posterior distribution will still be a beta distribution, but with different parameters:

$$p(R|k) \propto p(k|R)p(R) \propto Beta(k + \alpha, n - k + \beta)$$

An interesting fact is that the uniform case is a special case of the non-uniform case, where $\alpha = \beta = 1$. $Beta(1, 1)$ reduces to the uniform distribution.

Let's see the Python code to generate the graph with specific beta distributions:

```python
import numpy as np
import matplotlib.pyplot as plt
from scipy.stats import beta

# Define the specific parameters for the Beta distributions
specific_parameters = [(1, 1), (2, 1), (5, 5), (2, 8)]

# Generate a range of values for R between 0 and 1
R_values = np.linspace(0, 1, 1000)

# Initialize the plot
plt.figure(figsize=(12, 6))

# Plot each Beta distribution using the specified parameters
for a, b in specific_parameters:
    # Calculate the probability density function for each Beta
distribution
    beta_pdf = beta.pdf(R_values, a, b)
    # Plot the distribution
    plt.plot(R_values, beta_pdf, label=f'Beta({a},{b}) Distribution')

# Add titles and labels
plt.title('Beta Distributions with Specific Parameters')
plt.xlabel('R (Conversion Rate)')
plt.ylabel('Probability Density')

# Add a legend to the plot
plt.legend()

# Display the plot
plt.show()
```

We can see the output of multiple beta distributions in *Figure 13.2*:

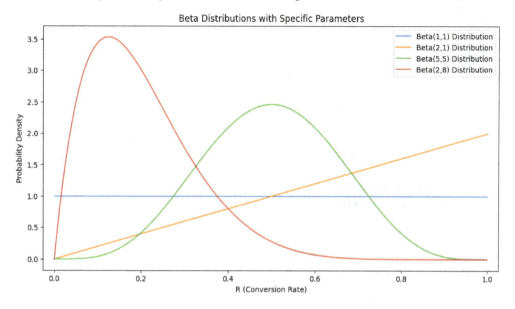

Figure 13.2 – Examples of beta distributions with specific parameters

Probability of conversion rate in some interval

The probability that the conversion rate sits in some interval $[a, b]$ is given as follows:

$$Pr(a < R < b) = \int_a^b beta(k + 1, n - k + 1)dR$$

This equation can be estimated either analytically or numerically, via Monte Carlo simulation:

1. The inputs n, k and the confidence level $0 < q < 1$ are given.

2. Generate a large number of random values with the distribution $beta(k + 1, n - k + 1)$.

3. Estimate the $q/2$-th and $1 - q/2$-th percentiles to obtain the desired credible interval. For example, for $q = 95\%$, we would estimate the 2.5th and 97.5th percentiles.

Let's go through the Python code to implement this algorithm in the following snippets. First, we need to define the functions to calculate the credible interval:

```python
import numpy as np
import matplotlib.pyplot as plt
from scipy.stats import beta

# Function to calculate the credible interval
def credible_interval(n, k, q):
```

```
    """
    Calculate the credible interval for Beta distribution with given
parameters.

    Parameters:
    n (int): Total number of trials.
    k (int): Number of successes.
    q (float): Confidence level.

    Returns:
    tuple: Lower and upper bounds of the credible interval.
    """
    # Calculate the distribution
    distribution = beta(k + 1, n - k + 1)

    # Calculate the percentiles
    lower_bound = distribution.ppf(q / 2)
    upper_bound = distribution.ppf(1 - q / 2)

    return lower_bound, upper_bound
```

Now that we have the required function, let's run the simulation with some example values for n, k, and q:

```
# Example values for n, k, and q
examples = [
    (10, 2, 0.95),   # Example 1
    (20, 5, 0.95),   # Example 2
    (50, 25, 0.95),  # Example 3
    (100, 50, 0.95)  # Example 4
]

# Plotting
plt.figure(figsize=(12, 6))

for n, k, q in examples:
    # Generate values for R
    R_values = np.linspace(0, 1, 1000)

    # Calculate the probability density function (PDF)
    beta_pdf = beta.pdf(R_values, k + 1, n - k + 1)

    # Plot the distribution
    plt.plot(R_values, beta_pdf, label=f'Beta({k + 1},{n - k + 1})')
```

```
# Calculate credible interval
lower_bound, upper_bound = credible_interval(n, k, q)

# Highlight the credible interval
plt.fill_between(R_values, beta_pdf,
    where=(R_values >= lower_bound) & (R_values <= upper_bound),
    alpha=0.3)
```

Finally, let's label and plot:

```
# Labels and legend
plt.title('Credible Intervals for Different Beta Distributions')
plt.xlabel('R (Conversion Rate)')
plt.ylabel('Probability Density')
plt.legend()

# Show plot
plt.show()
```

We can see the credible intervals for the different beta distributions in *Figure 13.3*:

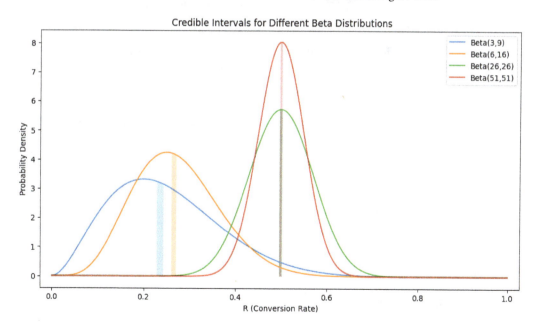

Figure 13.3 – Credible intervals for different values of k and n

Let's now move on to a discussion on what uplift modeling is and how it ties with experimentation.

Uplift modeling

Measuring the conversion rate is not enough as a good measure of effectiveness. We also need to measure the uplift, that is, the difference between the conversion rate of the treatment and the control group.

The conversion rate of the treatment group is $R_t = k_t/n_t$, and the conversion rate of the control group is $R_c = k_c/n_c$. The uplift is then as follows:

$$L = \frac{R_t}{R_c} - 1 = \frac{k_t n_c}{k_c n_t} - 1$$

We also want to measure how accurate our estimate is, that is, $Pr(R_t > R_c|data)$. We want to ensure that the lift is explained by the treatment and not by chance or unobserved factors. The standard approach is to make use of randomized experiments.

Experimentation

For a randomized experiment, you split the users into two groups (test and control), and then you apply the treatment to the test group, and you measure the conversion rate of both groups. Random selection of who is in each group is essential and ensures that the groups are comparable and that you are controlling for unobserved factors.

To find the credible interval of lift, we can do the following:

$$Pr(a < L < b) = \iint_{a<L<b} L(R_t, R_c) Pr(R_t, R_c) dR_t dR_c$$

If the random experiment is done correctly, then the distribution of R_t and R_c is independent, and we can write the following:

$$Pr(R_t, R_c) = Pr(R_t|k_t, n_t) Pr(R_c|k_c, n_c)$$

Now, we can simulate. We know that rates R_c and R_t will follow a beta distribution, so we can simulate a large number of values for R_c and R_t, and then calculate the lift for each pair of values. Then, we can estimate the credible interval of the lift:

1. Draw R_t from $Beta(k_t + 1, n_t - k_t + 1)$.
2. Draw R_c from $Beta(k_c + 1, n_c - k_c + 1)$.
3. Calculate $L = \frac{R_t}{R_c} - 1$.
4. Estimate the $q/2$-th and $1 - q/2$-th percentiles to obtain the desired credible interval. For example, for $q = 95\%$, we would estimate the 2.5th and 97.5th percentiles.

Let's see how to implement this in Python. First, we need to define the function to calculate the lift credible interval:

```python
import numpy as np
import matplotlib.pyplot as plt
from scipy.stats import beta
```

```python
def calculate_lift_credible_interval(k_t, n_t, k_c, n_c, q):
    """
    Calculate the credible interval of lift for two Beta
distributions.

    Parameters:
    k_t, n_t (int): Number of successes and total trials for test
group.
    k_c, n_c (int): Number of successes and total trials for control
group.
    q (float): Confidence level.

    Returns:
    tuple: Lower and upper bounds of the lift's credible interval.
    """
    # Draw samples from Beta distributions for test and control groups
    R_t_samples = beta.rvs(k_t + 1, n_t - k_t + 1, size=10000)
    R_c_samples = beta.rvs(k_c + 1, n_c - k_c + 1, size=10000)

    # Calculate lift for each pair of samples
    L_samples = R_t_samples / R_c_samples - 1

    # Calculate the percentiles for the credible interval
    lower_bound = np.percentile(L_samples, q / 2 * 100)
    upper_bound = np.percentile(L_samples, (1 - q / 2) * 100)

    return lower_bound, upper_bound, L_samples
```

Now let's run the function with example values for each input variable:

```python
# Example values for k_t, n_t, k_c, n_c, and q
k_t, n_t = 50, 100  # Test group
k_c, n_c = 45, 100  # Control group
q = 0.95  # Confidence level

# Calculate the credible interval of lift
lower_bound, upper_bound, L_samples = \
    calculate_lift_credible_interval(k_t, n_t, k_c, n_c, q)
```

Finally, let's plot the results:

```python
# Plotting
plt.figure(figsize=(12, 6))
```

```python
# Histogram of lift samples
plt.hist(L_samples, bins=50, color='blue', alpha=0.7,
    label='Lift Samples')

# Indicate the credible interval
plt.axvline(x=lower_bound, color='red', linestyle='--',
    label=f'Lower Bound ({lower_bound:.2f})')
plt.axvline(x=upper_bound, color='green', linestyle='--',
    label=f'Upper Bound ({upper_bound:.2f})')

# Labels and legend
plt.title('Credible Interval of Lift')
plt.xlabel('Lift')
plt.ylabel('Frequency')
plt.legend()

# Show plot
plt.show()
```

The chart in *Figure 13.4* illustrates the credible interval of lift calculated for two beta distributions corresponding to a test and control group in a randomized experiment:

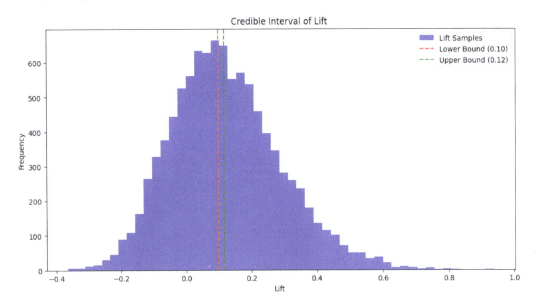

Figure 13.4 – Credible interval of lift

Here are the observations:

- The blue histogram shows the distribution of lift values, $L = \frac{R_t}{R_c} - 1$, where R_t and R_c are drawn from beta distributions $Beta(k_t + 1, n_t - k_t + 1)$ and $Beta(k_c + 1, n_c - k_c + 1)$, respectively.

- The lift is calculated 10,000 times to create a distribution of possible lift outcomes.

- The red and green dashed lines represent the lower and upper bounds of the credible interval for the lift, calculated at the specified confidence level (95% in this example). These bounds are the 2.5th and 97.5th percentiles of the lift distribution.

- The chart provides a visual representation of where the true lift is likely to lie, given the observed data from the test and control groups.

Observational studies

Randomization is critical. In online advertising, the standard approach to achieve this is to leave choosing which users enter the test and control groups to the end of the ad delivery pipeline, after the targeting and bidding.

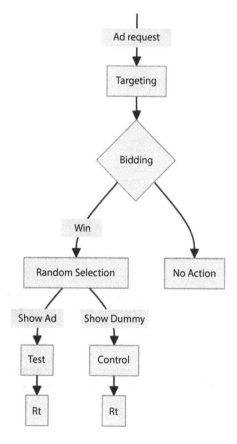

Figure 13.5 – Flow of an ad request for testing split

We have at least three rates we can measure:

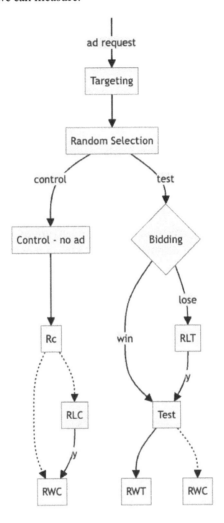

Figure 13.6 – Flow of an ad request for testing split 2

We have R_c for the control group, R_T^L for the test group that lost the bid, and R_T^W for the test group that won the bid. We want to find R_C^W, that is, the conversion rate for the users who would have won even if they weren't served with impressions.

We can estimate it with some assumptions. Note that the ratio, y, is the observable ratio of the number of users who won the bid and were served with impressions, over the number of users who lost the bid. By assuming that the distribution of the users is the same in both groups, we can write the following:

$$R_C = y R_C^W + (1 - y) R_C^L$$

The last equation relates to the estimation of conversion rates in the context of an online advertising platform, specifically within an A/B testing scenario. In this scenario, users are randomly assigned to either a test group (who are shown the ad) or a control group (who are not shown the ad). The equation is focused on understanding the conversion rate for the control group.

Let's break down the equation and its components:

- R_C: This is the overall observed conversion rate in the control group. It includes all users in the control group, regardless of whether they would have won or lost the bid had they been in the test group.

- R_C^W: This is the hypothetical conversion rate for users in the control group who would have won the ad bid if they had been in the test group. It's a conditional rate based on the assumption that these users had the opportunity to see the ad.

- R_C^L: This is the conversion rate for users in the control group who would have lost the ad bid even if they were in the test group. Essentially, these users never had a chance to see the ad.

- y : This ratio represents the proportion of users in the test group who won the bid and were served with impressions (ads), compared to those who lost the bid.

The equation is as follows:

$$R_C = y R_C^W + (1 - y) R_C^L$$

It is a weighted average that estimates the overall conversion rate in the control group R_C by combining the conversion rates of those who would have won the bid R_C^W and those who would have lost the bid R_C^L, weighted by the ratio y.

The logic behind this is to approximate what the conversion rate in the control group would be, considering the different probabilities of users winning or losing the ad bid. It's a way to understand the potential impact of the ad on users by comparing the observed conversion rate against the estimated rates had the circumstances been different (winning or losing the bid). This helps in isolating the effect of the ad from other factors that might influence the conversion rate.

We can also assume that R_C^L is the same as R_T^L, since both groups contain users who are losers and were not exposed to the ad. That means we can derive the following:

$$R_C^W = \tfrac{1}{y}\left(R_C - (1 - y) R_T^L\right)$$

Now uplift can be calculated as the ratio between R_T^W and R_C^W.

Let's consider the following DAG:

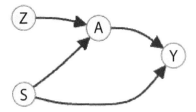

Figure 13.7 – DAG with a latent factor S

Here, Z is the test or control, A is the one being shown an ad, Y is the observed outcome, and S is for latent factors not accounted for:

$$Z \in \{0{:}test, 1{:}control\}$$
$$A \in \{0{:}\text{bid lost}, 1{:}\text{bid won}\}$$
$$Y \in \{0{:}\text{no conversion}, 1{:}\text{conversion}\}$$

Under this model, we want to calculate the joint distribution $p(Z, A, Y, S)$. Assuming that Z and S are independent, due to randomization, and that Z and Y are conditionally independent given A and S, we can write the following:

$$Pr(Z, A, Y, S) = Pr(Z)Pr(A)Pr(A|Z, S)Pr(Y|A, S)$$

Quasi-experiments

Although the gold standard of experimentation is the randomized controlled trial, there are many cases where it is not possible to run a randomized controlled trial, be it for technical or practical reasons. Here are some examples:

- **Market-wide changes or rebranding efforts**: When a company undergoes a complete rebranding or introduces market-wide changes to its branding strategy, it's often impractical to isolate variables and randomly assign different treatments (for example, old versus new branding) to consumers in a real-world setting. The impact of these changes needs to be assessed across the entire market without the possibility of controlling exposure.

- **Legal or ethical restrictions**: In some cases, the nature of the marketing experiment might involve manipulations that are ethically questionable or legally restricted. For example, experiments involving price discrimination (offering different prices to different individuals at the same time) may face legal challenges or public backlash, preventing a fair and controlled test.

- **Historical data analysis**: Marketing decisions are often informed by analyzing historical data where the conditions were not controlled by the marketer, for example, understanding the impact of a past advertising campaign on sales without having a control group. In these cases, marketers rely on quasi-experimental designs, such as time-series analysis, to infer causality.

- **Platform or channel limitations**: Some digital platforms or advertising channels may not support the implementation of a controlled experiment. For instance, a specific social media platform might implement algorithm changes affecting all users simultaneously, making it impossible to create a controlled group that is not exposed to the changes.

- **High-cost or logistical challenges**: Certain marketing interventions, such as opening a new retail store format or launching a large-scale marketing campaign, involve significant costs and logistical efforts that make it impractical to conduct in a randomized and controlled manner. The inability to create multiple, comparable test scenarios due to budgetary constraints often leads to reliance on observational studies or quasi-experiments.

- **Long-term branding campaigns**: The effects of long-term branding campaigns are difficult to measure in a controlled environment because they unfold over months or years, influencing consumer perceptions and behaviors in ways that are hard to isolate and attribute to specific interventions.

- **Consumer privacy concerns**: With growing concerns and regulations around consumer privacy, certain types of personalized marketing experiments may be limited. For example, experiments that require detailed tracking of individual consumer behavior across multiple touchpoints may face restrictions due to privacy laws, making a randomized controlled trial infeasible.

Also, sometimes, even if technically you can run an experiment, running it would violate the **Stable Unit Treatment Value Assumption** (**SUTVA**), which states that one unit's potential outcomes are not affected by another unit's treatment assignment.

An example is in e-commerce and travel, if you are experimenting with algorithms that decide which item the user will view, such as personalization engines or search algorithms. If you think about Airbnb, for instance, if an algorithm decides to show a listing to a user, and the user goes on to book that listing, that listing is no longer available to be shown to another user. This means that the potential outcome of one unit (listing) is affected by the treatment assignment of another unit (user).

The alternative is to run quasi-experiments, where although you are not randomizing the treatment, you are trying to control for the confounding factors.

There are several different types of quasi-experiments, and they all have different assumptions and limitations.

A common approach is to use geography as the differentiator, that is, to find a synthetic control unit that is geographically close to the treated unit.

Conceptually, you are launching a feature in one geography, as the treatment, and using another geography, or a weighted average of geographies if you are using synthetic control, as the control.

This is called geo lift experiments.

Difference in differences

The most popular quasi-experiment is the difference in differences. The idea is to compare the difference in the outcome between the treatment and control groups before and after the treatment. However, there is an assumption that the treatment and control groups would have followed the same trend if the treatment had not been applied, known as the parallel trends assumption.

In a difference in differences study, you will be modeling the following variables:

- a: Control pre-release
- x: Control post-release
- b: Treatment pre-release
- y: Treatment post-release

The difference before the treatment is $a - b$, and the difference after the treatment is $x - y$. The difference in differences, or the uplift, is $(x - y) - (a - b)$. We can see a graphic example in *Figure 13.8*:

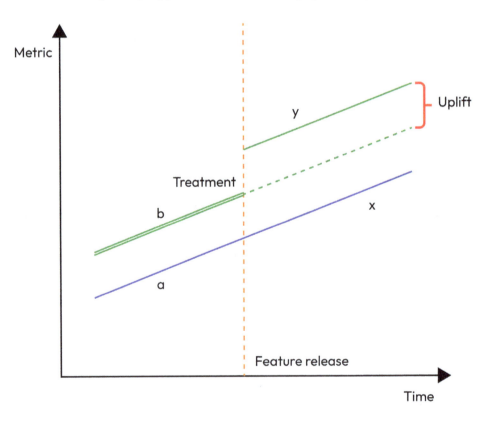

Figure 13.8 – Difference in differences diagram

As we can see from *Figure 13.8*, it is assumed that in the absence of the treatment, the difference over time between the control and treatment groups, would remain constant. In other words, without the treatment, $y - b$ would have been the same as $x - a$. The difference in differences estimator is calculated as $(x - a) - (y - b)$, which is the difference between the two groups' changes over time.

This calculation nets out the effect of time that affects both groups equally and isolates the **treatment effect**, which is attributed to the intervention itself. The uplift is the estimate of the causal effect of the intervention. A positive uplift indicates that the treatment had a positive effect compared to what would have happened without it. If the uplift is negative, it suggests that the treatment had a detrimental effect compared to no treatment.

The validity of the difference in differences estimate hinges on the parallel trends assumption. If this assumption does not hold, the difference in differences estimate may be biased. Researchers often examine trends in the pre-treatment period to check whether the assumption is plausible. If the groups were on different trends before the treatment, this suggests that the parallel trends assumption may be violated, and the difference in differences estimate may not accurately reflect the causal effect of the treatment.

To strengthen the design, researchers may include multiple pre-treatment periods to demonstrate parallel trends, or they may use additional statistical techniques to control for observable and unobservable differences between the groups that could violate the parallel trends assumption.

Synthetic control and causal impact

Synthetic control is a method for estimating the effect of a treatment on a unit by comparing it to a weighted average of similar units that did not receive the treatment. The idea is to find a weighted average of the control units, a counterfactual, that best matches the outcome of the treated unit before the treatment. The difference between the actual outcome and the predicted outcome after the treatment is the estimated effect of the treatment.

One advantage of this method over difference in differences is that, since it relies on panel data, one can account for confounders changing over time.

Summary

In this chapter, we deep-dived into A/B testing and experimentation. We reviewed what the purpose of experimentation is, the different types of experiments, and the different types of errors that can happen. We delved deep into what a p-value is and is not and how to interpret it. We review the math on calculating power and false positive risk, to measure the risks on our experiments. We also reviewed the common pitfalls of experimentation and how to avoid them.

Equipped with the necessary knowledge, you can plan and conduct reliable experiments, recognize and address potential issues from poor design, select alternative study types when RCTs are impractical, and implement your analysis in Python.

We have now reached the end of our journey into marketing analytics with Python. From here, you should have a sense and understanding of the basics of the most common methods currently available to you. This book is not, however, exhaustive. As mentioned in the *Preface*, each chapter of this book could be, and most often is, a separate book. However, the aim of this book was not to be exhaustive, but to open your skill set as much as possible to the wide range of possibilities in the field of analytics applied to marketing. Armed with the contents of this book, I hope that you can keep on your journey to deepen your knowledge of your chosen topics, equipped with the basic knowledge to make sense of the complexities ahead. As a fellow analyst on this journey, I wish you Godspeed on your analytics journey!

Further reading

- *Introduction to Algorithmic Marketing*, by Ilya Katsov

- *R for Marketing Research and Analytics*, by Chris Chapman and Elea McDonnell Feit

- *Marketing Analytics*, by Robert W. Palmatier, J. Andrew Petersen, and Frank Germann

- *Bayesian geo-lift in Python*, by Benjamin Vincent, `https://drbenvincent.medium.com/bayesian-geo-lift-in-python-79180525449d`

- *Trustworthy Online Controlled Experiments*, by Ron Kohavi, Diane Tang, and Ya Xu

- *A/B Testing Intuition Busters: Common Misunderstandings in Online Controlled Experiments*, by Ron Kohavi, Alex Deng, and Lukas Vermeer

- *Why Most Published Research Findings Are False* by John P.A Ioannidis

- *Beyond Power Calculations: Assessing Type S (Sign) and Type M (Magnitude) Errors* by Andrew Gelman and John Carlin

Index

www.packtpub.com

Subscribe to our online digital library for full access to over 7,000 books and videos, as well as industry leading tools to help you plan your personal development and advance your career. For more information, please visit our website.

Why subscribe?

- Spend less time learning and more time coding with practical eBooks and Videos from over 4,000 industry professionals

- Improve your learning with Skill Plans built especially for you

- Get a free eBook or video every month

- Fully searchable for easy access to vital information

- Copy and paste, print, and bookmark content

Did you know that Packt offers eBook versions of every book published, with PDF and ePub files available? You can upgrade to the eBook version at packtpub.com and as a print book customer, you are entitled to a discount on the eBook copy. Get in touch with us at customercare@packtpub.com for more details.

At www.packtpub.com, you can also read a collection of free technical articles, sign up for a range of free newsletters, and receive exclusive discounts and offers on Packt books and eBooks.

Other Books You May Enjoy

If you enjoyed this book, you may be interested in these other books by Packt:

Becoming a Data Analyst

Kedeisha Bryan, Maaike van Putten

ISBN: 978-1-80512-641-6

- Get to grips with data collection techniques, including surveys, interviews, and experiments
- Start cleaning and pre-processing data by removing duplicates, dealing with missing values, and handling outliers
- Use visualization and statistical techniques to gain insights from data
- Understand basic statistical concepts such as probability distributions, hypothesis testing, and regression analysis
- Transform data into a format that is suitable for analysis
- Apply machine learning algorithms to build predictive models, evaluate them, and interpret the results
- Create and communicate effective visualizations and dashboards
- Ensure that your analysis is conducted in an ethical and responsible manner

Essential Statistics for Non-STEM Data Analysts

Rongpeng Li

ISBN: 978-1-83898-484-7

- Find out how to grab and load data into an analysis environment
- Perform descriptive analysis to extract meaningful summaries from data
- Discover probability, parameter estimation, hypothesis tests, and experiment design best practices
- Get to grips with resampling and bootstrapping in Python
- Delve into statistical tests with variance analysis, time series analysis, and A/B test examples
- Understand the statistics behind popular machine learning algorithms
- Answer questions on statistics for data scientist interviews

Packt is searching for authors like you

If you're interested in becoming an author for Packt, please visit `authors.packtpub.com` and apply today. We have worked with thousands of developers and tech professionals, just like you, to help them share their insight with the global tech community. You can make a general application, apply for a specific hot topic that we are recruiting an author for, or submit your own idea.

Share your thoughts

Now you've finished *Data Analytics for Marketing*, we'd love to hear your thoughts! Scan the QR code below to go straight to the Amazon review page for this book and share your feedback or leave a review on the site that you purchased it from.

`https://packt.link/r/1-803-24160-8`

Your review is important to us and the tech community and will help us make sure we're delivering excellent quality content.

Download a free PDF copy of this book

Thanks for purchasing this book!

Do you like to read on the go but are unable to carry your print books everywhere?

Is your eBook purchase not compatible with the device of your choice?

Don't worry, now with every Packt book you get a DRM-free PDF version of that book at no cost.

Read anywhere, any place, on any device. Search, copy, and paste code from your favorite technical books directly into your application.

The perks don't stop there, you can get exclusive access to discounts, newsletters, and great free content in your inbox daily

Follow these simple steps to get the benefits:

1. Scan the QR code or visit the link below

https://packt.link/free-ebook/9781803241609

2. Submit your proof of purchase
3. That's it! We'll send your free PDF and other benefits to your email directly

www.ingramcontent.com/pod-product-compliance
Lightning Source LLC
Chambersburg PA
CBHW060646060326
40690CB00020B/4533